THE
SECOND X

Sex Role and Social Role

JUDITH LONG LAWS

Elsevier · New York

NEW YORK · OXFORD

Exclusive Distribution
throughout the World by
Greenwood Press, Westport,
Ct. U.S.A.

ELSEVIER NORTH HOLLAND, INC.
52 Vanderbilt Avenue, New York, New York 10017

Distributors outside the United States and Canada:
THOMOND BOOKS
(A Division of Elsevier/North-Holland Scientific Publishers, Ltd.)
P.O. Box 85
Limerick, Ireland

Library of Congress Cataloging in Publication Data

Laws, Judith Long.
    The second X: sex role and social role.

    Bibliography: p.
    Includes index.
    1. Women—Socialization.   2. Sex role.
I. Title.
HQ1206.L38   301.41′2   75-40649
ISBN 0-444-99023-2
ISBN 0-444-99071 pbk.

Manufactured in the United States of America

Designed by Loretta Li

To my Mother
and other Sisters

Contents

v

Acknowledgments

This book began humbly, as a collection of the articles (many of them part of the fugitive literature of the Women's Movement, few of them published) I used in my first course on the social psychology of women, taught at the University of Chicago in 1968. The project burgeoned as the field of sex roles exploded; my sources moved from the "women's shelf" in my bookcase to fill my work shelves.

I am indebted to many who helped me and the book along the way. I received timely encouragement from Jackie Wiseman, Bill Gum, Martha Mednick and Joe Pleck. I profited from the comments of a number of colleagues on various chapters: Alan Berger, Barbara Bergmann, Jessie Bernard, Pepper Schwartz, Sandra Schwartz Tangri, Phyllis Wallace and Jacqueline Wallin. The interchange and support I received from Carolyn Hoffman, Lee Lee, Jean Long, Jill Long and Margaret Bain Long, Barbara Richardson and Sandy Tangri was invaluable. Gleeful exchanges of current work with Mary Beth Norton sustained me for seven long years. Daniel Napthali Tapper saw me through the worst, elegantly.

I owe a great deal to the vast sisterhood who are not individually named here. The contributions of a vital network of feminist scholars are underestimated by the works cited in the book. For the title I owe an apology to Simone de Beauvoir, and thanks to Pauline Bart, who modeled the permissibility of wit in professional social science. Bill Gum has no responsibility for the remaining solecisms. Finally, I must acknowledge the contribution of my eminence grise, Rasputin, whose imprint is on every page.

JUDITH LONG LAWS
Syracuse, New York
December, 1978

Introduction

The aim of this book is to trace the systematic consequences of being born female—that is, of bearing the second X on the genetic code. The differences that are attributed to gender help us analyze sex roles—behaviors, attributes, demeanors and emotions in which women and men are expected to differ. The genetic patterns XX (the female) and XY (the male) do not, of course, stand for femininity and masculinity, but only for femaleness and maleness. *Sex roles, or the social significance attached to femaleness and maleness*, are social constructions to which members of the culture impute reality. Gender constitutes a master status—one that is visible and consequential in all institutional realms; and one that is so socially significant that the perceptions, expectations and reactions of others are likely to be organized around this aspect of the person rather than any other. Age, too, organizes perceptions and triggers scripts for social behavior; but age is not constant over the life cycle; hence its effect is more variable. There is mobility among age statuses, but not among gender statuses. Gender status is thus ascribed and there is little an individual can do through achievement to alter this basic fact of her or his social identity.

Society organizes human activity into a number of distinctive spheres or social institutions. Within these, women and men are assigned different functions. They inherit different expectations, opportunity structures and esteem. A woman worker faces a different probability of promotion from the male peer who begins work the same day, with the same qualifications. Her lifetime earnings curve will be much different from his, even if she has no long absences from paid employment. Co-workers and employers will hold the expectation that her work motivation will be deficient, even before they have seen her perform on the job. A male parent, similarly, faces demands and prerogatives that are different from those of the female parent. He seldom has specific job assignments in child care or housework. The prestige of his job entitles him to pursue leisure pursuits in his nonpaid hours. He does not have a second, unpaid, full-time workweek in addition to his income-bearing job. His job as a parent is the same as his job as an adult: to bring home the paycheck that supports the family.

Unlike other social roles, sex role is not tied to a specific behavior context: it intersects many institutional spheres. *Sex role behavior thus requires a separate script for each behavior sphere.* Early sex role socialization prepares the individual only in general ways. The monitoring and shaping of sex role behavior is a continuous process much in evidence in adulthood.

Gender status has its independent effect: to be female or male is to inherit quite a different pattern of opportunity, expectations and esteem. In addition, gender articulates with other roles so as to produce interaction effects that differ with gender. Being a female conditions all social interactions; whether or not the individual is conscious of her femaleness, others are. The ascribed status as female impinges on the enactment of achieved roles. For example, in the occupational sphere, femaleness can neutralize other status-bearing attributes. Thus, increasing the percentage of females in any occupation can cause a reduction in its perceived prestige (Touhey, 1974); similarly, the percentage of females is inversely related to hourly wage of an occupation.

Every role is defined in partnership with other roles (e.g. mother–child; husband–wife). The behaviors of role partners are expected to mesh; they are complementary. The existence of mother implies that of child: one cannot enact the mother role without a child. These expectations mean that each role constrains the other: the child *must* act childlike if the mother is to be a mother. Just so, feminine and masculine are defined with reference to each other. The enactment of the female sex role presupposes a complementary role performance on the part of a partner. Feminine helplessness relies on the foil of masculine competence, just as masculine bluster requires an appreciative feminine audience. Sex roles are so much tailored to each other that either masculine or feminine, in the absence of the other, appears inadequate and maladaptive. This constitutes a major problem in contemporary society where sex role change has begun among women without corresponding changes in men.

The achievement of femininity or masculinity requires much rehearsal and coaching. In the process of learning sex roles and identifying as female or male, the other sex is held up as a negative category. The other sex thus becomes as the "opposite" sex; boys and girls *learn to be different*. We learn that to be feminine is to be unmasculine, and—with particular emphasis—that to be masculine is to be *non*-feminine. The sex role scripts emphasize that girls and boys are *supposed* to be different, and once they have mastered the scripts, girls and boys have a part in enforcing differences.

All role partners have a stake in the role enactment of the partner: in the case of sex roles, one person's departure from the sex role script threatens the established femininity/masculinity of the partner. As sex role polarization advances through adolescence and early adulthood, women and men are even more likley to enforce sex role conformity than are children. To some extent, other role partners (e.g., in-laws) also engage in sanctioning sex role adequacy. Such ongoing role pressures are probably more important in effecting sex role conformity than any "internalization" of early sex role socialization.

Dominant and Deviant: Gender Classes

Although sex roles are complementary, they are not symmetrical. The two gender classes are not equivalent in social power, in participation in the society or in benefits. Males as a group constitute the dominant class and females are the deviant class. Sex roles incorporate the differing attributes, attitudes and demeanors held appropriate to the gender classes. In our society, male is normal (not merely different) and female is deviant, or Other.[1] Preschool and primary school children learn, as part of the sex role script, a misogyny that survives into adulthood. In our society, women seem through the eyes of male fantasy as men desire us to be or as they fear us to be. Rarely is women's experience, expressed by women, to be found in official documents, including research and theory in social science. Rather, the power of naming—defining how women are and should be—is held by men.[2]

At the simplest level, the distinction between dominant and deviant is reflected in language: a male professor is a professor; a female professor is a lady-professor. So it is with doctors, lawyers and prime ministers; it is otherwise with poetesses, but it is not different. A lawyer is judged to have more prestige than a lady-lawyer (particularly by men). That is to say, being female carries a stigma in and of itself, independent of other attributes with which it may be hyphenated. When other attributes are the equivalent of those of men, the evaluation of the "equivalent" female is reduced, in reflection of her gender status. Interactions with the deviant must include routines for the management or

---

[1]This analysis of gender classes is introduced in Laws (1975) The psychology of tokenism; an analysis, *Sex Roles* 1(1): 51–74.

[2]The power of naming is discussed by Daly (1973) and Roberts (1976). It is discussed at length in Chapter 5.

4

neutralization of stigma.[3] Institutional spheres in which men predominate are characterized in terms of the attributes of the dominant class rather than in terms of task requirements. In business, politics, the professions and manufacturing, therefore, a woman practitioner may be disqualified because she lacks masculine qualities, not because she cannot do the job. The lack of correlation between objective performance and ratings of effectiveness of women in sex-atypical jobs can be explained by these factors.

Issues in the Study of Sex Roles

There are two fundamentally different perspectives on sex roles. They correspond to two different realities, both of which exist contemporaneously in the United States. The two realities view the sexes in terms of a double versus a single standard, by emphasizing, respectively, ascription versus achievement; derived status versus achieved status for women; productive versus "nonproductive" labor; multiple role occupancy as norm versus crisis; emphasis on difference versus similarity; overlap versus divergence; androgyny versus masculinity "versus" femininity.

The dominant perspective in contemporary America emphasizes differences between the sexes, incorporating these into rationales for institutionalized practices of sex segregation in many spheres of life.

CHAPTER 1: SEX SEGREGATION

Doctrines of deviance are used to rationalize the restriction of women to spheres that are less rewarding (in terms of incentives

---

[3]It is sometimes argued that any individual in a sex-atypical job suffers the same fate, and causes discomfort to his co-workers and superiors. However, males in sex-atypical occupations do not pay the same penalty in income as women in "masculine" occupations. Indeed, males in librarianship and secondary education tend to be paid more than their female peers, and can anticipate accelerated career advancement. Furthermore, the male worker in a "feminine" job can neutralize stigma merely by asserting his masculinity (i.e., membership in the dominant class).

esteemed by men) than those that men monopolize. Such sex segregation is a major organizing principle of social life in our culture. Women and men are segregated into different spheres; rationalizations are offered in the form of characterizations of women in one way and men in another with the differences elaborated upon. In Chapter 1 we will find these features present in the labor market. Women and men are actually segregated into two virtually nonoverlapping labor markets, differing greatly in terms of the kinds of work and kinds of reward they offer. The allocation of women and men in the labor market follows sex role scripts, rather than task requirements. For example, labor market myths understate the role of on-the-job training. Research, however, indicates that women and men are not given equal access to on-the-job training and this, more than initial qualifications, has impact on lifetime earnings and promotions. Studies of employers' attitudes indicate that they believe women are less desirable employees than men, largely because of presumed motivational deficits. In other words, women's opportunities are being curtailed on the basis of sex role stereotypes, rather than on the basis of their characteristics as workers.

The myths of women's work motivation imply a question of whether women (too) are people, or whether they are qualitatively different from men. This issue recurs throughout the book, as issues of equity arise in different contexts. In the context of economic production, perceptions of an equitable distribution of effort and reward rely on social comparison processes. Workers compare the ratio of their input (effort or qualifications) and reward to those of others. Perceptions of relative deprivation, equity or relative gratification have implications for effort, aspiration and discontent.

It is well documented that individuals make comparisons within their own group. However, cultural doctrines of difference would seem to militate against social comparisons of women and men. The occurrence of such social comparison is potentially revolutionary in its effects. The implications of this tension can be seen in every institutional realm explored in this book: the labor market, the family, courtship, sex, education and childrearing.

The institutional arrangement of sex segregation thus bolsters the division between dominant and deviant, underlining the differences. Conversely, integration—whether of schools, social clubs or athletic facilities—undermines categorical prejudices and permits comparison. Sex segregation is perhaps less apparent in the labor force—since women are present in numbers although not in the same jobs as men—than it is in the home. A moment's reflection will reveal that men are even more absent from child care, domestic labor and the identity of spouse than women are from paid employment.

CHAPTER 2: THE "WOMAN'S WORLD" OF FAMILY ROLES

The lack of equal opportunity for women in the paid workforce, now commonly acknowledged, is rationalized by the claim that women come into their own in the sphere dedicated to them: the home and family. Since women are characterized (or named) in terms of giving priority to their "needs" to give nurturance and contribute to the wellbeing of others, there should be no disjunction between needs and the life of those who are thoroughly immersed in the family sphere. Yet, it is here where the greatest pain, role overload and problems of self-worth are felt, as the literature reviewed in Chapter 2 shows: the "woman's sphere" of home and family, far from being exempt from naming by the dominant group, is portrayed in terms of men's needs. The activities that women "should do" and the ways they "should be" reflect the ways men need or desire them to be. The family life of most women does not appear to reflect women's design.

In this sphere, perhaps more than any other, women's efforts are unreciprocated and their personal needs overridden by the demands of others. One scans this literature in vain for any report of women's needs being met. Hence, *the paradox of women's disappearing needs*: in this, the realm devoted to women, women's needs are invisible.

Some attempt is made to elevate the role of housewife to a "career," thereby establishing equivalence between woman's sphere and man's world. A serious assessment of domestic labor as an occupation, however, appears to backfire on those who expect women to be satisfied with restriction to this sphere. Analysis of the activities involved in this job and the rewards available makes it clear that domestic labor does not compete favorably with other jobs available to women—or men. Moreover, the research of Oakley (1974a) and Arnott and Bengston (1970) indicates that housewives engage in social comparison, which is associated, predictably, with dissatisfaction.

Chapter 2 also discusses the other institutional components of being a housewife: marriage and motherhood. The institutional aspect of marriage emphasizes derived status as the accepted way of defining the identity of an adult woman. The literature on mothering underscores the cultural assumption that a woman exists for the benefit of others. While this theme can be seen in the scripts for sexual interaction and for marriage, it is stated in exaggerated form where the role partner is presented as a helpless child.

The capacity and the willingness to respond to role expectations such as those aimed at the wife and mother require socialization for vicariousness—a central attribute in "feminine personality" as analyzed here. While "feminine personality" and its antecedent sex role socialization are analyzed in greater detail in Chapters 3 and 4, the materials of Chapter 2 focus upon two issues. One is the way in which elements of the sex role script, like the feminine quality of vicariousness, serve the purposes of the dominant group and uphold the status quo. The other is the sharp contradiction between the sex role script and women's personal reality. This disjuncture perturbs the status quo and fuels the Women's Movement—in ways that are explored in Chapter 5.

Chapter 2 contains some notable examples of bugaboos incorporated in the sex role script. Such cultural bugaboos are mechanisms of social control that can be invoked to keep women on the sex role track and warn them away from actions and identities that are not on the itinerary. The "maternal deprivation" bugaboo is a case in point. Oakley (1974b) has pointed out that "maternal

8

deprivation" is an artifact of our cultural arrangements for child-rearing, which assume (and create) children's dependence on a sole caregiver. The specter of maternal deprivation is engineered to exploit the vicariousness and the fears of "selfishness" that are built into "feminine personality" via socialization. Similarly, we find in the literature that the mother who is employed outside the home is *assumed* to suffer from (or even be disabled by) role conflict. The role conflict bugaboo warns women not to undertake too much: specifically, to stay away from the especially demanding (and rewarding) male-dominated professions.

Chapter 3: Objectivity and Subjectivity

In Chapter 3, the notions of objectivity and subjectivity are developed with reference to sexual scripts and sexual interaction. The role requirements for Object (or Other) readily translate into the components of "the" feminine personality—the conventional triad of masochism, narcissism and passivity. Masochism as defined by Sartre (1966)—i.e., as alienation of the will—bears close relationship with the idea of vicariousness. To be cast as the object is to be reactive—not initiating; the individual who is cast as agent expects us to respond to his initiatives and to facilitate his goal attainment, rather than offering our own. Facilitating outcomes for others includes the cheerleading and soothing expressive functions as well as the handmaiden function. The traits of the "feminine personality" facilitate women's being used as objects. The fit of these traits into the sex object role in courtship is apparent enough, and a similar process occurs in other spheres as well. The objectification of women—and the assumption of subjectivity by men—is particularly apparent in transactions involving women and their bodies: contraception, abortion and birth.

Chapter 4: Sex Role Socialization

Socialization is defined as the set of processes aimed at shaping the individual toward a given destination—in this case the adult sex roles of feminine and masculine. "Feminine personality" can be viewed as the product of sex role socialization, if by personality we mean a set of learned adaptations to the socially significant environment. Personality, in this approach, lacks the fixity of earlier approaches. Change and growth can be expected, in response to environmental demands or personal choice. Moreover, change can be facilitated via the same means that facilitate stasis: social support.

Chapter 4 reveals a pattern of increasing divergence between the sexes as they become more socialized. Initially high overlap between the sexes in interests and activities gives way to specialization and polarization. While girls and boys sit in the same classrooms, exposed to the same teachers and the same curriculum, girls are acquiring the posture of incapacity for which they will later be complimented. Both girls and boys are learning a double standard for the sexes in achievement and aspiration. Thus the paradoxical "problem of achievement" in women. It seems paradoxical because it is in code: under the single standard, *failure* to achieve is a problem; under the double standard, achieving is the problem, for a female. The responses in Horner's (1968) original research on the Motive to Avoid Success reflect this paralyzing ambivalence: to achieve like-a-man is to become not-a-woman. It remained for Monahan et al. (1974) to confirm that the ambivalence is in the culture—in fact, in the sex role script.

Chapter 4 shows socialization to be a two-edged sword. The direction of sex role socialization is toward increasing sex differences, yet as socialization continues, the lifecycle affords many inflection points where this direction could be reversed. However, it is clear that the individual's subjective connection between sex role orthodoxy and personal worth, established in primary socialization, must be broken before personal sex role liberation is possible.

Chapter 4 also reviews the considerable evidence for an androgynous repertoire that most children possess. While it is clear that sex role socialization works against this early androgyny, it is not clear that the broader repertoire extinguishes. This issue is discussed at length in Chapter 5.

CHAPTER 5: ANDROGYNY

In Chapter 5 the idea of androgyny is pitted against the constraints of sex roles. The literature that contains glimpses of androgyny is examined: the treatments of personal liberation in humanistic psychology, the psychological profiles of unusually creative individuals, the effects of having same-sex versus opposite-sex siblings in the early years, and feminist thought. The existence of a repertoire of both feminine and masculine attributes is witnessed not only in the child development literature but also in the ability of both women and men to score "masculine" and "feminine" on standard measures of these concepts. In rating of actual and ideal self and typical individual of one's own sex both women and men report an ideal self that is more androgynous than the sex role stereotype. The desire to own and to utilize both "feminine" and "masculine" aspects of the self finds expression in many ways.

Although the idea of androgyny is itself devoid of political content, the differing paths that women and men must take to androgyny will necessitate confrontation with a sexist society. The most powerful routes for women involve contexts that are divorced from patriarchal, social and nomological patterns. They involve experiences with female solidarity, including consciousness-raising groups; inspiring and subversive images of female goddesses, heroes and lives; feminist scholarship and theory. Inevitably these experiences lead to personal change and personal risk.

The women's community now claims the power of naming and reclaims women's history, women's religion and women's healing. It reverses the disapprobation of feminine attributes and the restrictions on women's lives that we inherit along with citizenship. Feminism moves women toward interdependence with other women and toward independence (or "selfishness"), but away from the illusion of dependence upon men. Once women are occupying a new space, they must deal with the issue of how to relate to the male-dominated society.

Social Science: A Mirror for Man

For the most part, the professional social science literature on which this book is based acts more as a mirror than as a conscience to sexual inequality in America. We find many instances in which social scientists use their license for authoritative opinion to espouse rationalizations for the status quo.

In Chapter 1, we will be introduced to the function of social and behavioral science as mirror and myth-maker for the status quo. We will discover a substantial body of theory that imputes a different and inferior sort of work motivation to women, as opposed to men.

It will become clear in Chapter 1 that most scholarly work about careers and occupations reflects the experience and expectations of men. Men are the normal case; indeed, most of social science literature is about men. Treatments of women appear in footnotes, afterthoughts or variants on the main theme. The reader will become aware of an intellectual double standard which operates in two ways. First, women are, relative to men, neglected as objects of study. In none of the disciplines that contribute materials to this analysis are women and men subjected to even-handed and symmetrical analysis. The bulk of what we know about human societies and human beings is about men: the bulk of social scientists' time and effort have been applied to inquiries that, implicitly or explicitly, exclude women. The second feature of the double standard of scholarship is a consequence: the quality of research on women, by ordinarily reputable individuals, is likely to be slipshod, failing to meet scholarly standards of evidence and logic. Thus, many social scientists feel free to make assertions about women that do not reflect the considerable empirical evidence available. Instead of operating as scholars and experts, many academicians allow cultural stereotypes to substitute for well-researched statements, appropriately qualified. Lack of interest appears to result in lack of effort. Moreover, the "herd of studious men," (Mill, 1869) who make up the academic establishment, seem ready to accept careless work that concerns women, especially if the authors are well-respected men.

In reviewing the data on women available in the professional literature, we found gaps where basic questions must be researched. The existing evidence is not adequate to the questions. However, the solution to this problem will be more complicated than filling the gaps: it has to do with how the gaps got there. Appropriate scholarship that takes women as its subject matter would exhibit two features lacking in much published work: it would specify existing theory for the case of women, showing which propositions from existing knowledge do and which do not hold for women; and it would incorporate women's experience, so that what is distinctive to women and what is common to humans can be seen. However, it can be argued that in such strategy, scholars would be starting from the wrong point. Correcting gaps and misinformation in the existing literature is, implicitly, to accept the existing research agenda. If social science is patriarchal in form and content, as I have argued elsewhere (Laws, 1976), then in this context the important questions about women will come up by chance—or else not at all.

Thus, there is an epistemological dilemma. Work that is distant from women's experience will not provide a valid knowledge base for understanding women's lives. Insofar as scholars have a monopoly on the techniques for acquiring valid knowledge, or on the means for disseminating information, the sex composition of the academic profession warrants pessimism about the scholarly study of women. If this work is left to men, a negligible amount, of indifferent quality, may result.

However, since the revival of the Women's Movement in the late 1960s, the scholarly study of women has emerged as an area of specialization in the social sciences. Much has been written about this new feminist scholarship (Long, 1969; Laws, 1972, 1976;

Millman and Kanter, 1975). The availability of academicians who made the study of women a priority depended on the brief spurt of "affirmative action" hiring in the early 1970s. With cutbacks and backlash, such young women are no longer being hired. The fates of those who are already in the pipeline are determined by factors sketched by Kuhn (1970) in his analysis of paradigm conflict in science.

There is a conflict between the images of women that result from the new feminist scholarship and those accepted by the dominant majority of the academic profession. The challenge of feminist scholarship is a threat to claims that social science is objective, complete and valid. The relative power of the two factions has implications for the future study of women.

However, it is possible that the atmosphere of academe retards thinking about women. In many instances feminists who are not part of the academic profession have been far in advance of the scholars in identifying the fundamental issues in the study of sex roles. Most often, it is real-world feminists, rather than ivory-tower feminists, who have initiated essential critiques of accepted doctrine, long before the research is completed, proving them to be correct.

In part, this reflects a difference in style and in evidentiary standards. Scientists are conservative with respect to reaching conclusions and the amount and kind of evidence that is required to convince one's scholarly colleagues far exceeds the requirements of the proverbial "reasonable man." Perhaps more to the point, male scholars have a vested interest in the status quo—in the larger world, that affords them many privileges as members of the dominant class and in the social system of the university, which supports their claims to expertise even while they are uninformed with regard to women.

These considerations affect the place, significance and the content of a work such as this. In a sense, it might be obsolete as it comes off the press. In the ten years when this book had been germinating, many of the epiphenomena of women's status have altered decisively. Yet the basic processes of sexual stratification

14

are only now becoming apparent, crying for study and remedy. The question of timeliness or validity haunts all social science like a conscience, and it is one of the fundamental dilemmas for feminist scholarship.

At present two additional dilemmas immure feminist scholarship. The first is the division between the feminist scholar and her academic colleagues; the second, between the feminist scholar and her feminist colleagues. More and more, feminist scholarship is diverging from traditional scholarship, with its characteristics of "normal science." It is now common knowledge that feminist activism or involvement in Women's Studies or focussing on the study of women can compromise or extinguish one's chances for tenure in the university. Moreover, the past ten years have seen an enormous increase in knowledge about women and the emergence of a knowledge base and research agenda. The parent disciplines have not assimilated the new knowledge or kept up with evolving emphases in the new specialty. Consequently, a knowledge gap divides the feminist scholar from her disciplinary peers.

The sex composition of the academic profession guarantees that the feminist scholar's commitments to women find little resonance within the university. However, established prejudices against "academic experts," on the part of feminist activists and policy makers, distance the feminist scholar from these publics. There are real differences between the goals, methods, vocabulary and standards of evaluation of these disparate groups. In accepting the necessity to communicate with and be answerable to both groups, the feminist scholar places herself in the crosshairs of the gunsight. In reviewing the existing wisdom, she seems to make herself responsible for its errors and distortions. In formulating ideas that are not part of this corpus, she appears either irresponsible or "speculative."

Here I have tried to abstract, as well as to critique, the dominant contributions to scholarly knowledge about women. In drawing them together, I have made clear the gaps and errors that need attention and which require study that is new—and bold. In many places I comment on the process of knowledge-getting itself and on the assumptions that thwart knowledge-getting. Many issues are raised where the answers are not known. Many of the factors analyzed have a bearing on whether those questions will *ever* be answered. It is clear, however, that basing education and policy on existing knowledge is an error whose consequences we cannot afford.

REFERENCES

Arnott, Catherine, and Bengston, V.L. 1970. "Only a homemaker:" Distributive justice and role choice among married women. *Sociol. and Soc. Research* 54 (4):495–507.

Daly, Mary. 1973. *Beyond God The Father*. Boston: Beacon Press.

Horner, Matina. 1968. The motive to avoid success in women. Paper presented at the meetings of The American Psychological Association, 1968. See also, Women's will to fail. *Psychology Today* (Nov. 1969):36–41.

Kuhn, Thomas S. 1970. *The Structure of Scientific Revolutions*. Chicago: University of Chicago Press.

Laws, Judith Long. 1972. The role of women's studies in general psychology. Paper presented at the meetings of the American Psychological Association, Honolulu, 1972.

———. 1975. The psychology of tokenism: An analysis. *Sex Roles* 1 (1): 51–74.

———. 1976. Patriarchy as paradigm: The challenge from feminist scholarship. Paper presented at the annual meetings of the American Sociological Association, New York, 1976.

Long, Judith A. 1969. Social psychology of women: Shibboleths and lacunae. Paper presented at the annual meetings of the American Psychological Association, 1969.

Mill, John Stuart. 1869. *The Subjection of Women*. London: Longmans, Green, Reader and Dyer.

Millman, Marcia, and Kanter, Rosabeth. 1975. *Another Voice: Feminist Perspectives on Social Life and Social Science*. Garden City, NY: Anchor Books.

Monahan, L., Kuhn, D., and Shaver, P. 1974. Intra-psychic vs. cultural explanations of the fear of success motive. *J. Pers. and Soc. Psych.* 29 (1): 60–64.

Oakley, Ann. 1974a. *The Sociology of Housework*. New York: Pantheon Books.

———. 1974b. *Woman's Work*. New York: Vintage Books.

Roberts, Joan I. 1976. *Beyond Intellectual Sexism: A New Woman, A New Reality*. New York: David McKay Co., Inc.

Sartre, Jean Paul. 1966. *Being and Nothingness*. New York: Washington Square Press.

Touhey, J.C. 1974. Effects of additional women professionals on ratings of occupational prestige and desirability. *J. Pers. and Soc. Psych.* 29 (1): 86–89.

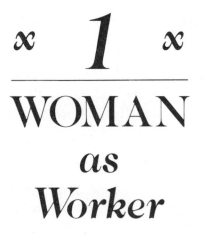

x *1* x
WOMAN
as
Worker

Women's Work Life

The history of America is the history of women hard at work. This is as true of earliest industrial production as it is of agrarian production and the frontier economy. At present, only paid employment is ordinarily considered "work" and it is paid employment that is the focus of this chapter.

In the light of complementary myths that all men work and most women do not, studies of women's labor force participation tend to focus on the simple fact of employment/nonemployment, and attempt to explain it.[1] Factors that predict women's participation in the labor force include education, marital status, number and ages of children, age and health, and employment opportunities. In general, education predicts participation and marriage predicts nonparticipation. However, the husband's earnings is a definite predictor as to whether a wife is employed: the lower the husband's earnings, the more likely it is that the wife will be

---

[1]For a discussion of myths of work motivation and labor force participation, see Laws (1976b). Kreps and Clark (1975) offer a series of tables illustrating labor force participation rates of women and men.

employed. The numerosity and youth of children also predict nonparticipation. Rates of participation are lower for older women and persons suffering from poor health.

Rates of employment for black women generally have exceeded those for whites. The effect of education on the probability of paid employment is magnified for black women. At all levels of educational attainment, the rate of labor force participation of black women substantially exceeds that of white: 49.6 percent of black, as contrasted with 28.4 percent of white women who completed eight years of schooling were employed. Of women who completed four years of college, 89.2 percent of blacks, as compared with 49.8 percent of whites, were employed (*Negro Women in the Population and in the Labor Force*. Women's Bureau, U.S. Department of Labor, 1968).

More and more, paid employment is becoming the majority phenomenon among women, whatever their age, education, race or marital status. Young women work: 47.9 percent of young women who are between 14 and 24 are employed. Older women work: 43.1 percent of women who are between 55 and 64 are employed. (U.S. Dept. of Labor, *Background Facts on Women Workers in the United States*, 1970, p. 7.) Single women work: 51.2 percent of them. Married women work: 39.6 percent of them (1970, p. 8). White women work: 45.2 percent in 1974; black women work; 49.1 percent in 1974 (*Employment and Earnings*, Jan. 1975, *21*(7), Bureau of Labor Statistics Washington, D.C., Government Printing Office). More than half of all women are employed at this moment. The trends indicate an increasing participation in all sectors of the female population.

In addition to the overall trend toward increase in labor force participation, some population segments have increased their participation dramatically. The most striking increase in labor force participation has been among married women living with their husbands. The participation of mothers with children in the home has increased nearly 300 percent in the period from 1940 to 1970 (Kreps and Clark, 1975, p. 8). Married women, husband present, with children in the home constitute the greatest increase in the labor force since World War II.

Although the presence of young children (under age 6) retards the labor force participation of mothers, the trend is toward increasing participation of these mothers in paid employment. In 1960, the labor force participation rate for mothers with children aged 3–5 at home was 25.1 percent, as compared with 39.1 percent in 1974. Fifty-one percent of mothers having children between 6 and 17 at home were in the work force in 1974, as compared with 31 percent of mothers with children under the age of 3. Even for mothers with preschool children at home, however, the rate has doubled between 1960 and 1974 (Kreps and Clark, 1975, p. 17).

Participation rates for all married women have shown a steady increase since 1940, rising from 14 percent in 1940 to 43 percent in 1974 (Kreps and Clark, 1975, p. 8). Thus, the trends indicate a change in the characteristics of the female labor force. The modal woman worker in 1920 was young and single. The modal woman worker in 1968 was 40 years old, and according to Peterson (1957) approximately 40 percent of all female workers were 45 or older.

In addition to changes in the composition of the female labor force, it appears that the shape of women's work lives is changing as well. In earlier times young women worked from the time they left school to the time they married or perhaps until the birth of their first child. Another common pattern was to interrupt labor force participation for a protracted period, returning to paid employment after all the children had left home. Only the never-married woman was likely to remain in the work force throughout her adult life. Increasingly, women have been reducing the amount of time out of employment with childbearing and childrearing. Current data indicate no decline in participation rates among women in the childbearing years (Kreps and Clark, 1975, p. 11).

Thus another major focus in discussing women's work is the proportion of posteducation adult life that is spent in paid employment, or labor force attachment, as it is called. Paid employment is coming to occupy an increasingly large part of women's adult lives. It can be expected that it will become an increasingly important part, as well.

When women's and men's patterns of labor force participation were—or could be presumed to be—substantially different, the question of comparing the rewards they received for work, or the conditions under which they worked, seldom arose. However, one group of women has always resembled men in labor force participation rates and labor force attachment. Single women traditionally have had the highest labor force participation rates: in 1974, 57 percent of never-married women were employed and so were 73 percent of divorced or separated women, as contrasted with 43 percent of married women with husband present (Kreps and Clark, 1975, p. 32). By way of comparison, single men's labor force participation has been declining since 1940 (85 percent). In 1970, only 71.6 percent of single men were in the work force (Kreps and Clark, 1975, p. 39); the rest are assumed to be in college. Labor force participation rates for all married men have generally exceeded rates for women. However, women and men show opposite trends in labor force participation: while the rate for all women is increasing, that for all men has declined from 92.6 percent in 1947 to 83.9 percent in 1974.

The trends we have been examining suggest that the work histories of all women are coming to resemble those traditionally associated only with single women. A number of factors appear to coincide to produce a trend toward increasing work experience in women. Women have been marrying later, which can extend the duration of the first period of paid employment. Trends toward smaller families and delayed childbearing also contribute to the same effect. In 1974, 11 percent of the married women between 14 and 24 intended to remain childless, in addition to 27 percent of childless married women between 25 and 29 (Van Dusen and Sheldon, 1976, p. 110).

Women are attaining ever higher levels of education, which means more employment. Divorce rates continue to increase, with remarriage rates for women substantially lower than those for men. Some estimates suggest that the average American woman will spend a third of her adult years without a partner, although 95 percent of women marry at least once. The proportion of never-married women has increased from 28 percent in 1960 to 39 percent in 1974, and is particularly marked in the group under 35 (Van Dusen and Sheldon, 1976, p. 109). In 1973, 42 percent of the women in the work force were widowed, divorced or separated or never married. Moreover, most divorced women must support themselves and often their children. Comparatively few men comply with court-ordered alimony and child-support obligations.

One of the most dramatic demographic trends of recent years is the growth of households headed by a woman. In 1974, 10 percent of all U.S. households were headed by a woman.[2] More than half of these households were living below the poverty level. The situation of female-headed households throws into sharp relief the economic issues involved in the female labor market and associated wage discrimination. Mean family income data for 1973 reported by Ross and Sawhill reveals the double penalty in the economics of female-headed families. For all ages of household head reported, the male household head does substantially better than the female—almost twice as much. Husband–wife families do better yet (1975, p. 10).

The economic costs of being female are muffled to some degree in two-earner households. However, the economic motivation for wives' employment is strong. Bell (1974) has calculated that the modal year-round, full-time employed wife contributed between 30 percent and 40 percent of family income in 1970. Peterson's (1975) estimate is that women's contribution to total family income is between 35 percent and 40 percent. A contribution of this magnitude is indispensable; loss of the second wage-earner or her income would spell economic disaster to many households. Al-

---

[2]A detailed picture of the phenomenon of female-headed households is to be found in Heather L. Ross and Isabel V. Sawhill, *Time of Transition: The Growth of Families Headed by Women*. Washington, D.C.: The Urban Institute, 1975.

though Table 1.1 does not indicate wives' and husbands' contributions, it indicates a tremendous economic advantage of husband–wife households.

Although the myth that married women work for "pin money" persists, quantitative data make it clear that female workers are a large, permanent and indispensable part of the economy. Recognition of the importance of this sector of the work force has begun to expand the focus of researchers' and policy makers' interest. In addition to labor force participation and labor force attachment, concern now extends to occupational choice, level of aspiration, the earnings gap, work history and lifetime earnings.

Although more women are working, for longer periods of time, they are not working in more jobs. Women are concentrated in relatively few jobs, while men are spread over a much broader range. Moreover, the concentration in "women's jobs" has increased with the increase in female labor force participation. Women are not finding their way into all sectors of the labor market; they are restricted to one corner. It is commonly conceded that family responsibilities inhibit many women's entrance to the labor market. However, once a woman does enter the paid work force, she is confronted by a number of social practices that restrict where she can work; how much she can earn; and how far she might advance. *Foremost among these is occupational segregation by sex.*

TABLE 1.1

Mean Family Income, 1973

| AGE OF HEAD | HUSBAND–WIFE FAMILIES | SINGLE-PARENT FAMILIES | |
		Male-Headed	Female-Headed
Under 25	$ 8,922	$ —	$3,198
25–44	15,114	11,931	5,951
45–64	17,761	12,078	7,205

SOURCE: "Money income in 1973 of families and persons in the U.S.," *Current Population Reports*, Series P-60, No. 97, table 29, Washington, D.C.: U.S. Bureau of the Census.

Sex Segregation in Occupations

The basic fact of life in the occupational world is the extent of sex segregation of the work force. Occupational segregation is the prototype for sexual stratification—that is, the allocation of inequalities by gender. Although the central focus of occupational segregation consists of structures located in the labor market, there are sociological and psychological aspects of the problem as well. Economic, sociological and psychological theories can be adduced to explain or rationalize occupational segregation; economic, sociological and psychological consequences of occupational segregation can be identified. The objective manifestations of occupational segregation consist in the allocation of women and men to different labor markets. These labor markets differ in many conditions of employment, as well as long-term opportunity structures and levels of reward. Lifetime earnings of workers in the segmented labor market reflect the initial allocation of workers more than they reflect the individual work histories or qualifications. The same is true for career mobility: the initial allocation to one or the other labor market effectively rules out access to training or experience which is required for jobs higher up on other career ladders.

Sex concentration or sex specialization in specific occupations is one consequence of occupational segregation. This gives rise to sex-typing of jobs, a cultural phenomenon that is reflected in the socialization of females and males for the occupational world. Although women and men may receive different pay for the same job, a much more common form of wage discrimination is to pay "female" jobs less than "male" jobs. Sex segregation in occupations is more pronounced and more consequential than racial segregation (Fuchs, 1970). This "balkanization" of occupations has prompted some writers to conclude that there are really two labor forces, one female and one male (Oppenheimer, 1970).

23

When gender is used as the basis for assigning workers to one labor market rather than the other, the issue of sex discrimination arises. Largely because of this concern, considerable attention has been devoted to the topic of occupational segregation in recent years. Piore (1970) has described the characteristics of "primary" and "secondary" labor markets, and the relationship between them. As an economist, he relates these differences to wages. The primary labor market is characterized by high wages, good working conditions, job security, employment stability, opportunities for advancement and work rules that include due process and equity (1970, p. 91). In short, the primary labor market offers the worker most of the incentives that have been shown by research to affect worker morale and productivity.

The rules are quite different in the secondary labor market. First of all, worker productivity is not reflected in wages. In other words, a basic mechanism of worker productivity (the anticipation of reward based on effort or results) is rendered inoperative. Jobs in the secondary labor market are characterized by low wages, poor working conditions, harsh and sometimes arbitrary discipline, variability in employment and low chance for advancement.

Piore points out that it is not jobs themselves that are "primary" or "secondary," for the degree of flexibility in the technology defining actual tasks is considerable. Moreover, within each labor market there are both jobs having "primary" characteristics and jobs having "secondary" characteristics. Rather, the characteristics of the labor market define the field of eligibles, who are then placed in jobs within the "appropriate" labor market.

Workers are assessed as "belonging" to the primary or secondary labor market on the basis of cultural characteristics such as "world of work" values and behaviors—e.g., promptness, dependability—more than actual work skills. Piore observes that employers may err in assigning workers to one or the other labor market on the basis of visible but task-irrelevant ascribed attributes such as race, demeanor or accent. These attributes serve as a cheap (cost-free) but, of course, discriminatory selection device.

Discriminatory procedures are the key to relations between the primary and secondary labor markets. On the one hand, mono-polization of the desirable primary labor market jobs by a few workers (e.g., white males) and exclusion of other workers from competition for these jobs causes wage inflation in the primary sector. On the other hand, "crowding" of minorities and women into the secondary labor market depresses wages in this sector.

SEX CONCENTRATION IN THE MAJOR OCCUPATIONAL GROUPINGS

It is not uncommon to read in the media that the growth in female employment signals an improvement in the status of women. Behind such assertions lies the incorrect assumption that the influx of women workers flows to all jobs in the economy proportionally. This kind of thinking overlooks the basic fact of occupational segregation. In fact, the impressive numbers of women entering the labor force are, for the most part, entering traditional "women's jobs." As a consequence, a labor oversupply or "crowding" occurs in these occupations, which may result in further driving down wages.

The picture for the labor force as a whole can be seen in Table 1.2, where time trend data on sex concentration are shown for the major occupational groupings covered by the census. Table 1.2 shows the trends toward sex segregation from 1940 to 1970. The proportion of occupations with a high female concentration (70–90 percent) have increased markedly over the last 30 years, as have those with a high concentration of males. This means that the polarization of female and male labor forces has *increased*. The proportion of all occupations with a more nearly equal sex ratio has not increased. Sex segregation has decreased only in those occupations with the highest male concentration, and there only a little.

By looking at sex concentration across the major occupational categories used by the census, we can pinpoint where the changes have taken place. At one end of the occupational pyramid, the proportion of draftspersons, nonfarm laborers and farm workers

TABLE 1.2

Detailed Occupational Categories by Percent Male, 1940–1970: Percentage Distribution

PERCENT MALE	PERCENT OF ALL OCCUPATIONS			
	1940	*1950*	*1960*	*1970*
10 and under	3.3	4.9	4.9	6.9
11–20	1.3	1.6	2.2	3.2
21–30	2.3	2.2	2.5	3.2
31–40	2.0	3.0	3.8	3.6
41–50	3.0	4.1	3.3	2.5
51–60	5.6	6.0	5.7	5.5
61–70	3.3	6.8	6.3	8.0
71–80	6.3	6.0	6.8	11.8
81–90	13.8	16.6	16.3	14.7
	$N=304$	$N=367$	$N=367$	$N=476$
Percent Male in Labor Force	75%	72%	67%	62%

SOURCE: U.S. Bureau of the Census, *U.S. Census of the Population: 1940. Detailed Characteristics. United States Summary*, table 58, pp. 75–80; U.S. Bureau of the Census, *U.S. Census of the Population: 1960. Detailed Characteristics. United States Summary.* Final Report PC (1)-1D, 1963, table 202, pp. 1-528–1-533; and U.S. Bureau of the Census, table 223. "Detailed Occupation of Employed Persons by Race and Sex: 1970," unpublished.

who are women (a small percentage) is less than half what it was in 1940. At the top of the pyramid, the professional and technical worker groups show some gain. In between, the pattern is for occupations dominated by females to become even more heavily concentrated with women, and those that had few women to become even more heavily male.

A summary statistic that expresses this trend is the Index of Sex Concentration (Duncan and Duncan, 1955) which, for 1970 data over all occupations, is 68.9. When the value of the Index is 100.00, it reflects an approximately equal distribution of female and male. The higher the number, the greater the concentration of males. The lower the number, the higher the proportion of females in the occupation. Table 1.3 shows the Index of Sex Concentration for each of the major occupational categories for 1940,

TABLE 1.3

Concentration Index for Major Occupation Groups, 1940, 1950 and 1968

	INDEX OF MALE CONCENTRATION		
MAJOR OCCUPATION GROUP	*1940*	*1950*	*1968*
Professional, Technical	73.7	82.3	96.8
Managers, Officials Proprietors (except farm)	119.2	120.5	132.0
Clerical Workers	64.0	57.6	43.2
Sales Workers	97.3	86.3	95.1
Craftsmen, Foremen	132.1	138.0	152.5
Operatives	100.3	103.4	110.6
Nonfarm Laborers	130.6	138.3	152.2
Private Household Workers	8.4	11.2	3.8
Service (except private household)	80.8	77.2	67.8
Farmers, Farm Managers		133.7	151.3
Farm Laborers, Foremen	124.2	102.7	113.6

1950 and 1968. The interpretation of the overall statistic is that 69 percent of the men would have to change occupational groups in order for the distribution of men and women in each of the major occupational categories to be the same as in the labor force as a whole. In a sense, this is an estimate of the degree of social change that would be required to achieve a sex-fair allocation of workers to jobs in the economy. In a sex-fair economy, achieved attributes (or qualifications) would be the basis of allocation, rather than ascribed attributes such as sex and race.

ECONOMIC EFFECTS OF OCCUPATIONAL SEGREGATION: WAGE DISCRIMINATION

The overall statistics on sex concentration within occupations can be matched with aggregate statistics on wages for the same occupational groupings. Table 1.4 shows annual income for women and men who worked year-round and full-time in 1970. The economic penalty for being female varies by occupational group-

TABLE 1.4

Median Earnings of Full-Time Year-Round Workers[a], by Sex, 1955–1970[b]

YEAR	MEDIAN EARNINGS		WOMEN'S MEDIAN EARNINGS AS PERCENT OF MEN'S
	Women	Men	
1970	$5,323	$8,966	59.4
1969	4,977	8,227	60.5
1968	4,457	7,664	58.2
1967	4,150	7,182	57.8
1966	3,973	6,848	58.0
1965	3,823	6,375	60.0
1964	3,690	6,195	59.6
1963	3,561	5,978	59.6
1962	3,446	5,794	59.5
1961	3,351	5,644	59.4
1960	3,293	5,417	60.8
1959	3,193	5,209	61.3
1958	3,102	4,927	63.0
1957	3,008	4,713	63.8
1956	2,827	4,466	63.3
1955	2,719	4,252	63.9

[a]Worked 35 hours or more a week for 50 to 52 weeks.
[b]Data for 1967–1970 are not strictly comparable with those for prior years, which are for wage and salary income only and do not include earnings of self-employed persons.
SOURCE: U.S. Department of Commerce, Bureau of the Census: *Current Population Reports*, P-60.

ing, but there is a substantial difference between female and male wages within each major occupational grouping.

As with sex concentration in occupations, so with the earning gap: trend data show an increase. As Table 1.5 reveals, when earnings of the female and male labor forces as a whole are compared through time, the earnings gap increases. During the period of growth of the female labor force, no corresponding increase in opportunity can be seen in earnings data.

It is easy for many people to assume, even in the absence of concrete evidence, that sex differences in pay reflect different job qualifications or productivity. However, the pay differential re-

TABLE 1.5

Median Wage or Salary Income of Full-Time Year-Round Workers, by Sex and Selected Major Occupation Group, 1970

MAJOR OCCUPATION GROUP	MEDIAN WAGE OR SALARY INCOME		WOMEN'S MEDIAN WAGE OR SALARY INCOME AS PERCENT OF MEN'S
	Women	Men	
Professional and Technical Workers	$7,878	$11,806	66.7
Nonfarm Managers, Officials and Proprietors	6,834	12,117	56.4
Clerical Workers	5,551	8,617	64.4
Sales Workers	4,188	9,790	42.8
Operatives	4,510	7,623	59.2
Service Workers (except private household)	3,953	6,955	56.8

SOURCE: U.S. Department of Commerce, Bureau of the Census: *Current Population Reports*, P-60, No. 80

mains even when women and men within the same occupation are compared. Worker quality is often indexed by educational attainment: wages are expected to reflect the value the worker has acquired through training. When income of female and male full-time, year-round workers are compared by educational level, a substantial difference favoring men is found at all educational levels. When women and men who have completed less than eight years of schooling are compared, women's median income is only 62.8 percent of men's; when those with five or more years of college are compared, women's median income amounts to 65.0 percent of men's (*Current Population Reports*, P-60, No. 80).

Sex differences in pay within occupations are commonly explained by the higher ranks that men attain as compared with women. Whether the greater rate of promotion for men reflects merit or sex bias is a much debated question. When systematic comparison of qualifications and pay is made by sex, however, the merit hypothesis fares ill (cf. P. A. Wallace, ed. *Equal Employment Opportunity and the A.T.&T. Case*, Cambridge: MIT Press, 1976).

Research on the micro-economic level sheds further light on the workings of occupational segregation. Although the separation of women's and men's jobs makes it easy to assign unequal pay for jobs that appear different, it is apparently more difficult to maintain and defend sex differentials in pay when workers are not physically segregated by sex.

Hamilton (1970) and McNulty (1967) both found that the discrepancy between pay rates of women and men is less when persons of both sexes are employed in the same establishment. The wage differential is higher when women and men are not employed within the same establishment. Thus it appears that physical segregation facilitates wage discrimination by impeding social comparison. Social comparison, in turn, is the basis for judgments of equity or inequity, a major factor in work motivation.

What Hamilton and McNulty observed at the level of the micro-economic unit (the firm) is true of the labor market as a whole. The segregation of jobs from each other impedes comparison, which is essential for the determination of equivalence. The Equal Pay Act (as amended in 1972) provides for equal pay for equal work. However, the practices of sex labeling of jobs and sex segregation of jobs and workers severely limit the applicability of this statute. In practice, it can curtail only sex discrimination in *identical* work. In order to enforce equal pay for *equivalent work*, systematic and objective assessment of jobs would have to be carried out, independent of sex-typing.

SEX LABELING OF JOBS

Sex labeling of jobs is a phenomenon related to but distinct from the concentration of women or men in particular jobs. Certainly sex concentration contributes to the formation of an image of a job as "feminine" or "masculine," as characteristics of the typical job-holder become associated with the job. Once sex labeling of a job has occurred, however, it has consequences that are independent of the actual characteristics of job or job incumbent. An expectation arises that the job will continue to be filled by a succession of similar persons. Violating this expectation is considered to be a potential "problem" for the anomalous worker and her/his co-workers. In this way, an informal tradition grows up that a job is a man's or a woman's job.

The sex labeling of a job may be entirely arbitrary, as two examples show. Within the craft divisions of the operating companies of the Bell Telephone system, there is a job which is labeled exclusively female *or* male in two different locales. At the time of the Equal Employment Opportunity Commission suit against AT&T (Wallace, 1976), this job was known as frameman in most localities. It was a "male" job, paying between $7,500 and $8,500. In Detroit, the identical job was called switchroom helper; it was a "female" job, paying $7,000 maximum. In another instance, a pair of jobs appear to be sex-typed, but the sex labeling varies by region. In the midwest, cornhuskers are traditionally women and the trimmers are usually men; in the far west, cornhuskers are men and trimmers are women. The principle seems to be sex segregation, rather than task specialization: men and women should be doing different things, whatever those things might be.

Ideas about the "appropriateness" or "suitability" of particular jobs for one sex or the other are widespread (Oppenheimer, 1970, p. 45 ff.). Judgments about the "appropriateness" of a job for a given individual may have nothing to do with the specific features of either the job or the individual but may be based instead on very general notions of "masculinity" and "femininity."

Projecting personal or cultural attributes like femininity/masculinity onto a job has the double consequence of defining what jobs are considered "appropriate" for the individual worker and also which workers are considered "appropriate" for which jobs. It is widely assumed that individuals are not attracted to jobs that are staffed predominantly by the "opposite" sex. This is a gross oversimplification, for it overlooks the many other considerations that enter into occupational choice. For a man to be attracted to elementary teaching or a woman to engineering is viewed as highly unusual. This is not solely because the individual would be a statistical anomaly but because such a choice would be viewed as sex role incongruent. However, as the research on work motivation and occupational choice shows, individuals predominantly cite other factors in explaining their choices. The question of sex-atypical occupational choice is particularly interesting in this light. Occupations that are sex role atypical for women are also occupations with higher pay and prestige than the "feminine" choices. Economic factors top the list in most studies of both women's and men's job incentives. The seeming paradox of men's entering the lower-paid "female" occupations is explained, at least in part, by the fact that they are usually paid more than the women in those fields.[3]

Sex role considerations may play a part in occupational choice and ought not be overlooked in the research on this topic. However, to the extent—as yet unsubstantiated by research—that sex role congruency is problematic, it is a problem created by the sex labeling of jobs.

Although it is nonsensical to talk about jobs as possessing gender—i.e., as "female" or "male"—such beliefs can have real effects. One consequence of the sex labeling of occupations is that choosing an occupation in which most practitioners are of a different sex may impugn the individual's femininity (or masculinity). Even given the cultural sex labeling of jobs, however, it is possible for an individual who is attracted to a sex-atypical occupation to compensate for the lack of congruency between the sex labeling of self and of job. Thus female engineers and female physicians can engage in "cognitive feminization" by emphasizing a sequence of female practitioners they have known, or the opportunities provided by these professions to engage in female-valued behaviors like the betterment of humankind. Similarly, the role can be enacted in culturally feminine (or masculine) ways. A more serious problem may arise when potential co-workers or supervisers at-

---

[3]Oppenheimer (1970) provides a case study in the instance of elementary school teaching. Men who enter this predominantly female field receive higher pay and have expectations of advancing to higher ranks than do females. The same is true of librarianship, an occupation with a high concentration of females, and one in which the majority of top jobs are held by men (Kronus and Grimm, 1971).

tempt to exert social control over "deviant" recruits, (Kanter, 1977). Attacks on the individual's femininity or masculinity are more likely to come from co-workers than from internalized self doubts, as research on solo or token women in work groups reveals.

The experience of the first or only woman in a male work group draws attention to another consequence of sex labeling and sex concentration. The first or only woman may be not only unexpected but unwelcome. Co-workers and supervisers can harass and sabotage the interloper in many ways that affect her work performance, morale and persistence (Wolman and Frank, 1972; Laws, 1975; Kanter, 1977). The survival or extinction of the first or only woman has consequences for the recruitment and morale of those who follow, as well. Although the sex labeling of jobs can contribute to the scarcity of women and men in sex-atypical jobs, the operation of prejudice and discrimination against the few can add to this problem. The highly visible token woman may provide a role model for aspiring women, but if they observe that she is harassed, discriminated against and miserable, they are unlikely to follow in her footsteps.

The sex labeling of jobs contributes to the prior problem, as well. The lack of visible examples of women in many occupations gives rise too easily to the perception that women cannot do certain jobs, or that some occupations have nothing to offer women. Recent research on various forms of media (including TV, movies, advertisements and textbooks) shows that the media exaggerate this sort of distorted perception in failing even to represent occupations in their true statistical sex compositions (Himmelweit, 1960). Many occupations are thus hidden from young women and do not appear as options in occupational planning.

Given the sex segmentation of the labor market, once jobs are sex labeled, the whole panoply of features discussed by Piore comes into play. "Male" jobs are careers with expectation of increased earnings, responsibility and prestige over the work-life. Starting wages are higher and the wage differential is maintained. The converse holds for "female" jobs. In addition, "overcrowding" and competition characterize many "female" jobs. However, females may not compete for "male" jobs.

IS SEPARATE NECESSARILY UNEQUAL?
CHARACTERISTICS OF "FEMALE" OCCUPATIONS

We have seen that "women's occupations" are characterized by an extreme degree of sex concentration. Women are concentrated in comparatively few occupations, and the degree of concentration is high. Thus, Lyle and Ross (1973) have compiled a list of occupations in which women predominate, which illustrate both the sex-typing of jobs and the degree of sex concentration. Women are

97.89 percent of all kindergarten and preschool teachers;
97.62 percent of all secretaries;
96.85 percent of domestic workers in private households;
95.82 percent of all airline stewardesses;
94.76 percent of all receptionists;
93.01 percent of childcare workers;
89.76 percent of key punch operators;
86.21 percent of bank tellers;
84.82 percent of nurse's aides, orderlies and attendants;
81.94 percent of file clerks;
75.27 percent of clothing ironers and pressers (Lyle and Ross, 1973, pp. 4–7).

We have also seen the degree of wage discrimination that accompanies sex segregation in occupations.

In addition, Oppenheimer (1970) has listed attributes that characterize virtually every job in the female occupational ghetto. These, like the characteristics already reviewed, have substantial consequences for women's work careers. Characteristics of women's occupations include the following.

1. Women's jobs usually offer low pay. Women's wages are low both in absolute and in relative terms. Of families below the

34

poverty line, a full 43 percent are headed by women (Ross, 1973). Women's wages make it very difficult to support a family. In a two-earner household, wage discrimination against women perpetuates the myth of "the" breadwinner and the power relationships that are rationalized by economic dominance. Relative to men, as we have seen, women are drastically underpaid, even with education and occupation controlled. Relative to their qualifications, women are underpaid: their years of education do not bring the same rate of return as do men's. Relative to their time in the work force, women are underpaid: their lifetime earnings curves never equal those of men, even when their labor force attachment is the same. Finally, low pay is one factor in female underemployment, which is widespread in the labor force as whole.

In addition to the material consequences of living on female wage scales, there are psychological consequences as well. The sense of equity or fairness, which affects job performance, arises from the comparison of one's own ratio of qualifications and outcomes to those of others. The worker who feels she is being unfairly treated may well reduce her effort, reduce her work quality or quit. Moreover, the sense of one's value as a worker is influenced by the material value placed on the work.

2. Jobs reserved for women usually utilize skills that women are assumed to possess already. Consequently women receive little on-the-job training. On-the-job training is significant in that it increases the worker's "value" and potential for raises and promotions. It also increases the employer's investment in the worker and makes her less dispensable. Conversely, when an employer makes no investment in the workers, they can be treated as interchangeable and dispensable. Where there is no labor shortage (as is the case with "female" occupations), turnover is no threat to an employer. Even with the high turnover, one can get the job done. The lack of training costs minimizes the penalty to the employer of worker turnover. The perception of the workers as interchangeable and low-skilled insulates the employer from de-

35

mands to improve working conditions or wages. A job defined in terms of such worker characteristics is a minimal job, with virtually zero incentive value or career potential for the worker.[4]

3. *Women's jobs require no career continuity.* The lack of career continuity is related to the minimal job, one in which worker quality makes little difference. The worker's contribution is not unique; the work does not cumulate over her working life; it is not progressively more demanding. Such work does not have distinct, marked-off stages or statuses within it; there is no increasing curve of competence, achievement or reward. Thus, the term *career* is a misnomer when applied to the minimal job, no matter how long its timespan. A worker could be employed continuously for many years in one of these jobs and could still readily be replaced by a new-comer.

This feature is reflected in many women's work histories. Where a family moves many times, a woman worker may continue to pursue the same occupation, or equivalent ones, in different locations. Often, the move will not occasion a promotion, and many women remain at nearly the same level of earnings and responsibility throughout a long work history.

4. *Women's jobs require little specialization.* On the assumptions that all women workers are married and will move from one job to another as a function of their husband's job mobility, women's jobs are frequently structured so as to minimize specialization. This, of course, permits interchangeability but also militates against the development of valuable and transferable skills.

These job characteristics reflect ways of structuring tasks, rather than the essential nature of the tasks themselves. Jobs can be and are engineered and re-engineered, as a function of many changing

---

[4]Such a job is that of telephone operator, as analyzed by Laws (1976a). At the time of the Equal Employment Opportunity Commission suit, turnover in this job was 200 percent per year in some localities.

factors, including labor force. The features structured into women's jobs, however, have consequences for job satisfaction, aspiration, income and promotability. The effect of these factors, in concert, is so strong that for many women, the female job ghetto is incescapable once entered.

There is no evidence that women perceive the dimensions of the occupational ghetto, either at the stage of occupational planning or later during the work history. Rather, both personal and professional accounts emphasize psychological variables like preference or motivation, ignoring the structural constraints within which these operate. The phenomonology is in a sense the mirror image of reality. As we shall see, the structural variables exercise strong effects on the psychological, but there is no evidence that the psychological can avail against the structural.

The tendency to see the world in terms of personal action—individualism—is part of American culture. So is the belief in America as the land of opportunity, a myth which explicitly denies the existence of categorical discrimination. The psychological emphasis is compatible with and supported by these threads of culture, which are so much a part of the individual's social environment that the structural realities remain invisible.

Processes of Occupational Choice in Women

The factors that make up occupational segregation affect every working woman every working day. However, sex segregation is an institutionalized cultural pattern, with psychological and social as well as economic consequences that extend beyond the workplace. Thus the outline of the female job ghetto is incorporated into the thinking of those who, as yet, have not even chosen a future occupation. A sex segregated labor market is part of the culture to which the individual adapts; it is learned without being questioned. Long before true occupational choice occurs, a field of possibilities has been absorbed, along with its boundaries. Children acquire occupational maps in the course of sex role socialization, and these are highly differentiated by sex. Nursery school children name sex-typed occupations as their preferences (Papalia and Tennent, 1975). Interestingly, adult roles they actually expected to attain differed from their preferences only for girls, not for boys. The roles preschool girls actually expected to attain were family roles, rather than occupational roles (1975, p. 198).

By the time they are in second grade, girl and boy children can reproduce for researchers the separate labor markets for which they are being psychologically prepared. The female job ghetto can readily be discerned in the occupations anticipated—"chosen" is clearly an inappropriate term—by girl children throughout the school years (Iglitzin, 1972).

Thus, sex role scripts form the background for women's occupational choice. Occupational choice processes operate within a context of options presented and constraints accepted. It makes little sense for researchers to think in terms of careers that are not real options for most women, or of models that do not fit the shape of women's lives. Yet this female context is most often ignored in discussions of work motivation, aspiration and occupational choice.

Most studies of occupational choice among women focus upon adolescents who have not yet entered the work force. The professional literature errs in treating occupational choice as a discrete event, analogous to the menarche, which occurs once in a lifetime. Quite the contrary: making occupational choices is a dynamic, continuing process, in which the information, options and constraints operative at a period in time influence occupational behavior. Occupational choice can occur whenever any of these factors changes. Research on women's labor force behavior makes it clear that major changes in life contingencies—for example, marriage, divorce, family members' becoming dependent or independent, moving to a new locality, changes in health status— occasion occupational planning and choice. Each of these discontinuities should be the focus for research on women's occupational choice. Failure to research the multiple phases of women's occupational choice results in an unrealistically static, exaggeratedly conventional picture—one which, not surprisingly, results in poor predictive validity. To some degree, the process involved in occupational choice operates in between major shifts, as well.

The appropriate questions for research on this process are as follows:

1. How do occupations come to be perceived as options?
2. By what mechanisms are options eliminated? By what mechanisms are options maintained, encouraged?
3. How do options acquire positive and negative valence for the individual?
4. How do positive and negative valences change?

Given this expanded, life-cycle framework for studying women's occupational decision-making, it becomes evident that the existing research can profitably be divided into three types of studies. *Prospective* studies elicit occupational preferences or intentions from young people who have not yet entered full-time employment. *Retrospective* studies query individuals about their past work history. *Concurrent* studies investigate contemporaneous determinants of labor force behavior among employed persons.

As I have indicated, the bulk of research on women's occupational "choice" takes the form of prospective studies. Although this research rarely takes a process perspective, there are a few studies that shed some light on the question of how the field of possibilities comes to be defined.

PROSPECTIVE STUDIES OF WOMEN'S OCCUPATIONAL
ORIENTATIONS

Not so long ago, the intention of women to engage in paid employment during the adult years was viewed as problematic by some. It was assumed that all women would marry, stay married, have children and be occupied full-time in the home. Attitudes continue to lag behind the facts of women's labor force participation, as Oppenheimer documents (1970, pp. 45 ff).

The expectation of participation in paid employment seems virtually universal at present. Even a decade and a half ago, adolescent women were oriented toward paid employment during the adult years (Davis, 1964; Siegel and Curtis, 1963). The outlines of the field of occupations considered is apparent from research with very young individuals, as we have seen. Table 1.6 illustrates the range of popular occupations nominated in three studies of adolescent women. Of particular interest is Harmon's study of the occupations college freshwomen reported ever considering. Those which emerge as most popular options in Table 1.6 were the *earliest* ones considered by the women in this sample. Housewife and actress were both adopted at median age 6–9. Artist, nurse and dancer (among others) were adopted at median age 10–12. Both teacher and the "glamor" occupations of model and stew-

TABLE 1.6

Comparison of Percentages Choosing Specific Occupations in Three Studies of Adolescent Women

OCCUPATION	PROJECT TALENT[a]	HARMON[b] (1971)	DAVIS[c] (1964)
Housewife	10.4	51	5.5
Elementary Schoolteacher	9.5	36	13.2
Secretary/Clerical/Typist	30.3	20	27.4
Actress/Entertainer	—	44	1.2
Artist	—	33	1.3
Social Worker	—	33	1.2
Nurse	10.1	28	10.9
Interior Decorator	—	31	1.1
Model	—	27	1.9
Stewardess	—	27	3.4
Author	—	26	—
Beautician	4.2	—	6.8
H.S. Teacher	7.3	25	—
Doctor	—	—	1.9

[a]SOURCE: Rand and Miller (1972).

[b]SOURCE: Harmon, L. The childhood and adolescent career plans of college women, *J. Vocat. Behav.* 1, (1) (January 1971). Percentages refer to respondents *ever* considering this occupation.
[c]SOURCE: Davis, E. (1964, p. 156).

ardess were adopted as occupational intentions at age 14. Social worker, interior decorator, dietitian and dental assistant—more technical "women's professions"—were adopted at age 15. The traditional male-dominated professions—judge, college professor—were adopted as options later, at age 16 (Harmon, 1971, p. 50). Harmon (1971) concludes, on the basis of her data, that what we are calling occupational maps have crystallized by the time the individual is ten years old. Sex-atypical occupations enter the list of occupational intentions comparatively late (in early adolescence) and drop out rather quickly. Rand and Miller's (1972) study showed a contraction of the range of occupations that young women were considering, as younger adolescents were compared with older. Preferences for some stereotypically "feminine" jobs (e.g., secretary) declined with age, but so did sex-atypical choices.

Tyler (1964), in a study of the development of occupational preferences from kindergarten to high school, proposes a model of this process. She concludes that the process of "choice" involves excluding whole categories of options, until alternatives are progressively narrowed down. This implies a rather conservative outcome, if the earliest-acquired categories have the greatest chance of surviving the process of elimination. On the other hand, these findings draw attention to the need for research on the factors that support choice and persistence in a broader range of occupational preferences. Some relevant research is reviewed later in this chapter.

Research on preadolescent females makes it clear that the occupational map is substantially sex-bound, becoming part of the individual's thinking at an early age. Another feature of socialization for occupations is equally significant, and equally sex-differentiated. Once again, research on elementary school age children demonstrates that sex role scripts prescribe different responsibilities for females and males in the family, and that grade school children are aware of these prescriptions. Thus, only girl children, in describing a hypothetical future day of their adult life, made mention of family roles; boys did not (Iglitzin, 1972). Hartley (1960) studied the expectations of and feelings toward adult jobs in girls and boys aged 5–11. Hartley found that although girls, like boys, intended to work when they grew up, boys expressed disapproval of their future wives' working outside the home. Perhaps coincidentally, the older girls in this study (the 11-year-olds) expressed less intention to work after marriage than did the younger (from age 5).

Some elements of a process of formation of occupational intentions in women are apparent even here. First, the cognitive map of the job ghetto is present from earliest years. Second, planning for dual roles is present in females (but not males). Hartley's data indicate the addition of a third element: as the girl child approaches nubility, the sex role agenda begins to gain ascendancy, at the expense of occupational ambition. A large number of studies show a tendency for young women to lower their occupational aspirations as they grow older. Sometimes it is educational aspiration that is reduced; sometimes "career commitment," usually indexed as the intention to remain continuously in the labor force.

The impetus for the retreat seems often that women are presented with a conflict between occupational ambition and sex role adequacy (or orthodoxy). Sometimes the message is crude, as when a researcher asks young women their preferences for career versus marriage (Empey, 1958). Bugaboos regarding child welfare are mobilized early on. Generalized attitudes of disapproval toward working wives or mothers may be voiced in the presence of young women. As a consequence, young women begin backing away from full employment participation.

A study of junior and senior high school women and men of blue collar backgrounds illustrates some of the factors involved. Davis (1964) found that, among the young women, 60 percent believed most women want a job as well as a family. Only 25 percent of this sample, however, *expected* to obtain their most preferred job. The other 75 percent most commonly listed marriage as the major obstacle to accomplishing their occupational aspiration.

Other findings from this study cast light on the considerations that influence the work orientation of women, in its formative

42

stages. (1) The girls, contrary to the stereotype that women are casual about employment, had given more thought to their future occupation than had the boys in this study. (2) Boys showed less tolerant attitudes toward women working than did the girls. (3) Although the girls were able to rate the prestige of occupations, they did not choose the high-prestige occupations for themselves. (4) Considerations of sex-appropriateness appeared as a determinant in several ways: in addition to the anticipation of marriage and concern about potential mates' attitudes, certain job-relevant self-attributions differed by sex. Davis found that only a third of the young women wanted to be known as ambitious, while 49 percent of the young men did. (5) The females' choices piled up in certain traditional female occupations: secretary, teacher, nurse and beautician accounted for more than half of their choices. (6) The incentive values that the young women attributed to the jobs they chose seem to fall into three groups: the most frequent was intrinsic interest in "the work itself"; a second group included people-orientation (helping others plus congenial co-workers); and a third, bread-and-butter considerations such as job security and pay. Opportunities for promotion ranked sixth.

In Davis' study, the conflict between achievement and femininity was conscious. In other studies conflict may be expressed in indecision. Watley and Kaplan (1971) report a follow-up study of 883 females who had been National Merit Finalists in 1956 to 1960. Their current plans were distributed as follows: Marriage only, 8.6 percent; marriage and deferred career, 32.8 percent; marriage and immediate career, 46.4 percent; career only, 6 percent; uncertain, 6.2 percent. When SAT scores were cross-tabulated with future plans, a distinct pattern emerged. The "marriage now" groups had the lowest aggregate scores; the "career now" groups were intermediate and the highest SAT scores characterized the "uncertain" group. This latter relationship is particularly interesting, suggesting that the conflict between achievement and femininity is most severe for women of greatest ability.

In today's climate, both marriage only and career only are deviant choices. Rand and Miller found that young women's lifestyle choices changed even within the preemployment, adolescent period. Rand and Miller (1972) compared lifestyle preferences of three groups of young women: junior high school students, high school students and college students. Students were asked their preferences for lifestyle options from "To never work" to "To work most of the time and remain single" or "To work most of the time combining a career, marriage and motherhood." Each respondent was also asked to indicate her preference at age 12, as she recalled. This comparison revealed a dramatic drop in the popularity of the marriage-only option and nearly as great a decrease in the proportion choosing the career-only option. Lifestyles that gained adherents were those involving marriage and motherhood, including curtailed employment.

Rand and Miller's data indicate that taking dual role expectations into account causes women to abandon certain future options. The implications of this are emphasized in Angrist and Almquist's longitudinal study of life planning in college women. Women adopt a "contingency approach" in life planning, according to which elements (or commitments) for future life are added one at a time, and adjustments made (1975, pp. 30–44). Angrist and Amquist opine that, much as men elect a lifestyle when they choose an occupation, women do so when they choose a spouse. Although their approach is limited by the traditional assumption that women give first priority to marital selection and lesser emphasis to occupational planning, Angrist and Almquist's data do not support such an interpretation. It is equally consistent with the contingency approach for a woman with an occupational commitment to a demanding profession to delay marriage and/or childbearing until it fits in with the established direction of her life.

We can go further than Angrist and Almquist, and propose that, in fact, *the unit of analysis for women's planning is the lifestyle, rather than the occupation.* Occupational choice may be moderated by family planning, just as fertility planning reflects employment considerations. Moreover, marital dissolution often provides the opportunity for occupational retooling.

The focus on lifestyle as the unit of analysis requires correction in many research traditions. The bulk of literature on occupational aspiration and work motivation, for example, assumes a life-cycle that has the shape of the male, rather than the female experience. Some of the difficulties of trying to fit women into these models will be discussed below. Another topic deserving of additional attention is that of role models. In my own longitudinal research with college women, I found it necessary to collect data about both *occupational role models* and *lifestyle role models*. For the professions to which my respondents aspired, the two categories of role models were virtually nonoverlapping. This kind of finding has serious implications for women's socialization for and enactment of dual roles. The changing effects of maternal employment on women's occupational aspiration may more profitably be analyzed in terms of role modeling effects than, as has been the practice, in terms of labor force participation per se.

If further evidence were needed, it could be found in a comparison of the predictive validity of research that focuses on lifestyle planning versus research that focuses on "occupational choice." In the Watley and Kaplan study of women who had listed marriage only as their future choice, 95 percent were married by the time of the followup; of those choosing marriage and deferred career, 80 percent; of those choosing marriage and immediate career, 65 percent were already married. In Tangri's followup of the college women studied in 1968, the actual age at marriage corresponded very closely with the intended age at marriage reported at the time of the first data collection. By way of contrast, Harmon (1969) found little predictive validity for the Women's Strong Vocational Interest Blank (SVIB) when the college scores (taken in 1953–1955) were compared with postcollege occupational histories (taken in 1966–67). Of two groups selected for study, 44 percent of those scoring high on the Social Worker scale, and 40 percent of those scoring high on Lab Technician Scale reported having had no usual occupation in the intervening years. Obviously, the failure to take into account the other contingencies that could be anticipated rendered prediction nearly useless.

In a longitudinal study of boys' and girls' vocational interests, Tyler (1964) found that specific scales of the SVIB did not differentiate girls who were not career oriented. Although Tyler expected that these would score high on scales whose content corresponds to work the housewife actually does, this was not the case (1964 p. 205). Women aspiring to become housewives were, apparently, choosing a status, not an occupation.[5]

Retrospective and concurrent studies of women's labor force participation and occupational planning underscore the importance of contingencies.

RETROSPECTIVE AND CONCURRENT STUDIES OF WOMEN'S OCCUPATIONAL ORIENTATIONS

Retrospective studies are useful in uncovering patterning in women's careers, which prospective studies fail to predict. Sometimes the failure is in the respondents, as when they fail to anticipate the effects of divorce or bereavement on labor market activity. In a study of 310 Chicago widows, Lopata and Steinhart found that 40 percent had not been employed outside the home while their husbands were alive. Presumably, they had not planned to work. Indeed, Lopata and Steinhart (1971) found that even at the time of the study, the widows were doing essentially no planning for the future.

Sometimes the shortcomings of prospective studies lie in the researchers' failure to conceptualize alternative lifestyles or lifestyle planning strategies of women. Retrospective research permits post hoc construction of such models, and can provide an estimate of the relative influence of a variety of factors. Thus Mulvey (1963) studied 475 female high school graduates 20–27 years after graduation, when they were 37–47 years of age. Mulvey developed a twelvefold behavioral typology based on the

---

[5]The issue of whether it is appropriate to consider housewifery a "career" is discussed at length in Chapter 2.

temporal ordering of marriage and employment contingencies plus "career orientation" (work primary versus marriage primary).

Three categories (totalling 39 percent) comprised those who had not been employed since marriage. Interrupted work patterns accounted for 20 percent of the sample. Stable Working groups (17 percent) were composed of single women who had worked continuously. Double track (dual role) workers comprised 8 percent of the sample. Another 16 percent included a group entering employment after a long period of homemaking, a group with a history of casual and episodic employment, and women who had worked for their husbands since marriage.

Mulvey's data indicated that in every group there were women whose work behavior and preference were inconsistent. There were employed women who would have preferred to be at home, and women at home who would have preferred to be at work. Although it is possible to characterize work histories from such data, it is not possible to infer preference, "career commitment," "level of aspiration" or any such motivational entity from data on where women end up in the labor force. Outcome data reflect contextual constraints as well as individual intentions. In a labor market characterized by categorical discrimination, the former has considerably more effect. In order to evaluate women's work motivation (as compared, say, with men's), we would have to examine those cases—very few, in a sex stratified economy—where the constraints are controlled and the effects of preference can be specified independently. Thus for Mulvey's respondents, neither personality ratings, socioeconomic background nor school achievement predicted the course of their postgraduation histories. Individual differences on all these factors appear to have been overshadowed by the effects of marriage and family life.[6]

---

[6]Other studies reinforce the awareness of the potency of family life constraints on women's occupational achievement. When Terman (Terman and Oden, 1947) followed up 671 intellectually talented young women (IQs of 150) in their 40s he found that fewer than half were employed outside the home.

Concurrent studies offer a snapshot of a work force or a sample, rather than a series of observations of the same population. These can be valuable for understanding the allocation of individuals over positions, but cross-sectional studies cannot really be used to assess "change." Concurrent studies are particularly useful, however, when they permit comparison of outcomes for samples operating under different constraints. A study by Baruch (1967) illustrates how the possiblities for action in women's lives varies with the constraints of domestic responsibilities. The respondents in Baruch's study were Radcliffe alumnae who were at varying stages of the family life-cycle: before children, child-intensive and family-established. These cohorts were respectively, five, ten and 15–25 years out of college. Measuring achievement motivation (n Ach), Baruch found it highest in the cohort most recently graduated, lowest in those ten years out of college and intermediate in those 15–25 years out of college. Although it is incorrect to infer, as Baruch does, that n Ach "drops" with years away from the university and then rises again, an alternative interpretation suggests itself. As a recalculation of Baruch's data shows, n Ach is lowest when family constraints are highest: the cohort ten years out of college had both the highest mean and highest absolute number of children. Perhaps measured achievement motivation reflected a realistic accommodation to real-world constraints. However, these constraints are not permanent. There is much research—including Mulvey's and Baruch's studies—indicating that women in their late 30s or 40s whose children are nearing independence, are planning renewed labor force activity. The opportunity structure they confront is, in the main, not adapted to utilize these workers fully.

Work Motivation in the Individual

In ordinary usage, occupational choice, job performance and success are considered to be consequences of individual attributes—ability, achievement motivation, persistence, creativity and the like. Structural factors such as those we have discussed are not taken into account in explaining behavior. Too often, the professional literature perpetuates the same errors, polysyllabically.

A certain amount of confusion is apparent even in the terms in which work motivation is defined. The term work motivation is sometimes used interchangeably with achievement motivation—although the latter term has a specific definition and an associated tradition of research that overlaps little with the real world of work. Often, work motivation is inferred post hoc from outcomes such as labor force attachment or from the attributes of the individual's occupation. Those who have "inferior" jobs or interrupted work histories are assumed to have inferior motivation. The terms "career orientation" or career salience are sometimes inferred from level of occupational aspiration, persistence or promotion history, with no attempt to measure personal constructs or obtain self-reports.

Yet motivation is a psychological process, not a behavior. The relationship of behavior to motivation is as variable as the relation of attitudes to behavior. Behavior is an outcome, and a multiply determined one; motivation is one putative determinant. The relationship between the two is not a simple one of cause and effect, or independent and dependent variable. Motivation is, in fact, a realm of study unto itself, with its own scientific laws, premises and essential constructs. The "explanation" of behavior by reference to motivation, without understanding of basic motivational processes, is simply superstition.

A basic and workable model of motivation can be found in the tradition of Lewin (1951), McClelland and Atkinson (1953) and Vroom (1964). Motivation can be viewed as a field of forces operating on the individual at a point in time, within a context of interpersonal influences and material constraints. Expectancy/Value theory contains an information term (Expectancy) and an incentive term (Value). Vroom's formulation specifies that Expectancy and Value, multiplied together, produce a motivational force that can be expressed in behavior. Behaviors commonly predicted are effort and productivity. The basic principle of Expectancy/Value theory is commonly expressed in this way:

$$F_i = (E_{ij} \times V_j),$$

where E = the subjective probability that the individual's act i will lead to outcome j, and V = the anticipated gratification associated with outcome j. At any moment in time, the motivational process may involve many such forces being generated, corresponding to the number of outcomes that the individual is considering. According to the theory, behavior is determined by the strongest resultant force.

This model assumes that any outcome or option known to the individual has a valence or incentive value associated with it. It should be noted that valences can be negative as well as positive; when the valence is negative, the direction of the resultant force is avoidance rather than approach. Theoretically, any course of behavior can be the resultant of forces toward one outcome or set of outcomes and away from others. It is also possible for approach and avoidance forces to operate simultaneously with reference to the same outcome. This notion of approach/avoidance conflict is very useful in understanding the motivation of some women toward achievement.

It should be noted that information and incentive(s) interact in a multiplicative rather than an additive manner. In other words, the theory predicts zero effort or resultant force if either Expectancy or Value is zero. (An additive model would predict resultant force equal to some fraction representing the nonzero term.) An outcome with a known probability of attainment will not motivate behavior if its valence is zero. Similarly, if the probability of success is zero, no resultant force is predicted even for an outcome with high positive valence. The first of these formulations may be useful in understanding the rather lukewarm response of many women to the lackluster career options presented to them. The second may help to explain the failure of some women to "choose" the most highly rewarded and competitive jobs in the occupational hierarchy.

The information term may be thought of as including qualitative information (e.g., what options are perceived by the individual) as well as quantitative (e.g., the subjective probability of attaining a given outcome). The issue of role modeling, often discussed in the context of women's occupational aspiration, can be viewed in a new light here. If a schoolgirl has never seen or been exposed to a female engineer, does she think of this as a possibility? If this outcome does not appear among the options in her motivational equation, then all questions of valence and instrumental behavior become moot. The sex composition of the occupation (or the individual's perception of it) might serve as an estimate of the probability of success in that field. However, if there are so few females in a field that the individual is unaware of them, then both terms operate essentially as zeros.

Sex role socialization, as well as formal vocational training and general education, all contribute to the information term in the motivational equation. It is easy to see how these processes limit the occupations that appear as options in most females' motivational equation. Sex labeling of jobs communicates valence: positive for occupations sex-typed for one's own gender, and negative for "opposite" sex-typed occupations. Some authors have argued that the whole realm of occupational achievement is sex-typed masculine. Hence any occupational success undermines femininity and carries a negative valence for this reason. At the same time, achievement carries a positive social valence. In part because of women's dual roles and in part because of contradictory valences, women's motivation toward occupational performance is complex. These complexities have largely been overlooked in research to date.

POSITIVE AND NEGATIVE INCENTIVES AS
FACTORS IN WORK MOTIVATION

Positive and negative job factors can easily fit into this option/incentive framework. Thus, it is possible to characterize specific jobs in terms of how "motivating" they are, by examining the positive and negative incentives they make available. And indeed, there is a large literature on the factors that workers like and dislike about their jobs. It should be noted, however, that the research in industrial psychology focuses exclusively on the valence term of the equation and does not consider how information enters in.

The characteristics of jobs in the primary and secondary labor markets constitute a good introduction to positive and negative incentives, respectively. Positive incentives include high pay, opportunities for promotion, challenge, interest in the task itself, congenial co-workers, autonomy, the opportunity to be useful or help others, working conditions, fringe benefits, convenience and self-actualization. Negative incentives include the absence or converse of these.

The type and amount of incentives available on the job bears a well-documented and persistent relationship with job satisfaction, which in turn predicts productivity. Conversely, negative incentives predict to job turnover, absenteeism, wastage, pilferage and dispensary visits. Consequently, industrial psychologists have shown a lively interest in incentive factors.

In the literature of industrial psychology, there has been a tradition of distinguishing intrinsic and extrinsic motivation and associated incentives. In intrinsic motivation, the rewards are under the individual's control and relatively independent of environment. Extrinsic motivation is thought to be governed by rewards controlled outside the person. The contrast—which is by no means clearcut in terms of empirical data—is between the sense of accomplishment resulting from achievement and the material reward for achievement.

Earlier scholarship frequently made the mistake of reifying workers' reports of the incentive afforded by their jobs into motivational types. These became further confounded with the social attributes of persons typically filling the jobs, so that instead of a psychology of female jobs authors slipped into talking about the psychology of female workers. From there it is but one step further to the kind of prejudice described by Piore, in which employers' assumptions about the characteristics of a whole category of workers blocks their access to high-incentive jobs.

The expectation of finding differing "female work motivation" and "male work motivation" has died at the hands of empirical data. With the accumulation of evidence, it now appears that some *jobs* afford more in the way of "intrinsic" incentives (e.g., autonomy) than others. Not surprisingly, people in these jobs cite intrinsic satisfactions among their major job incentives. It no longer seems justifiable to assert that some kinds of *people* (e.g., white males who predominate in these jobs) are more "intrinsically motivated" than kinds of people less likely to hold such jobs (e.g., blacks, women, blue-collar workers). Thus in Rand and Miller's (1972) study, the most commonly cited incentives affecting occupational preferences were "own interests and abilities"—an indication of intrinsic motivation. "Personal satisfaction" and "enjoyment of the work" were closely followed by salary (an extrinsic incentive). These do not reflect "masculine" motivation so much as the incentives that persons entering the labor market of college-trained workers can expect to enjoy. It is worth noting that these young women's aspirations do not reflect any foreknowledge of wage discrimination or of the attributes of the jobs they will inherit. The lack of such knowledge is significant in terms of the adequacy or realism of information they possess.

Workers' reports of the satisfactions they find in their work reflect what is available. Thus, Morse and Weiss (1955) found that bases for job satisfaction varied by occupation: professionals and sales persons cited the content of the job itself; managers cited salary; and service workers cited contacts with co-workers and customers. Centers and Bugental (1966) failed to find overall sex differences when they interviewed 692 employed adults concerning the aspects of their jobs they valued. Rather, they found effects of occupational level: workers at lower levels valued extrinsic factors more, while workers at higher levels valued intrinsic factors more.

Occupations appear to differ in the extent to which workers feel the job is central to their lives. Dubin (1955) discovered that for

75 percent of industrial workers in a large-scale study, neither work nor the work place was numbered among central life interests. In this same study, the great majority (91 percent) of workers made family and friends, rather than co-workers, the focus of their social life. Blauner (1960) has shown that a majority of jobs in our occupational structure are neither demanding nor intrinsically rewarding, and the job incumbents do not show a pattern of intense work involvement. Rather, the values they find in their work are often extrinsic ones—pay, benefits, congenial co-workers, seniority.

Morse and Weiss (1955) studied a national sample of employed men. The most common reason men gave for persisting in employment was "to keep occupied." The authors note that 36 percent of those who report they want to keep working give only negative reasons for it, seeming to view their jobs as a means of warding off isolation, idleness or "trouble" (1955, p. 192). When asked what they would miss most if they stopped working, the largest proportion (31 percent) said friends and contacts. Only 12 percent said they would miss "the kind of work I do." Among the positive reasons for working, enjoyment of the kind of work was mentioned by less than seven percent of the men.

Some writers (e.g., Tyler, 1972) opine that the proportion of working women who exhibit "career orientation" is a minority, while implying that career orientation is a majority phenomenon among men. The "myth of the heroic male professional" (Laws, 1976b) is invoked as a standard against which women's work motivation and labor force behavior are compared—a standard to which, as we have just seen, the majority of workers fail to measure up. This kind of invidious comparison exemplifies the way in which a psychological interpretation of social inequalities bolsters the status quo, by finding inadequacies in the individual rather than injustices in the system.

If the model of the hardworking, intensely committed worker with a lifetime involvement with a career fits anyone, it fits the professional (Hall, 1969)—and the research here shows that women professionals do not differ from men in what they put into their work, nor do they differ in their productivity. This tends to be true across the professions, whether we are considering law (White, 1972), academia (Simon et al., 1966), medicine (Phelps, 1968) or secondary school teaching (Kuhlen, 1963).

The professions appear to represent the ideal situation, in terms of work motivation. Besides affording high pay and prestige, these occupations commonly allow the worker a high degree of control over her work, responsibility and the opportunity to use and develop valued skills. In addition, they offer a succession of ranks, with increasing pay and perquisites. These inducements seem to have the same effect on women's work motivation and performance as on men's. Occupations offering these inducements are commonly called careers, and those who are fortunate enough to occupy them are often called career-oriented.

Research on job incentives indicates that women and men respond in the same ways to the same inducements. The research we have reviewed thus far has emphasized job satisfaction, hence positive work incentives. Research on behaviors indexing job dissatisfaction—mainly quitting—give a picture of negative job incentives. In the studies of job attrition conducted in the operating companies of the Bell Telephone Company, dissatisfaction with the pay was cited as the major reason for quitting by terminating operators in Houston, with lack of opportunity for advancement being the second most frequent reason. Terminating operators in the Chesapeake system gave lack of opportunity as the first reason, and salary as the second. Women's reasons for quitting were the same as those of men. A study in Houston indicated that when operators who had quit for these reasons were compared with a group who stayed, the leavers were found to be more intelligent and more independent than the stayers. The Bell system data indicate not only that women will quit when inadequate incentives are offered them, but that the employer loses the best employees this way.

Both positive and negative incentives mobilized in the work situation feed back upon motivation and work-related behaviors. High levels of reward and high expectancy of reward reinforce job attachment and loyalty. High autonomy and control over the work increase the intrinsic satisfaction enjoyed by the work. Among the organizational variables that can be manipulated in order to increase job satisfaction are worker participation in decision-making, e.g., the Scanlon Plan (Coch and French, 1948), strengthening the work group (Cartwright, 1951), varying supervisory style (Bowers and Seashore, 1966; Fiedler, 1961; Patchen, 1962); job enlargment (Killbridge, 1960) and communication (Katz and Kahn, 1966). The emphasis is on the work situation itself, rather than prior experiences or inner personality.

Contemporaneous determinants of work motivation have a social as well as an individual aspect. Since the 1940s it has been known that the roots of psychological satisfaction and dissatisfaction lie in social comparison. Stouffer et al. (1949) discovered that a feeling of "relative deprivation" resulted when soldiers serving in World War II perceived that their outcomes were worse than the outcomes of others in a comparable situation. More recently, industrial psychologists have investigated the relationship between task requirements, rate of pay and feelings of equity or fairness. According to equity theory (Adams, 1963; Lawler, 1968), the individual compares the ratio of her inputs (including skill, education and so forth) to outcomes (or reward) with that of her neighbor. Work motivation and work output are affected by the individual's judgment of the fairness of her rewards relative to those of other workers. The most common way the worker has of adjusting the input: outcome ratio to achieve equity is to reduce output. Another way of seeking equity is to change jobs. In a recent study of the computer industry, Shuster and Atchison (1973) found evidence of variation in ways of coping with inequity, depending on the worker's position vis-à-vis the labor market. These authors found greater length of employment associated with equity, as well. Finally, they found that equitably paid workers were hard-working and loyal.

Another implication of feelings of inequity is the potential for social activism. Occupational discrimination against women is a phenomenon with the potential for developing major social protest. Some aspects of the current situation, however, militate against collective action. There is no evidence at present that women are aware of the extent and nature of sex discrimination in employment. Sex segregation, as we have seen, militates against women's acquiring the knowledge of men's qualifications and pay rates, which sets in motion the psychology of relative deprivation. On the other hand, public opinion polls show that the majority of Americans now support equal pay for equal work. When they realize that inequality is the status quo, will they be ready to take action consistent with their values? Another predictor of increasing activism is the increased labor force attachment of women. As women become more invested in their work life, it is to be expected that a sense of their own self-interest will develop. This will lead to heightened demands with respect to working conditions, benefits (e.g., on-the-job training) and career opportunities, as well as wages.

Achievement Motivation and Sex Role Conflict

The achievement motive (need for achievement or n Ach) has been widely studied throughout the 1950s and 1960s. McClelland et al. (1953) define n Ach as a relatively stable disposition within the individual to strive for sucess in any situation where standards of excellence are applicable. Performance on competitive tests, aspiration level on games of skills and chance, and occupational aspiration have come under study as manifestations of the motivational tendency.

The framework for achievement motivation is Expectancy/Value theory (Lewin, 1951; McClelland and Atkinson, 1953; Atkinson and Raynor, 1974). Research on achievement motivation has discovered that, given a choice, persons high in the need for achievement prefer to work in situations where the probability of success or failure is about the same (Atkinson, 1958). For these persons, a task having too high a probability of success is too easy to arouse the achievement motive; the payoff of winning at an easy task is too low. Conversely, although a very difficult task may be challenging enough to arouse the motive, the threat of failure that accompanies a very low probability of success diminishes motivation. This theory predicts that individuals high in the need for achievement will shun both the very risky and the riskless, preferring odds approximating 50/50. This prediction may appear unexpected to those who imagine the high n Ach individual as one who strives for the most difficult goal. However, it merely underscores the importance of the expectancy term (subjective probability of success).

The achievement motive is an acquired or learned motive (Atkinson, 1958). Both the Expectancy and Value terms reflect the individual's learning about relevant social conditions. Much of this chapter has been devoted to a review of the conditions reflected in women's occupational choices. The conditions confronting women are, as we have seen, substantially different from those confronting men. Moreover, the Value term assumes comparable values for women and men; there is no evidence of an initial difference in the degree to which females and males are attracted to highly rewarded and highly competitive occupations.

The failure to comprehend the different opportunity structures confronting women and men may account for the well-documented neglect of women in the early achievement literature. That literature implicitly presupposes a male work history and a male opportunity structure as the context for studying aspiration and striving. Not surprisingly, measures and operations that provided good prediction for male behavior failed to predict for females. With equal parts lack of chivalry and lack of creativity, the authors of this tradition decided to omit women from their research until the late 1960s when women were rehabilitated through the discoveries of Matina Horner.

The striving for excellence need not be restricted to activities dominated and esteemed by men, although that is the scope of the achievement research tradition. There has been an early and persistent tradition focusing on women s ambition, which attempted to assess achievement motivation in the context of female tasks. For the laboratory and academic achievement contexts depicted in the standard Thematic Apperception Test picture series, these authors substituted pictures of women sewing, baking and so forth. The results of these studies have always been equivocal, perhaps because women who have acquired the achievement motive have done so in a sexist context. They have learned to esteem science more than sewing, and brain work more than baking; the image of success is for them, as for other creatures of our culture, the white male's.

Another research strategy is implied in the work of Stein and Bailey (1973). They defined achievement motivation as involving a general pattern of striving for excellence *in self-selected areas*. This definition preserves the motivational dynamic—striving behavior, associated with the idea of excellence—without restricting it to arenas in which women's efforts are traditionally discouraged. Veroff and Feld (1970) said that parenthood fits the definition of an achievement situation. How many other endeavors are there in which the individual strives for excellence, overcoming obstacles and persisting to the ultimate triumph, without ever coming to the attention of a researcher? What is the scope of achievement motivation and achievement behavior that is not chronicled in *American Men of Science*?

An answer to this question must await the accumulation of research that does not share the flaws of the existing research tradition. However, there are complexities in women's achievement behavior even within the restricted male corral that require further analysis. These are rooted in sex-typing of occupations and its multiple effects on Expectancy and Value. The significance of the sex composition of an occupation has already been mentioned. The sex ratio of the work group on the job has the same significance. The most prestigious and demanding jobs in our occupational hierarchy are not only sex-typed masculine but are dominated by men as well. On both counts, women's aspiring to such an occupation threatens the "masculinity" of the job and of those who hold the job. Their response is often to challenge the femininity of the woman seeking entrance to the occupation. The fear of sex role invalidation is at the heart of the sex role conflict involved in the Motive to Avoid Success (M_ Succ). This sex role invalidation is exactly parallel to the male fear of symbolic "emasculation." Any achievement situation—for instance, academic performance, sports competition or striving for occupational success—can potentially arouse a conflict, for women, between social acceptance as an adequate female and recognition for achievement.

THE MOTIVE TO AVOID SUCCESS

This dilemma came to light with Horner's (1968) dramatic findings on the Motive to Avoid Success. Horner discovered that situations where the achievement motive is aroused have additional meaning for women. In the presence of cues that define an achievement situation, n Ach is aroused but for many women, the M_ Succ is simultaneouly aroused. This motive reflects fears that to succeed is to fail as a woman, and suffer social rejection. Horner developed her idea of the M_ Succ from the stories college students wrote to the following cue:

> After first term finals, Anne finds herself at the top of her medical school class.

Horner conceived of the Motive to Avoid Success as a stable property of the person, acquired in conjunction with sex role socialization. Subsequent development of the theory has emphasized the cultural elements of M_ Succ. If the expectation of negative outcomes of achievement *for women* is part of the cultural script, men should have learned this too, and should generate fear of success stories in response to the standard M_ Succ cue. In fact, this is what happens. Monahan et al. (1974) found that males as well as females told M_ Succ stories, and only to the "Anne" cue. A parallel cue with a male protagonist elicited few fear of success stories from either females or males. Negative consequences of success are expected only for females. The confirmation of the cultural script hypothesis is important, but an equally significant implication of Monahan et al.'s findings relates to the behavioral relevance of the script. The ways women and men act on this script are different: men may act to make the anticipated negative consequences of female achievement real, while women must try to avoid these negative consequences. Put another way, men's success does not invalidate their masculinity or inspire social rejection; quite the contrary. Their achievement striving and enjoyment of success are unaffected by what this cultural script prescribes for women.

Monahan et al.'s findings are particularly important in view of the controversies within the research tradition concerned with M_ Succ. Fear of success is, first of all, not a motive to seek failure, nor a repudiation of success as a goal, as some authors have claimed (Tresemer, 1974). Although there is evidence that some individuals hold a negative valence for success, this is a different phenomenon from M_ Success, which is a true approach/avoidance conflict. In terms of Expectancy/Value theory, the repudiation of success could be represented by a simple negative valence associated with success. The motive to avoid success, on the other hand, involves both positive and negative valences associated with success, and only among women.[7] Behavioral manifestations of these two distinct motivational patterns are also distinguishable. Simple avoidance of achievement would suffice for those motivated by the need to repudiate success. However, the approach/avoidance motivation is more complex.

A study by Weiss (1962) illustrates this complexity. In an experiment involving squeezing a dynamometer, women were told

---

[7]This is in part an artifact of the sex tested and the sex-typing of tasks investigated. It would certainly be possible to study a situation in which succeeding at a female sex-typed task puts a male's masculinity in threat and requires him to resolve a quandary parallel to the motive to avoid success.

that they were squeezing harder than the men. Their behavioral response was to cut back on the pressure they were exerting, but their self-reports indicated the presence of a feeling of guilt for slacking off. If the motivation were simply to remain in good standing as a feminine person by demonstrating incompetence, the accompanying psychological state would be one of satisfaction or relief at having evaded the threat to femininity. In the situation created by Weiss, however, the solution to the sex role dilemma satisfied the avoidance motive at the expense of the approach motive; hence, the guilt.

It should not be surprising, in the light of sex role socialization, that in many cases the achievement motive is compromised to make peace with sex role standards. Existing research shows, however, that there are several ways of resolving or adapting to the sex role dilemma. Additional research is required in order to specify the conditions under which an individual will adopt one rather than another. One response to the conflict between achievement and femininity is to abandon the sphere of competition—in fantasy and in fact. Thus, in Horner's original study, some respondents wrote that "Anne," the medical student protagonist, becomes a nurse. The lowering of occupational aspiration (Schwenn, 1970), in high-ability college women who have not experienced failure, is presumably a real-life parallel to this fantasy "solution." Another solution generated by Horner's respondents was vicarious achievement: Anne drops out of medical school and marries her boyfriend, who becomes a successful doctor. Another solution is to deny responsibility for success (Kanter, 1977). Interestingly, research on processes of attribution reveal sex differences that are consistent with this strategy. Women tend not to take credit for their successes, attributing these to transitory or external causes rather than their own stable attributes, while men do the reverse (Unger, 1975; Dweck, 1975).

Both the failure to take credit and the reluctance to compete with men may be responsible for the "confidence gap" that appears consistently in studies of women's aspirations and expectations.

When compared with males, females tend to report lower aspiration *relative to past performance*. Girls' expectancy is lower than that of boys, even when their achievement is higher (Crandall, 1969; Baird, 1973). In an Educational Testing Service study of college seniors, Baird found that 44.6 percent of the men but only 29.4 percent of the women intended to go to graduate school. The sex difference held true up and down the scale of past achievement, so that the proportion of men with C+ averages who planned to go on in school equaled that of women with B+ or A averages.

The conditions for the arousal of the motive to avoid success are nearly ubiquitous in the world of work. In any job that is sex-typed masculine, in any instance of striving for achievement, in any success experience, a woman worker is vulnerable to this immobilizing conflict. However, the conflict requires a specific trigger. The identification and neutralization of these triggers could do much to remove this threat to women's effectiveness.

Current research has revealed only some of the factors associated with the arousal of sex role conflict in achievement situations. The physical presence of males appears to be such a factor. Girls perform better in all-girl schools than in coed schools (Sutherland, 1961; Fahrner and Cronin, 1963). Horner (1968) found that women students high in n Ach/M_ Succ performed worst in a situation where they were tested along with male peers. Komarovsky (1946) found that college women reported they "played dumb" on dates. Peplau (1973) found that college women were unwilling to compete with their boyfriends. These findings spell out the sex role dilemma that women confront in the occupational world: women fear to perform successfully in front of men or to compete with men. They fear even the appearance of doing so. A number of studies show that women are motivated to deny or dissemble their ability on the basis of what they *think* men desire of them (Steinman and Fox, 1966; Hawley, 1971; Matthews and Tiedeman, 1964). Matthews and Tiedeman found that older adolescent women reported lower career commitment than did younger ones. The strongest predictor of low career commitment was the belief that males disapprove of women's using their intelligence.

These studies of unmarried women suggest a connection between concern with social rejection and nubility. This leads to a prediction that marital status is a factor in how vulnerable or protected a woman is to having her feminine identity undermined. In cultural terms, the married woman is certified; hence, she is under less of an obligation to "prove" her femininity by satisfying the nontask expectations of her male peers. The single woman who is not part of a couple is more vulnerable. Moreover, she is more of a threat, as Wolman and Frank (1971) observe, since the possibility of her forming a sexual bond with one of the group threatens their male solidarity. It may be that realistically she can expect a more punitive response from male peers than does her married counterpart.

Another factor affecting the vulnerability of a woman worker to sex role invalidation is the sex ratio of the occupation and of the work group. The more skewed the sex ratio in favor of men, the more difficult it will be: the sole woman carries an excessive burden as the target of all her colleagues' projections.

Finally, the possibility that male co-workers will explicitly and deliberately arouse sex role conflicts by baiting the woman recruit cannot be ruled out. Research on women in nontraditional occupations document a whole range of harassment and sabotage by male co-workers and sometimes supervisors. Of these studies, we will cite here only those relating specifically to sex role issues.

Although the literature on the motive to avoid success has provided a detailed picture of women's side of the sex role dilemma, it is silent on the topic of men's contribution. Yet the motive to avoid success is not a female paranoid delusion. As Monahan et al. have shown, the theme of negative consequences for female achievement is widely known. It is available for manipulation by anyone. How and under what conditions men manipulate this fear to disarm women's competition in task situations is revealed in the following studies.

Male Resistance to Female Participation
in Achievement Situations

In a classic paper, Wolman and Frank (1972) studied the experiences of task groups in which there was a single woman participant. Although the women attempted to achieve the role of regular group member (and in one case, group leader), all were ultimately forced into one of two roles: isolate or deviant. Both roles effectively prevented the woman's contributions from being taken into account by the group and blocked her from receiving the benefits of group participation.

Wolman and Frank analyze the male-culture aspects of the way work gets done in groups.[8] Although this is only one of several possible ways of organizing work, it is one that produces predictable problems when women are introduced into groups structured in this way. Wolman and Frank observed that the woman member was excluded from the normal group processes in a male group: jockeying for power, competition for leadership, coalition formation and the emergence of a clear pecking order. In most instances, male members did not risk violating the group norm by forming coalitions with the female member. The women were excluded from the competition, although they were occasionally treated as audiences for or prizes in male competition.

Wolman and Frank point out that much of the group's attention and energy were consumed in dealing with the female member, although the problem was not recognized as such nor dealt with constructively. Rather, the means adopted by the men were extremely painful and stressful to the woman member. In all cases, the women experienced anxiety, anger and/or depression. "Suc-

---

[8]An analysis of men's problems in dealing with women in a task setting fails outside the scope of this chapter. However, one aspect of this problem is dealt with in Judith Lorber's paper, "Trust, loyalty and the place of women in the informal organization of work" (paper presented at the annual meeting of the American Sociological Association, 1975).

cessful" participation was simply staying in the group; however, working under such conditions afforded none of the rewards usually associated with professional occupations.

Mayes (1976) studied self-analytic groups composed of professionals brought together for workshops for varying lengths. Mayes studied follower–leader and follower–follower relationships as a function of sex of the group leader. Males led by a female refused to play by the rules: they did not cooperate in the task and did not follow her leadership. They attempted to stage a coup and urged each other not to cooperate. In contrast to the overt behavior, the verbalized concerns focused almost exclusively upon sex role contents unrelated to the task. Male followers adopted either a hostile or a dependent posture toward the female leader, sometimes combining both in an overtly seductive posture.

Toward their female peers, male followers adopted a strategy of sex role invalidation, demanding a loyalty oath of heterosexuality and manipulating female guilt and/or nurturance by claiming to be wounded and castrated in the situation of female leadership. The effect of this sex role pressure on the female followers was immediate and definitive. They retreated from active participation in the groups, and engaged in ritual behavior by changing to dresses, appearing in makeup and the like. The initial effectiveness of their participation in female-led groups was extinguished. Mayes notes that female group members who did not capitulate to the sex role pressure withdrew before the end of the workshop; they dropped out. Mayes does not comment on the unenviable situation of the female leader.

Pleck has analyzed a personality trait or predisposition he calls Male Threat from Female Competence (MTFC), which casts further light on the male-club atmosphere in which some individuals strongly prefer to work. Males who scored high on this psychological variable showed the lowest liking for the experimental task and the least willingness for future participation with their partner—even though their partner was their long-term girlfriend (1976). These results underscore the difficulty some males have in dealing with women on any basis other than sex role interaction.

This difficulty presents an obstacle to women's participation in the labor market which no amount of assertion training can change. It is questionable whether changing the *manner* of women's participation in a male world of work will have any effect, in view of the substantial resistance to the *fact* of their participation.

LABOR MARKET MYTHS AND THEIR FUNCTIONS

In addition to the obstacles posed by objective social arrangements, working women suffer from the effects of a whole host of subjective beliefs that compromise their success in the workplace. These are myths: counterfactual beliefs or stories that yet retain some currency among the population. Myths of primitive peoples often serve the function of providing an acceptable (though inaccurate) explanation of observable phenomena that are incompletely understood (for example, the seasons, biological paternity, the origin of the physical world). The myth is made plausible by its connections with other elements of culture, including the practices for which it provides the rationalization. So it is with myths about women workers. Myths about women in the work force support and rationalize the major cultural themes of male dominance/female inferiority and sexual segregation. In a secular society, myths are accorded no ritual significance, nor even awareness. Rather, they masquerade as facts. Myths about women workers constitute a somewhat coherent set of definitions about women workers—all of them distorted in varying degrees: definitions of who *is* the woman worker, what *are* her goals and capabilities. These constitute a nonconscious ideology (Ryan, 1971). As Ryan notes, the function of a nonconscious ideology is to support the status quo (and discredit challenges to the status quo). However, it must remain nonconscious; otherwise the element of self-interest would become apparent to both those supporting the status quo and its challengers. The labor force myths serve the function of suppressing the potentially threatening competition of women with men for jobs.

Some of the most popular myths have been compiled by the

Women's Bureau of the U.S. Department of Labor (1971). They include the idea that women are casual laborers rather than bread-winners; that women lose more time from work than men for illness; the fear that women take jobs away from men. All of these are false. Some myths have been prefigured in the literature reviewed earlier in the chapter—for example, the belief that women are characterized by a distinctive and inferior type of work motivation. Other myths are really value statements rather than statements of fact: the idea that woman's place is in the home. Others are value statements masquerading as factual statements: for example, the assertion that when mothers work, children become delinquent. Such myths castigate women for not occupying themselves fully with home and family. Such beliefs—and the actions stemming from them—operate as social control mechanisms which punish women for departing from traditional sex roles and priorities. As we have seen, the sex role script requires women to give priority to family responsibilities, at the expense of labor force performance if necessary. The "choice" is influenced by threats that family relationships or the wellbeing of family members will suffer if a woman persists in job involvement. This cultural myth is so powerful that even scientists who have made a specialty of studying the achievements of women of talent assert, without citing evidence, that job success may interfere with marital success (Terman and Oden, 1959, p. 106). This is another example of through-the-looking-glass thinking: the evidence is that marriage may interfere with career success. Evidence that supports the myth is still lacking.

Some myths are best understood as projections. In this type of myth, problems exhibited by men are projected into women. The objection that a woman cannot be both feminine and competent is a projection of men's preoccupation with sex and their preference for dealing with women as sex objects rather than peers. The claim that women cannot supervise men is men's desire to maintain dominance, turned inside out to resemble an objective fact. The myth that women work for "pin money" appears as a kind of wishful thinking: a denial that women's labor market activity is essential coupled with a nostalgia for the role of male breadwinner and the power monopoly it entailed.

The factual basis for such myths is nil. What is impressive, however, is the degree to which they are believed. Many of them emerge as "reasons" for discriminating against women on the part of men who are in a position to do so.

One example is the belief that women cannot supervise men, or lack leadership qualities in general. In the extensive research on supervisory styles that is by now available, there are no clear-cut or consistent sex differences (Roussel, 1974; Boehm, 1975). In Lyle and Ross's (1973) study, *male* managers reported that they had different modes of management for female and male employees; *female* managers treated both groups the same. (There are special difficulties confronting women in leadership positions, but these have nothing to do with skills or credentials.) Strodtbeck and Mann (1956) found that women exhibiting leadership traits were rejected; Whitaker (1965) found that males were perceived as a more credible source of influence than females. Male subordinates react differently to supervision by women and by men, as we have seen. Eskilson and Wiley (1976) found that male subjects (Ss) working with a female leader in an experimental situation made fewer requests for leadership than did male Ss working with a male leader. Nevertheless, female-led groups performed as well on the task as male-led groups, and better on some measures.

A factor analysis of male managers' attitudes toward women's roles, especially in the world of work, was reported by Bass et al. (1971). The pattern of endorsement of attitude items indicated that the greatest obstacle to women's acceptance was sex role ideology rather than belief in women's lack of capability. The factor accounting for the largest proportion of the variance comprised negative attitudes toward women's combining work and family roles. Concerns with male dominance, predictably, figured in a factor reflecting women's potential for supervisory positions. Myths about absenteeism figured in the third factor, and a fourth was concerned with deference behavior between the sexes. In this study, managers who showed the most negative attitudes toward women workers were those who worked with women *subordinates* only. However, mere exposure to women at work does not affect these negative attitudes.

A study of male managers' attitudes within the Bell Telephone Company (E.E.O.C. 1289) echoed myths about female mobility, and also indicated some shortcomings of male managers which, by a process of projection, become stumbling blocks for women attempting to handle their jobs. Objections to women in management included:

1. fears about what others would think if women are promoted;
2. men's sexism ("men cannot consider women as equals"); and
3. males' feelings of threat from women's competence or competition.

None of these refer to women's behavior or qualifications, and hence are outside of women's control. Nevertheless they are obstacles to women's career success, because of the power structure of male-dominated management.

Thus, the most serious obstacle to women's occupational success may well consist in counterfactual prejudices—myths—held by men who have the power to evaluate and promote them. Rosen and Jerdee (1974) found that sex role stereotypes affected the evaluation of women's promotability, the willingness to select young females for training opportunities and selection for a management position requiring travel. Although the job history and personnel evaluations of the female and male candidates were exactly the same, respondents perceived them to be enough different that they found the woman less suitable for the job and less likely to remain with the organization (1974, p. 55).

The Rosen and Jerdee study, which utilized alternate forms of a questionnaire that involved either a female or a male protagonist in a variety of organizational situations, uncovered clear effects of traditional sex role expectations for women. Respondents *expected* women to sacrifice their careers for their families. Greater valuing of males was made evident by the greater efforts to retain a male employee whose job was threatened by his personal conduct (1974, p. 47). Similarly, less severe sanctions for infringements were recommended for male than for female executives. Spouses of career women were expected to provide much less support than were spouses of career men (1974, p. 49).

Interestingly, Rosen and Jerdee found women respondents much less prejudiced against women in some areas than were the males (1974, p. 57). A number of other studies have found the same result (Mead and Kaplan, 1965; Haavio-Manila, 1969).

Belief in labor market myths and neglect of empirical data are not limited to ordinary citizens or practical men of affairs. Academic scholars show the same astigmatism as those lacking special expertise in work motivation or occupational choice. Thus, Psathas' (1968) often-quoted theory of women's occupational choice attempts to correct for the neglect of women in the occupational literature. He does so, however, by taking into account only those aspects of women's lives that are circumscribed by traditional sex roles: marriage, childbearing and family income adequacy. There is no attempt to explore women's motivation for work in terms of incentives related to the job; paid employment is presented as a temporary expedient instrumental for the attainment of traditional family (rather than personal) goals. Psathas' work exemplifies the intellectual double standard of scholarly work on women. Although traditional models of occupational choice are reviewed, no attempt is made to integrate women. Rather, Psathas' "theory" takes the form of a footnote (or deviant case) to the "normal" theories. No attempt is made to substantiate Psathas' assumptions concerning the nature of and priorities in women's motivation for employment. Finally, Psathas makes no use of the empirical evidence available at the time of writing.

Zytowski (1969) provides another example of a theory about women's vocational behavior that ignores the data. Zytowski asserts as axiomatic that the modal life role for women is that of homemaker. He does not specify whether "modal" is operationalized in terms of time budgeting, exclusivity, personal commitment or the possession of ovaries. A lifecycle model presented by Zytowski has no entry between age 6 and age 20: no data on the formation of occupational intentions, sex-typing, role modeling or educational preparation for occupation are introduced. In developing a typology of degrees of vocational participation, Zytowski labels female-dominated occupations as "low participation" by definition. He also asserts that homemaking and employment are mutually incompatible (1969, p. 662), apparently overlooking the statistics on labor force participation of married women, husband present, with young children at home. Lacking a theory of work motivation, Zytowski permits himself to assert that women's preferences for patterns of vocational participation "is determined mainly by internal, motivated factors" (1969, p. 663). He does not recognize the necessity of ascertaining both expectancy and value data, and makes the error of confounding the resultant (or choice) with one predictor (value).

The persistence of myths about women workers irresistibly draws attention to the functions that they serve. If the content of the myths does not constitute information—and we have seen that it does not—then it must communicate something else, perhaps an inventory of concerns. In this connection it is interesting that most of the myths appear to be directed more at the employed wife and mother than at the single woman. One may speculate that the greater threat posed by single women is being denied. Certainly the single woman is freer to pursue the male model of career ambition than is the woman with family responsibilities (though she may not choose to do so). She can travel; she can work overtime; she can take risks; she can go back to school. There is no question of her husband's "letting" her work. There are no child victims to her ambition, who can be used to arouse debilitating guilt.

Myths about women in the work force also overlook the female head of household. By focusing on the working wife, these myths obscure, and hence are unresponsive to, the distinctive needs of this large group of working women. The "invisibility" of these two large groups of women workers is an example of the paradox of women's disappearing needs, which is seen again in Chapter 2.

The paradox is explained by the peculiarities of male vision: what is not seen can be presumed not to exist.

However, it can be argued that the average man (and men as a class) have more to lose if wives escape the strictures prescribed by labor market myths than if single women do.

The myths about working mothers are perhaps the most insidious, because many of them are plausible—they just are not factual. It is frequently quoted, for example, that women who live in families do not have the freedom to move that similarly situated men do. Hence, the argument goes, they will refuse transfers and promotions. If they are bound to refuse, they have poor promotion potential; hence, they should not be offered the opportunity. Only one study has come to my attention that actually puts these assumptions to the test. In a study of civilian employees of the United States Army, it was found that most employees, male and female, had never been asked to move for the job (1973, p. 13). Of civilian employees asked to relocate temporarily in the course of their duties, 89 percent of the men had always accepted, as compared with 87 percent of the women (1973, p. 14). An employee's willingness to move, like so many related questions, is better viewed as a function of the incentives mobilized in the choice situation. Where payoffs are equalized for women and men, gender will no longer be a basis for prediction.

This, of course, implies a single standard rather than a double standard—for opportunity, for evaluation and for reward. The labor market myths, however, exemplify the other tradition: the double standard, spelled out in doctrines of difference. Doctrines of difference are employed both to distance and differentiate women and men, and to rationalize their unequal treatment. Doctrines of difference operate within the framework of male as dominant, female as deviant. As we have seen, doctrines of difference are used to exaggerate or even fabricate sex differences (e.g., in turnover and absenteeism). Where sex differences do exist (e.g., in childbearing responsibilities of parents of young children) the male pattern is regarded as the norm and the female pattern as problematic or nonconforming.

It is clear that, in the absence of doctrines of difference, the treatment of males as the dominant and females as the deviant group would arouse feelings of inequity and protest. At the ideological level, doctrines of difference operate in a way parallel to the structural arrangements of occupational segregation: to inhibit social comparison between the sexes. Similarly, attempts to bring about integration in the labor market imply an ideology of individual merit and equal opportunity.

We have seen that the labor market myths misrepresent working women. Universally defining women workers as wives and as secondary wage earners or financial dependents is at variance with the facts of women's work histories. However, defining women in the way they ought to be is an instance of the preemptive power of naming. When a definition is already present, all competing initiatives are in reaction to it. Moreover, as we have noted, the power of naming, or the power to define, carries with it the power to prescribe behavior consistent with the definition. Thus, labeling is a more economical means of social control than is coercion.

The masculine view of women's work motivation and employment behavior differs substantially from accounts of women's experience. A large part of the distortion derives from the tendency to see women in ways that are instrumental to men's goals. The larger process is objectification of women, where man defines himself as Subject and woman as Object. Male self-interest is clearly served in a situation where women can be induced to take jobs that increase family income without threatening male monopoly and at the same time retain responsibility for all the work of the home. These issues are developed in Chapter 2.

REFERENCES

Acker, J., and Van Houten, D.R. 1974. Differential recruitment and control: the sex structuring of organizations, *Administrative Science Quarterly* 19: 152–163.

Adams, J.S. 1963. Toward an understanding of inequity, *Journal of Abnormal & Social Psychology* 67, 5: 422–436.

Almquist, E., and Angrist, S. 1970. Role model influences on college women's career aspirations. Paper read at the meeting of the American Sociological Association.

———. 1971. Role Model influence on college women's career aspirations, *Merrill-Palmer Quarterly* 17: 263–279.

Almquist, Elizabeth, and Angrist, Shirley. 1970. Career salience and atypicality of occupational choice among college women, *Journal of Marriage and the Family* 32, 2: 242–249.

Angrist, Shirley. 1972. Changes in women's work aspirations during college, *International Journal of Sociology of the Family* 2, 1: 1–11.

——— and Almquist, Elizabeth M. 1975. *Careers and Contingencies: How College Women Juggle with Gender*. Port Washington, New York: Kennikat Press Corp.

Atkinson, J.W. 1958. Towards an experimental analysis of human motivation in terms of motives, expectancies, and incentives. In *Motives in Fantasy, Action and Society*, ed. J.W. Atkinson, pp. 288–306. Princeton: D. Van Nostrand Company, Inc.

——— and Raynor, Joel O. 1974. *Motivation and Achievement*. Washington, D.C.: V.H. Winston and Sons.

Bailyn, Lotte. Notes on the role of choice in the psychology of professional women. In *The Woman in America*, Robert Lifton, ed., pp. 236–246. Boston: Beacon Press.

Baird, L.L. 1973. *The Graduates*. Princeton: Educational Testing Service.

Baruch, G.K. 1972. Maternal influences upon college women's attitudes toward women and work, *Developmental Psychology* 6, 1: 32–37.

Baruch, R. 1967. The achievement motive in women: implications for career development, *Journal of Personality and Social Psychology* 5: 260–267.

Bass, B.M., Krusell, J., and Alexander, R.A. 1971. Male managers' attitudes toward working women, *American Behavioral Scientist*, pp. 221–236.

Battle, E.S. 1966. Motivational determinants of academic task persistence, *Journal of Personality and Social Psychology* 4: 634–642.

Bayer, A.E. 1973. Teaching faculty in academe: 1972–73. Washington, DC: American Council on Education, Research Rep. #2.

Becker, H.S., Geer, B., Hughes, E.C., and Strauss, A.L. 1961. *Boys in white: student culture in medical school*. Chicago: University of Chicago Press.

Bell, Carolyn Shaw. 1974. Working women's contributions to family income, *Eastern Economic Journal* 1, 2–3: 185–201.

Bem, S.L., and Bem, D.J. 1972. Do sex-biased job advertisements discourage applicants of the opposite sex? Testimony before the Federal Commerce Commission.

Bergmann, B. 1973. The 1973 Report of the President's Council of Economic Advisors: The economic role of women, *American Economic Review* 63: 509–514.

Bernard, J. 1971. *Women and the public interest: an essay on public policy and protest*. Chicago: Aldine Atherton.

Birnbaum, J.A. 1971. *Life patterns, personality style and self-esteem in gifted family oriented and career committed women*. Unpublished Ph.D. dissertation, University of Michigan.

Blauner, R. 1960. Work satisfaction and industrial trends in modern society. In *Labor and Trade Unionism*, eds. W. Galenson and S.M. Lipset. New York: Wiley.

Boehm, Virginia. 1975. The competent woman manager: will success spoil women's lib? Paper presented at the annual meetings of the American Psychological Association.

Bowers, D.G., and Seashore, S.E. 1966. Predicting organizational effectiveness with a four-factor theory of leadership, *Administrative Science Quarterly* 11: 238–263.

Brayfield, A.H., and Crockett, W.H. 1955. Employee attitudes and employee performance, *Psychological Bulletin* 52: 396–424.

Campbell, Patricia. 1973. Feminine intellectual decline during adolescence. Ph.D. dissertation, Syracuse University.

Caplow, T. 1954. *The Sociology of Work*. Minneapolis: University of Minnesota Press.

Carey, G.L. 1955. Reduction of sex differences in problem-solving by improvement of attitude through group discussion. Ph.D. dissertation, Stanford University, unpublished.

Cartwright, D. 1951. Achieving change in people: some applications of group dynamics theory, *Human Relations* 4: 381–392.

Centers, R., and Bugental, D.E. 1966. Intrinsic and extrinsic job motivations among different segments of the working population, *Journal of Applied Psychology* 50: 193–197.

Coch, L., and French, J.R.P. Jr. 1948. Overcoming resistance to change, *Human Relations* 1: 512–532.

Conant, E.H. and Kilbridge, M.D. 1965. An interdisciplinary analysis of job enlargement: technology, costs, and behavioral implications. *Industrial and Labor Relations Review* 18: 377–397.

Constantinople, A. 1967. Perceived instrumentality of the college as a measure of attitudes toward the college, *Journal of Personality and Social Psychology* 5: 196–201.

Coser, R.L., and Rokoff, G. 1974. Women in the occupational world: social disruption and conflict. In *The Family: Its Structures and Functions*, ed. Rose Laub Coser, 2nd edition. New York: St. Martin's Press.

Crandall, V.C., and Battle, E.S. 1970. The antecedents and adult correlates of academic and intellectual achievement effort. In *Minnesota Symposium on Child Psychology*, ed. J.P. Hill, Vol. 4. Minneapolis: University of Minnesota Press.

David, D.S. 1974. Occupational values and sex: the case of scientists and engineers. Paper presented at the annual meeting of the American Sociological Association.

Davis, E. 1964. Careers as concerns of blue-collar girls. In *Blue Collar World: Studies of the American Worker*, eds. A. Shostak and W. Gomberg, pp. 154–164. Englewood Cliffs, NJ: Prentice-Hall, Inc.

Douvan, E., and Adelson, J. 1966. *The Adolescent Experience*. New York: Wiley.

Dubin, R. 1955. Industrial workers' worlds: a study of the "central life interests" of industrial workers. *Social Problems* 3: 131–142.

Duncan, O.D., and Duncan, B. 1955. A methodological analysis of segregation indexes, *American Sociological Review* 20: 210–217.

Dweck, C.S. 1975. The role of expectations and attributions in the alleviation of learned helplessness, *Journal of Personality and Social Psychology* 31: 674–685.

Empey, L.T. 1958. Role expectations of women regarding marriage and a career, *Marriage and Family Living* 20: 152–155.

Epstein, C.F. 1969. Women lawyers and their profession: inconsistency of social controls and their consequences for professional performance. Paper read at the meetings of the American Sociological Association.

———. 1970. Encountering the male establishment: sex-status limits on women's careers in the professions, *American Journal of Sociology* 75: 965–982.

———. 1971. *Woman's place: options and limits in professional careers*. Berkeley: University of California Press.

Equal Employment Opportunity Commission. 1969. I Quit! a study of short tenure losses in the plant department. (R-791) Washington, DC: U.S. Government Printing Office.

———. 1970a Plant force retention project interviewing summary. (Z-728) Washington, DC: U.S. Government Printing Office.

———. 1970b. Psychological factors affecting operator turnover. (R-798) Washington, DC: U.S. Government Printing Office.

———. 1970c. The service representative: her story. (Z-727) Washington Commercial Personnel. Washington DC: U.S. Government Printing Office.

———. 1970c. The utilization of women in the management of the Bell System. (#1289) Washington, DC: U.S. Government Printing Office.

———. 1972. A unique competence: a study of equal employment opportunity in the Bell System. Washington, DC: U.S. Government Printing Office.

Erikson, E. 1964. Inner and outer space: reflections on womanhood. In *The Woman in America*, ed. R. Lifton. Boston: Beacon Press.

Eskilson, Arlene, and Wiley, Mary G. 1976. Sex composition and leadership in small groups, *Sociometry* 39, 3: 183–194.

Fahrner, C.J., and Cronin, J.M. 1963. Grouping by sex, *Nat. Educ. Association J.* 52: 16–17.

Farmer, H.S., and Bohn, M.J. 1970. Home-career conflict reduction and the level of career interest in women, *Journal of Counselling Psychology* 17, 3: 228–232.

Feather, N.T., and Simon, J.G. 1975. Reactions to male and female success and failure in relation to the perceived status and sex-typed appropriateness of occupations, *Journal of Personality and Social Psychology* 31: 536–548.

77

Festinger, Leon. 1954. A theory of social comparison processes, *Human Relations* 7: 117–139.

Fichter, J.H. 1964. Young Negro talent: survey of the experiences and expectations of Negro Americans who graduated from college in 1961. Chicago: N.O.R.C.

Fidell, Linda S., and DeLamater, John, eds. 1971. Women in the professions: what's all the fuss about? *American Behavioral Scientist* 15, No. 2.

French, E., and Lesser, G.S. 1964. Some characteristics of the achievement motive in women, *Journal of Abnormal and Social Psychology*. 68: 119–128.

Fuchs, V.R. 1971. Differences in hourly earnings between men and women. *Monthly Labor Review* 94: 9–15.

Ginzberg, Eli, Ginsburg, Sol W., Axelrad, Sidney, and Heuna, John L. 1951. *Occupational Choice: An Approach to a General Theory*. New York: Columbia University Press.

Glenn, H.M. 1959. Attitudes of women regarding gainful employment of married women, *Journal of Home Economics* 51: 247–252.

Goode, W.J. 1960. A theory of role strain. *Am. Sociol. Rev.* 25, 4: 483–496.

Goodman, Paul, and Friedman, A. 1971. An examination of Adams' theory of inequity, *Admin. Sci. Quart.* 16: 271–286.

Gubbels, Robert. 1972. The supply and demand for female workers. In *Woman in a Man-Made World*, ed. Nona Glazer-Malbin and Helen Youngelson Waehrer, pp. 208–218. Chicago: Rand McNally and Company.

Gurin, P., and Katz, D. 1966. *Motivation and aspiration in the Negro College* Ann Arbor: ISR.

Haavio-Manila, E. 1969. Some consequences of women's emancipation, *J. Marr. Fam.* 31: 123–134.

Hall, R.H. 1969. *Occupations and the Social Structure*. Englewood Cliffs, NJ: Prentice-Hall, Inc.

Hamilton, M.T. 1970. Woman power and discrimination in the labor market. Chicago: University of Chicago. Unpublished.

Handbook of Women Workers. 1969. Women's Bureau Bulletin 294 Washington, DC: U.S. Department of Labor.

Harmon, L.W. 1967. Women's working patterns related to their SVIB Housewife and "own" occupational scores, *Journal of Counseling Psychology* 14: 299–301.

———. 1969. Predictive power over ten years of measured social service and scientific interests among college women, *Journal of Applied Psychology* 53: 193–198.

———. 1970. Anatomy of career commitment in women. *Journal of Counseling Psychology* 17: 77–80.

———. 1971. The childhood and adolescent career plans of college women, *Journal of Vocational Behavior* 1: 45–56.

Hartley, Ruth E. 1960. Children's concepts of male and female roles, *Merrill-Palmer Quarterly* 6: 84–91.

———. 1964. A developmental view of female sex role definition and identification, *Merrill-Palmer Quarterly* 10, 1: 3–16.

78

———— and Hardesty, F.D. 1964. Children's perceptions of sex roles in childhood. *J. Genet. Psychology* 105: 43–51.

Hawley, M.F. Relationship of women's perception of men's views of feminine ideal to career choice.

Hawley, P. 1971. What women think men think: does it affect their career choice? *J. Couns. Psychol.* 18, 3: 193–199.

Hedges, J.N. 1970. Women workers and manpower demands in the 1970's, *Monthly Labor Review*, pp. 19–29.

Heer, D.M. 1958. Dominance and the working wife, *Social Forces* 26: 341–347.

Hennig, M.M. 1973. Family dynamics for developing positive achievement motivation in women: the successful woman executive, *Successful Women in the Sciences: An Analysis of Determinants, Annals of the N.Y. Academy of Sciences* 208: 26–81.

Herzberg, F., Mausner, B., and Snyderman, B. 1959. *The Motivation to Work.* New York: Wiley

Himmelweit, H. 1960. *Television and the Child.* New York: Oxford University Press.

Hodge, R.W., and Hodge, P. 1965. Occupational assimilation as a competitive process, *American Journal of Sociology* 71: 249–264.

Hodge, R.W., Siegel, P.M., and Rossi, P. 1964. Occupational prestige in the United States, 1925–1963. *American Journal of Sociology* 70, 3: 286–302.

Hoffman, L.W. 1974. Fear of success in males and females: 1965 and 1972, *J. Consulting and Clinical Psychology*, 42: 353–358.

———— 1963. The decision to work. In *The Employed Mother in America*, eds. Nye, F.I., and Hoffman, L.W., Chicago: Rand McNally.

Hornaday, J.A., and Kuder, G.F. 1961. A study of male occupational scales applied to women. *Educational and Psychological Measurement* 21: 859–864.

Horner, M.S. 1968. Sex differences in achievement motivation and performance. Unpublished doctoral dissertation, University of Michigan.

———— 1969a The motive to avoid success in women. Paper read at the meetings of the American Psychological Association, 1968.

———— 1969b. Women's will to fail, *Psychology Today* 3 (November): 36–41.

———— 1970. Femininity and successful achievement: a basic inconsistency. In *Feminine Personality and Conflict*, eds. Bardwick, J., Douvan E., Horner, M., and Gutman D., Belmont, California: Brooks-Cole.

———— 1970. Follow-up studies on the motive to avoid success in women, Paper presented at the annual meetings of the American Psychological Association.

———— 1972. Toward an understanding of Achievement related conflicts in women. *Journal of Social Issues* 28, 2: 157–175.

Hulin, C.L., and Blood, M.R. 1968. Job enlargement, individual differences, and worker responses. *Psychological Bulletin* 69: 41–55.

Iglitzin, L.B. 1972. A child's eye view of sex roles, *Today's Education* 61: 23–26.

Inkeles, Alex. 1960. Industrial man: the relation of status to experience, perception and value, *American Journal of Sociology* 66: 1–31.

Kahn, R.L., Wolfe, D.M., Quinn, R.D., and Snoek, J.D. 1964. *Organizational Stress: Studies in Role Conflict and Ambiguity.* New York: Wiley.

Kanter, Rosabeth. 1977a. *Men and Women of the Corporation*. New York: Basic Books.

――――. 1977b. Some effects of proportions on group life: Skewed sex ratios and responses to token women, *A.J.S.* 82, 5: 965–990.

Katz, D. 1964. The motivational basis of organizational behavior, *Behavioral Science* 9,2: 131–146.

Katz, D., and Kahn, R.L. 1966. *The Social Psychology of Organizations*. New York: Wiley.

Katz, Daniel. 1960. The functional approach to the study of attitudes, *Public Opinion Quarterly* 24: 163–204.

Katz, M.L. 1973. Female motive to avoid success: a psychological barrier or a response to deviancy? Unpublished Ms., Educational Testing Service.

Kemper. T. 1968. Reference groups, socialization and achievement, *American Sociological Review* 33: 31–45.

Keniston K., and Keniston, E. 1964. An American anachronism: the image of women and work, *American Scholar* 33: 355–375.

Killbridge, M. 1960. Reduced costs through job enlargement, *Journal of Business* 33: 357–362.

Klein, Viola. 1961. Attitudes to work and marriage of 600 adolescent girls, *British Journal of Sociology* 12: 176–183.

Klemmack, D.L., and Edwards, J.N. 1975. Women's acquisition of stereotyped occupational aspirations, *Sociology and Sociological Research* 57: 510–525.

Komarovsky, Mira. 1946. Cultural contradictions and sex roles. *A.J.S.* 52: 184–189.

Kreps, Juanita, and Clark, Robert. 1975. *Sex, Age and Work: The Changing Composition of the Labor Force*. Baltimore: The Johns Hopkins Press.

Kriesberg, Louis, 1964. Occupational controls among steel distributors. In *Social Organization and Behavior*, eds. A.L. Simpson and I.H. Simpson, pp. 274–281. New York: Wiley.

Kronus, Carol, and Grimm, James. 1971. Women in librarianship: The majority rules? *Protean*, December 1971.

Kuhlen, R.G. 1963. Needs, perceived need satisfaction, opportunities, and satisfaction with occupation, *Journal of Applied Psychology* 47, 1: 56–64.

Lawler, E.E. 1970. Equity theory as a predictor of productivity and work quality, *Psychological Bulletin* 70: 596–610.

Laws, Judith Long. 1972. A feminist analysis of relative deprivation in academic women. *The Review of Radical Political Economics* 4: 107–119.

――――. 1975. The psychology of tokenism: An analysis, *Sex Roles* 1, 1: 51–67.

――――. 1979. Work motivation and work behavior of women: New perspectives. To appear in *Psychology of Women: Future Directions in Research*, ed. J. Sherman and F. Denmark, New York: Psychological Dimensions, Inc.

Levine, A., and Crumrine, J. 1975. Women and the fear of success: A problem in replication, *American Journal of Sociology* 80: 964–974.

Levitin, T., Quinn, R.P., and Staines, G.L. 1971. Sex discrimination against the American working woman, *American Behavioral Scientist* 15: 237–254.

Levitt, E.S. 1971. Vocational development of professional women, *J. Voc. Behavior* 1: 375–385.

Lewin, Kurt. 1951. *Field Theory in Social Science*. New York, Harper and Brothers.

Lipman-Blumen, J. 1972. The development and impact of female role ideology. Paper presented at the Radcliffe Institute.

Lipinski, B.G. 1965. *Sex role conflict and achievement motivation in college women*. Unpublished Ph.D. thesis, University of Cincinnati.

Looft, W.R. 1971. Sex differences in the expression of vocational aspirations by elementary school children, *Developmental Psychology* 5: 366.

Lopata, H.Z., and Steinhart, F. 1971. Work histories of American urban women, *The Gerontologist* 2: 27–38.

Lorber, Judith. 1975. Trust, loyalty and the place of women in the informal organization of work. Paper presented at the annual meeting of the American Sociological Association.

Loring, Rosalind, and Wells, Theodora. 1973. *Breakthrough: Women into Management*. New York: Van Nostrand Reinhold Company.

Lyle, Jerolyn R. 1971. *Affirmative Action Programs for Women: A Survey of Innovative Programs*. EEOC, OR contract # 71–45.

———— and Ross, Jane L. 1973. *Women and Industry*. Lexington, MA: Lexington Books.

Maccoby, E.E., and Jacklin, C.N. 1974. *The Psychology of Sex Differences*. Stanford: Stanford University Press.

Maccoby, Eleanor, ed. 1966. *The Development of Sex Differences*. Stanford: Stanford University Press.

McClelland, D.C., Atkinson, J.W., Clark, R.A., and Lowell, E.L. 1953. *The Achievement Motive*. New York: Appleton-Century-Crofts.

McNulty, D. 1967. Differences in pay between men and women workers, *Monthly Labor Review* 90: 25–29.

Maslow, A.H. 1943. A theory of human motivations, *Psych. Review* 50: 370–396.

Matthews, E., and Tiedeman, D.V. 1964. Attitudes toward career and marriage and the development of life style in young women, *Journal of Counseling Psychology* 11: 375–383.

Mayes, Sharon S. 1976. Women in positions of authority: an analysis of changing sex roles. Paper presented at the annual meeting of the American Sociological Association.

Mednick, M.S. and Tangri, S.S. 1972. New perspectives on women, *J. Soc. Issues* 28: 2.

Mill, John S. 1896. *The Subjection of Women*. London: Longmans, Green, Reader and Dyer.

Miller, D., and Form, W. 1964. *Industrial Sociology*. New York: Harper and Row, Publishers.

Mills, C.W. 1940. Situated actions and vocabularies of motive, *American Sociological Review* 5: 904–913.

Milton, G.A. 1959. Sex differences in problem solving as a function of role appropriateness of the problem content, *Psych. Reports* 5: 705–708.

Monahan, L., Kuhn, D., and Shaver, P. 1974. Intrapsychic vs. cultural explanation of the fear of success motive, *J. Pers. and Soc. Psych.* 29: 60–64.

Mooney, J.D. 1968. Attrition among Ph.D. candidates: an analysis of recent Woodrow Wilson Fellows, *J. Human Resources* 3: 47–62.

Morse, N.C., and Weiss, R.S. 1955. The function and meaning of work and the job, *American Sociological Review* 20: 2.

Mulvey, M.C. 1963. Psychological and sociological factors in prediction of career patterns of women, *Genetic Psych. Monographs* 68: 309–386.

National Manpower Council. 1957. *Womanpower.* New York: Columbia University Press.

Nye, F.I., and Hoffman, L.W. 1963. *The Employed Mother in America.* Chicago: Rand McNally and Company.

O'Hara, R. 1962. Roots of careers, *Elem. School J.* 62: 177–180.

O'Hara, R.R., and Tiedeman, D.V. 1959. Vocational self-concept in adolescence, *J. Counsel, Psychol.* 6: 292–301.

O'Leary, L.R. 1973. Fair employment, sound psychometric practice, and reality, *Am. Psychol.* 28: 147–50 (February).

Oppenheimer, V.K. 1970. The female labor force in the United States: Demographic and economic factors governing its growth and changing composition. University of California at Berkeley: Population Monograph, Series No. 5.

———. 1972. Testimony before the Federal Commerce Commission, August 1972.

Paige, K. 1974. The effects of sex, children and dual careers on the uses of time. Paper presented at American Psychological Association Meeting.

Palmer, Gladys L., and Brainerd, C.P. 1964. Labor mobility in six cities: A report on the survey of patterns and factors in labor mobility, 1950–1960. Committee on Labor Market Research, SSRC.

Papalia, D.E., and Tennent, S.S. Vocational aspirations in preschoolers: a manifestation of early sex role stereotyping, *Sex Roles* 1, 2: 197–201.

Patchen, M. 1962. Supervisory methods and group performance, *Administrative Science Quarterly* 7: 275–293.

Peplau, L.A. 1973. The impact of fear of success, sex-role attitudes and opposite sex relationships on women's intellectual performance: An experimental study of competition in dating couples. Unpublished doctoral dissertation, Harvard University.

Peterson, Esther. 1964. Working women. In *The Woman in America*, ed., R.J. Lifton. Boston: Beacon Press.

Phelps, C.E. 1968. Women in American medicine. *Journal of Medical Education* 43: 916–924.

Piore, Michael, 1970. The dual labor market: theory and implications. Reprinted from Michael J. Piore, Jobs and Training, in *The State and the Poor*, eds., Beer and Barringer. Winthrop Publishing, Inc.

Pleck, J.H. 1973a. New concepts of sex role identity. Paper read at the Society for the Scientific Study of Sex.

————— 1973b. Social science and sex role change. Cambridge: Harvard University. Unpublished.

————— 1976. Male threat from female competence, *J. Consulting and Clinical Psychology* 44: 608–613.

Pasathas, George. 1958. Toward a theory of occupational choice for women, *Sociology and Sociological Research* 52: 254–268.

Rand, L.M., and Miller, A.C. 1972. A developmental cross-sectioning of women's careers and marriage attitudes and life plans, *Journal of Vocational Behavior* 2: 317–331.

Raph, J. Goldberg, M., and Passow, H. 1966. *Bright Underachievers*. New York: Teachers College Press.

Rosen, B., and Jerdee, T.H. 1973. The influence of sex role stereotypes on evaluations of male and female supervisory behavior, *Journal of Applied Psychology* 57: 44–48.

Rosenberg, M. 1965. *Society and the Adolescent Self-Image*. Princeton: Princeton University Press.

Ross, H. 1973. Poverty: Women and children last. Washington, DC: The Urban Institute.

Ross, Heather L., and Sawhill, Isabel V. 1975. *Time of Transition: The growth of families headed by women*, Washington, DC: The Urban Institute.

Rossi, A.S. 1965. Barriers to the career choice of engineering, medicine, or science among American women. In *Women and the Scientific Professions*, eds., Jacquelyn Mattfeld and Carol Van Aken. Cambridge: MIT Press.

————— 1972. Women in Science: Why so Few? In *Toward a Sociology of Women*, ed., Constantina Safilios Rothchild. Lexington, MA: Xerox College Publishing.

Rousell, Cecile. 1974. Relationship of sex of department heads to department climate, *Admin. Sci. Quart.* 19: 211–220.

Sawhill, Isabel, 1974. The earnings gap: Research needs and issues. Washington DC: The Urban Institute.

Schwenn, M., 1970. Arousal of the motive to avoid success. Cambridge: Harvard University. Unpublished junior honors thesis.

Shaw, M., and McCuen, J. 1960. The onset of academic underachievement in bright children, *Journal of Educational Psychology* 51: 103–108.

Shuster, J.R., and Atchison, T.J. 1973. Examining feelings of pay equity, *Business Perspectives* 9: 14–19.

Sieber, S.D. 1974. Toward a theory of role accumulation, *American Sociological Review* 39: 567–579.

Siegel, A., and Curtis, E. 1963. Familial correlates of orientation toward future employment among college women, *Journal of Educational Psychology* 54: 33–37.

Simon, R.J., Clark, S.M., and Tifft, L.L. 1966. Of nepotism, marriage and the pursuit of an academic career, *Sociology of Education* 39: 344–358.

Simpson, L. 1970. A myth is better than a miss: Men get the edge in academic employment, *College and University Business*, pp. 72–73.

Stafford, R.E. 1961. Sex differences in spatial visualization as evidence of sex-linked inheritance, *Perceptual and Motor Skills* 13: 428–438.

Stein, A.H. 1971. The effects of sex-role standards for achievement and sex-role preference on three determinants of achievement motivation, *Developmental Psychology* 4: 219–231.

Stein, E., and Bailey, M. 1973. The socialization of achievement orientation in females, *Psychological Bulletin* 80: 345–366.

Steinman, A., and Fox, D.J. 1966. Male–female perceptions of the female role in the United States, *Journal of Psychology* 64: 265–276.

Stouffer, S.A., Suchman, E.A., DeVinney, L.C., Star, S.A., and Williams, R.M. Jr. 1949. *The American Soldier: Adjustment During Army Life*. Princeton: Princeton University Press.

Strodtbeck, F.L., and Mann, R.D. 1956. Sex role differentiation in jury deliberation, *Sociometry* 19: 3–11.

Strong, E.K. Jr. 1943. *Vocational Interests of Men and Women*. Stanford: Stanford University Press.

Suppes, Patrick. 1968. Computer technology and the future of education, *Phi Delta Kappan*, 1968.

Sutherland, M.B. 1961. Co-education and school attainment, *British Journal of Educational Psychology* 31: 158–169.

Sweet, J.A. 1973. *Women in the Labor Force*. New York: Seminar Press.

Tangri, S.T. 1972. Determinants of occupational role innovation among college women, *Journal of Social Issues* 28: 177–201.

Tenopyr, M.L. 1970. Dimensions of the now generation's attitudes toward working women. Paper read at the meetings of the American Psychological Association, September 1970.

Terman, L.M., and Oden, M. 1947. *The Gifted Child Grows Up*, Stanford: Stanford University Press.

Thompson, J.D., Carlson, R., and Avery, R.W. 1962. *Occupations, Personnel and Careers*; Pittsburgh: Administrative Science Center, University of Pittsburgh.

Tresemer, D. 1974. Fear of success: Popular but unproven, *Psychology Today* 7: 82–85.

——— and Pleck, J. 1972. Maintaining and changing sex-role boundaries in men (and women). Paper presented at Radcliffe Institute Conference: Women, Resource for a Changing World.

Tyler, L. 1964. The antecedents of two varieties of vocational interests, *Genetic Psychological Monographs* 70: 177–227.

———. 1972. Sex differences in vocational interests and motivation related to occupations. Testimony before the Federal Commerce Commission, August 1972.

Unger, R. 1975. Status, power and gender: An examination of parallelisms. Paper presented at the Conference on New Directions for Research on Women, Madison, Wisconsin.

U.S. Department of Labor. 1966. *1965 Handbook on Women Workers*, Bulletin 290. Washington, DC: U.S. Government Printing Office.

———. 1969. Facts about women's absenteeism and labor turnover. Washington, DC: U.S. Government Printing Office.

The Utilization of Civilian Women Employees Within the Department of the Army: Civilian Personnel Pamphlet CPP 79. Washington, DC: Department of the Army, 1973.

Van Dusen, R.A., and Sheldon, Eleanor. 1976. The changing status of American women: a life cycle perspective, *American Psychologist* 106–116.

Veroff, J. and Feld, S. 1970. *Marriage and Work in America: A Study of Motives and Roles.* New York: Van Nostrand-Reinhold.

Vroom, Victor. 1964. *Work and Motivation.* New York: Wiley.

Wahrman, R., and Pugh, M.D. 1972. Sex, nonconformity and influence, *Sociometry* 35: 376–386.

Waldman, E. 1970. Changes in the labor force activity of women, *Monthly Labor Review*, pp. 10–18 (June).

Wallace, Phyllis A. 1976. *Equal Employment Opportunity and the AT&T Case.* Cambridge: MIT Press.

Watley, D.J., and Kaplan, R. 1971. Career or marriage? Aspirations and achievements of able young women, *Journal of Vocational Behavior* 1: 29–43.

Weil, M.W. 1961. An analysis of the factors influencing married women's actual or planned participation, *American Sociological Review* 26: 91–95.

Wells, Theodora. 1973. Equalizing advancement between women and men, *Training and Development Journal*, pp. 1–4 (August).

Whitaker, James O. 1965. Sex differences and susceptibility to interpersonal persuasion, *Journal of Social Psychology* 66: 91–94.

White, J.J. 1972, Women in the law. *Michigan Law Review* 65: 1051–1122.

Wilensky, H. 1968. Women's work: economic growth, ideology, structure. *Industrial Relations*, pp. 235–248.

Wolman, C., and Frank, H. 1972. The solo woman in a professional peer group. Philadelphia: The Wharton School, University of Pennsylvania, Working paper #133.

Zinberg, D. 1973. College: When the future becomes the present. In *Successful Women in the Sciences: An Analysis of Determinants. Annals of N.Y. Academy of Sciences* 208: 115–124.

Zytowski, D.G. 1969. Toward a theory of career development for women, *Personnel and Guidance Journal* 47: 660–664.

WOMAN
as
Housewife

Many of the myths that are used to disqualify women in the labor market are rationalized in terms of women's family obligations. These myths assume that wifely responsibilities take first priority in a woman's life and are incompatible with full-time (and over-time) pursuit of a career. The family obligations of married women, in fact, divide into four roles, each carrying expectations that may be incompatible with each other, even without the complicating factor of paid employment. Here we will examine the components of married women's role obligations as spouse, mother, consumer and domestic worker.

This complex of roles constitutes the normal expectation for adult women in our society—or "the" female sex role. Sex role ideology specifies different ways for women and men to participate in all institutional spheres of society. The female sex role pre-scription is based on the premise that women will be both wives and mothers having primary responsibility both for childcare and housework. It is assumed, further, that the normal household includes a male breadwinner: not merely *a* male earner, but *the* breadwinner who is the head of household. It is assumed that the male earner's occupation determines the social status of the entire household. Part of the wife's obligation is to enhance the husband's occupational role performance and his status. All these elements of the sex role script constrain women's activities in spheres that are defined as peripheral—her own career advancement, personal growth, community service, social and political action. The potential flexibility and variation with which women might combine their multiple roles are truncated by the dictates of sex role ideology. The way a woman enacts and organizes her behavior as spouse, mother, housekeeper and consumer is taken as a reflection on her "adequacy" as a female. She judges herself and is judged by children, spouse, in-laws, neighbors and others, with reference to the sex role script. Conformity, rather than originality, is the basis of successful sex role performance.

The Wife Role

Although "the" adult female sex role is composed of distinct parts, women enter this status through one of them. Women are recruited to the role of wife—not that of a mother, a domestic worker or a consumer. Recruitment is accomplished in two stages. The first is sex role socialization, which begins early and is pervasive. Virtually all young women desire and expect to marry from preschool on (Angrist and Almquist, 1975). Some women list housewife as their preferred occupation: some, from an early age, mother. Their aspirations for adult life are linked to the status of wife and they become part of the pool of eligibles. The second stage of recruitment is through courtship, marriage representing the selection stage.

The English philosopher John Stuart Mill wrote, more than a hundred years ago,

> Marriage being the destination appointed by society for women, the prospect they are brought up to, and the object which it is intended should be sought by all of them, except those who are too little attractive to be chosen by any man as his companion; one might have supposed that everything would have been done to make this condition as eligible to them as possible, that they might have no cause to regret being denied the option of any other. (1869, Vol. 2, p. 1).

Mill is describing a process that forms not only women's preference for marriage, but a whole set of attitudes and postures that give precedence for marriage. This process of socialization or shaping is treated later. Ideas of femininity are central to the influence process. The manipulation of these ideas is tied to the individual's gender identity and sex role identity, which are early, central and valued parts of the self. Once this link is made, to repudiate femininity is to repudiate part of the self. Thus, women are locked into traditional life scripts. Labeling is a vehicle for social control and women feel the obligation to conform to scripts that are labeled feminine.

One paramount consequence is the orientation of young women toward romantic love and a focus upon the partner to the exclusion of other aspects of the intended role of wife. This gives rise to a paradox: in many cases women are choosing a "job" about which they know next to nothing. Insofar as marriage is a woman's "career," she enters it unprepared and almost under false pretenses. The script advertises for a wife: the job is that of a domestic worker. Current research (Lopata, 1971) reveals that many housewives believe that they received no preparation for this—the central role of their adult lives. Although marriage is the most heavily scripted outcome our culture provides for women, it is presented as the destination—not the starting point. Marriage is the end of the line: "And they lived happily ever after." Yet to marry is to become a wife—for the great majority a housewife. Mill's language is apt, as women are tracked toward marriage as if on rails. Moreover, marriage (and particularly motherhood) costs women their other options, at least for the period when childcare demands are intensive. Mill also draws our attention to the process of persuasion (or brainwashing) which makes marriage most women's first choice of adult lifestyle. This is not rape, after all; women are not married against their will. Rather, other options are foreclosed or made less attractive. The process by which this is accomplished is presented in detail in Chapter 4, dealing with early sex role socialization and in Chapter 3 dealing with courtship. Now we should note that socialization processes shape women's behavior and desires toward some goals *and also away from others*. Women are tracked away from competitive achievement and toward marriage and motherhood. Traditional attitudes make this explicit: married women should not work; mothers should not work when their children are young; women should not neglect their household responsibilities and the wellbeing of their husbands and children.

Most women, when they choose marriage as a goal, accept this system of priorities. An available language of love and selflessness, characterizing the transactions of courtship, facilitates a shifting of focus from one's own life to those of others.

The language of romance and love constitutes the accepted vocabulary of motive for courtship and marriage. Individuals explain their involvement in relationships in terms of this motivation. An explanation of marital behavior in these terms obscures another, equally real level of interaction: the exchange of goods, services and the power relations that determine the rates of exchange. To characterize the marital relationship exclusively in terms of emotions is to engage in mystification; that is, to substitute one definition of reality for another. Mystification involves the shifting of meaning or position, with the consequent denial of the individual's experienced reality. The result of mystification is the invalidation of personal experience and sometimes the substitution of some socially accepted definition of the situation. Often shifting ground takes the form of an attack on the individual's competence to assess reality, as a substitute for a confrontation on the nature of reality (Laing and Esterson, 1964). Mystification also means that it is impermissible to analyze marriage as exchange, or to discuss the housewife's role in terms of the job it really is—domestic labor. Marriage "means" lifelong love and commitment but it also "means" unacknowledged daily drudgery. Confronting the latter reality would mean different implications for the conduct of the marital relationship from dealing only with the former.

In our culture, preparation for marriage is confined almost entirely to the courtship process and to mate selection, rather than skill learning. Characteristics of courtship are carried over into marriage. Traditionally, men bear the costs of courtship; women are guests, not partners in entertainment, and they receive, more than they give, substantial gifts. The economic dominance of men in courtship is carried over into marriage, in the complementary scripts of male breadwinner and female parasite. Power of another sort arises from the male's traditional initiative in proposing marriage. If a woman desires marriage, she must persuade a man that she is lovable enough to merit marriage. It is her obligation to please her partner—the husband. The obligation to please carries over into marriage.

In the courtship script, men retain the initiative; the woman's role is basically reactive. When a woman accepts a suitor as a husband, she moves into a role relationship in which he is implicitly in the center of the picture. Vicariousness is a central element in the female sex role script. The wife is the man's helpmeet, dearest friend, his consolation and ornament. Ordinarily, her ambition is subordinated to his. This is certainly true of her occupational ambitions. Often these are supplanted entirely, as many wives function vicariously with respect to achievement. She directs her energy and talent to facilitating attainment of her husband—as in Papanek's (1973) analysis of the two-person career—and/or her children. The point here is not that her behavior is not instrumental (it may be exceedingly instrumental) but it is directed to others' ends—not her individual needs. If this occurs, the wife is doing what she has been socialized to do. Her attitudes support this. As we will see in Chapter 4, women learn to overestimate men and to underestimate themselves; this is good training for a marriage that features a vicarious role for the wife. Many wives, we suppose, believe that their husbands deserve their contributions. Men, to be sure, verbalize a belief that they advance themselves for the benefit of their families. Both partners believe the appropriate unit of analysis is the family. Particularly for the wife, the family's interest is expected to supplant self-interest.

These commonplace beliefs form a foundation for the conduct of marital and familial relations. We might anticipate that social scientists would critically analyze the taken-for-granted definitions of reality in terms of the benefits and functions of traditional arrangements. We find, instead, that social science echoes old husbands' tales. Sociological analysis of women is virtually confined to their familial roles. Moreover, the emphasis is on relationships rather than on tasks. Marriage is seen popularly within a privatized context, as though it were a personal relationship rather than a social institution. The sociology of the family perpetuates this shortsighted view. Furthermore, women in families are treated almost entirely in terms of roles rather than as persons. In a class-bound middle-class sociology, the "normal" family is portrayed as an intact nuclear family with male breadwinner and female housewife who is not employed outside the home. The housewife's job, hours, compensation and working conditions are strikingly neglected in the professional literature. The family's status is characterized in terms of the husband's occupation and the wife's status attributes are generally ignored or effaced within the collective context. When the wife's status attributes (e.g., education) are analyzed, it is in a way that reflects the vicariousness of her role: in terms of her contribution to the husband's or children's "human capital accumulation." The wife is assumed to reflect her husband's status, her children's needs and other people's expectations. She is viewed in terms of the functions she serves for others. She is portrayed not as an agent within the context of the family, but as an essential glue that oozes into cracks and interstices as needed. In short, the picture of women is constructed from a masculine perspective and reflects the interests of adult males.

DISTORTIONS IN SCHOLARSHIP

Scholarly work on women's roles incorporates biases that have systematic consequences for research and theory. Implicitly, it is assumed that the allocation of adults' time and effort follows sex role lines. Thus, it is assumed unquestioningly that investment in paid employment, domestic labor and child rearing is determined by traditional priorities. One important consequence is that since this allocation is fixed by custom, the family and child development are now regarded as feminine spheres—characterized in terms of concepts totally discontinuous with those used to characterize the concerns of men and "society." We will observe three consequences of the intellectuals' segregation of topics bearing on women's lives: (1) ignorance of the realities of women's lives; (2) the falsification of women's realities, resulting in part from this ignorance; and (3) a double standard in theory and research bearing on women as contrasted with men. As we examine theories about women in their familial and extrafamilial roles, we will see a discontinuity between analyses of women and men. They are analyzed in different terms, hence systematic comparison is impeded. Women are treated as a special case or, more often, as qualitatively different from other social beings. A double standard is also apparent in the tendency of theory regarding women to be underdeveloped, ad hoc and sketchy. As the traditional theories of society are male-centered, they reflect priorities and values of the traditional paradigms. Scholars who are uninterested in phenomena regarding women devote less effort to their formulations and explanations of these phenomena, and it shows.

Some recent analyses have cogently documented the invisibility of women in the social sciences and the distortions in our knowledge that result (e.g., Millman and Kanter, 1975). Ignorance is a factor (although not an excuse): it is doubtful whether the typical social scientist could enumerate the usual housework tasks; almost certainly he would grossly underestimate the time and skill requirements of the job. The same can be said of the actual phenomena of parenting. This ignorance is, however, motivated; it is accompanied by indifference—often contempt. Low prestige is attached to women's work, whether paid or unpaid. (This is an instance of the generalized misogyny of our culture.) Mainardi's possibly apocryphal husband dubs her analysis of the politics of housework trivial: the topic is trivial, hence any study of it is a waste of time. (Mainardi, 1971). Further to persist in such study is thought to reflect unfavorably on the discernment or professional qualifications of the researcher and is likely to hurt her career.

A number of examples of social science theories illustrate these points.

Sociological Perspectives on Women's Familial Roles

One of the most influential traditions in the sociology of women has relied on a polarized distinction between "instrumental" and "expressive" roles that exemplifies the tendency to characterize women and men in qualitatively different ways. This dubious dichotomy was introduced by Talcott Parsons (1949) and was widely adopted. Parsons distinguished between an expressive function—having to do with building and maintaining morale, for example—and an instrumental function—having to do with building things, for example. These had emerged as factors in the functioning of laboratory groups in the social psychological experimentation of the time (Bales, 1950).

Laboratory research on task groups confirmed that both functions are essential for groups to continue functioning. In these artificial groups there was a tendency for one individual to emerge as the "task leader" and another to emerge as the "social–emotional leader."

Parsons extrapolated from the experimentally created groups of five strangers to the intimate, ongoing dyad of the family. He assigned a marital division of labor, based on the instrumental/expressive distinction. Thus instrumentality became identified with the male, expressivity with the female—though in Bales's laboratory groups, both functions were fulfilled by males.

Parsons may appear to have overreached the bounds of scientific caution in this extrapolation, perhaps to the point of outlandishness. Yet, this formulation fits so well with many cultural assumptions that it hardly seems outlandish at all. It must be the cultural, rather than the scientific, considerations that account for the popularity of the expressive/instrumental polarity in the sociological literature of the last generation.

93

In Parsons' analogy, the wife was like the family's Secretary of Commerce and the husband was like the family's Secretary of State. Parsons did not comment on the asymmetry of these two cabinet positions and his ingenuous aggrandizement of the male function has remained unanalyzed. In his choice of analogy, Parsons implied that the woman's sphere is virtually limited to the home, all other institutions falling within the male purview. A generation of social scientists has uncritically echoed Parsons' analysis and rigidified it to the point of caricature. Male sociologists have been content to relegate women to this restricted sphere and to devote their attention to a whole world of topics in which women are invisible. Recent work of feminist scholarship (Millman and Kanter, 1975) has documented the shortcomings of such androcentric sociology.

Regrettably, this sociology is as inaccurate in rendering the woman in "her sphere" as it is in omitting her from other spheres. Women's functioning within "their" sphere is not realistically represented. To characterize women and women's work, as "expressive" betrays not only ignorance but falsification. Family sociologists have been consistent in overlooking the demands for instrumental functioning in the mother, wife, houseworker and paid-worker roles that most married women manage. We find there is a complementary blind spot in the lack of analysis of the need for expressive functioning in males, not only in intimate relations, but in work, politics and the marketplace. Many social scientists have succumbed to a grotesque personality theory that holds that women "are" expressive (emotional, nurturant, altruistic and perhaps not serious) while men "are" instrumental (ambitious, task-oriented, knowledgeable, rational and serious). We recognize this version of "human nature" as the one used to rationalize occupational segregation and the dramatically different opportunity structures confronting women and men in paid employment, as was shown in Chapter 1.

In an early study of domestic labor, Blood and Wolfe (1960) relied on the instrumental/expressive polarity to posit a natural division of labor in household tasks. Blood and Wolfe concluded that sexual specialization exists: husbands were more likely than wives to shovel walks, mow lawns and manage minor repairs. Wives were more likely to wash dishes, straighten the living room and fix breakfast. Childcare, shopping, clothing care and heavy housecleaning were omitted from the study. Blood and Wolfe are quoted as demonstrating an egalitarian division of domestic labor, evidence in its turn for the egalitarian "colleague family." This formulation is appealing, but misleading. It implies that both sets of responsibilities are accepted by those to whom they are assigned and are equally valued and equally rewarded. The idea of a domestic division of labor fits the pattern of different models for women's and men's functioning. It is important to note that the underlying principle is *separate but equal*: separate, in order to protect male perquisites, but "equal," in order to avoid the appearance of inequity.

Blood and Wolfe's selection of household tasks helps them to report an apparently equitable, if sex-typed, domestic division of labor. If husbands and wives take responsibility for the same number of tasks, it appears their contribution to domestic labor is equivalent—always assuming this parity holds for not just a sample of tasks, but for all the housework. A more revealing statistic is the effort distribution, based on the amount of time a task takes and how often it must be done. (Blood and Wolfe, 1966). When Blood and Wolfe's data are examined in the light of this index, even the appearance of equality is lacking.

Blood and Wolfe anticipate the human capital theory of the 1960s with their discussion of the way "the" husband and wife (ideal types, rather than the respondents in the study) allocate their time. They present as normal the picture of a wife who "retires" from employment soon after marriage and "specializes" in housekeeping. The husband, of course, continues to "specialize" in wage labor. This "normal" situation is disrupted if the wife, in addition to her job as housewife, seeks employment outside the home.

95

Studies of Family Power

Blood and Wolfe's speculations on "employment outside the home" have been carried forward by a series of studies on family power. Interestingly, power relations in the one-earner family have not attracted the professional attention of sociologists. Rather, the question of family power has become problematic only when the status quo is "disrupted" by the wife's entering the paid work force. The acknowledged focus of the research has been the distribution of power in the family. An underlying concern seems to be a threat to the husband from the employed wife. The second wage earner brings added resources to the family unit and employment often has noneconomic gains for the wife, in addition. Nevertheless, the tone of sociological speculation on this phenomenon is doleful. It reflects unacknowledged concerns of men over potential loss of advantages they enjoy when a wife is not employed outside the home. We can only speculate that some of this apprehension reflects the threat of competition from women in the job market. Another threat may be the anticipated loss of the wifely attention that fosters "expressive dependence" in men.[1] Similarly, an anticipated reduction in domestic services may, in part, account for this peevish tone.

It should be noted, however, that the domestic division of labor is not a major focus in the literature on family power. Here, social scientists reflect the traditional views prevalent in the culture: since the existence and significance of domestic labor are not acknowledged, a shift in allocation of this function is not debated. Since housework is considered as trivial, market substitutes have been little discussed. The shortsightedness of social scientists fol-

---

[1]Tresemer and Pleck (1972) have developed the idea of men's "expressive dependence" on women. That is, men sometimes seem to experience emotion, regression, tenderness, etc. only vicariously, through a female partner. Lacking a female partner, a man may be cut off from his expressive side, as women are sometimes assumed to be lacking in instrumentality unless they are paired with an instrumental male.

lows from the viewpoint that a woman is *primarily* a wife. House-work is seen as a role obligation of wife: neither the nature of housework nor the responsibility for it is likely to change as long as this role definition persists. Thus, it should not be surprising that the bulk of domestic labor continues to be borne by wives, even when paid employment doubles their burdens. Adjustment occurs *within* the wife role, not between family roles. Though sociologists tend not to acknowledge explicitly that power in the family is based on economic dominance and dependency, they predict a diminution of husband's power relative to wife when the wife is employed. There is a tendency for employed wives to enjoy greater power—usually indexed by family decision-making—than wives who are not employed outside the home, but this relationship is powerfully conditioned by social class. Working-class wives appear to gain more by employment, relative to their husbands' power, than middle-class wives. The middle-class husbands manage to maintain their dominance in the face of the "threat" of wives' employment.

It is apparent that economic power is only one of the factors in the allocation of family power. In the light of what we know in the 1970s about occupational segregation, the early predictions about the effects of wife employment seem naive. Most working women are restricted to job and salary levels that would limit them to subsistence. The younger a wife at marriage (Campbell, 1967), the earlier her first pregnancy, and the more numerous her children, (Heer, 1958), the lower her power in the family. Overall, it appears that the more a wife reduces her options relative to the world outside marriage, the more she disadvantages herself within marriage. One of the consequences is an increasing share of the domestic labor as the number of children increases (Blood and Wolfe, 1960; Campbell, 1967; Heer, 1958). To turn it around, one way to keep an "uppity" wife in her place is to "give" her lots of children. We will be reminded of this old "barefoot and pregnant" adage when we examine the human-capitalist argument for women's investing themselves in child-rearing. For the middle-class woman, the argument takes the form of an insistence on quality, rather than quantity—on child-rearing rather than child-bearing. However, in all classes it is the wife who makes the "investment," and it is on her that the burden of domestic labor falls.

HUMAN CAPITAL THEORY AND THE ALLOCATION OF TIME TO HOME AND EMPLOYMENT

A "new look" in theory on familial division of labor turns out, on closer inspection, to be a new rationale for the old sex-role script. Human capital theory developed from the writings of Theodore Schultz in the 1960s. His 1963 book focused upon education, and women do not even appear as an entry in the index. Subsequent development of theory and research have, however, focused upon the family and upon the allocation of adults' time to paid work and household production (Schultz, 1973). Within the latter category, housework tends to be neglected and child-rearing emphasized. Human capital theory holds that individuals invest in education, which is their human capital. They exchange this in the marketplace for wages. The more education individuals amass, the higher their value in the marketplace. Workers are portrayed in this theory as minicapitalists, who make their resources work for them. An assumption of economic rationality is also made. Indeed, the family is assumed to operate like *a* rational decision-maker, seeking and evaluating information that helps it deploy its collective resources for optimal gain. It is questionable whether family members can be compressed into one person. Given the assumption, what person represents the family? The answer in human capital theory parallels a traditional view of marriage: husband and wife become one, and that one is the husband. In human capital theory, the family is represented by economic *man*.

Human capital theory accords well with the Protestant Ethic values that serve as the official value system of American society—society comprising those spheres associated with men. The Protestant Ethic emphasizes individualism and competition, assuming merit and equal opportunity. Individuals can (and should) increase their resources through education; by this means they can better themselves. Since it is possible to sacrifice present resources in anticipation of future profit (i.e., invest), persons who choose not to do so have only themselves to blame. This reasoning extends not only to the acquisition but also to the utilization of education. Human capital, like money, only earns if it is put to use. Consequently, it must be sold in the market if there is to be profit.

In economic theory, a distinction is traditionally made between "productive" labor (in the cash market) and "nonproductive" labor (in the home). This unfortunate labeling reinforces the idea that men's work is real work and women's work is not. In fact, the home is the site of two kinds of productive labor: housework, which includes the production of noneconomic goods, and reproduction. The latter is emphasized at the expense of the former, and women are thought of as investing their human capital in order to produce new workers. Their investment, of course, pays off not to the mothers but to the new workers as they become human-capitalists. Within the framework of human capital theory, then, women's behavior is explained in ways that are at variance with the theory.

Human capital theory has been criticized for ignoring the indirect contribution of wives to productive labor, as they service the breadwinner. Under our economic system, that breadwinner sells his labor for wages. The family system that articulates with capitalist production is responsible for keeping the breadwinner functioning—rather like the maintenance of productive machinery—and capable of bringing in wages. The work of the home is not paid and hence is left out of most calculations concerning productivity. Work done in the home is not counted as part of the Gross National Product. The costs to the breadwinner of purchasing domestic services in the market are not taken into account—although the purchase of substitute labor *is* considered when a wife becomes a paid employee. Interestingly, substitute services are commonly paid for out of the wife's and not the husband's earnings. Both these observations reflect the assumption that the normal state of affairs is for a wife to remain at home and provide unpaid domestic services. The issue of allocation of husband's and wife's time to paid and unpaid work is not seen as problematic so long as home and family are seen as the female sphere.

One explanation attributes the failure to value domestic labor as a consequence of advanced monopoly capital. (Secombe, 1963.) The financial structure of capitalism determines that when home labor and industrial labor are no longer housed under the same roof, only the latter is assigned a price. Wage labor produces surplus value, or profit for the capitalist, in the commodity market. The contribution of domestic labor to the wage worker's readiness to work is not acknowledged. Similarly, because domestic labor is considered "unproductive" (i.e., it does not produce surplus value), it is left out of the advances of the world of "real" work— e.g., unionization, benefits and technological advances.

Secombe makes the point that the housewife is separated not only from the means of production (insofar as she is not employed outside the home) but from the means of exchange. The redistribution of the wage that results from her efforts jointly with those of the wage-earner is a private, unregulated exchange. Secombe does not analyze the potential for exploitation in this situation. Indeed, he fails to explore the possibility that the male breadwinner in the single-income family is a petty capitalist who exploits (i.e., realizes profit from the surplus labor of) his wife. Development of this analysis would be valuable. The wage-earner supports his wife (upon whose labor the family's status as an income-producing unit rests) at a subsistence level, sufficient to keep her alive and working. Above and beyond this cost, anything he "saves" is profit for him. It seems curious that socialist scholars, so critical of capitalist exploitation of workers, have not analyzed this possibility. The socialist perspective, like the human capital perspective, treats domestic labor as nonproductive. Although Marx asserts that fundamentally all labor has value, the socialists, no less than their adversaries, accept the framework of capitalist pricing theory. If work does not command a wage and produce surplus value (i.e., profit), it is "nonproductive."

The socialist critique of domestic labor has its own limitations. It overemphasizes the contribution of the housewife in reproducing labor power, leaving out the central function—housework. Moreover, the Marxist perspective does no better with the employed housewife and the single woman than do the more conventional analyses. Each woman is contributing to her own capacity to work, yet this function is not valued (priced), leaving the implication that it is only male labor that is "productive."

The treatment of women in human capital theory has additional shortcomings. On the face of it, if human capital is productive only when employed for profit, then the wife (and mother) who is not employed outside the home is wasting her education. Some human capitalists have morbidly estimated that a housewife "loses" 4 percent of her human capital each year that she stays at home. This leaves us to contemplate the horrifying prospect of the long-married housewife accumulating a human capital *deficit*.

However, the intellectual double standard comes to the rescue. Although there is little disagreement that time out of the paid work force depresses women's earning ability, the focus in human capital theory shifts away from the woman as economic actor (or worker) and to her function as reproducer. When the focus is women, as we have seen, an unquestioned traditional sex-role ideology is in fact substituted for the economic calculus of human capital theory. The wife is not treated as an economic actor but only as a member of the family. When the family is taken as the unit of analysis, the wife's time and education become merely resources that the family can deploy. It is assumed that the husband "specializes" in market production and the wife in home production. In effect, human capital theory applies only to him, and a new theory emerges to account for the wife. The nature of this theory is, in essence, noneconomic. The new vocabulary of motives that is introduced relies on feelings: wellbeing or "psychic gains"—not income maximization. Epstein (1970) observed the tendency for women to be "paid off" in the "coinage of compliments," even for their contributions to task accomplishment in the work sphere. This tendency, apparent in the human capital approach to mothering, brings us full circle back to women's expressive function.

If human capital theory were consistent in the analysis of women's and men's contributions, one might expect that the wife's investment in home production would be justified in terms of children as a source of future income or support for their aging parents. However, this argument is not made; rather, consistency and economic rationality are abandoned. After all, this version of the theory applies to women. According to human capital theory, the gains to be realized from investing in children are *psychic*. In other words, a totally different rationale is advanced for women's behavior.

Of course, many objections to the human capital approach can be raised. Surely it is solipsistic to maintain that only economic values and economic outcomes should be taken into account.[2] Fathers as well as mothers can derive "psychic gain" from having children, although what parents "pay" for this gain may differ a great deal. Some important issues are overlooked altogether by human capital theory. The actual forms of reallocation within the household have not been studied, although some theoretical formulations have been offered (Becker, 1973). Decision-making within the family is central to the theory, but no attempt has been made to study it empirically. The question of "child quality," of great theoretical interest not only to economists but to sociologists and psychologists, is raised, but human capital theory offers only a trivial answer. Child quality is indexed by the amount of education "invested" in the child, which is assumed in turn to predict future earnings of the child. Human-capitalists have applied con-

---

[2]An exception is Becker's attempt to include a formulation of "caring" as a factor in his theory of marriage (1973, p. 328).

cepts both of quality and quantity to reproduction. Blake (1968) has critiqued the resulting logic, which treats a decision to have children and what "quality" children to have, as a consumption decision rather like buying a major appliance. Child-rearing is labor-intensive and the assumption is made that some quality (or quantity?) of mother's time is related to quality of child outcome. Yet as we shall see, without a means of assessing quality of child outcomes, we cannot asses the rationality of the mother's investment.

Women present an anomaly for human capital theory in several ways. We have raised the question of the "rationality" of women's investing in their children's human capital. A question may be raised, as well, concerning the rationality of investing in girl-child "quality." Research reports challenge the empirical validity of the contention that investment in education "pays off" in income. Certainly it does so to a greater extent for white males than for any other group in society. The private rate of return on the investment in education is lower for women than for men. A number of conclusions can be drawn from this, using the logic of human capital theory. One might argue that the education dollar— parent's or public's—is better spent on men, since it will guarantee a higher rate of social return. One could also argue that for women the return on the investment is indirect. Education for women is often seen as an investment in husband-hunting; attending the "right school" exposes the young woman to "good" husband material—that is, it facilitates the maximization of her future income stream through marriage. Indeed, it has been argued that women invest in no more than that level of education required to catch the highest-status husband, rather than investing in the level of education required to catch a high-status occupation (Benham, 1973). This line of thinking once again illustrates the tendency to shift the grounds of argument when the focus is upon women. It reveals more about the author than of the women about whom he is writing—that the ground to which he chooses to shift is *courtship*. This human capital analysis of women's investment in education takes woman out of the serious realm of economics and places her in the frivolous realm of courtship—out of the public sphere, back into the private.

An even more basic issue with the human capital approach is the defensibility of making inferences about decision processes and preferences in the absence of psychological data. This is characteristic of much writing in economics and is not restricted to human capital theory. However, human capital theory offers some glaring examples. Economists commonly employ explanations at the psychological level, which implies the individual as the unit of analysis. However, they seek to validate their formulations, using data from large aggregates. Rarely do they spell out or index the intervening variables—largely at the structural level—that must link the two for the explanation to be meaningful. Failure to develop the connections between individual behavior and social structure produces a basic flaw: the constraints on behavior are systematically overlooked, and an empirically unjustified individualism is systematically exaggerated. Gronau's (1973) interpretation of nonparticipation rates of women in paid employment illustrates these shortcomings. He assumes that nonparticipation results from a discrete decision based in turn on the woman's placing higher value on her nonmarket production than on the wage offered to her for market production. The many considerations and constraints that affect such decisions are sweepingly overlooked in such formulations (see Chapter 1).

Approaches such as human capital theory rationalize the segregation of women in the familial sphere and contribute to the characteristics of a double standard in theory. The scholarly literature tends to neglect a whole range of phenomena that figure in women's experience. The gap is greatest in areas where male scholars have least experience.

Unpaid Domestic Labor: The Buck Stops Here

Of all the understudied aspects of the "female role," surely domestic labor is the most invisible. Traditional social science perspectives have emphasized the relational aspects of the wife and mother roles, almost totally ignoring the solitary labor that takes up most of the housewife's day and makes her work week almost double the length of the ordinary worker's. The reality of Occupation: Housewife is unpaid domestic labor. This ugly phrase may upset some readers, as its web of connotations is radically different from those of the common term, *housewife*, or the even more euphemistic *homemaker*. The term underscores the difference between a focus on the wife role, with its vocabulary of civility and sentiment, and the focus upon the housewife role. The idea of labor is at variance with images of ease and graciousness. We sometimes subdivide work into "mental" and "manual"; manual labor connotes arduous, often dirty work; work without glory, work without thanks and often, low-paid work. The service occupations exemplify what we mean by labor. In addition to their other attributes, they are most often nonunionized, so that service workers lack the protections and benefits of most workers in our society. When a distinction is made between "work" and "labor," it is said that work results in a product, while labor is the repetitive, invisible effort by which waste is disposed of, machines are maintained and supplies obtained.

There is little acknowledgment of the realities of the housewife's job. Laymen tend to think of domestic labor as an easy job and the housewife as a privileged and leisured person. The belief is prevalent that "labor-saving devices" have made the housewife's job an undemanding, part-time occupation—almost child's play. The life of the frontier woman, who shared her husband's farm work as well as baking, scrubbing, sewing and so forth, is often contrasted with that of the privileged suburban housewife. As is often the case, research findings directly contradict the old husbands' tales. Oakley (1974) has surveyed studies of domestic labor going back to 1929, in the United States, Great Britain and France. These data (Table 2.1) show that, contrary to what is commonly assumed, urban housewives have a longer work week than rural wives. There has been no appreciable decrease in the housewife's work load during this period. It is interesting to note that the same decades have seen a progressive

TABLE 2.1

A Comparison of Data on Housework Hours

STUDY, AND COUNTRY IN WHICH STUDY WAS CARRIED OUT	DATE	AVERAGE WEEKLY HOURS OF HOUSEWORK
I. **Rural studies**		
Wilson: United States	1929	64
U.S. Bureau of Home Economics: United States	1929	62
Cowles and Dietz: United States	1956	61
Girard and Bastide: France	1959	67
II. **Urban studies**		
U.S. Bureau of Home Economics: United States	1929	51
Bryn Mawr: United States		
(i) Small City	1945	78
(ii) Large City	1945	81
Stoetzel: France	1948	82
Moser: Britain	1950	70
Mass Observation: Britain	1951	72
Girard: France	1958	67
Oakley: Britain	1971	77

SOURCE: Oakley, Ann. 1974. *The Sociology of Housework.* New York: Pantheon Books, p. 94. Copyright, Pantheon Books, a Division of Random House, Inc.

reduction of the work week in paid employment from 50 to 40 hours. The husbands' leisure has been increasing while wives' leisure is vanishing.

The activities that take up the housewife's time have changed somewhat but the housewife's working day is as long now as it was 30 years ago. The price tag of our steadily rising standard of living is paid for by women's nonwage labor. Diets are more varied and nutritious, wardrobes more extensive and standards of cleanliness higher now. Many housewives wash every day; clothing is often washed after every wearing, and the distinction between "good" and "everyday" clothes seems almost to have disappeared. In the home, as in the larger economy, the demand for services has increased. Many women spend hours each week chauffeuring their children to their activities. Many women cook separate meals for different family members. Although families differ in the demands they place upon their live-in domestic worker, almost all of the work generated by the family falls upon this one individual.

Most persons outside the occupation would have difficulty in specifying what it is that a housewife does. This ignorance makes it easy to underestimate the housewife's job. A first step toward understanding is to obtain a census of the tasks that make up domestic labor and the associated time budget. What are the tasks of housework? How much time do they take? How often do they need to be done? Beyond such basic social accounting, we may ask, does a week of housework vary with the number and age of children—and the spouses' job obligations? What is the contribution of the husbands, children and others to domestic labor? Is the responsibility ever shared? The research of Walker and her associates shows the dimensions of this job (Walker and Woods, 1975). In 1967–68, they collected detailed records of housework in 1296 households in the Syracuse, New York, area. Although this is not a representative national sample, the Walker data contain variety and numbers sufficient for a picture of the factors affecting housework. Walker was particularly interested in how much housework is done in the household and who does it. She was interested in the extent to which the housework burden and its distribution among family members is altered by age of children, the number of children and the employment status of the wife.

With Walker's method, housewives were asked to recall housework activities of the day before, which were recorded in ten-minute time segments for a whole day. Such records were completed for each member of the family. The 2592 records produced were equally distributed over days of the week and seasons of the year, so that the effects of unusual weekend or vacation pattern of time would not distort the pattern. Respondents were asked about the following thirteen housework categories:

1. Regular meal preparation
2. Special food preparation (e.g., preparation of food for special use, canning, and so forth)
3. After meal cleanup
4. Regular house care
5. Special house care and maintenance (including repairs, painting and papering and so forth)
6. Care of car and yard
7. Clothes washing
8. Ironing
9. Sewing and care of household linens, hand wash, mending, and so forth
10. Physical care of family members (including escorting them to medical appointments)
11. Other care of family members (including pets)
12. Marketing
13. Management and record keeping

Specific, standard examples were available for each category, to facilitate the respondent's coding.

The results of Walker's study shatter the myth of the indolent housewife. The average workweek of housewives in the sample was 63 hours, including both housework and paid employment. Looking at the housewife's working week, we find variation by number of children and by the wife's employment status. Wives with no children managed 34 hours of housework weekly, on the average, while mothers with one child averaged 48, mothers with four, 57 and mothers of five or more averaged 61 hours weekly. Wives who were not employed outside the home averaged 8.1 hours of housework per day; those employed outside the home averaged 7.3 hours if they worked from 1 to 14 hours a week, and 6.3 hours a day if they worked from 15 to 29 hours a week. Only for those employed over 30 hours a week (i.e., full time) was the housework load appreciably reduced; these wives averaged 4.8 hours of daily housework. While other family members are sleeping, watching TV or engaging in other leisure activities, the housewife is working.

Who Does the Housework?

A number of studies have shown that employed wives do less housework than women who are not employed outside the home (Robinson and Converse, 1966; Vanek, 1974). Some attribute the difference to greater efficiency of women who cope with two jobs. Others have assumed that other family members, especially the husband, step in to fill the gap left by the mother during her working hours. Walker's research shows no significant variation in the husband's contribution whether the wife was employed full time, part-time or not at all: husbands spent 1.6 hours on housework each day. The average contribution of children was 1.1 hours when the mother worked from 0 to 14 hours each week, and 1.2—essentially no increase—when she worked 15 hours a week or more. The age of children seemed to make no difference: although there was virtually no contribution from children under six, their contribution did not increase as they grew older and presumably more competent. Thus, in the Walker study, children do not appear to be a major resource for domestic labor. We might note that although the advent of children increases the housewife's work load, there is no offsetting contribution from children to domestic labor. Housework remains "women's work," not "family work" or women and children's work.

One traditional perspective on the family holds that spouses are "colleagues" (Miller and Swanson, 1958), specializing in different spheres. If husbands refrain from involvement in domestic labor, it is due not to contempt for women or for "women's work," but because they specialize in different work. The hypothesis of sex role specialization leads us to predict that certain household tasks will be performed more by men than women.

Blood and Wolfe (1960) discovered a degree of sex role specialization in a selection of household tasks. Oakley found that couples differ in the degree of segregation (sex role specialization) or jointness (interchangeability, "togetherness") of their intimate lifestyle but that this did not carry over to housework.

Walker's data show some evidence of specialization in the husbands' contribution to domestic labor. Their greatest contribution was to tasks in the traditionally "masculine" outdoor sphere: yard and car care. Very little indoor housework fell to husbands in this sample. The husband's contribution to the preparation of food doubled when the wife was employed; up from six minutes a day to 12. In the category of clothing care, the husband's contribution was too small to be tabulated (that is, less than six minutes a day). The husband's contribution to child care tended to be about 20 minutes a day, concentrating on chauffeuring children, helping them with schoolwork or other nonphysical care. The bulk of physical child care remained the wife's responsibility. When marketing and management activities are combined, husbands contribute an average of 24 minutes a day.

Walker's dramatic findings stem from a straightforward tradition of work in home economics. This work is without ideological premise but it provides the basis for a radical materialist analysis of an important, overlooked economic function: domestic labor. Economic analyses have traditionally focused on monetary exchanges. In the fast-paced, complex life which is typical of advanced industrial nations, time is another highly valued resource. Often tradeoffs between time and money are explicitly made. Walker's research gives us concrete estimates of the cost in time of unpaid domestic labor, showing unequivocally who pays.

Walker's research is concrete and narrowly focused. The social context of domestic labor falls outside Walker's focus. Questions such as the impact of sex role ideology on domestic labor and the degree to which domestic labor is organized as a work role require additional kinds of data. To examine these questions we turn to the research of Oakley (1974).

Occupation: Housewife

Oakley (1974) has undertaken a study of housewife as a work role. Unlike sociologists who treat the legal status of wife (i.e., one legally bound to a man) as central to this role, Oakley focuses upon the work itself—that is, upon domestic labor. As with any study of an occupation, she investigates conditions of work, technology employed and worker morale. In particular, Oakley attempts to specify the aspects of the household worker's job that are perceived as satisfiers, and those perceived as dissatisfiers. Oakley's study affords a sense of how the context of domestic labor—working conditions in the broadest sense—affects the housewife's "job satisfaction."

Oakley's is a small-sample study of 40 London housewives, aged 20–30, all mothers. Six of the women had paid jobs, all but one of these part-time. Respondents were designated by being selected alphabetically from the patient lists of two London physicians: one who practiced in a predominantly working-class area and one in a middle-class area. Respondents were interviewed regarding their feelings about housework in general, and about specific housework tasks (cleaning, shopping, cooking, washing up, washing, ironing). Other questions investigated the degree to which the housewife had explicit routines and standards for housework, the degree of shared leisure activity and decision-making in the marriage, the husband's contribution to domestic labor and identification with the housewife role. Background data included the number and ages of children, child care or schooling arrangements for these, the husband's occupation, the respondent's occupation prior to marriage and the respondent's educational attainment. A number of other questions were omitted from the report.

Like Walker, Oakley found that her respondents had a long workweek, averaging 77 hours. The preponderant sentiment was job dissatisfaction, as measured in this study. Seventy percent reported that they disliked housework. The terms in which they discussed their job indicated clearly that they thought of it as labor, not productive work. These interviews contain no images of housewifery as creative or expressive. Yet, domestic labor was seen as a job. The respondents compared their job with their husbands' and with jobs they had held before marriage. Of the 40 women, 26 felt they worked harder than their husbands did. Moreover, they had no relief, no work breaks, no friends to have a beer with after the day's work; and, of course, there was no coming home after the working day to unwind and take it easy. The housewives were aware that their husbands did not see it this way but generally thought the housewife's job was easier. When they discussed their husbands' contribution to domestic labor, it was clear that wives whose husbands "helped" felt fortunate, and those whose husbands did not were resentful. Yet sex role ideology set definite limits on both spouses' ideas as to the kind and degree of help from husbands that were appropriate.

In Oakley's study, domestic labor seems to be the defining component of the housewife role for women. When asked what were the best and worst aspects of the job, most of the worst, but also more than half of the best, focused upon housework. It is interesting to note that although housework is central in these women's "job satisfaction," it is not an undifferentiated lump. Housewives' reactions to their job showed that they discriminate among a number of aspects of the job and differentiate among different housework tasks as well. There was agreement that ironing was the most disliked task and that cooking was the least disliked. Housewives ranked shopping next to cooking, which was followed by washing, cleaning, washing up, and ironing. Seventy-five percent of the housewives disliked ironing: only 5 percent liked it. Table 2.2 shows the like and dislike responses for each of the tasks. When the respondents discussed what they liked or disliked about the tasks, the dimensions of the housewife job emerged.

Dissatisfaction with housework was associated with monotony, fragmentation and work overload. Monotony arises from the rep-

TABLE 2.2

Answers to Questions About Housework Tasks

	PERCENTAGE OF WOMEN GIVING ANSWER ($N = 40$)		
HOUSEWORK TASK	*Dislike*	*Do not mind*	*Like*
Ironing	75	20	5
Washing up	65	28	8
Cleaning	50	20	30
Washing	33	35	33
Shopping	30	20	50
Cooking	23	18	60

SOURCE: Adapted from Oakley (1974, p. 49). Copyright, Pantheon Books, a Division of Random House, Inc.

etitious nature of housework tasks and also from their characteristic of "producing" no palpable, lasting outcome. Housework must be repeated frequently; the goals, once attained, are impermanent. The food, once cooked, is consumed; the cleaned room becomes untidy and dirty. The experience of fragmentation arose from the constant interruptions that are a condition of the housewife with young children at home. The housewives complained that they could not expect to get a job finished. Housework, particularly when combined with child care, has the quality of flow (and of being diverted), rather than being composed of discrete tasks that, like building blocks, can be assembled into the day's work. Moreover, housework does not require the worker's whole attention, but requires enough concentration so that the worker cannot concentrate on something else. Most of the women found no intrinsic meaning in domestic labor. Finally, the multitude of tasks to be done and a sense of time pressure contributed to the sense of overload.

Ironing was seen as an endless series of similar tasks. Isolation, considered as a condition of the housewife's job, colored most tasks. By way of contrast, shopping was liked: it afforded the occasion to get out and to have contact with other adults, as brief and mundane as this might be. Some women's isolation was broken by visits with relatives and friends, but there were no accounts of women doing housework together. Much of the housewife's job consists of direct service to others, and when such service was appreciated, the task was not disliked as much. The possibility of a compliment seemed to be a factor in the high ranking of cooking. Conversely, housework appears to be little appreciated. Eight of the women reported that their husbands never commented on the house; another 24 of the 40 reported that the husband commented only negatively (Oakley, 1974, p. 105).

The satisfactions and dissatisfactions that Oakley's respondents found in their work appear to stem from three sources. First, the work itself appears to generate negative feelings in most workers. Second, working conditions interact with the tasks. It seems likely that changes in working conditions could materially affect the job satisfaction of domestic workers. A third influence is compensation for the work: the income, in both wages and esteem, that house-wifery commands.

Occupation: Housewife clearly lends itself to study in much the same terms as other occupations; yet this topic is virtually un-researched. Scholarly interest in domestic labor is recent and tends to originate outside the social science mainstream, within systematic radical perspectives (e.g., feminism, socialism). The exception to this generalization is the tradition of research in home economics, which is generally ignored by social scientists (Steidl and Bratton, 1968).

We may ask why orthodox social scientists have ignored do-mestic labor and its enormous working population. Why are there no studies comparing domestic labor and other manual occupations? Why is there no systematic analysis of the working conditions of domestic laborers and their outcomes? Why are not the complex issues of remuneration and reallocation of resources dealt with? The failure to study domestic labor thoroughly may be explained in part via the traditional mystification that concerns the role of wife. Mystifying the wife role serves the unacknowledged function of maintaining the separation between work and home, and separation between the rewards "appropriate" to each.

Analyzing domestic labor as a job flies in the face of this mystification and the social science treatments that reflect it. Such analysis opens the Pandora's box of social comparison between women and men; specifically, a comparison of their respective inputs and outcomes. Analysis of the prestige and compensation of the housewife's job is doubly taboo. It violates the civility of the view of the woman as wife, in the context of personal relationships and sentiment. It also brings her into the marketplace and threatens the economic monopoly that is central to men. And it raises questions of justice, when rewards are shown to be determined by gender more than qualifications.

SOCIAL STATUS OF AND FOR WOMEN

The question of the social status of married women involves several distinct issues. An initial question is this: *What is the housewife's social status?* And a second is, *What are the determinants of her social status?*

Looked at from one perspective, all housewives have the same status. Insofar as being a housewife is an occupation, it is generally assigned a low status. In the Duncan Index (Duncan, 1961) of socioeconomic status it is conventionally coded at the bottom of the list. In assigning this status to the married woman, traditional stratification theory essentially strips her of her individual attributes, reducing her to the lowest common denominator. Sociologists take a woman's individual status attributes into account when discussing courtship and assortative mating, but when she is married, it is as if these attributes cease to have any effect. Of course, they do not; this blind spot has been a weakness in sociologists' treatments of married women. The other component of a wife's status is her husband's occupation, according to traditional stratification theory: his occupational status "places" her in the stratification system. Ordinarily the low status of housewifery is ignored; the wife is "characterized" primarily by her husband's occupational status.

The gospel of traditional stratification theory, that a wife's social status is determined by her husband's occupation alone, has recently been much questioned. Acker (1973) has stressed that this dogma has contributed to our lack of knowledge about women. Barth and Watson (1967; Watson and Barth, 1964) have published data showing that, in a national sample, many women attribute to themselves a different social class membership than that to which they would be assigned on the basis of their husband's occupation. A study by Arnott and Bengston (1970) challenges the assumption that a woman's individual status attributes are obliterated in the context of her marriage.

The Marriage/Mobility Paradox

Social science treatments of Occupation: Housewife illustrate, while at the same time obscuring, a major paradox in the role of wife. The paradox is that marriage seems to make a woman upwardly mobile, but, in reality, it makes her downwardly mobile. Traditionally, marriage is viewed as a means to upward mobility for a woman: *wife* is a desirable status. Marriage further enhances a woman's social status by linking her with a male occupation. This thinking covertly acknowledges the differential opportunity structures resulting from occupational segregation. The conventional assumption is that derived status (i.e., through the husband's occupation) is comparable or interchangeable with direct or earned status, which the husband gains from his occupation. Status assigned to married women has been higher *on a categorical basis*. Although this traditional thinking may be on the wane, there are many who still believe "Married is better." On an individual basis, marriage may mean downward mobility for a woman. Traditionally, her own status attributes are ignored once she is married and the social status of the family unit that she forms with her partner is calculated on the basis of his status attributes alone. Women are bound-in to marriage because the cultural script tells them it is the means to social mobility. The means is, however, not through their own agency but through their husbands' achievement. This factor perpetuates their dependency and vicariousness. The cultural formulation involves mystification but there is also a reality that is involved. The marriage/mobility paradox rests on the fact that while domestic labor is assigned low status and a woman's own occupation is likely to have higher status, her husband's occupation is likely to have higher status yet. To the extent that the individual perceives derived status as equivalent to achieved or direct status, the wife/domestic worker combination might appear the most attractive option. When we recognize that the housewife's job is that of a domestic laborer, it becomes apparent that, restricted though the range of women's paid occupations is, most paid jobs outrank unpaid domestic labor. *Marriage means downward occupational mobility for almost all women.*

The marriage/mobility paradox is obscured in two ways. First, the status of wife is inflated: for example, by promulgating such models as the "colleague marriage" and by neglecting to question the validity of the derived status idea. Second, domestic labor is ignored, permitting its low status to be negated.

DERIVED STATUS

Sociological discussions of the status of women illustrate the familiar intellectual double standard. In a sense, sociologists treat status as a concept that applies only to men. When applied to women, it is a different phenomenon, governed by special rules rather than those that characterize "real" status. Hence, *derived status*. Marriage is the great leveler for women: the wife is stripped of her individual status attributes and her husband's occupational status is used to place her in the stratification system.

Many sociologists act as though the man's occupational status "becomes" the wife's, but the evidence suggests that this is an oversimplification. It overlooks the fact that the prestige a wife derives from her husband's occupation is derived, rather than direct. Derived status or power exists in virtue of the role incumbent's relationship with a powerful person. The basis of the prestige may be in the position or in the attributes of the powerful person, but the derived prestige is contingent upon the relationship. The secretary of a powerful man is, to be sure, a force to be reckoned within an organization. But she can, of course, be fired. When this happens, she loses all status. Status that does not stem from the accomplishments or skills of the individual is perishable. Lopata's research on widows bears this out: not only do women lose a husband and the associated status, but also the social life and the routines that were predicated upon the relationship (Lopata, 1973).

It might be difficult to see the parallel between the wife and the secretary. The particular kind of relationship involved in marriage (and even more, mystification about this relationship) blinds many people to the structural similarities. It is easier to see how derived status works in the status system of the work organization. Ordinarily, the secretary of a high-ranking man is paid more than other secretaries, and when her boss is promoted, she is also. Both of these events are independent of her own attributes or performance, for they are determined by the vicissitudes of the boss's career. Many successes and distinctions fall to wives as a function of their husband's status.

Wives get fired, too. Many women are not aware that when a man retires or dies, a divorced wife is not eligible for Social Security benefits if she was married for less than 25 years. In this respect marriage is somewhat like a mortgage: the equity you build up on your investment accumulates slowly; if you don't pay off the mortgage, you don't realize a profit.

The idea of derived status reflects traditional sex role definitions. It reflects reality only for the wife who is not employed outside the home, and reflects the preferences of those, both women and men, who favor segregation of women's and men's spheres. It follows that challenges to this ideology are more likely to come from persons in less traditional lifestyles. An interesting study by Haavio-Manila (1969) is an example. In a study of Finnish workers, Haavio-Manila found that women and men working in the same plant differed significantly in the status they assigned to a range of occupations, depending on the sex of the person in the occupation. The ratings reflected variation in prestige that is common to the culture, but sex differences also appeared. *Women tended to rate the status of women in an occupation significantly higher than men did, and, in some cases, higher than they rated the man in that occupation.* Another set of ratings evaluated the status of wives of men in the selected occupations. Here the sex difference was also clear: *women rated the woman in the occupation higher than the wife of the man in the occupation and men did the reverse.* A important extension of this study would be to obtain ratings from the wives of the male workers. Are women who do not have an occupation of their own more likely to reflect the traditional stratification gospel in their responses than women who are employed? Will they evaluate wife-of-occupation more highly than female-in-occupation, and male-in-occupation more highly than female-in-occupation, and male-in-occupation more highly than either? Such a pattern raises again the fascinating issue of women who think as men do, found here in the most traditional corner of the stratification system.

The predicted pattern of responses would be consistent with existing research. Negative attitudes toward the employment of married women have repeatedly been found among housewives who are not employed outside the home. Oppenheimer (1970) has tabulated national surveys of such attitudes in the period of 1936–1960. A more informal assessment of attitudes might be obtained by examining the organized resistance to the Equal Rights Amendment. Some proponents in this resistance have expressed the belief that women are advantaged by a system that excludes them from equality, and stand to lose status and benefits *if* equality is mandated.

It seems that husbands with traditional wives benefit from the shared belief in derived status by being spared the economic competition, at least from this quarter. The inflation of the status of the male breadwinner, evident in Haavio-Manila's data, is a little-noticed feature of such sex-role segregation. It parallels the

119

male wage inflation that accompanies occupational segregation discussed in Chapter 1.

The sociologists' notion of derived status thus fits cosily with traditional family form and with the economic institution of occupational segregation. Attitudes and lifestyles are systematically related and mutually reinforcing. Will the same be true on the other side of the issue? Will the attitudes of husbands with employed wives be consistent? A study by Axelson (1963) found that husbands' attitudes toward the employment of married women vary systematically with the employment status of their wives. Husbands whose wives were employed outside the home were more positively inclined toward employment of married women, and they were considerably more liberal on other issues related to relations between the sexes. We should note that Axelson collected his data at a time when the employment of wives was a minority phenomenon. Because a broader range of women are now employed, we should expect that their husbands' attitudes might not line up so clearly. The best exposure to a systematic set of attitudes that express the perception of benefit with nontraditional lifestyles might be found in the writings of male feminists. And, indeed, in one of the earliest writings of the male liberation movement, Farrell (1974) sets forth 21 reasons why symmetrical marital roles, rather than segregated roles, benefit men. Most of these have to do with the greater resources and flexibility in lifestyle afforded partners who trade off participation in home and market production.

Farrell's argument seems far from radical, directed as it is toward traditional men, couched in the conventional male vocabulary of motives of economic self-interest. Yet, it is radical in advocating a breakdown in the separation of female and male spheres. Farrell, like other feminists, applies a single standard, rather than a double standard, to women and men.

There is evidence for two contradictory approaches to women's roles and women's status. They define different perspectives on another component of women's familial roles, that of consumer.

Woman as Consumer

In the traditional script, the wife is a financial dependent. As that script becomes modified in response to the realities of married women's employment, the job is considered ancillary and the myth that women work for "pin money" persists. The wife's resources are supposed to be applied to home production. The "new look" in human capital theory concedes that commodities are in fact produced, not merely consumed, in the home. The wife combines commodities bought in the market with her own skills and time to produce goods such as nutritious meals, family health and quality children.

One tradition in viewing woman as consumer dates from Veblen (1953). The wife is one among many proofs of a male's occupational success: he buys a high-quality wife and she proceeds to buy and display a number of commodities that, because of their rarity or price, further testify to the male's success. It has come to be understood that this function of conspicuous consumption requires, in its turn, certain training. The upper-class wife must know quality and must have the skills requisite to supervising servants, managing houses, travel and entertainment.

The idea of conspicuous consumption applies, strictly speaking, only to the rich. The ideology, however, appears to affect conceptualization of the middle-class housewife as well. Because her work of domestic labor is ignored, she is considered idle. Often, the housewife is portrayed as a parasite: her job is to be an effective consumer. Thus Lopata (1971) finds that the consumer segement of the housewife role (as indexed by the use of services delivered to or performed by others in the home) increases with income and with the presence of children. Galbraith (1973) has trenchantly analyzed the way that housewives are manipulated by the media in ways that inflate sales of the sponsors' products.

Pronatalist Images and the Reality of Motherhood

The paradox of married women's status is emphasized if we add the role of mother to that of wife and domestic worker. In our pronatalist society, motherhood is an honorific status. It confers higher status on a woman than does the domestic worker role. For most women, it powerfully reinforces feminine identity in a way that housewifery does not. Women value this component of their role (Lopata, 1971). Society tells them that their contribution to the development of their children is of great value and some women do experience motherhood in this way.

Peck and Senderowitz (1974) have analyzed the complex of practices and values that exalt parenthood and encourage reproduction. Peck and Senderowitz note that our culture tacitly expects that the individual's first loyalty will be to the family unit. The father/breadwinner demonstrates his loyalty by occupational success while the mother is expected to be absorbed in household and child care.

Pronatalist culture emphasizes expectations and prescriptions for the woman much more than for the man. Rehearsal for adult roles in the family is much more common in girls than boys, and the accessories of "child's play" illustrate this. Girl-children's doll play is pronatalist conditioning. Consistent conditioning creates a sense of the inevitability of parenthood and the appropriateness of this "choice." Common pronatalist ideas include the idea that feminine fulfillment is through maternity, and its converse, that the childless woman is unfulfilled. The idea of a "maternal instinct" presents as natural or inevitable that which is merely socially expedient.

No evidence for the existence of a "maternal instinct" exists although this is a time-honored myth. A genuine maternal instinct would have to appear in all women and would presumably have a genetic basis. If a maternal instinct had survival value, it would presumably cause women to behave in a way that fosters the best interests of the helpless infant. Such behavior would theoretically be triggered automatically at birth, or at exposure to an infant, or during pregnancy—or at whatever point that serves the interests of the mythmaker. Though the "theory" of maternal instinct is not rigorously spelled out, the existing facts fail to support any part of it. As we know, the physical event of conception does not depend on any desire to be a mother. The automatic process of pregnancy and birth can be similarly free of intention. If mothering behavior, or "nurturance," came naturally to all biological mothers, we would not have to worry about the young. In fact, it appears that both the biological aspects of mothering (e.g., nursing) and the psychological (e.g., attachment) require learning in the human female. Some research suggests that close and sustained contact between the mother and the newborn is required for maternal attachment to develop. Standard obstetrical practice in most hospitals separates mother and child immediately after birth, and may thus routinely undermine the development of the critical mother–child bond.

We suspect that many other experiences mothers have might affect the mother–child bond in similar ways. With respect to maternal attachment, as with many other maternal behaviors, *the conditions under which a woman must do her mothering will determine how she does it.* In their study of mothers and children in six cultures, Minturn, Lambert et al. (1964) discovered that the more help a mother has with child care, the more nurturant she is toward her children.

Obviously, if adequate mothering is not guaranteed by instinct, it must be socially engineered. The study of pronatalism identifies the mechanisms by which pronatalist allegiances are formed and conforming behavior ensured. Hollingworth (1922), in an early and classic paper reprinted in Peck and Senderowitz, likens motherhood to military service—a function necessary to the state, but hazardous and profitless to the individual. There are many ways to transform consciousness so that the individual's preferences match society's mandate. Two that affect women's experience of motherhood in America deserve special mention. One manipulates the positive incentive of esteem, and the other, the negative of guilt.

The glorification of motherhood serves to enhance the appeal of this life option, while setting up unrealistic expectations for gratifications to be derived from it. In a recent Ann Landers survey of parents, an overwhelming majority reported that, if they had known at the outset what they knew now, they would not have decided to have children. The reason voiced by many of these disillusioned parents is that they had expected their offspring to reciprocate, as the parents grew older, the care and selflessness that the parents had lavished on them as children. This disappointment made parenting seem, to many, a misplaced effort.

In the official image of motherhood, children are portrayed in smiles and clean clothes, rather than in tantrums and dirty diapers. They are portrayed as affectionate and healthy. The images imply that it is in the nature of children to be loving, adorable, appreciative and helpful, rather than implying that these attributes emerge only under certain circumstances. The image of perfection as the child's natural state sets the mother up for a guilt trip and grossly underestimates the difficulty of her job. Of course the official image fails to mention that the company of the very young, their conversation and their pastimes can bore the normal adult. The child, however adorable, inspiring or affectionate, cannot reciprocate an adult relationship with her mother. Once again the conditions under which mothering takes place influence the outcomes for the mother and affect outcomes for her child. Unrelieved company of and responsibility for very young children constitute a deprivation for the mother.

The pronatalist image is the dominant view of motherhood that is afforded to women and men in our culture. The liabilities and costs of motherhood are little publicized. The unpublicized underside of motherhood resembles in some respects the "invisible" reality of domestic labor. Child care, like domestic labor, is an activity that demands much time and vigilance. Much of it is repetitious drudgery and, like housework, it is work in which men take a comparatively small share. The labor components of child care are not widely recognized. Much child care is done under conditions of isolation and unremitting responsibility. Parents of young children lose sleep and mobility. To the extent that child care is not shared, the primary caregiver loses more. For many mothers, there is chronic anxiety about whether they are doing an adequate job. The possibility of traumatizing the child is a threat that hangs over the head of every mother who has ever heard of Freud (or Spock). As feminists have observed, the mother is the "fall guy" for any negative outcomes that befall her child.

While the event of motherhood officially confers honorific status on a woman, we may note that at the same time it renders her least independent of any time in her lifecycle. Having children may keep her out of the work force or may disadvantage her even as she remains in paid employment. Divorced women who are mothers are less likely to remarry than child-free women. The economic burden on divorced mothers is severe, as most husbands default on court-ordered child support and alimony payments. These various forms of dependence also emerge as a factor in the helplessness of women who are victims of domestic violence. Often they cannot find or pay for any other domicile nor find a way to support their children, should they leave their assaultive partner.

The effect of pronatalist values and propaganda is to inflate misleadingly the incentives associated with motherhood and presumably influence women to have children who might not make this decision with fuller information. It may also lock women into motherhood as an activity, keeping them at it longer or more exclusively than would be the case in the absence of pronatalist influences. Scholars who analyze pronatalism tend to focus upon the positive images by which women are manipulated. These rosy images are effective in getting women to "choose" maternity, but by themselves might not be adequate to induce women to *limit* themselves to this option. Consequently, if women are to be excluded (often voluntarily) from other spheres of endeavor, additional influences must be brought into play. This is where the bugaboo of "maternal deprivation" is manipulated in order to control maternal behavior. Mothers who do not devote themselves full time to motherhood are subject to the threat that their children will develop social and psychological maladjustment, will fail to achieve and/or fail to develop normally. Employed mothers are subject to guilt, whether self-generated or in response to others' accusations. The idea that children are entitled to 24-hour service by their mothers has rarely been challenged—although perhaps it has rarely been expressed explicitly. This assumption appears to be embedded in the role definition for mothers.

The role expectations for the mother are consistent with some of the basic elements of female sex role script, most notably vicariousness. It is understood that when a woman undertakes the responsibility of parenthood, she subordinates her own needs, desires or priorities to the welfare of her child. Ironically, it is usually male experts who specify what is in the best interests of the child and, consequently, what is the mother's obligation. We are not speaking here of a parent role, but of the mother role. Obligations for the father are seldom spelled out. His obligations as a parent seem to be satisfied in the same way as his obligations as a spouse: by the wage-earning function. He is exempted from directly meeting the needs of partner or children. As we found with domestic labor, so it is with child care: although the wife increasingly shares the wage-earning function, the husband does not reciprocate by sharing child care and domestic labor.

STUDIES OF MATERNAL EMPLOYMENT

This specification of priorities for the wife is seldom made explicit. It can be readily inferred, however, from the focus of research on employed mothers. Very little emphasis is placed on outcomes *for the mother*; the overwhelming bulk of concern is about outcomes for the children. The "maternal deprivation" thesis is concerned only with child outcomes, and not at all with the interrelationship of outcomes for mother and child. The history of the "maternal deprivation" hypothesis is an interesting one. The idea gained currency just at the time when men were being demobilized at the end of World War II, and began to displace women from jobs they had occupied during the war (Tobias, 1973). Child care facilities, provided to induce women to enter employment, were disbanded. Women were being pushed out of the paid work force by men, at the same time they were having full responsibility for child care "restored" to them. The "maternal deprivation" thesis provided a convenient rationale for these changes.

This hypothesis found its way into the mainstream by a rather dubious route. During World War II, Spitz (1945) studied the functioning of war orphans who had been institutionalized. In addition to the trauma of being orphaned, with its consequent disruption of primary ties, these children were cared for in an institutional environment that was stimulus-poor and afforded little physical care and contact. The children showed severe decrements in intellectual functioning and social adjustment. With unseemly haste, social scientists rushed to predict that children of mothers who reentered paid employment would show the symptoms of Spitz's hospitalized children. In 1943, Ribble, in a book provocatively titled *The Rights of Infants*, attributed to "inadequate mothering" horrid infant behaviors including refusal to nurse, screaming, vomiting, hypertension, diarrhea and negativism.

One of the most influential proponents of the maternal deprivation hypothesis was Bowlby, whose 1946 study of young thieves alerted him to the dimension of inadequate supervision as a factor in delinquency. Since only women have responsibility for children, of course, women's neglect of their duties was blamed for this problem. In subsequent work, Bowlby (1953, 1969) focused on child development, underlining the importance of maternal care.

Interestingly, virtually all of those who joined in the outcry about "maternal deprivation" ignored a contemporaneous study by Anna Freud, dealing with a population much more similar to that of Spitz than were the American children about whom concern was being expressed. Freud and Dann's (1970) study of World War II orphans reared in a group-care setting showed that the children provided much nurturance for each other, exhibiting neither intellectual deficit nor social maladjustment.

Nevertheless, in the 1950s, "maternal deprivation" became doctrine. The movement of mothers into the paid work force, already evident in the postwar years, was seen by some as a dangerous trend—even as a social problem. Two prominent researchers on juvenile delinquency wrote, unabashedly: "As more and more *enticements* in the way of financial gain, excitement and independence from the husband are offered married women to *lure* them from their domestic duties, the *problem* is becoming more widespread and acute" (Glueck and Glueck, 1957, p. 350, italics mine). The language of this quote seems archaic and melodramatic, rather like an old temperance handbill. But unlike temperance tracts, this hypothesis of "maternal deprivation" is still with us. This is so in spite of the body of research findings that have accumulated since the "maternal deprivation" hypothesis was first broached. Its persistence is a clear example of the function of myth discussed in Chapter 1.

From the beginning, the verdict of research has been that maternal employment does not produce detectible negative effects on children. Burchinal and Rossman (1961), in one of the earliest of the careful studies, examined personality characteristics of children with employed mothers and those whose mothers were not employed outside the home. They found no differences even where mothers had been employed before the child was three years old (presumably a critical period for development).

Nevertheless, the concern with effects of maternal employment on children persists. Current research is characterized by an appropriate specification of the *conditions under which* a variety of effects may be observed. As of today, research indicates that this is a more realistic approach. Glueck and Glueck were eager (as were many of their generation) to blame any negative child outcomes on the mother. Yet their data revealed that many mothers who were employed outside the home, in that decade, were laboring under disadvantages that were antecedent to their employment status. More careful research has uncovered the variables that disadvantage both mothers and children. Income inadequacy, for example, has its effect independent of mother's employment status. *It is not children of "broken homes" who suffer, but children growing up in homes below the poverty line.* Mothers who are the sole support of their children are often employed outside the home, but the wage levels commanded by most women are not adequate to support a family in comfort. Economics underlies much of the "familial disorganization" with which social scientists are, from time to time, concerned. Women who, through personal choice or other events are living in non-standard families, continue to incur economic as well as social penalties. Public policy has not met the needs of this large group of American citizens (Ross and Sawhill, 1975). In an early review of the research on maternal employment, Stolz listed the assumptions prevalent in 1960: working was presumed to result in "deficiencies in mothering," i.e., insufficient supervision of the child, less dedication, less effectiveness and less interaction between mother and child. The child of the working mother was expected to be both overly dependent *and* subject to too much achievement pressure. The undermining of sex role socialization was also suspected. (Employment of fathers was not, however, predicted to result in deficient fathering or child deprivation.)

Yarrow et al. (1962) examined child-rearing practices as reported by 100 middle-class white mothers who had children between the ages of 4 and 11. The mothers were matched on family characteristics, and varied by employment status, educational attainment and motivation for working or not working. Yarrow et al. found relatively few differences in child-rearing practices that were attributable to employment status alone. Employed mothers with a high-school background differed markedly from working mothers with a college background. Yarrow et al. found substantial social-class differences in the reported strictness of fathers, in the degree to which mothers encouraged independence in the child, in sensitivity to the child, in the clarity of limit setting and in the consistency between child-rearing principles and practice. College-trained mothers were more permissive toward their children, while high-school-educated mothers were more demanding.

Rather than focusing solely on outcomes for the child, current research on the effects of maternal employment examines all the role relationships within the family. Thus marital satisfaction, divorce and the domestic division of labor are included in current research, as well as attitudes of family members toward maternal employment.

In a recent review, Howell (1973a,b) expands the focus to employed mothers and their families. She includes effects on husband–wife sociability and role flexibility. The most common reason given for maternal employment is income needs of the family. Howell does not question this response, although we might expect that, if husband, wife and children agree that she is employed in order to further family goals (rather than her personal goals), there will be greater acceptance of maternal employment. Vicarious achievement and vicarious consumption are more consistent with wife and mother role expectations than is personal ambition or self-actualization.

Insofar as a wife's employment increases a husband's domestic burdens or decreases the attention he commands from his wife, we might predict higher rates of marital disruption in families where the wife is employed outside the home. However, divorce rates do not vary for marriages with an employed wife as compared with marriages where the wife is not employed outside the home. A number of studies find wives perceiving support from their husbands in the multiple responsibilities of the home. Attitudes tapped in these studies are consistent with those found by Axelson (1963). However, we may well gain an inflated view of the degree of family members' acceptance of maternal employment when we sample only employed mothers. The reader should remember, however, that husbands' opposition may have its effect in keeping women out of paid employment; wives of such men will not be found in a sample for research on maternal employment.

Research generally finds that children of mothers employed

outside the home are more accepting of maternal employment, while children whose mothers are not employed generally have more negative attitudes. Children's attitudes toward maternal employment seem to be conditioned by the structure of family life. When the father takes a greater share in domestic labor, children seem more accepting of their mothers' employment (Duvall, 1955; King et al., 1968; Mathews, 1933). Children of mothers not employed outside the home perceive maternal employment as threatening the marital relationship to a greater extent than do children whose mothers are actually employed. In one study of adolescents' attitudes, it was found that adolescents were more accepting of maternal employment when the father participated more in domestic labor. This possibility of *fathers* as role models for non-sex-stereotyped attitudes and behaviors has received little consideration in the literature.

The father's attitude toward his wife's employment (or others' perception of his attitude) appears to be critical in the family's acceptance of maternal employment. This acceptance may have long-term consequences for female and male children's choices of adult lifestyle. Thus Baruch (1972) found that college women's expressed intention to pursue role-innovative occupations was mediated not only by mother's employment status, but even more by their perception of the father's acceptance of maternal employment.

Although the father's attitude is influential, we know very little about the ways in which men's sex role attitudes are formed or changed. Existing research marks only the tip of the iceberg. We have much to learn about the negotiations that go on between spouses concerning women's exercise of extended options.

Reports of marital satisfaction should be taken with a grain of salt in all cases, since it is socially conventional to claim marital happiness publicly—whatever one's private feelings. Responses to marital happiness scales are always highly skewed toward the positive end (Orden and Bradburn, 1968). Thus, Nye, while he found no differences in marital happiness reports by employment status, found that among employed wives there was a higher incidence of reported conflict between spouses and thoughts of divorce. It is possible that employed wives, having demonstrated earning capacity, felt freer to admit these feelings than wives not employed outside the home, whose status of financial dependence provides no alternative to marriage. Early studies tended to show some tradeoff of household responsibilities when the wife was employed, but the meaning of these for "family power" is ambiguous. When a husband takes responsibility for some day-to-day family concerns, is he "gaining" or "losing" power? Is family power the right to make decisions binding on others or the freedom from involvement in family affairs (Hoffman, 1960)?

In an exemplary review of the literature, Hoffman (1973) keeps both mother and child in focus as she examines a number of theories of the the effect of maternal employment. The conditions under which a woman enters the paid work force, characteristics of the job and the family climate are only a few of the variables that affect the mother–child nexus. Of course maternal employment is not a single variable, and Hoffman points out the futility of trying to predict *anything* on the basis of so gross a category. In meticulously differentiating the phenomena of maternal employment and in specifying their several outcomes, Hoffman brings us up to date on this persistent question.

Hoffman concludes that for all the child outcomes she analyzed—social attitudes and values, social adjustment and mental health, independence/dependence, and achievement motivation, ability and performance—maternal employment shows benefits to *daughters*. Several studies, however, show a deficit in academic performance of sons of employed mothers. Supervision of the child seems to be a critical factor in at least one child outcome, delinquency. McCord et al. (1963) and Glueck and Glueck found that inadequate supervision contributed to delinquency; unstable employment seemed related to supervision. Nye found, however, that too much supervision also contributed to a child's delinquency (1958). Moreover, supervision has different effects on female and male children: too much supervision affects girls negatively while too little affects boys negatively (Becker, 1964; Bronfenbrenner, 1961; Hoffman, 1972).

Effect of Maternal Employment on Sex Role Orientations of Offspring

Although most studies have asked mothers "why" they work, few have asked why they stay home. There is some indication that women whose behavior is motivated by healthy "selfishness" feel better about their choices and themselves than those who are motivated by "duty." Kappel and Lambert (1972) found that when mothers were employed because of desire for self-actualization, daughters had higher self-esteem than when mothers worked for family-oriented reasons. In Birnbaum's (1971) study of able housewives and professionals, the lowest scores on adequacy of mothering were found among women who had chosen to be full time homemakers but had done so out of a sense of duty rather than positive motivation. Studies like this have something to tell us about role modeling. What is the effect on a daughter of seeing her mother do something she manifestly does not feel good about doing? And what is the effect if, added to this impression, she is told that this is the right thing to do? In assessing the impact of their children on their lives, Birnbaum's homemakers stressed the necessity for sacrifice. The mothers employed professionally outside the home saw motherhood in terms of enrichment and self-fulfillment.

The Birnbaum study also casts some light on the question of "smother love." (Hoffman, 1973). Birnbaum observed strong differences between the homemaker and professional groups in their reactions to the developing independence of their children and the prospect of the empty nest.

Mothers serve as a direct role model for their daughters and as a model of possible partners for their sons. Various studies have shown that the daughters of employed mothers have higher occupational aspirations than daughters of mothers not employed

133

outside the home (Tangri, 1969; Almquist and Angrist, 1971). A related finding is that daughters of employed mothers hold less sex-stereotypic attitudes (Baruch, 1972; Meier, 1972) than daughters of mothers who are not employed outside the home. Some studies also find a similar effect for sons (Vogel et al., 1970; Broverman et al., 1970; Meier, 1972). Yarrow et al. (1972) found no differences in the degree of sex-typing of children by mother's employment status.

It appears that mothers who do not restrict themselves to a single adult role are walking advertisements for an enriched lifestyle. Their daughters are more likely to admire and wish to emulate them (Douvan, 1963; Baruch 1972); their sons are less likely to impose traditional role expectations on women with whom they relate. The offspring of employed mothers perceive their own sex in a more androgynous and less rigidly sex-stereotyped way (Vogel et al., 1970). A number of studies have found that daughters of working mothers have a higher opinion of women in general. Finding more to admire in an enriched role model, these daughters are less chauvinistic toward other women, as well as more ambitious for themselves. Hoffman observes that there is no reason to expect that maternal employment will affect female and male children in parallel ways. Employment per se is no sign of nontraditional sex role orientation in the mother (and to the extent that maternal employment has become the norm rather than the exception, this will be more true in future). Consequently the employed mother may socialize her children to traditional sex roles and serve as a model of the exceptional only for her daughter. A boomerang effect may occur for boys of working-class background, as suggested by the finding that sons respect the father less when the mother is employed (Kappel and Lambert, 1972). Presumably the wife's employment reflects badly on the father's male role as breadwinner and so has an indirect effect on the father–son relationship.

134

Yarrow et al. (1962) examined the motivational context of the mothers' employment/nonemployment status. When the mothers were doing what they preferred to do—whether staying home or working out side the home—there were few differences in their reported child-rearing practices. Difference appeared, however, when those dissatisfied with their status were compared. Sixty-seven percent of the dissatisfied nonemployed mothers reported a continuous battle for control with the child, while only 18% of the dissatisfied employed mothers reported this problem. Interviewer ratings of the mother's confidence in her mothering favored the employed mothers: 50 percent of the employed while 11 percent of the nonemployed showed high confidence. A similar pattern was found with respect to the mother's emotional satisfaction in the relationship with the child and with the interviewer's rating of maternal adequacy.

The motivational context also made a difference among the nonemployed mothers. Those who were dissatisfied with their work status showed inconsistency between their child-rearing principles and practices; they were also lower on clarity of limit setting for the child. The question of whether a woman is exercising her *preferred* employment option seems more important than whether she is working full time, part time or not at all. Thus in the Yarrow et al. study, the mothers not employed outside the home, but who wished to be, had the lowest scores on adequacy of mothering. Orden and Bradburn (1968) found that satisfaction and not employment status per se mediated marital satisfaction and the mother's rating of her own adequacy as a mother.

These findings demonstrate that, traditional sex role ideology aside, women who want to work during their mothering years suffer if they are prevented from doing so. It appears their children may suffer in addition.

However, the traditional sex role script takes its toll even from those who are employed outside the home in accordance with their own wishes. Yarrow et al. found some evidence of a guilt script for employed mothers: almost twice as many employed mothers expressed misgivings and anxious concern about possible interference of the work role with the maternal role. In a study of employed mothers with elementary-school-age children, Hoffman (1974) found that those who reported enjoying their work paid a price of guilt. Their children helped less with domestic labor than did the children of mothers who were not employed outside the home. Hoffman suggests that the mother who enjoyed employment compensated for her guilt by overindulging her children to the extent that they were socially less mature than their peers. This mother was conscious of quality concerns in her relationship with her children and had more positive feelings toward them than did the nonemployed mother. The results of this study, however, show no emphasis on training for self-sufficiency. Yet in Birnbaum's study it was the professionally employed mothers who encouraged independence in their children, while mothers remaining at home did not like the child's increasing independence. In Yarrow's findings, independence training is as much related to social class (educational attainment) as to employment status. Her middle-class mothers who were not employed emphasized independence training more than those with high-school backgrounds. Employed mothers with a high-school background emphasized independence training more than nonemployed mothers, and here a college background did not differentiate. Birnbaum did not have variation in social class in her study, which may account for the difference in findings. The interaction between social class and independence training deserves further study.

Employed mothers appear to do obeisance to the maternal deprivation myth, by consciously compensating their children for any deprivation that may result from their working outside the home. Yarrow et al. found that middle-class mothers employed outside the home consciously compensated for any deprivation by planning special activities with their children. Similar efforts were reported by the respondents in other studies (Kliger, 1954; Jones, Lundsteen and Michael, 1968; Rapaport and Rapaport, 1972).

It is apparent from these results that mothers' compensatory behaviors can have positive (enriching) effects or negative effects (where children are overindulged and independence training suffers).

ROLE STRESS UNDER CONDITIONS OF MULTIPLE-ROLE OCCUPANCY

The phenomenon of role stress in employed mothers deserves more analysis. There is empirical support for the idea that mothers working two full time jobs experience role overload. Yet as we have seen, this demanding situation is not always perceived as stressful and it rarely has measurable effects on the adjustment of children. The adjustment of mothers is a topic largely avoided in the social science literature. We will examine the evidence on this point later. Here we will try to uncover some of the conditions under which multiple-role occupancy—the normal situation for most adults in our society—is endurable and those under which it is unendurable.

One possibility is role conflict, the clash of competing expectations or demands on the mother's time, attention or energy; another possibility is the kind of support or validation she receives from role partners. Both of these questions direct our attention to the mother's role partners. Here we encounter some surprising findings. Woods (1972) found children of the full-time employed mothers were the best adjusted. Even more surprisingly, her sample included a number of single-parent households. Not only did these women carry the heaviest work burden, but, in addition, they lacked the usual support of a husband. How is it that their children showed no ill effects? Although the question cannot be answered definitively on the basis of the available data, one possibility is that single mothers are not exposed to harassment from role partners, specifically husbands. Although their work load is heavy, their total stress may be less than that of a woman who is exposed to obstructive behavior from a husband. Woods's finding is thus reminiscent of Feldman's (1973). In his study of experienced stress in graduate school, Feldman found, contrary to expectation, that divorced women had an easier time of it than married women. Married men, of course, had the easiest time of all. The explanation seems to be that while wives do support and facilitate their husbands' efforts, husbands do not reciprocate. Expressed another way, those who have wives benefit therefrom and those who lack husbands also benefit.

Another sidelight is provided in a study of Lyerly (1969). Lyerly found that single mothers spent less time on housework than mothers with husbands. In addition, the children of single mothers contributed more to domestic labor than did children in husband–wife households. These findings raise two possibilities, both pointing to the necessity of future research. One possibility is the question of how much additional work is generated by a husband's presence in the household. Although Walker has estimated the increase in domestic labor generated by each successive child, no one has raised the question of how much work is required with a husband. The failure to ask this question is probably best explained by traditional sex role expectations, which assume that every man is entitled to a domestic servant and that domestic labor is a component of the wife role. The second possibility raised by the Lyerly data is that the mother–child household develops a more rational (and more equitable) division of domestic labor than is possible in most households that contain an able-bodied adult male. It would be interesting to know specifically how the nonparticipation of children in housework is modeled or mandated in husband–wife households.

The problem of role overload is acknowledged (only implicitly) in research that focuses on full-time versus part-time maternal employment. Researchers in this tradition assume that relationships within the family do not readjust in response to reduced availability of the employed mother. If we accept this constraint, we can see why they argue that part-time employment is the optimal solution for the mother. *If* the mother accepts exclusive responsibility for domestic labor *and* accepts the motherhood myths, this may be the only solution and hence (as with Hobson's choice) the best. It is more likely to be the "best" solution for husband and children (if they hold traditional views) than for the mother. If, by chance, the mother wants a career, it is a poor solution, since career interruption badly compromises achievement in many fields. Many occupations (and many career lines within occupations) will not adapt to part-time role enactment.

Thus, the findings of Orden and Bradburn that the satisfaction of mothers and spouses was highest under conditions of part-time employment must be seen in this context. Douvan found that adjustment problems were more common among the children of mothers who were employed full time. However, in her study these were also working-class families, in which problems of income adequacy and other factors might contribute to difficulties, independent of the effect of maternal employment. Other researchers have found no negative effect of full-time employment. *It appears that the role conflict of the employed mother is situational and contingent.* Some mothers are made to feel guilty or inadequate by specific others in their social circle. If the stay-at-home mother is held out as the norm (though she is now a statistical minority), those who violate the norm will be punished by others in their social circle. Landers (1973, personal communication) reports that children of a business and professional women's association, when asked what their mothers did all day, replied, "Nothing . . . she watches TV." This distortion of perception not only shows the power of the stereotyped image, but also suggests the kinds of pressures that children exert on their mothers. It seems likely that the guilt reported by employed mothers is manipulated, in many cases, by their children. Very little research has addressed the question of whether children resent their mother's job and how they make her feel it.

Of course, the role expectation of the stay-at-home mother can be communicated through role pressures from neighbors, in-laws, or TV, as well as by children or spouse. Pleck (1976) suggests that the norm has shifted so that the employed mother is no longer deviant, but the *career* woman still is. As long as a woman is employed in a low-status job, one that is inferior to her husband's, and/or she subordinates work concerns to family concerns, she will not be subject to sanctions. However, the woman who violates either the motherhood mandate (Russo, 1976), the career taboo or the traditional domestic division of labor may be criticized.

Are negative sanctions of this sort inescapable? Coser and Rokoff (1971), building upon the work of Merton, analyze the mechanisms by which individuals buffer themselves against competing role pressures. They describe ways by which the individual localizes and segregates roles, so that each has its time and place and, under normal conditions, does not interfere with the others. Coser and Rokoff assert, rather disingenuously, that employed mothers are not permitted to avail themselves of the accepted means of role articulation. They argue that society assigns top priority to the mother role where women are concerned, and hence society will not tolerate working women's segregation, scheduling or prioritizing pressures stemming from this role. This unconscious sexism weakens the validity of Coser and Rokoff's analysis of role conflict in women. They take the theoretical position that women cannot be analyzed in the same terms as the situation of men. Factual evidence, however, contradicts this conservative assumption. Rapoport and Rapoport (1972) find that their dual-career couples do in fact insulate themselves from sanctioning by persons with traditional values. They quite consciously associate with others like themselves. Research on career women, similarly, suggests that they organize their lives and their role obligations much as men do. They do not mix the role sets of their family life and their occupational life; they schedule periods where they cannot be interrupted; they plan; and they delegate responsibility. The differences between employed mothers who role-articulate and those who do not appear to lie in the leeway their position affords. In other words, we can specify the conditions under which means of muffling role conflict are available to working women and conditions under which they are not. Many occupations do not permit the kind of autonomy that is required by the standard mechanisms of role articulation. We may speculate that the characteristics of many typically "feminine" jobs, or the working conditions in which many women find themselves, militate against this. For example, many women with school-age children choose jobs that are near their homes; this increases the possibility of their children's dropping in on them at work, a possible disruption or cause of role conflict.

Outcomes for Children/Outcomes for Mothers

Concern with the outcomes of role enactment for mothers have consistently been overshadowed by concern with outcomes for children. This ordering of priorities is as American as pronatalism and apple pie, but the desired outcome itself—successful child rearing—remains elusive.

It is clear that women have a good deal of concern about the quality of their mothering. At this state of knowledge, however, we have very little certainty about what kind of parenting produces healthy, well-adjusted, achieving, and/or happy children. In the absence of adequate knowledge, of course, myth often fills the gap. Theoretically we can make a distinction between quality and quantity of parenting, but we often make a simple-minded assumption that quantity is the best proxy for quality.

Traditional views that hold that constant availability of the biological mother is optimal for child development do not make a distinction between quality and quantity. They imply that more is better and assume that the mother who is not employed outside the home is really "there" for her child full time. This thinking involves the assumption that a mother who is available all the time provides better inputs to her child than one who is not. Of course, it additionally assumes that the full-time homemaker actually is available to her child full time.

These assumptions about quality parenting are hard to test since, as we have said, we have no reliable way of measuring "quality" input, "desirable" outcomes or the relationship between them. There is evidence, however, that is relevant to the assumptions equating quantity with quality. Time-budget research shows that homemakers spend much less time with their children than one would expect (Matthews-Taormino and Paige, 1974). Other research shows that while mothers and children may spend many hours under the same roof, they are more often in coaction (doing different things not requiring interaction) than actual interaction. Moreover, the employed mother often spends more time and attention on her child than the full-time housewife. The conclusion to be drawn from these data is not that homemakers are "bad" mothers, but rather that *full-time motherhood is a myth*. A more viable reformulation of this issue would be to ask, on the one hand, What are children's needs for adult input? and on the other, What are the mothers' *tolerances for interaction with young children?* On this latter point data are accumulating that suggest that six hours a day is probably the limit of toleration for the company of young children. Gray (1962) compared mothers who used day-care facilities, mothers who did not, and mothers who were in psychotherapy, expecting to find differences in their attitudes toward children. She did not find any differences; rather, women in all three groups reported that their preferred quantity of interaction with their children was six hours a day. Fitzsimmons and Rowe (1971) report the observation of professional child-care personnel that most adults cannot handle more than six hours of interaction with children a day. Many adults, of course, would prefer much less. Fitzsimmons and Rowe's finding corresponds to the results of Gray's study of mothers.

TOLERATION FOR MOTHERHOOD

Radl (1973) points out that mothers love their children but find motherhood intolerable. Judging from Gray's data, we can say that the lucky ones find motherhood intolerable only at times. The tolerability of motherhood is a function of many factors, some of which we have already discussed: the work load, the degree of isolation/sociability, the degree of sharedness/soleness of responsibility and family climate. In this section we will focus on the ways in which motherhood impinges on personhood.

One aspect of motherhood is drudgery, combined with unremitting responsibility. In Oakley's study, respondents seemed at first reluctant to admit any negative feelings. As they detailed what child care involved, however, much "job dissatisfaction" emerged. Some women saw their children mainly in terms of their own servicing function and were aware of the addition to their work load contributed by each child. A few mentioned the entertainment value of the child as an emerging entity.

These mothers were tied to their children not only by the material conditions of their lives but by their ideology as well. In their view, the "good mother" is one who refuses to be separated from her children during their waking hours. This self-enforced restriction increases the effect of isolation and houseboundness and might affect the evaluation of the role overall. Interestingly, although these mothers give lip service to the sacred value of motherhood, there is little spontaneous expression, in their interviews, of children as a source of positive feelings. The lack of pleasure in these women's number-one life priority suggests that mothering 24 hours a day, seven days a week is "too much of a good thing."

There is a startling discrepancy between the role requirements of maternity and the personal preferences of the role incumbents. When we begin to focus on outcomes of maternity *for mothers*, we open a Pandora's box on unacknowledged costs and frustrated needs of mothers. The true victim of maternal deprivation in our society is the mother—not the child.

MOTHERS' NEEDS FOR POWER

So little attention has been paid to issues of female power and power needs that we do not have an adequate conceptualization of relations between mothers and children on this dimension. As usual, writers who portray mothers as villains have claimed the stage first (cf. Mailer, 1971; Rheingold, 1967; Wylie, 1942). Some of these express the rebellion of the small boy against his more powerful mother. The other side of the picture, however, remains unexamined: the mother's powerlessness and her reactions against it. Both sides of the picture may reflect the results of the way the mother–child interaction is structured in our society. Under the conditions of isolation that constitute the "ideal" nuclear family context, the child may be forced to orient overmuch to the mother, as she is to the child. Yet, the study of Freud and Dann reminds us that it need not be so. The group of children they studied formed only minor ties with their adult caretakers. Their emotional life was centered in the group, which governed itself in cooperative and complementary role-taking. Nurturance was reciprocal and complementary, rather than being the obligation of one individual and the right of another.

The evidence we have reviewed suggests that too much maternal attention may impede the young person's development of self-reliance and social skills. The impetus for the oversupply of maternal attention need not be some dark, twisted motive to power but rather the absence of anything better to do or the absence of anything other to do. The idealized motherhood script defines motherhood as a full-time occupation and as one that demands the mother's very best. Women who try to live up to this script may fall into the trap of "smother love."

It is possible that to the extent mothers have no options outside of their mothering role, they will resist or fail to facilitate their children's growth toward competence and independence. To the extent that motherhood is a career chosen in perpetuity, becoming obsolescent is threatening to one's preferred lifestyle. A mother whose children become self-sufficient is out of a job. Conversely, mothers with multiple options, or those who view mothering as an episode rather than a lifelong occupation, can facilitate and enjoy such growth in their children. Such, in fact, are the findings in some studies comparing full time homemakers with employed mothers (Birnbaum, 1971). Moreover, there is some evidence that women who are most immersed in the mother role suffer most

144

from its obsolescence as children leave home (Le Masters, 1957; Bart, 1971). Specifically, those who have not maintained other identities during the child-intensive years are more likely to suffer a crisis when the demands of the mother role taper off. Restriction to the mother role appears to engender some learned incapacities. When other competences are squeezed out or cut off, a mother loses facility in them. If a mother puts all her eggs in one nest, then (and only then) is the empty nest a crisis. Just as those who enjoy multiple options experience transition to parenthood as a greater crisis (Le Masters, 1957), so those who maintain multiple options find the transition to the postparental period easier.

MOTHERS' NEEDS FOR SELF-ACTUALIZATION

It is obvious that the conditions of mothering do not provide for many of women's basic needs as persons. The need for efficacy may be served by controlling the activities of the young and managing a household, but the sense of personal identity suffers. Persons need to feel that they are doing work that is worthwhile, that is valued. One may be personally convinced of the value of one's efforts and yet suffer from the lack of validation. In the ceaseless round of unremarked activity, the sense of the self can be worn away and the positive sense of one's individuality obliterated. Evidence that this is an effect of the mother role, and not of the female person, can be found in the personal testimony of a father who assumed this role (Sarda, 1975). This "househusband" entered into a division of labor with his partner that had all the hallmarks of economic rationality. The wife's profession required market work; the husband's permitted him to work at home and combine work and child care. While both partners found the arrangement viable, over a period of years the husband found himself slipping into an identity crisis. His account might have been written by any wife:

> The years had passed, and somewhere along the way I had started to feel that I was being consumed by those around me. It wasn't a particularly dramatic feeling, but I felt it just the same. Somehow I

didn't have enough energy to combat the sensation that I was starting to shrink, to disappear.

There seemed to be tangible reasons connected with my mood, but they were of the which-came-first-the-chicken-or-the egg? variety. One of these reasons was the first serious cold I'd had since I was a child. It took hold of me in autumn and held on until spring. Another was that I'd been unable to get started on a second book—the first, at long last, was finished. The mounting pile of rejections slips wasn't nearly as distressing as my not being able to write. I needed the escape and the sense of accomplishment that writing afforded me. Writing was my private tranquilizer.

I knew that somehow I had to muster the energy to get rid of my cold and begin writing again, but there didn't seem to be enough energy for everything and everyone. Lynn, Sigrid and Inga had first claim on me. I didn't want to skimp on whatever portion of me each of them needed to keep fit and happy. The bigger they all grew— both inside and out—the more of me and my energy each seemed to require. It had reached a point where there was hardly any of me left for *me*. I was becoming, I feared, a faded nonperson (1975, p. 47).

While Sarda recognized the problem, the constraints of the role blocked him from asking for validation and relief. After all, the role was essential and he had chosen it. "Maternal" guilt silenced his dissatisfaction.

After two and a half years of 24 hours a day of parenting, my sense of myself and my defenses were low, Something had got past my guard, sneaked into my spirit and pulled the drain plug. It was a slow drain, but constant. I was being quietly consumed, and the rest of the family was so busy growing that they didn't even notice.

Not that I wanted them to notice. Surely if I became openly moody and loaded down my wife and children with my private frustrations, it would be counterproductive for us all. Lynn would feel lousy about going out to work; the girls would feel lousy about growing up; and I'd get even more frustrated because not only was I being consumed but also I wasn't doing my job properly. How could I be doing a good job if everyone felt lousy? (1975, p. 48).

Sarda was a captive of the role expectation of maternal vicariousness. Mothers' needs for achievement are supposed to be fulfilled via the successes of their family. A "maternal instinct" is assumed to impel the mother to serve and nurture others, without the expectation of reciprocity. It appears that family members accept personal service and sacrifice from mothers and do not think of it as remarkable. Although assumptions about a maternal instinct may not have been applied to Sarda, the role expectation of vicariousness was. From within the confines of that role it is very difficult to voice a claim that one is not getting what she deserves.

Sarda's loss of identity and feeling of overload were exacerbated by having to forego work that was important to *him*. This specific pain has not received study in the social science literature, perhaps because it is assumed that motherhood is women's true vocation and paid work is peripheral. In this context of professional neglect, a few voices speak to the struggle between the need for self-expression in work and the overwhelming demands of motherhood.

It is perhaps not surprising that these are the voices of poets. The work of a writer is not a "job." The work of a writer is experienced as a need; it is compelling, not contingent. While not a "job," neither is it a "career," requiring orderly advancement in a highly structured work setting. In theory, it is possible for a writer to work at home. But under what conditions? And what conditions render it impossible? Earlier women writers have shed some light on these questions. The dimension of the compelling need to write, the agonies of the demands of craftsmanship and perfectionism, and the analysis of the contradictions of the conditions needed for this work and the conditions of the housewife's life are to be found in Virginia Woolf and in Sylvia Plath—but in both cases they are to be found in separate writings.[3] In two current writers, Alta and Rich, the issues are brought together.

Alta's book is called *Momma: A Start on All the Untold Stories.*

---

[3] Sylvia Plath's poetry characterized housewifely settings in sinister images (e.g., "Lesbos," 1961) and wrote longingly of being freed from the "hooks" that are part of living ("Tulips," 1961). Her letters, however, exalted both her life and her achievements. Virginia Woolf wrote of the requirements of a writer's life (*A Room of One's Own, 1929*), but in her journal (*A Writer's Diary*, 1953) recorded the distractions of her own domestic life.

Alta takes as her central focus this dilemma: "We can either live it or write it. We cannot do both simultaneously. & no one can write it who has not lived it" (1974, p. 37). The context of this passage speaks for itself:

> (retyping this, i stopped to read the rest of this section & forgot to put the pages in order, as if my life were in order, who am i kidding.) . . . .
>
> Everyone was asleep by 11:00 & so i have had 3 hours to myself this week. one i spent writing letter; one, writing this; the other, i read poetry sent to me by a woman . . . 3 private hours in 6 days. i have had the snatches of solitude that most of us have the minutes when everyone else is out of the house, or when we are alone in the yard. these moments. but the rest of the time i am on call (indeed, am still on call: if the baby coughs, this paragraph will end) & altho this story, this very story that i am writing, that of being a mother, is going on, i have not had the chance to tell it. *that is why our story has not been told.* we can either live it or write it. we cannot do both simultaneously. & no one can write it who has not lived it.

Adrienne Rich (1976) holds that institutional and relationship aspects of motherhood have been confounded. Relationships include that between the woman and her powers of reproduction and that between the mother and her children. The institutional channeling of motherhood is organized, not around these relationships, but around the relationship of male control to female reproduction.

Rich's book opens with excerpts from her personal journals in the years when her children—three sons, spaced at the conventional two-year interval—were young. They convey the ambivalence and dividedness of the women with a vocation as a writer, who accepts the feminine mystique. Rich traces the personal/history that led her to this place:

> To be like other women had been a problem for me. From the age of thirteen or fourteen, I had felt I was only acting the part of a feminine creature. At the age of sixteen my fingers were constantly ink-stained. The lipsticks and high heels of the era were difficult-to-manage disguises. . . . There were two different compartments, already, to my life. But writing poetry, and my fantasies of travel and

self-sufficiency, seemed more real to me; I felt that as an incipient "real woman" I was a fake (1976, p. 25).

The institutions of marriage and motherhood seemed powerful enough to overcome a self-orientation that had been made to feel wrong. The day after she was married Rich was sweeping a floor.

> But as I swept that floor I thought: 'Now I am a woman. This is an age-old action, this is what women have always done.' I felt I was bending to ancient form, too ancient to question. *This is what women have always done*. (1976, p. 25).

The very rigidity of the form had the power to undo the negatives that her achievements had created. Rich continues,

> As soon as I was visibly and clearly pregnant, I felt, for the first time in my adolescent and adult life, not-guilty. The atmosphere of approval in which I was bathed—even by strangers in the street, it seemed—was like an aura I carried with me, in which doubts, fears, misgivings met with absolute denial. *This is what women have always done* (1976, p. 26).

The disapproval and friction generated by doing what Rich uniquely could do was magically cleared up by doing what all women can do. The approval was for conformity; the disapproval was for individuality.

Yet during her mothering years Rich continued to feel love for her children *and* the desire to write *and* frustration at being prevented from doing so. She continued to feel guilt over the anger occasioned by frustration, as though the frustration were natural and her anger unnatural instead of the other way around.

> But I do know that for years I believed I should never have been anyone's mother, that because I felt my own needs acutely and often expressed them violently, I was Kali, Medea, the sow that devours her farrow, the unwomanly woman in flight from womanhood, a Nietzschean monster. . . . I feel grief at the waste of myself in those years, and at the mutilation and manipulation of the relationship between mother and child, which is the great original source and experience of love (1976, p. 33).

The culture provided Rich with a wealth of terms for denouncing and denigrating herself, even while she accepted the burdens of an impossible role. She was guilty, not of rejecting the motherhood mandate, nor of neglecting her duties, but simply of retaining a will of her own. Female anger, as Rich observes, threatens the institution of motherhood (1976, p. 46). We might go further and say that any of the natural human needs that we have just discussed threatens the institution of motherhood, as it is now constructed. Women's familial roles are constructed for the benefit of others— at the mothers' expense. It is becoming apparent that a conflict exists between the mother's self-interest and those of others.

THE REAL VICTIMS OF MATERNAL DEPRIVATION

Oakley (1976) observed that the bugaboo of "maternal deprivation" can only be a problem in a culture that assumes an exclusive mother–child bond. However, the same structural arrangements that focus too much attention on the child focus too little on the mother. The overworked and isolated American mother does not receive physical help or emotional support. It is perhaps not surprising that research has found that the measured IQ of women who stay home with preschool children declines, presumably as a function of stimulus deprivation. Mothers suffer directly as a function of their devotion to others. Mothers' unmet needs for nurturance, for physical contact and comfort, and for intellectual stimulation have begun to attract the concern of feminist writers. As we have come to understand that "illegal abortion" is a crime against women, not a crime against society, so we are now prepared to recognize that mothers and not children are the victims of "maternal deprivation."

Rich adds a dimension to the analysis of costs to mothers. In addition to the problem of unmothered mothers, Rich sees a link between these mothers and their unmothered daughters. Rich attributes both effects to the shaping of the institution of motherhood in a male-controlled world. Males have first claim on the mother's attention, and mothers shape their behavior to the wishes of the dominant males. The mother's victimization mutilates her daughter as well as herself. A deep alienation pervades the deep bond between mother and daughter. In the experience of the girl-child in such a world, the relationship with the mother incorporates the deepest mutuality and the most painful estrangement (1976, p. 226). Rich suggests that many daughters perceive their mothers as models for compromise and self-hatred that they themselves repudiate. The young girl's fear is not of motherhood or of her own mother but of becoming her mother. It is not the mother so much who is being rejected, but rather the posture she adopts under patriarchy.

To contradict the affronts of patriarchy against women, Rich proposes, a mother must have a strong sense of self-nurture in order to nurture her daughter (1976, p. 245). Abdication of all *"self*-ishness" is called for by the sex role script, and it is conformity to this script that causes the abandonment of the unmothered daughter. In this reasoning Rich has turned around the traditional prescriptions for women. Where the traditional script exhorts them to be selfless and blames them for any sign of ego, Rich exhorts them to be selfish, for only in this way do they present to their daughters the model of a life worth living. She suggests, too, that only in this way can the breach between mothers and daughters be healed, and both be mothered.

> This is the core of my book, and I enter it as a woman who, born between her mother's legs, has time after time and in different ways tried to return to her mother, to repossess her and be repossessed by her, to find the mutual confirmation from and with another woman that daughters and mothers alike hunger for, pull away from, make possible or impossible for each other (1976, p. 218).

Women's Class Interests

This question of *"self*ishness" in women is both subversive and essential. The idea of a woman's self-interest has been slow to develop. The American belief in individualism has been expressed, "A man [sic] makes his own luck." An emphasis on achievement and competition is embedded in the American system of universal free education, and girls are exposed to these forces as well as boys. Our society, unlike some others, does not overtly declare women to be nonpersons; indeed, much of socialization is the same for girls and boys.[4] Our cultural values on achievement, on education and on self-actualization are impressed on girls as well as on boys. However, girls are derailed from the achievement train when they approach nubility and a competing set of expectations assumes preeminence. These are the role expectations we have been examining in this chapter, which are attached to the nearly universal expectations of marriage and motherhood. When women adopt these goals, they are implicitly relinquishing their right to self-determination. Within the complex of familial roles the female person is defined as a woman rather than as a person. In our culture there is an inescapable contradiction between the rights of persons and the rights of women. Because women have been thought of first as wives and mothers, and only secondarily as persons, awareness of this contradiction has been slow to develop. We have seen it in housewives' envying their husband's leisure, and in women's adopting a class identification different from that defined by their husbands' occupation. The unequal responsibilities of two spouses who share a home and a family bespeaks a contradiction. Arnott and Bengston (1970) investigated how women feel about the status assigned to them as housewives. Arnott and Bengston's sample was composed of faculty wives, individuals with high educational attainment and a history of high-school achievement. They hypothesized that women who compared their share of social esteem with that of men would feel deprived. Feeling deprived in the role of Housewife Only would lead women to add roles that took them outside the home, they predicted. As predicted, Arnott and Bengston

[4]See Maxine Hong Kingston, *The Woman Warrior: Memoirs of a Girlhood Among Ghosts* (1976) for an account of explicitly misogynistic attitudes among the Chinese.

found that the women who added the role of student, paid worker or volunteer to that of homemaker were those who felt the most deprived in their status as housewife. In the Homemaker Only group, the feeling of relative deprivation was lowest: these women had not expected greater rewards from this role than they had in fact experienced, and hence they were not deprived. Interestingly, the women who were *involuntarily* Homemaker Only had the greatest feeling of deprivation.

The dissonance between person and role has a structural and a psychic aspect. The status dilemmas we have discussed throughout this chapter create contradictory definitions of the individual. Moreover, it appears that we are entering an era where statuses a woman may achieve (e.g., occupational status) bring more prestige than statuses that are ascribed to her (e.g., that of wife). Where a woman occupies both statuses, does she have to right to choose the one by which she will be identified? The gospel according to stratification theory says no. Furthermore, if wives are to be defined in terms of their husbands' status, a rule for mate selection is implied: no woman should have an occupational status higher than that of her spouse (Caplow, 1954; Oppenheimer, 1972). Yet new research shows that for substantial numbers of women, exactly this situation obtains (Barth and Watson, 1964; Watson and Barth, 1963). Does the woman in such a situation have a choice in how she defines herself? And, if this is the case, would she not define herself in such a way as to maximize her status (i.e., define herself in terms of the higher of the two)? Here again, female self-interest and the vested interest of the male order diverge. The wife is obliged to protect her husband's status, which involves, among other things, not outshining him. *The person is obligated to make the most of herself; the wife is obliged to make more of her husband.*

We have found the feelings of dissatisfaction expressed by Oakley's and by Arnott and Bengston's housewives relate to social comparison and concerns with equity, topics that we dealt with first in Chapter 1. It is not surprising that satisfaction (or, more commonly, dissatisfaction) with the job of housewife should be a function of the relationship of inputs to rewards and of a comparison of one's own input:outcome ratio to "the going rate." If housework is viewed as a job, such comparisons are facilitated. By the same token, an analysis that denies that housework is work, and claims that housewifery is about relationships, is an attempt to prevent such comparisons and the claims for equity that arise from them. Scholarship is "politicized" on this point: that is, different positions have implications for (or against) the status quo.

In the feelings of housewives about their job, two forms of equity seem to be at issue. One is an individualistic concern with the question, What am I worth? The effort to attach a dollar value to the housewife's labor and the demand for pay for housewives are attempts to bring domestic labor into the nexus of wage labor and commodity exchange. All of us have this vocabulary at our command, and although Blood and Wolfe may speak wishfully of the wife's "retirement" from this world, contemporary social forces seem to help rather than hinder the making of such connections. Many working mothers have in fact, not in theory, the experience of substituting wage labor for their own unpaid labor, when they purchase child care or housekeeping services. Human capital theory approves this kind of substitution, when the mother's time is "worth more" than the surrogate's. But a woman whose occupation is nonprofessional may not be able to "afford to" work, when the price of substitute labor and services approximates the income she can gain from paid employment. What the individual is "worth" is not based on humanistic principles of the inherent worth (and equality) of all individuals, but rather is based on the market test: what the individual (or commodity) can command in the marketplace. This is the reason, I think, why normally persons do not think of the husband as available substitute labor: because his time is spoken for, and priced far above that of the wife or her surrogate. The market standard also accounts for the social-class effects found in Oakley's and in Arnott and Bengston's data. Middle-class background is a proxy for a position of relative privilege vis-à-vis others and the expectation of greater prestige that goes with it. Another way of putting it is that women possessing greater resources expect to drive a more advantageous bargain in marriage than those with fewer resources. In Arnott and Bengston's study, wives whose previous occupation was higher status than domestic labor were comparatively more dissatisfied with their current job than those who had not suffered a status loss. Similarly, Arnott and Bengston found that the housewives most reluctant to designate themselves "just a housewife" were those whose previous social-class position was superior.

A second set of concerns with equity has as its referent not the marketplace but the family system itself. Here the concern is with a balance or ratio between *benefits derived* and *contributions made*. Comparison here is not between home and market but among those benefiting from home production. Even if we suppose that all family members share equally in the benefits, we have observed that the wife makes the overwhelming majority of the contributions. The family is very likely an arena in which the wife compares her inputs and outcomes with contributions and benefits of others. Once both adults are in the labor force, they are subject to comparable demands from that source. Job demands have traditionally accounted for the "unavailability" of husbands for housework and child care. Surely wives could offer the same argument. I have mentioned above that, to date, it appears that accommodation within the wife role, not between the wife and others, is the expected solution to the shortage of time for domestic services. Kreps (1976) notes that the price is paid in women's leisure, which is becoming a vanishing phenomenon. Yet men's leisure time is expanding, both over the work life and during the workweek. This discrepancy exacerbates wives' feelings of inequity. If wives contribute their leisure to the family good and wives themselves derive no benefit from it, they will perceive it as inequitable if their husbands invest their leisure only in themselves and the family derives no benefit. It is via such processes of social comparison that the sense of equity or inequity arises.

As long as wage discrimination and occupational segregation persist, a wife's time will be "worth less" (by the market test) than her husband's. This line of thinking provides support for the traditional family allocation decision, or division of labor. The "value" of a wife's home production is similarly pegged to her market wage. Hence the wife with higher educational attainment is "worth more" as a housekeeper and mother, and the woman whose market earning power is less is worth less. On the other hand, as Kreps (1976) points out, the greater the family income inadequacy, the greater the value to the family of the wife's participation in paid employment and the less the value of her domestic services. The difference between these two approaches is that between a fixed-price valuing of a woman's labor and a relative valuing. The more realistic approach, particularly as women spend more of their adult lives in paid employment, is to look at an optimum mix of home and market production. A question that remains is, Who controls the decision about a woman's mix of home and market production? Still a further question is, Who benefits from her home and market activity?

These questions are disruptive of the status quo—subversive, if you will. They emphasize the discrepancy between social programming of women's roles and women's rights and needs.

The evidence reviewed in this chapter makes it clear that the traditional sex role script does not reflect women's "nature" or preferences. Women's preferences state clearly that the optimum hours per day of child care probably do not exceed six (and this for women who put a priority on assuming primary responsibility for child rearing). It is abundantly clear that the supply of housework far exceeds women's demand for it. Left to their own devices, many women might prefer to lower their housekeeping standards or subcontract domestic labor, rather than to put in the typical 70+ hour week. New research suggests that when once-married women have alternative means of financial support for themselves and their children, they tend to pass up remarriage. With respect to motherhood, housewifery and marriage, women are defecting from the traditional script. When other options become available, women choose them. Among women highest in occupational status and earning ability, the proportion *ever* married is dramatically lower than among the population of all women.

Among women holding graduate degrees, the marriage rate is about 50 percent (Bernard, 1971, p. 187); among all women, greater than 90 percent. If we accept Becker's interpretation that the act of marrying signifies the partners' perceptions that they better their lot thereby, how are we to interpret the booming popularity of divorce?

Dissatisfactions and strains in all the components of women's familial roles contribute to a strong impetus for change.

Forces for Change in Women's Familial Roles

While we could take any of the familial roles as a starting point for assessing the potential for change, we will return to domestic labor. Domestic labor is the full time occupation of all married women, whatever their additional jobs. It is thus the pivotal element among familial roles. Single women keep house too. The consistent neglect of this work in the professional literature and the tendency to underestimate and trivialize it make it an irresistible target for consciousness raising. Changing this component of the family role constellation will of necessity bring about changes in all the other roles.

Oakley remarks on the revolutionary potential of housewives as a class. Secombe (1973) observes that, next to the split between capital and the working class, the split between industrial and domestic workers is the major class division. This view is powerfully in opposition to an approach that excludes and trivializes this enormous group of workers from consideration. Housewifery is a condition that, as we have seen, all female flesh is heir to and it must for this reason be a basic concern in any attempt to organize women on a large-scale basis. Oakley's data make it clear that the discontent is already present. However, the discontent is tied to housework tasks and working conditions; there is no evidence of class consciousness as such. Indeed, the unquestioning acceptance of the status of wife, in the face of dislike of the job, could be taken as evidence of false consciousness. The explanation for this false consciousness can be found in the sex role ideology that legitimates the sexual division of labor and the working conditions of the housewife and in the socialization practices that instill this ideology.

However, class consciousness is arising among housewives. One manifestation is the current international Wages for Housework Movement. Housewives are demanding pay for the massive, invisible and essential layer of labor that makes possible the wage work of the society. They unequivocally demand parity with paid workers and refuse the coinage of love and compliments as "payment" for their labor. They reject servitude to men as the price of support for themselves and their children. They resent being assigned the stigmatized status of welfare "parasite" when they are in fact employed within the home. They refuse to be forced into a second low-paying job in order to get off welfare and join the ranks of the working poor. They are demanding that the government compensate them for the work they are doing and award back pay for the work they have done for years. Housewives have more catching up to do than any other segment of the work force.

Wages for Housework points out the similarities among women's occupations. They define housework as encompassing all the specific behaviors involved in servicing others. Agger (1975) draws the parallel between housewifery and waitressing. Others note that women's servicing function is supposed to be motivated by—and paid off by—love. Similarly, the work involved is not thought of as requiring skill but rather as being a direct manifestation of women's "nature" (Simister, 1975).

The Displaced Homemaker Movement focuses on another aspect of the problem. They are seeking support for women who, having devoted many years to the service of their families, are left unprepared to support themselves in the wage economy after divorce. The displaced homemakers are women who have chosen and lived a traditional lifestyle, a life of hard work devoted to other people's benefit. A sequence of events that is part of this lifestyle have made them, over the years, less and less prepared for self-sufficiency. The myths of financial security and the protected status of wife are the rules of the game they have played; they have played it straight and somehow lost. In several states, Displaced Homemakers have succeeded in getting legislation passed that supports life and transition for these women.

A number of voices have been raised to claim recognition for the service that wives perform for the society in their work at home. Alice Cook (1975) has proposed legislation modeled on the G.I. Bill that would provide compensation for advantages foregone by women during their homebound years. This is a logical development of the approach put forward by Hollingworth (1916), in which the parallels between mothering and soldiering are stated.

These social movements make the long overdue assertion that housewives are essential people and claim the compensation due them for the essential services they perform. Dalla Costa (1972) goes further, arguing that the role of housewife itself must be dismantled. Dalla Costa points out the many ways in which the isolation and privatization of housework in the home cuts women off from political consciousness and personal efficacy. Because she is outside the wage economy, the housewife does not have even the freedoms of the wage slave: to sell her labor for a price, to shop around among potential buyers of that labor and to quit an undesirable job. In wage work, technological advances provide at least the potential that the amount of necessary labor will be reduced and the time released for workers' leisure. This is not the case with housework. Indeed, as Dalla Costa notes, if the worker is not on an hourly wage, no one cares how long it takes her to do her job.

Dalla Costa gives us the vivid image of the housewife as one who is locked away in her family as the chrysalis in the cocoon, imprisoning itself by its own work, that dies in order to leave silk for capitalist production (1972, p. 46). Precisely because housework functions are confounded with femaleness, women will continue to be captive to the role as long as it persists.

This critique points to the need for solutions beyond simply upgrading the housewife role.

Reorganizing Domestic Labor

The institution of housewifery is only one way of organizing the provision of essential services. Many of the negative aspects of the housewife role are inessential and wasteful.

The isolation of the housewife's job is universally experienced as a negative aspect of the job. It seems unnecessary. The spatial arrangements of the traditional American nuclear family and the single-family dwelling are part of the problem, not part of the solution. Communal organization of domestic labor is one solution that has a long history. Social experiments that have concerned themselves with housework have almost all turned to some form of collective effort for many tasks. In the kibbutzim of Israel, meals, laundry and child care are collective. In other socialist countries as well, many services are provided to the family for which the housewife under capitalism has sole responsibility.

Social and psychological isolation can be as dangerous as physical isolation. The new mother who is housebound finds many ordinary tasks—e.g., shopping—beyond her grasp, without help in child care. It is this chore that appears to take precedence, and other housekeeping and personal items are taken up as child care demands permit. When the woman has no one to share child care, the interruptions of sleep and other necessities can produce feelings of being overwhelmed and hopeless. In such a mood Sylvia Plath took her own life. Isolation also fosters the sense of strain and no relief that is a factor in child abuse.

In accounts of the great social experiments of the nineteenth century, cooperative work arrangements seem to have had positive outcomes in terms of morale as well as production. The accounts of the Oneida community are particularly attractive. There most work was organized as "bees," and participants report that time flew as fingers (and no doubt tongues) flew. At Oneida, work assignments were rotated, and this militated against monotony for the worker and also against a rigid sexual division of labor.

Dalla Costa makes the point, often overlooked, that the sexual division of labor makes an officially heterosexual society mono-sexual in practice. Divorcing domestic labor from femaleness would permit partners to share these activities and thereby expand their time together.

Some of the housewives in Oakley's study found a benefit in the autonomy of their job: it gave them freedom from close supervision and work pacing imposed by someone else. This autonomy is the other side of isolation. When a wife has her "own" home, she is not sharing a roof with others and her spouse is not present most of the time. When she has children, she is "tied down"—often housebound. If she has a car, she is mobile but still tied down. Often, the responsibility for making arrangements that will help her break out of this web is hers. The "family vacation" is, of course, no vacation for her. It is not uncommon to hear mothers say that they haven't had a day off since the birth of their first baby.

For most housewives, asserting control over the job is a problem. Lopata's research indicates that for the most part, women are neither taught nor evaluated by others. The housewife must be self-taught and self-paced: self-motivating, in short. Role strain is common in the early stages of role acquisition (Lopata, 1973, p. 152).

One crucial challenge for the "self-employed" housewife is to structure time in a way that provides for satisfaction and leisure. Many women—although not Oakley's respondents—elaborate certain aspects of their household work in such a way as to add a self-expressive dimension—e.g., by gourmet cooking or by making gifts. Some women, paradoxically, "lighten" their work load by increasing it. They take on volunteer assignments which break the monotony and isolation of household work and in some cases serve to motivate greater efficiency in the household labor. These kinds of additions increase the housewife's social contact and usually her "income" of appreciation from others. Some household tasks seem to lend themselves more to this kind of elaboration than others. The "Tupperware party" is an interesting phenomenon from this point of view, for it appears to glorify an aspect of housekeeping that has little intrinsic appeal, and it creates a social occasion as the vehicle for selling a commodity.

Oakley found that some housewives, by means of work specification and scheduling, produced in themselves the monitor or foreman they had escaped by working at home. Satisfaction was associated with this for some: successfully completing self-set tasks was an occasion for a sense of achievement and well-being. Failure, on the other hand, could produce feelings of depression and lack of worth.

Cooperative housework would not only lighten the load but provide feedback and appreciation of the work. Moreover, sharing housework with a partner provides a basis for *joint* decisions about standards for commodities in which both must invest their labor, with an attendant opportunity cost of other desirable experiences foregone.

Another problem to be solved by the reorganization of domestic labor is that of prestige or esteem. Recent research indicates that regardless of its actual skill level, any job that is seen as women's work is downgraded and underpaid (Clarenbach, 1975). A recent study showed that college students downgrade the desirability of an occupation when informed that the proportion of women in the occupation will increase (Touhey, 1974). Destroying the association between domestic labor and femaleness will offset the undervaluation of this work to some degree. Doing it for money rather than for love may also increase the respectability of domestic labor. Another dimension is that of skill. To the extent that housework is an occupation, both the skill requirements of the job and the skill of the worker should affect job satisfaction. A highly skilled worker, other things being equal, will derive more satisfaction from the utilization of her work skills than a low-skilled worker, and will find satisfaction in work that permits skill utilization. The skilled worker has more pride in work than the unskilled, and skill differences should produce differences in job satisfaction (as well as self-esteem) in domestic laborers as in other workers. Other things being equal, a high-skilled job should command more compensation and more social esteem than a low-skilled job. This is one aspect of housework on which there is little research to date. Domestic labor has the reputation of a menial, low-skill job, but the tasks involved have not been subjected to job analysis or standards of competency investigated.

The level of technology defining a job is one factor that affects both its productivity (wages) and its ability to recruit workers. As long as domestic labor is excluded from the wage economy, no incentive exists for reorganization or innovation. The time of the unwaged worker carries no price tag. Not surprisingly, technology in the domestic realm is undeveloped.

Oakley examined the level of work technology available to her respondents as a factor in their "job satisfaction." Many of them performed their job without some of the aids most American housewives think of as basic: vacuum cleaner, washing machine, dryer, running hot water. Some, in their careers as housewives, had done their washing by boiling it in a pot on the stove. Thus the level of amenities was, on the average, considerably lower than what the American housewife is used to. However, the technology factor did not affect "job satisfaction" as measured in this study. In the future, when efficiency can win payoffs in terms of leisure, we may anticipate that technology will affect performance of domestic workers.

All the proposals for reorganizing domestic labor assume an end to the division between wage-earning and unwaged workers. When housework becomes a job, many women will give preference to other alternatives. Without a captive labor supply, getting the job done at all becomes problematic. Compensation and working conditions will have to be adjusted to the point where an adequate supply of qualified workers can be recruited and held in the job. This is quite appropriately a concern of the society as a whole and not the housewife's problem.

REFERENCES

Acker, Joan. 1973. Women and Social Stratification: a Case of Intellectual Sexism. *American Journal of Sociology* 78(4), 936–946.

Almquist, E., and Angrist, S. 1971. Role model influences on college women's career aspirations. *Merrill-Palmer Quarterly* 17(3): 263–279.

Alta. 1974. *Momma: A Start on All the Untold Stories*. New York: Times Change Press.

Angrist, Shirley S., and Almquist, Elizabeth M. 1975. *Careers and Contingencies*. Port Washington, NY: Kennikat Press.

Arnott Catherine, and Bengston, Vern L. 1970. "Only a Homemaker:" Distributive justice and role choice among married women. *Sociology and Social Research* 54(4): 495–507.

Axelson, Leland J. 1963. The marital adjustment and marital role definitions of husbands of working and non-working wives, *Journal of Marriage and Family Living* 25(2): 189–195.

Bales, R. Freed. 1950. *Interaction Process Analysis*. New York: Addison-Wesley.

Bart, Pauline. 1971. Depression in middle aged women. In *Women in Sexist Society: Studies in Power and Powerlessness*, ed. Vivian Gornick and Barbara K. Moran. New York: Basic Books.

Barth, Ernest A. T., and Watson, Walter B. 1977. Social stratification and the family in mass society, *Social Forces* 45: 392–402.

Baruch, G. K. 1972. Maternal influences upon college women's attitudes toward women and work, *Developmental Psychology* 6(1): 32–37.

Becker, Gary Stanley. 1962. Investment in human capital: a theoretical approach, *Journal of Political Economy* 70: 9–49 (supplement).

———. 1973. A theory of marriage. In *Economics of the Family*, ed. Theodore W. Schultz, pp. 229–345. Chicago: University of Chicago Press.

Becker, Howard S. 1963. *Outsiders: Studies in the Sociology of Deviance*. New York: Free Press.

———. 1964. *The Other Side*. New York: The Free Press.

Bell, Norman W., and Vogel, Ezra F., eds. 1969. *A modern introduction to the family*. New York: Free Press.

Bernard, Jessie. 1971. *Women and The Public Interest*. Chicago: Aldine-Atherton.

Benham, Lee. 1973. Benefits of women's education within marriage. In *Economics of the Family*, ed. Theodore W. Schultz, pp. 375–390. Chicago: University of Chicago Press.

Binstock, Jeanne. 1972. Motherhood: An occupation facing decline. *The Futurist* 6.

Birnbaum, Judith A. 1971. Life patterns, personality style, and self-esteem in gifted family oriented and career committed women. Doctoral dissertation. State University of Michigan, Ann Arbor.

Blake, Judith. 1968. *Are Babies Consumer Durables?* Population Reprint Series, reprint 278. Berkeley: University of California Press.

Blood, Robert O., and Wolfe, Donald M. 1960. *Husbands and Wives: The Dynamics of Married Living*, Chap. 3. Glencoe, IL: The Free Press.

———. 1966. The division of labor in American families. In *Role Theory*, ed. R. J. Biddle and E. J Thomas. New York: Wiley.

Bowlby, John. 1946. *Forty-four Juvenile Thieves*. London: Bailliere Tundall and Cox.

———. 1953. *Childcare and the Growth of Love*. Baltimore: Penguin Books.

———. 1969. *Attachment and Loss: Vol. I, Attachment*. London: Hogarth Press. New York: Basic Books.

Bronfenbrenner, Urie. 1961. Changing American child—a speculative analysis. *Journal of Social Issues* 17(1): 6–18.

Broverman, Inger K., Broverman, D. M., Clarkson, F. E., Rosenkrantz, P. S., and Vogel, Susan R. 1970. Sex-role stereotypes and clinical judgments of mental health. *Journal of Consulting and Clinical Psychology* 34: 1–7.

Burchinal, Lee G., and Rossman, Jack. 1961. Relations among maternal employment indices and development characteristics of children. *Journal of Marriage and Family Living* 23: 333–340.

Campbell, Frederick L. 1967. Demographic factors in family organization. Doctoral dissertation. University of Michigan, Ann Arbor.

Caplow, Theodore. 1954. *The Sociology of Work*. New York: McGraw-Hill.

Chesler, Phyllis. 1972. *Women and Madness*. Garden City, NY: Doubleday.

Clarenbach, Kathryn F. 1975. Women's Work: Up from .878. Report on the D.O.T. Research Project. Madison, WI: University of Wisconsin.

Cook, Alice. 1975. Working mothers: problems and programs. Ithaca, NY: Unpublished ms., School of Industrial Labor Relations, Cornell University.

Coser, Rose Laub. 1956. A home away from home. *Social Problems* 4: 3–17.

Coser, Rose Laub, and Rokoff, Gerald. 1971. Women in the occupational world: social disruption and conflict. *Social Problems* 18: 535–554.

Dalla Costa, Mariarosa. 1972. Women and the subversion of the community. Bristol, England: Falling Wall Press.

Douvan, Elizabeth. 1963. Employment and the adolescent. In *The Employed Mother in America*, ed. F.I. Nye and L.W. Hoffman. Chicago: Rand-McNally.

Duncan, O.D. 1961. Properties and characteristics of the socio-economic index. In *Occupation and Social Status*, ed. A. Reiss. Glencoe: The Free Press.

Duvall, Elise Barrett. 1955. Conceptions of mother roles by five and six year old children of working and non-working mothers. Doctoral dissertation. Florida State University.

Edmonds, Vernon H. 1967. Marital conventionalization: definition and measurement. *Journal of Marriage and the Family* 29(4): 681–688.

Epstein, Cynthia. 1970. Encountering the male establishment: sex-status limits on women's careers in the professions. *American Journal of Sociology* 75(6): 965–982.

165

Farrell, Warren. 1974. *The Liberated Man*. New York: Random House.

Feldman, Harold. 1974. Changes in marriage and parenthood: a methodological design. In *Pronatalism*, ed. Ellen Peck and Judith Senderowitz, pp. 206–226. New York: Thomas Y. Crowell Co.

Feldman, Saul D. 1973. Impediment or stimulant? marital status and graduate education. In *Changing Women in a Changing Society*, ed. Joan Huber. Chicago: University of Chicago Press.

Fitzsimmons, J.J. and Rowe, Mary. P. 1971. A study in child care, 1970–71. Cambridge, MA: Abt Associates.

Freud, Anna, and Burlingham, Dorothy. 1943. *Infants Without Families: The Case for and Against Nurseries*. London: G. Allen & Unwin.

Freud, Anna, and Dann, S. 1970. An experiment in group upbringing. In *Child Development and Behavior*, ed. F. Rebelsky and L. Douvan. New York: Knopf.

Galbraith, J. K. 1973. *Economics and the Public Purpose*. Boston: Houghton-Mifflin.

Glueck, Sheldon, and Glueck, Eleanor. 1957. Working mothers and delinquency. *Mental Hygiene* 41: 327–352.

Gray. H. 1962. The trapped housewife. *Journal of Marriage and Family Living* 24(2): 179–82.

Goode, William J. 1956. *Women in Divorce*. Glencoe, IL: The Free Press.

Gronau, Reuben. 1973. The effect of children on the housewife's value of time. In *Economics of the Family*, ed. Theodore W. Schultz, pp. 257–289. Chicago: University of Chicago Press.

Hardin, Garrett. 1974. *Mandatory Motherhood: The True Meaning of "Right to Life"*. Boston: Beacon Press.

Haavio-Manila, Elena. 1969. Some consequences of women's emancipation. *Journal of Marriage and the Family* 31: 123–134.

Heer, David M. 1958. Dominance and the working wife. *Social Forces* 36: 341–347.

———. 1963. The measurement and bases of family power: an overview. *Journal of Marriage and the Family* 25: 133–139.

Hoffman, Lois Wladis. 1960. Effects of the employment of mothers on parental power relations and the division of household tasks. *Journal of Marriage and Family Living* 22: 27–35.

———. 1963. Parental power relations and the division of household tasks. In *The Employed Mother in America*, ed. F. Ivan Nye and Lois W. Hoffman. Chicago: Rand-McNally.

———. 1974. Effects of maternal employment on the child—a review of research. *Developmental Psychology* 10: 204–228.

Hoffman, Lois W., and Nye, F. Ivan. 1974. *Working Mothers: An Evaluative Review of the Consequences for Wife, Husband, and Child*. New York: Jossey-Bass.

Hollingworth, Leta S. 1916. Social devices for impelling women to bear and rear children. *American Journal of Sociology* 22: 19–29.

Howell, Mary. 1973a. Employed mothers and their families. *Pediatrics* 52(2): 252–263.

––––––. 1973b. Effects of maternal employment on the child. *Pediatrics* 52(3): 327–343.

James, Selma, 1972. *A Woman's Place*. Bristol, England: Falling Wall Press.

Jones, J. B., Lundsteen, S. W., and Michael, W. B. 1967. The relationship of the professional employment status of mothers to reading achievement of sixth grade chidlren. *California Journal of Education Research* 43(2): 102–108.

Kappel, B. E., and Lambert, R. D. 1967. Self-worth among the children of working mothers. Waterloo, Ontario: Unpublished ms.

Kreps, Juanita M., and Leaper, R. J. 1976. Home work, market work, and the allocation of time, In *Women and the American Economy: A Look to the 1980's*, ed. J. M. Kreps. Englewood Cliffs, NJ: Prentice-Hall.

King, Karl, McIntyre, J., and Axelson, L. J. 1968. Adolescents' views of maternal employment as a threat to the marital relationship. *Journal of Marriage and the Family* 30(4): 633–637.

Kingston, Maxine Hong. 1976. *The Woman Warrior: Memoirs of a Girlhood Among Ghosts*. New York: Knopf.

Kligler, D. 1963. The effects of employment of married women on husband and wife roles: a study in culture change. Unpublished doctoral dissertation. Yale University (New Haven).

Laing, R. D., and Esterson A. 1964. *Sanity, Madness and the Family*. New York: Basic Books.

Laws, Judith Long. 1971. A feminist review of marital adjustment literature: The rape of the Locke. *Journal of Marriage and the Family* 33(3): 483–516.

LeMasters, Ersel Earl. 1957. Parenthood as crisis. *Journal of Marriage and Family Living* 19(4): 352–355.

Lopata, Helena. 1971. *Occupation: Housewife*. London: Oxford University Press.

––––––. 1973. *Widowhood in an American City*. Cambridge: Schenkman.

Mailer, Norman. 1971. *The Prisoner of Sex*. New York: Little. Brown.

Mainardi, Pat. 1971. The politics of housework. In *Sisterhood Is Powerful*, ed. Robin Morgan, pp. 447–455. New York: Vintage.

Mathews, S. M. 1933. The development of children's attitudes concerning mother's out-of-home employment. *Journal of Educational Sociology* 6: 259–271.

Matthews-Taormino, Mary, and Paige, Karen E. 1974. The effects of sex, children and dual careers on the uses of time. Paper presented at the annual meetings of the Western Psychological Association, San Francisco.

McCord, J, McCord, W., and Thurber, E. 1963. Effects of maternal employment on lower-class boys. *Journal of Abnormal and Social Psychology* 67(2): 177–182.

Meier, H. C. 1972. Mother-centeredness and college youths' attitudes toward social equality for women. Some empirical findings. *Journal of Marriage and the Family* 34: 115–121.

Miller, Daniel R., and Swanson, Guy E. 1958. *The Changing American Parent*. New York: Wiley.

Millman, Marcia. 1975. She did it all for love: a feminist view of the sociology of deviance. In *Another Voice*, ed. Marcia Millman and Rosabeth Moss Kanter, pp. 25–274. Garden City: Anchor Press.

———— and Kanter, Rosabeth Moss. 1975. *Another Voice*. Garden City: Anchor Press.

Minturn, Lambert, et al. 1964. *Mothers of Six Cultures: Antecedents of Child Raising*. New York: Wiley.

Neal, Arthur G., and Groat, H. Theodore. 1970. Alienation correlates of Catholic fertility, *American Journal of Sociology* 76(3): 46–473.

Neisser, Edith G. 1973. *Mothers and Daughters: A Lifelong Relationship*. New York: Harper and Row.

Nye, Francis Ivan. 1961. Maternal employment and marital interaction: some contingent conditions. *Social Forces* 40: 113–119.

————. 1963. Adjustment of the mother: summary and a frame of reference. In *The Employed Mother in America*, ed. F. Ivan Nye and Lois W. Hoffman. Chicago: Rand McNally.

———— and Hoffman, Lois W. 1963. eds. *The Employed Mother in America*. Chicago: Rand McNally.

————. 1958. *Family Relationships and Delinquent Behavior*. New York: Wiley.

Oakley, Ann. 1974. *The Sociology of Housework*. New York: Pantheon Books.

————. 1976. *Woman's Work: The Housewife, Past and Present*. New York: Vintage Books.

Oppenheimer, Valerie Kincaid. 1970. *The Female Labor Force in the United States*. Berkeley: Population Monograph Series, No. 5.

————. 1972. Testimoney before the Federal Communications Commission.

Orden, Susan, and Bradburn, Norman. 1968. Dimensions of marital happiness. *American Journal of Sociology* 73(6): 715–731.

Papanek, Hanna. 1973. Men, women, and work: reflections on the two-person career. In *Changing Women in a Changing Society*, ed. Joan Huber. Chicago: University of Chicago Press.

Parsons, Talcott. 1949. The social structure of the family. In *The Family: Its Function and Destiny*, ed. Ruth N. Ashen. New York: Harper.

————. 1956. The American family: its relations to personality and the social structure. In *Family Socialization and Interaction Process*, ed. Talcott Parsons and Robert F. Bales. London: Routledge and Kegan Paul.

Peck, Ellen, and Senderowitz, Judith, eds. 1974. *Pronatalism: The Myth of Mom and Apple Pie*. New York: Thomas Y. Crowell Co.

Plath, Sylvia. 1975. *Letters Home: Correspondence 1950–1963*, ed. Aurelia S. Plath. New York: Harper and Row.

Poloma, Margaret M. Role conflict and the married professional woman. In *Toward a Sociology of Women*, ed. Constantina Safilios-Rothschild, pp. 187–198. Lexington, MA: Xerox College Publications.

Radl, Shirley L. 1973. *Mother's Day Is Over*. New York: Charterhouse.

Rapoport, Rhona, and Rapoport, Robert N. 1972. The dual-career family: a variant pattern and social change. In *Toward a Sociology of Women*, ed. Constantina Safilios-Rothschild. Lexington, MA: Xerox College Publishing.

Rheingold, Joseph C. 1967. *Mother, Anxiety and Death: The Catastrophic Death Complex.* New York: Little.

Ribble, Margaret. 1943. *The Rights of Infants.* New York: Columbia University Press.

Rich, Adrienne. 1976. *Of Woman Born: Motherhood as Experience and Institution.* New York: W. W. Norton.

Robinson, J. R., and Converse, P. 1966. *Basic Tables of Time Budget Data for the United States.* Ann Arbor: Survey Research Center.

Ross, Heather L., and Sawhill, Isabel V. 1975. *Time of Transition: The Growth of Families Headed by Women.* New York: Urban Institute.

Rossi, Alice S. 1968. Transition to Parenthood. *Journal of Marriage and the Family* 30: 26–39.

Russo, Nancy. 1976. The motherhood mandate. *Journal of Social Issues* 32, 3: 143–153.

Safilios-Rothschild, Constantina, ed. 1972. *Toward a Sociology of Women.* Lexington, MA: Xerox College Publishing.

Sarda, Reese. 1975. Reflections of a father who became a mother. *Redbook* (November), p. 38 ff.

Schultz, Theodore W. 1963. *The Economic Value of Education.* New York: Columbia University Press.

————. ed. 1973. *Economics of the Family: Marriage, Children, and Human Capital.* Chicago: University of Chicago Press.

Secombe, Wally. 1973. The housewife and her labour under capitalism, *New Left Review* 83: 3–24.

Simister, P. 1975. Out of one kitchen into another. In *Wages for Housework,* pp. 13–16. Toronto: Amazon Press.

Spitz, Rene. 1945. Hospitalism: An inquiry into the genesis of psychiatric conditions in early childhood. *Psychoanalytic Studies of the Child* 1: 53–74.

Steidl, Rose E., and Bratton, Esther C. 1968. *Work in the Home.* New York: Wiley.

Stolz, Lois Meek. 1960. Effects of maternal employment on children: evidence from research, *Child Development* 31: 749–782.

Tangri, Sandra S. 1969. Role Innovation in Occupational Choice. Unpublished doctoral dissertation, University of Michigan.

————. 1974. Effect of background, personality, college and post-college experiences on women's post-graduate employment. U.S. Dept. of Labor, Manpower Administration.

Tobias, Sheila. 1973. What really happened to Rosie the Riveter? In *Demobilization and the Female Labor Force,* pp. 1–36. New York: Modular Publications, Inc.

Touhey, John C. 1974. Effects of additional woman professionals on ratings of occupational prestige and desirability. *Journal of Social Psychology* 29(1): 86–89.

Tresemer, David, and Pleck, Joe. 1972. Maintaining and changing sex role boundaries in women (and men). Unpublished paper.

————. Sex-role boundaries and resistance to sex-role change. *Women's Studies* 2: 61–87.

Vanek, Joan. 1974. Time spent in housework. *Scientific American* 231(5): 116–20.

Veblen, Thorstein. 1953. *The Theory of the Leisure Class*. New York: Mentor Books.

Vogel. S. R., Broverman, I. K, Broverman D. M., Clarkson F. E., and Rosenkrantz, P. S. 1970. Maternal employment and perception of sex roles among college students. *Developmental Psychology* 3(3): 384–391.

Walker, Kathryn E. 1970. *Time-use Patterns for Household Work Related to Homemakers' Employment*. Washington, DC: U.S. Department of Agricultural Research Service.

——— and Woods, Margaret E. 1976. *Time Use: A Measure of Household Production of Family Goods and Services*. Washington, DC: American Home Economics Association, Center for the Family.

Wallston, Barbara. 1973. The effects of maternal employment on children. *Journal of Child Psychology and Psychiatry and Allied Disciplines* 14(2): 81–95.

Watson, W. B., and Barth, E. A. T. 1964. Questionable assumptions in the theory of social stratification. *Pacific Sociological Review* 7: 10–16.

Woods, M. B. 1972. The unsupervised child of the working mother. *Developmental Psychology* 6(1): 14–25.

Woolf, Virginia. 1963. *A Room of One's Own*. New York: Harcourt Brace Jovanovich.

———. 1973. *A Writer's Diary: Being Extracts from the Diary of Virginia Woolf*, ed. Leonard Woolf. New York: Harcourt Brace Jovanovich.

Wylie, Philip. 1942. *Generation of Vipers*. New York: Farrar S. Rinehart.

Yarrow, Marion R., Scott, D., DeLeeuw, L., and Heing, C. 1962. Child-rearing in families of working and non-working mothers. *Sociometry* 25: 122–140.

3

WOMAN
as
Object

Perspectives on Women in Courtship

Courtship is the institutional means by which individuals are induced to assume roles in reproduction and take responsibility for the socialization of the new generation. Although the content of the courtship "game" has changed drastically over the short history of the United States, the function of courtship has not. Social science treatments place this tender subject in the context of the societal imperative to reproduce itself. The research focuses on the patterned and predictable ways of meeting and mating through which a particular society meets this need. The society—through its many agents of socialization—provides sexual scripts[1] for women, which focus upon marriage. As individuals wander through these scripts, which are intricate and absorbing in themselves, they find themselves at the destination: marriage.

Courtship (and its postwar cousin, dating) has often been described as a dance: a patterned sequence of reciprocal steps en-

---

[1]Sexual scripts comprise the set of positions, participants and behavior sequences that are accepted and expected among a given group of people. For an extended analysis of the idea of sexual scripts, see Laws and Schwartz (1977).

acted by two or more actors. Anthropologists, in studying dance in other cultures, have focused on the significance of the whole dance as a culturally-patterned phenomenon, rather than on the motivations or movements of individual dancers. Sociologists have viewed courtship in much the same way. The motivations of the individual dancers constitute a separate and perhaps contradictory level for analysis. The perspective of sexual scripts holds that the motivations and perceptions of the individuals are themselves patterned—through socialization. Moreover, the message of social constructions of reality is that they are *reality*, not convention; consequently unawareness of the social origin of feelings is built into socialization for such cultural dances as courtship.

The metaphor of game-playing is even more prevalent: it implies a rule-governed interaction motivated by the expectation of gain, and the duality of an ostensible and a latent set of moves or transactions. Adopting the actors' point of view, rather than society's, mating is often seen in terms of exchange.

This literature emphasizes the different stakes that women and men may have in such exchanges. Some writers suggest (Kanin et al., 1970; Kephart, 1967) that women as a group tend to construe dating as courtship, having permanent mating as their goal, while men as a group tend to view it as an opportunity for sexual expression and exploitation. This means, of course, that women and men are at odds when they enter into a dating relationship, holding different goals and different definitions of the situation.

From the earliest studies (Waller, 1937) to the more recent (Kephart, 1967; Kanin, 1970; Lever and Schwartz, 1971; Rubin, 1970) the dimensions underlying the exchange remain similar. One such theme is the relationship between scarcity and value. Traditional sex role scripts hold that sex—or, from a masculine perspective, sexual access—is one such scarce value. However, sexual access traditionally has been mediated by the rules and arrangements of courtship. Within this context, the manipulation of perceived scarcity involves techniques of impression management. Waller (1937), in a classic study, discusses the "college coed's" means of creating and maintaining the impression of being sought after, hence "hard to get" (scarce = valuable):

> . . . nothing succeeds like success. Therefore, the clever coed con-trives to give the impression of being much sought after even if she is not. It has been reported by many observers that a girl who is called to the telephone in the dormitories will often allow herself to be called several times, in order to give all the other girls ample opportunity to hear her paged. Coeds who wish campus prestige must never be available for last-minute dates; they must avoid being seen too often with the same boy, in order that others may not be frightened away or discouraged; they must be seen when they go out, and must, therefore, go to the popular (and expensive) meeting places; they must have many partners at the dances. If they violate the conventions at all, they must do so with great secrecy and discretion; they do not drink in groups or frequent the beer-parlors. Above all, the coed who wishes to retain Class A standing must consistently date Class A men (1937, p. 731).

Waller discusses the role of fraternities and sororities in reinforcing this particular organization of dating by restricting the pool of eligibles.

It is essential to bear in mind that we are talking about *perceived* scarcity and *perceived* desirability, and not about the true qual-ities of the object being perceived. A natural "experiment" re-ported by Waller reveals the arbitrariness of the conventional nature of the assignment of value and the pursuit behaviors that follow. On the campus he studied, the coeds departed in the summer term and were replaced by great numbers of women schoolteachers. The sex ratio—and consequently the scarcity phe-nomenon—was reversed and the whole pattern turned inside out. The men had the upper hand: the women wooed them, pursued them, spent money on them and so forth.

In the "rating and dating complex," every individual is rated (or assigned a value) on a variety of indicators, although these differ by sex. There is competition within sex, something on the order of a zero-sum game (i.e., what *A* wins, *B* loses). There is also a competition, somewhat like that between sports teams, between the sexes, as each tries to exploit the other without being exploited himself or herself (1937, p. 731). Status in one's own sex group depends on avoiding exploitation by the other sex. According to Waller's analysis, there is little same-sex solidarity among women, since they are in competition for the "best" men. Although the same might be expected to hold for men, there is evidence that the male peer group has special value in male sexual performance, and may, indeed, be its primary audience.

Waller also describes the dating cycles of women at the top and bottom of the pecker order. As long as a coed continues to follow the rules and date (rather than forming a permanent attachment and retiring from the marketplace), she inevitably experiences a "descending cycle of popularity." It is as though social activity, even of the approved sort, decreases her novelty—hence her scarcity, hence her value.

Blau's (1964) "Excursus on love" deals, like Waller's work, with courtship ritual rather than with the subjective and intersubjective events of love. Waller's analysis dealt with the social activity of dating in general, rather than with sexual transactions. Blau applies the same kind of logic to sexual transactions in dating.

Blau builds a case that men seek signs of affection (i.e., sexual intimacies) from women, but the value they assign to these signs is determined at least in part by the ease or difficulty of obtaining them. Blau notes, "How valuable a woman is as a love object to a man depends to a considerable extent on her apparent popularity with other men" (p. 79). Value-judgments are difficult to make, and persons tend to rely in making them on opinions of social others,[2] commonly their peers. The existence of a hidden audience for the exchanges between lovers is one of the critical points to

---

[2]Leon Festinger, in his theory of social comparison processes (1954), asserts that human beings have a drive to validate their opinions and abilities. When there is no absolute or objective standard, persons get the desired information from comparing notes with others. These are likely to be persons perceived as similar to the self.

bear in mind. Blau continues by examining the "evidence" on which the value-judgment is made:

A woman whose love is in great demand among men is not likely to make firm commitments quickly. . . . A woman who readily gives proof of her affection to a man, therefore, provides presumptive evidence of her lack of popularity and thus tends to depreciate the value of her affection for him. Her resistance to his attempts to conquer her, in contrast, implies that she is in great demand and has many alternatives to choose from, which is likely to enhance her desirability in his eyes (pp. 79–80).

Blau does not treat the underlying model of human relations as problematical, nor does he subject it to any searching analysis. He does, however, suggest strategies for "winning" under this model: "To safeguard the value of her affection, a woman must be ungenerous in expressing it and make any evidence of her growing love a cherished prize that cannot be easily won. . . . Of course, unless she finally does bestow these rewards, she does not profit from their increased value" (p. 80). Blau claims that the woman can engineer the transition from a relationship of extrinsic exchange to a love relationship by playing by these same rules. "By prolonging the challenge of the chase until a boy has become intrinsically attracted to her, a girl exploits the significance of conquest to promote a more fundamental attachment that makes this incentive for dating her superfluous" (1964, p. 81). Traditional sociological analyses, such as Waller's, document but do not analyze the operation of power relationships that are, in fact, based upon pervasive gender stratification. When, like Waller and Blau, they notice the operation of power in intimate relationships, they do not seek its causes nor remark upon the asymmetry of power relations between the sexes.

Like Waller, Blau proposes a Principle of Least Interest (1964, p. 78): the partner who cares less is in a stronger bargaining position, since the other fears the loss of the relationship more than he or she does and hence will yield in situations of conflict.

The suggestion of a potential for exploitation in such situations needs to be developed. The person who is more dependent on the relationship is easily "persuaded" to do the other's will, even when it is against his or her own best interests. Blau relates this to the Principle of Least Interest: a relationship governed by the Principle of Least Interest is nonreciprocal and, by implication, nondisclosing. A process of mystification also contributes to the lack of reciprocity. The Principle of Least Interest implies an unequal power relationship of which both parties are aware. However, when mystification takes place, a thing is labeled by a name other than its own. Unequal relations, which an objective observer might see as the result of power, may be explained instead by love. The victim of exploitation "wants to" do things for the other, once she or he accepts the definition of the situation that, "this is love." According to Blau, giving to the other is expressive of one's own feelings, not instrumental to securing a return; this is his definition of an intrinsic attachment (1964, p. 76).

Because love is valued in our culture, an individual might be motivated to demonstrate, to herself and to others, that she is in fact "in love." To be convincing, the individual will exhibit the behaviors that go along with being-in-love. If she takes Blau's hint, she will demonstrate her real feelings by giving. And because she is motivated intrinsically and not instrumentally, she will not look for a return. She is not entitled to complain, or even to feel aggrieved, if her giving is not reciprocated. The risk of being accused of exploitation is almost nonexistent for an object of attentions who has not requested them. Within the dyad, it seems, there is no check on nonreciprocity, as long as there is a disparity of desire and commitment.

The focus on giving without reciprocity is consistent with the female sex role script dissected in Chapter 2. The image of the female as existing for the benefit of others is found in the realm of sexual transactions as well as in the realm of family relations.

Not merely mystification but actual deception can occur in the context of dating and courtship. The grounds that "justify" sexual contact for women and for men may well be different, and these differences will be reflected in their language.

Blau says that much of the pursuit involved in dating is motivated, not by intrinsic attraction, but by the desire for conquest. The degree of intimacy "achieved" from a woman of specified desirability is used by the boy to gain status with his peers. One of the ironies of such transactions is that while for the woman the relationship may be of deepest emotional import and intensely private, it may very well have an audience of which she is unaware.[3] The language the male uses to persuade his partner to greater intimacy is quite different from the vocabulary he uses to report to his peers on how well he "scored." To her, he will use the language of intrinsic attraction: the intensity and singularity of his feelings for her, the uniqueness of her worth and lovableness, the joy that her love confers on him. To his peers, he will use the vocabulary of athletic competition and conquest.

The woman is thus subjected to extensive mystification. I use the term *mystification* in the same way Laing (1964)[4] does: logically inconsistent messages are thrust upon the target by one who asserts that he speaks for reality. The target person's own perceptions are discredited, which creates in her mind an ambiguity about the world and alienation from her own experience. The mechanism by which mystification is achieved is simply verbal

---

[3]"To be sure, men sometimes discuss women among themselves, their desirability and even their behavior on dates, the social taboo on doing so notwithstanding, but these discussions only increase the importance a woman's restraint has for protecting the value of her affections (Blau, 1964 p. 80).

[4]"Mystification entails a constant shifting of meaning and of position" (1964, p. 96). In an interaction, an assertion or definition of the situation is offered which strongly implies a certain meaning. If the other, in responding, confirms this premise, the interaction proceeds smoothly. If the target person challenges the implied assertion by disputing it or trying to make it explicit, the instigator shifts the grounds of the argument, so that it is impossible to pursue it logically from point to point and reach a conclusion that is provable or disprovable. Often the shifting of ground involves a movement from an assertion about objective reality to an attack on the target person's competence to assess reality. Laing treats this as the prototypical style of interaction that generates a schizophrenic personality. Mystification has similar effects, although in lesser degree, in persons who remain within the normal range.

labeling, which is one of the basic building blocks in symbolic communication.[5]

The woman experiences mystification in the context of normal courtship. She has been told that sex is meaningful only in the context of a committed, intimate relationship. She has been told that love is the crowning emotional experience in life; on the other hand, she has been schooled to be concerned about her "reputation." The ambiguity about which definition applies to her present reality haunts her. She is expected to refrain from sexual intercourse, but is given increasing freedom and privacy for her social contacts. In the intimate dyadic relationship she is presented one definition of the situation, with an accompanying pressure to be sexually expressive and to make an emotional commitment. In her roles as daughter, nubile maiden, and member of a peer culture, she is aware that she ought to put a price on both sexual and emotional commitment. An additional complication is that the price deemed appropriate varies across these reference groups (especially with parents as compared with peers).[6]

The dilemmas to which women are exposed in courtship are inherent in the female sex role, and do not pass away when the nubile woman marries. The restriction on female sexual expressivity is officially lifted once the woman is married, but there remains substantial control by the partner. Lillian Rubin (1976) discovered, in interviews with working-class women, that the premarital definitions of what is a "good girl" are not easily thrown off by a good wife. The early training may result in nonresponsivity or in sexual alienation that is hard to reverse.

In courtship, as in other spheres surveyed in this study, there

---

[5]"Unless one has a vantage-point outside this relationship, it must be very difficult to know where one is. She [mother] says, 'I am doing X: She then does Y; then she says she had been doing X, and expects [daughter] not to perceive that she had done Y" (Laing and Esterson, 1964, p. 87). The patient loses either way: if she plays the game by the other's rules, she experiences conflict with reality; if she resists, she demonstrates her "illness" to the family.

[6]Recent research on sexual standards indicates that "permissiveness with affection" (Reiss, 1967) is widely accepted among college students—that is, sexual intimacy (including coitus) is deemed appropriate for couples who are in love. Their parents, however, do not agree.

are different rules for women and men. The "shoulds" that can be gleaned from the sociological literature on courtship could not be used to guide male conduct. They emphasize the female's orienting toward and attracting attention from the male, with the initiative and control still resting with him. They retain the emphasis on derived status for women, and present women as commodities. They depict the women as objects; in fact as sex objects. Thus the role of the woman in courtship includes these elements:

1. She has the obligation to attract men.
2. She should attract as many men as possible.
3. She should concentrate her efforts on those with highest status, so that her own status may be maintained.
4. She should publicize the extent to which she is sought after, even magnify it.
5. She should withhold physical expression of desire, love or affection.
6. She should resist other attempts at exploitation (e.g., cheap dates, last-minute dates, non-prime-time meetings).
7. She is responsible for "setting a price" on herself and she gets conflicting advice about what that price should be.

The rules for women in courtship delineate an image of women as commodity. Her power to attract is her "capital,"[7] which she should invest frugally to assure an adequate future income. It is an absolute quantity and if she spends it unwisely, she will have nothing left. Moreover, her resource is prey to inflation: time diminishes it, and if she does not move quickly at the critical time, her currency may become worthless (or at the very least, devalued). Finally, it is of dubious liquidity: it does not retain its value when transferred from hand to hand. With successive transactions the capital is depleted.

The woman is thus rendered an object, for the sake of her

---

[7]An old nursery rhyme begins "And where are you going, my pretty maid? . . ." and ends, "'My face is my fortune, Sir,' she said."

sexuality, which is construed as a perishable commodity. Her value is defined in terms of one aspect only and that one is commercialized, pandered, discounted, advertised and oversold. The image that stays with us is "woman as Kleenex," a disposable, useful commodity, which is designed for a particular purpose, and so successful that all imitators are called by the same name. They are in fact interchangeable, and even those which do not carry the brand name are used—and used up—in the same way. The Kleenex is not saved, laundered, packed away in hope chests, handed down to granddaughters. It is made to be thrown away after one use, and no marginal difference of color or pattern can alter this. The Kleenex does not have a soul; it lacks volition; it has no control over its destiny or destination.

Traditional role prescriptions tie sex to marriage and to love for women, but the picture is different for men. The role obligations of sex object are not incumbent on men; rather, theirs is a complementary role of sexual subject or agent. The relationship between love, sex and marriage is different in the male script, as this imaginative exercise by Reiss (1960) makes clear.

> Picture how men would behave sexually if they were brought up as women are. Boys would be told quite young they would one day marry and raise a family and this state of affairs was very desirable. When they reached puberty, instruction would be given about the dangers of sexual intercourse outside of marriage. They would be told if they did allow themselves to step out of line sexually, their lives would be ruined—that no girl would marry a boy who had lost his virginity. Moreover, even on a dating basis, girls would not respect non-virginal boys. In addition, these boys would be taught it was a "girl's world" and girls were allowed more freedom than boys and one must accept this. The boy's role would be to marry, care for his family, and not be too upset when girls had special sexual privileges for, after all, girls will be girls. Suffice it to say that if boys were brought up in this fashion, which, in large measure, is the way many girls are brought up today, the male's sex drive would also be inhibited—so inhibited he could not give vent to his sexual desires as easily as he does today.

SEX OBJECT AS SEX ROLE

Although it may be argued that courtship, as conventionally analyzed, has been eclipsed by the "sexual revolution," sex role scripts have not changed. The central dimension of objectivity (as contrasted with subjectivity) is the defining characteristic of the female sex role in many spheres, only one of which is sex. Many of the behaviors prescribed by the sex object role have the function of inviting approach, initiative and control by another. Becoming an attractive object is a role obligation. A woman is given much credit if, by dint of sincere effort, she renders herself more attractive. In this respect the woman who is an "over-achiever" relative to her natural endowment may receive more credit than a woman who is naturally beautiful and need not work at it. By dint of effort, a woman can add to her capital by creating charm, beauty and sex appeal—commodities which have market value.

Value must, of course, be testified to by the intended consumer. In a society which does not have arranged marriages, the nubile female is an independent entrepreneur. Her marketing strategy is to beam her appeal to the widest possible audience. Since she does not know in advance who will choose her, or which is the most desirable fish, she must cast a wide net. Consequently her reliance on feedback is magnified, since she must always be asking as wide an audience as possible, "How'm I doing?" "How do you like me so far?"

Passivity is expected of the sex object. While we have seen that she actively strives to attain the role of object, once she has "arrived" she must wait to be noticed, to be approached, to be asked, to be chosen. Moreover, as an object, she is always some-body's sexual "property."[8] The traditional view of the woman is

---

[8] Cf. the Tenth Commandment.

that she passes from her father's vault to her husband's. The carryover of these attitudes has implications for women's sense of themselves as sexual beings, as we shall see in reviewing the research on premarital sexual behavior.

Appropriate demeanor (e.g., dress, posture) becomes important here. One set of skills involves being effectively attractive, but in the appropriate degree. There is finesse involved in communicating "approachability" without being "easy." Another set of skills involves signaling that one is indeed willing to assume the role of object and willing to be accommodating—not challenging. This is communicated by a set of demeanors which include traditional "feminine behavior"—appealing helplessness, selective incompetence, giggling, speaking softly and the like—which constitutes a form of deference behavior. The symbolic significance of a woman's evident effort to make herself more attractive may well consist of signaling her availability to be dominated by another. Conversely, the woman who refuses to dress up or make up is flouting this expectation. Refusing to play the game is, of course, subversive to the power rules of the game.

This signaling of docility (or compatibility, if you will) is important in the initial phases of attracting a particular partner, but it assumes even greater importance as the relationship develops. The basic premise is that the object's aims will be subordinated to the subject's. This includes occupational goals and sexual gratification, among others. A major continuity between the role of sex object and that of wife has to do with the dimension of *vicariousness*. The proposition is that a woman maximizes her own status by "catching" a man high in status-bearing attributes. Notice that his status is achieved, while hers is ascribed—i.e., as X's date, girlfriend or (if all goes well) wife. This vicariousness, as part of the role expectation for women carries over into marriage. Many women complain—jokingly, of course—that they feel eclipsed by roles in which they are known, as Ari's wife or Tricia's mother. The premise that underlies and "justifies" the role expectation of vicariousness is that Ari's or Tricia's achievements provide the same satisfaction to wife/mom as achievements of her own would.

The body is a particular focus of the sex-object role. It is a commodity: examined, handled, dissected, appraised, marketed. A woman is reduced to her anatomical components, some emphasized by her measurements (again, only some are "vital statistics"). She learns to think in terms of "maximizing" her good features and "minimizing" her bad ones, or totting up her "beauty assets" and "figure flaws." In all these calculations she is aware of an audience. Her role prescription is to display herself to advantage. The obligation to "look pretty" conflicts with the options of being strenuous or sweaty. The number of bodily postures a woman can adopt while keeping her knees together is severely limited.

The sex object role limits women's personal and sexual freedom. It denies initiative or choice, and penalizes sexual expressiveness. The only "power" it affords to women is the exercise of attractiveness to "make" someone with power want them. It is tied to the "achievement" of marriage, for only marriage is a good bargain in the sexual transaction, under the traditional rules.

Sexual Scripts and Sexual Standards

As long as the link between sex and marriage remains powerful in others' judgments of women or in their own thinking, sexual scripts will change but little. The "sexual revolution" of the 1960s may (arguably) have occasioned some change in sexual behavior and in expectations concerning sexual availability and sexual activity. A double standard in evaluations and sanctions attached to sexual activity does not, however, appear to have changed. As long as marriage is "the destination all women are intended for," failure to attain it will lower the estimation of a woman. To the extent that her marriageability is an inverse function of her degree of sexual experience, the "sexual revolution" may in fact decrease rather than increase the liberation of women. The idea of a sexual revolution is much discussed and little understood. A "sexual revolution" could involve massive changes in sexual behavior, sexual standards or both. It implies the displacement of one dominant sexual script by another.

One component of a sexual script is a code of normative (or normal, or appropriate or desirable) sexual behavior, specifying who may do what with whom. Ira Reiss (1960, 1963) has analyzed four such sexual standards that can be distinguished in current American sexual morality. They tend to be held by differing segments of the population (or differing sexual communities). They vary in the degree of permissiveness or restrictiveness. Of greater interest in the present context, perhaps, is the fact that they differ in being double standards (i.e., differing for women and men), or single (i.e., specifying the same expectations and the same sanctions for sexual behavior of women and men).

America's inheritance from Puritanism is the single standard of premarital abstinence, according to which no sexual congress before marriage is condoned for either women or men. The single standard of abstinence is a rigorous one, and a number of modifications have developed over time, including the twin institutions of petting and "technical virginity," the practice of raiding other communities other than one's own for sexual contact, and the double standard. In addition, Reiss notes two permissive single standards. One stipulates that sex is permissible for both sexes when a strong affectional bond is present, e.g., when the partners are in love. The other considers sex permissible between consenting partners who do not claim such a bond.

Reiss informs us that the double standard is the most prevalent in actuality; that means that the expectations associated with this standard are brought to bear on women. Under the double standard men are permitted sexual expression but women are denied it. The double standard really presents a syndrome of related behaviors and beliefs. These are, of course, particularly restrictive for women. When the double standard is the premise, the woman is caught in a number of dilemmas that have far-reaching effects on her self-esteem, her "reputation," her sexual development and her sexual adjustment.[9]

Figure 3.1 attempts to illustrate the way females and males interpret the cultural prescriptions regarding love, sex and marriage. The sexual standards provide differing emphasis for females and males. The double standard (applied to men) links love and marriage but allows for sex outside of the marital relationship (see Figure 3.1a). Sex does not overlap with *either* love or marriage as much as it does in the abstinence standard (Figure 3.1b). The standards governing women (abstinence and permissiveness-with-affection standards) are not as different as one might have expected. Under the abstinence standard, the overlap between sex and marriage is very great: only a little sexual expression (corresponding perhaps to petting standards) is permitted outside of marriage. Similarly one might have minor love experiences before marriage [perhaps the "infatuations" reported by Kephart (1967)]. Kephart suggests that women psychologically demote previous love experiences once they make a permanent mating that is aimed toward marriage. Thus the emotional experience is subject to "editing" just as the sexual behavior is, in such a way as to keep the woman's sexual identity congruent with the permissive/affection standard.

Among the consequences of the role assigned to the woman under the double standard script are (1) her role as policeman of the sexual interaction; (2) the threat of loss of public esteem if she violates the double standard; and (3) the sexual alienation resulting from the denial of her own sexuality. The double standard, and the conduct it prescribes, is consistent with the object role. The role of subject is reserved to the male.

Although other sexual standards are prevalent, the double standard exerts lingering effects. Moreover, the individual is not entirely free to govern her own sexual behavior according to whatever sexual standard appeals to her—particularly if she is a woman.

---

[9]Reiss (1960) has provided a detailed analysis of the intricacies of the culture of dating/courtship, with particular attention to features that derive from the double standard.

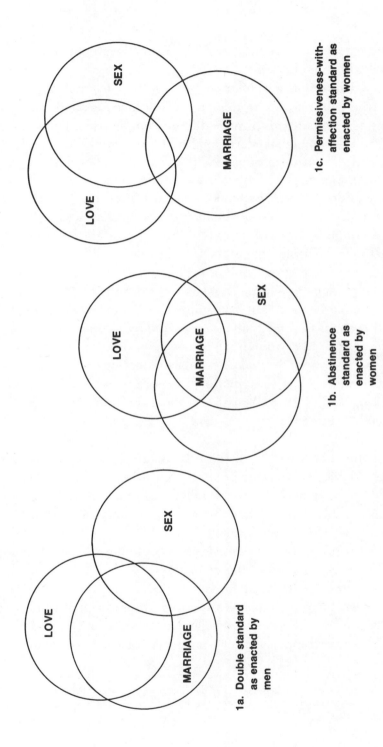

SEX

MARRIAGE

LOVE

1c. Permissiveness-with-affection standard as enacted by women

LOVE

MARRIAGE

SEX

1b. Abstinence standard as enacted by women

LOVE

SEX

MARRIAGE

1a. Double standard as enacted by men

FIGURE 3-1: Contemporary Sexual Standards

186

Sexual Pluralism and the Sexual Behavior of Young Women

A variety of sexual standards flourish simultaneously in America. Indeed, the contemporary sexual scene is a pluralistic one. However, it is not an open marketplace of sexual lifestyles, where the individual is free to choose. Rather, each sexual lifestyle is represented by a sexual community and these compete for legitimacy. Sexual behavior that characterizes one lifestyle is condemned by another. Women appear to be caught in this competition to a greater degree than men, since at least some of the sexual lifestyles embody a double standard—that is, they are more restrictive for women than for men.

Sexual standards represent a major component of sexual scripts; they specify what sexual behavior is permissible for which actors with which partners. These are generalized attitudes and do not in themselves constitute a complete guide to action. In fact, they are best thought of as providing categories of actors rather than sexual scripts for action. They do provide a scorecard for anticipating the evaluations of other people to sexual behavior. Data on young adults' anticipation of support or disapproval for sexual behavior provides evidence that individuals are aware of the content of such standards. However, such information is not the sole determinant of sexual choices that individuals make. Rather, the face-to-face relationships within which individuals experience definitions of themselves as sexual beings, share experiences and experience pressures toward (and away from) sexual behaviors are of major importance, as research cited below indicates.

In other words, individuals align their sexual behavior in conformity with the sexual community in which they operate. For young adults, this may no longer be the family but, with increasing age and independence, the peer group. For women the dating partner becomes an especially influential figure in defining their sexual identity and sexual behavior. Personal sexual decision-making takes place in a context of ambiguity. In addition to conflicts and confusion inherent in sexual pluralism, the heritage of sexuality in American culture is full of contradictions.

Ours is a society where there is no formalized exchange of property between lineages at marriage and where there is no arranged marriage. Young people choose their own mates, and personal preference is the major factor determining choice. Sexual attraction plays a central role in choice. However, within the context of a Puritan tradition, this influence has traditionally been covert. Sex has been a private behavior and a taboo topic until the last decade. Moreover, sex has been disapproved in general (with the sole exception of intercourse for the purpose of procreation within marriage)and viewed as a sin or a vice. This would seem the perfect context for the operation of pluralistic ignorance[10] and the resulting gap between sexual behavior and sexual standards. Research findings support the existence of gaps (a) between behavior and sexual standards; (b) between generations; (c) between self and others; and (d) between women and men.

The relationship between attitudes and behavior is not a simple, one-to-one predictive function; this is as true with respect to sex as it is in other areas. The factors that form attitudes (or sexual standards) and which motivate people to believe in them or to profess belief may be quite distinct from the factors which determine sexual behavior. Certainly authorities such as parents or the church instill sexual standards in the young with the intention of guiding sexual behavior. However, sexual behavior may be largely independent of the official standards. Sexual standards may

---

[10]Pluralistic ignorance refers to a situation where (a) the individual actor does not know the attitudes or behavior of others relevant to his own, and (b) the others are similarly in the dark about him and each other. A situation in which there is a severe, formal moral standard would seem to militate toward pluralistic ignorance, since persons violating the standard would be unlikely to share this information with others, for fear of disapproval. In the situation studied by Schank (1932), who coined the term, many citizens engaged secretly in illicit cardplaying, in a community with a strong moral stricture against gambling. Each cardplayer thought he was the only sinner. Given the traditional abstinence standard, it can be seen that sexual activity might be an area where pluralistic ignorance would flourish. Since the abstinence standard falls more heavily on women than on men, we would expect less communication among women about violations of the standard, greater pluralistic ignorance and greater guilt or ambivalence.

even change as a result of sexual experience—a reversal of the presumed relationship.

Kinsey's early research on male (1948) and female (1953) sexuality illustrates sexual behavior at variance with sexual standards. A single standard of abstinence (no extra- or premarital sex permitted for either women or men) is the official traditional code. Kinsey's (1953) study of sexual behavior in American women reveals a substantial degree of behavioral nonconformity with this standard, according to self-report data.

Kinsey compared rates of premarital coitus reported by women in different birth cohorts. Kinsey found a discontinuity in the percentage of women admitting to premarital coitus when he compared them by decade in which they were born. The break came between those born before 1900 and those born between 1900 and 1909. Among respondents born before 1900, Kinsey found a very high degree of behavioral adherence to the abstinence standard (92%). By this comparison, Kinsey may have discovered evidence for a "sexual revolution"—in behavior, not attitudes. If we look only at the rates for women 20 and 25 years old (in order to get some comparability with the college populations of other studies), we find the rate more than doubling, in both age groups, between these two cohorts. While only 8 percent of the 1900 birth cohort admitted premarital coitus by the age of 20, 18 percent of the 1900–1909 cohort did (Kinsey, 1953, p. 339, table 83). Fourteen percent of the 1900 cohort reported coitus by age 25, compared with 36 percent of the 1900–1909 cohort. While Kinsey reports no attitudinal data (we therefore do not know the proportions of the respondents espousing traditional sexual standards), it appears that women entering young adulthood before the "roaring twenties" behaved more in conformity with abstinence standards than did women born in the subsequent decade. After this initial leap, the percentages of women reporting premarital coitus leveled off, remaining under 40 percent through the 1940s and 1950s. Thus increase in premarital coitus has not been a linear trend, but, rather, appears to level off for a rather long period. Current data suggest that the seventies will see another substantial increase.

The change reported by Kinsey shows a behavioral violation of the sexual standard of abstinence, but there is no evidence of a "revolution" in attitudes. In fact, evidence from a recent study (Gallup Poll, 1969) suggests that women of the cohorts studied by Kinsey did not repudiate the standard, although a sizable minority of them violated it. That is to say, there was a discrepancy between their "public" adherence to the idea of what is moral behavior for a young woman and their private practice. In Reiss's (1963) study, college women and their mothers were asked whether intercourse was permissible between engaged couples (the permissiveness-with-love standard). Forty-four percent of the students, but only 17 percent of the mothers, replied yes. Mothers of women who are college students in the 1970s or late 1960s are women who reached their twenties in the 1940s and 1950s—that is, in the last cohort reported by Kinsey. We can infer that these women taught their daughters a conservative sexual standard, although they may not themselves have abided by it. This gap between attitudes and behavior has been noted by a number of students of American sexual practices (Reiss, 1960; Christensen and Carpenter, 1962; Kaats and Davis, 1970): a stringent standard is espoused, but more liberal behavior is practiced.

Kinsey's findings reveal that the "generation gap" with regard to sexual behavior is not so simple as many have supposed. Though parents espouse a sexual standard of premarital abstinence, it would be wrong to infer that this standard describes their own behavior. The fact that they tell their young not to engage in sexual behavior does not mean that they themselves are not sexually active. Nevertheless, this is what college students appear to believe. College students do not perceive their parents as sexually active beings. This perception may contribute to the generation gap and to the noncommunication between parents and young people concerning sex. The lack of communication, in turn, may have the consequence that parents are not an effective reference group for sex, and hence have little impact on their offspring's sexual decision-making. Sources of influence on sexual behavior are thus restricted to peers, impersonal sources (such as books and magazines) and perhaps an occasional adult.

The first major change, documented by Kinsey, was in behavior; sexual expression became more liberal, but attitudes remained traditional. During this period (roughly from the 1920s to the 1960s), the great majority of women who violated the abstinence standard did so with those who were to become their husbands. In other words, their modification of the prevailing sexual standard consisted only in putting the coital cart before the nuptial horse. This is a protomonogamous pattern of sexual behavior: women were following the rules of monogamous marriage, with the sole partner whom they intended as a marriage partner. We will see evidence of a protomonogamous pattern of sexual behavior among women in the studies of contemporary college students.

A number of authors contend that we are at present witnessing another change in the sexual mores. The nature of the current change is the liberalization of sexual standards and a reduction of the discrepancy between values and behavior. Davis (1970) compiled a summary of contemporary studies of premarital sexual behavior among college students. He found rates of coitus comparable to those reported by Kinsey—around 40 percent for women, and upwards of 60 percent for men. Based on his own research on the sexual behavior of college underclassmen and the predisposing attitudinal factors, he predicted substantially higher rates for the future. Davis expected coital rates of 70 percent for college women in the 1970s (1970, p. 6).

This suggests a convergence in the rates of premarital coitus for women and men. Davis has identified a number of factors that predict to young women's engaging in premarital coitus. Davis's findings illustrate the major role of sexual scripts and sexual communities in influencing sexual behavior. Factors that militate toward engaging in coitus, for college women, include (1) believing in the sexual standard of permissiveness with affection; (2) being in love; and (3) believing that one's close girlfriends are engaging in coitus. The sexual standard defines coitus as acceptable if the woman is in love; when she defines herself as being in love, the standard then applies to her. When she engages in behavior that is condemned under the more traditional standards, she anticipates support from peers whom she perceives as engaging in the same behavior.

Kaats and Davis find evidence for an increase in the popularity of a single, permissive standard among college students. Within this trend, however, sex differences remain. In addition, anticipated approval and disapproval for engaging in sexual behavior reveal persisting sex differences.

In Kaats and Davis's two samples, permissiveness was higher in men than in women, and men were more likely to apply a *single* permissive standard, while women applied a less permissive standard to themselves than to men. Another split between the sexes concerned permissiveness with or permissiveness-without affection. Men espoused both permissiveness-with and permissiveness-without affection, while women were considerably less permissive when no affection was involved. On the other hand, toward sexual intercourse when "in love," women were as permissive as men (Kaats and Davis, 1970, p. 393, table 1). Love is still the condition that ligitimates coitus for women, while men judge it permissible for themselves under a broader range of conditions.

Both men and women perceive more support for the sexual activity of males than females; both perceive most disapproval from grandparents and parents. A woman would expect most support from close personal friends if she had intercourse while in love, but not if she had intercourse with a casual date. Women students perceived faculty members as having the most liberal (libertine?) attitudes under this condition, followed by the population in general. Sorority sisters were perceived as more disapproving than either of these groups. With respect to all reference groups, however, women anticipated far less support for sexual activity than did men.[11]

---

[11]Kaats and Davis fail to note that many of the reference figures about whose attitudes the respondent is asked are men, who can be expected to hold different (and more liberal)

Kaats and Davis also found evidence of pluralistic ignorance. When the *actual* standards held by total groups were compared with the proportions just reported, it became clear that the students in the study underestimated the prevalence of the permissiveness-with-affection standard. As might be predicted, women underestimated more than men. Of the men in the study, only 64 percent anticipated that their close friends would approve of "intercourse with a girl they love," while 81 percent personally accepted it. Among the women, only 28 percent anticipated acceptance, yet 57 percent personally found permissiveness-with-affection acceptable.

The expectation of disapproval from others can be seen as evidence of the lingering effects of the abstinence and double standards. The sex difference is a direct carryover from the double standard, for the anticipation is that women will be judged more severely than men for the same sexual behavior. These attitudes are not limited to college populations. In a study of British working-class adolescents, Schofield (1965) found a much greater insistence on the desirability of a virgin bride among the females than among the males (85 percent versus 64 percent). Schofield's respondents exhibited other attitudes and behaviors that are consistent with a double standard script. Females clearly held a different standard for themselves and for males: they did not want their partner to be virginal at marriage. They believe that a woman who engages in sex before marriage gets a bad reputation. In all of these matters the females held more restrictive standards than did the males. Behavior also reflected the double standard: about twice as many of the males were coitally experienced in both the younger (15–17) and older (17–19) age groups. In addition, contraceptive behavior (or rather, lack of it) reflected the reactivity and lack of agency that go with the role of Object rather than Subject in sexual relations. The women in Schofield's study

---

attitudes toward the sexuality of men than women. Even "liberal" men (like college professors) would be more tolerant of male sexuality than female. This leads to the prediction that men will receive more support *from all sources* than will women—a prediction borne out by Kaats and Davis's data (1970, p. 397, table 5).

thought contraception was "a man's business." Of those who were coitally experienced, 43 percent of males reported they "always" used some method of birth control, as compared with 20 percent of the females. Conversely, 25 percent of the males "never" used any, and 61 percent of the female. Thirty-five percent of the women reported they always insisted the man use something, but many neither practiced any method themselves nor insisted their partner do so. Not surprisingly, 70 percent of the coitally experienced women expressed fears of pregnancy; yet as we see, they did not actively take steps to protect themselves against unwanted pregnancy.

The failure to take charge of contraception creates a problem for coitally active youth. The solutions provided in the sexual scripts followed by Schofield's respondents indicate some basic processes of sexual politics. The "honorable" solution to premarital pregnancy was marriage—although both females and males expressed the expectation that marriage was dreary and signaled the end to fun (1965, p. 128). Abortion was the dishonorable solution to premarital pregnancy (1965, p. 109).

In the U.S., abortion is an "old" issue. Yet women's right to this solution for an unwanted pregnancy is constantly being challenged, as part of the continuing fight to control women's sexuality. These issues are dealt with in depth in a later section which is concerned with women and their bodies.

In addition to illustrating the double standard, Schofield's data reveal the operation of pluralistic ignorance. In all of the female—male comparisons, the females' attitudes indicate that they believe their sexual behavior is more consequential than do the males. If women are simply uninformed or misinformed concerning the standards their male peers use in evaluating them, then the lesson of Schofield's research is that females hold themselves to an unnecessarily high standard of sexual behavior. If a single, permissive standard is in actuality the operative principle, then women may be as sexually expressive as men, without penalty.

However, current research in American settings suggests that the situation may not be so simple. The discrepancy between attitudes and behavior has the potential for inconsistent messages. The instigation to sexual freedom appears to be directed at both sexes equally (cf. the *Playboy* philosophy), but the consequences for acting upon the message may be different. This seems particularly likely in the light of the importance that marriage has traditionally had in defining women's lives and in the light of the historic link between female chastity and marriageability.

Marriage enjoys a better reputation among American youth than among the British youth who were studied by Schofield. The permissive standard espoused by American college youth applies to premarital behavior only; monogamy is the standard for marriage (Reiss, 1960, p. 128). Insofar as unmarried women are looking ahead to a monogamous future, their premarital sexual behavior will reflect that. In fact, we have already reviewed evidence that, within a sexually permissive climate, college women follow an essentially protomonogamous script.

Three elements define a protomonogamous sexual script. First, as Davis's data indicated, intercourse occurs only when the woman defines herself as being in love. Second, the number of partners is limited; in the ideal, intercourse is shared only with one's lifetime marital partner. Third, women tend to sustain intimate and exclusive partnerships as though they were married to their partners.

With respect to each of these three elements, research shows women and men to differ. In a 1967 study involving freshmen, sophomores, juniors and seniors from 12 varied colleges and universities around the country, Simon, Berger and Gagnon asked the persons who were coitally experienced about their partner on the occasion when they first had intercourse. They also asked about the duration of this relationship and the number of subsequent partners. When females in all years of college were averaged together, a total of 59 percent had first intercourse with someone they "planned to marry." Another 22 percent had intercourse with someone with whom they were "in love" but had no marriage plans. In contrast, the corresponding proportions from the men students were 14 percent and 17 percent respectively. The bulk of first coital experiences for these college men came with "Pickup or casual date" (26 percent), "Dated often, no emotional attachment" (16 percent), or "Emotional attachment, not love" (23 percent). (Simon et al., 1972). In Schofield's study, 62 percent of the women as compared with 52 percent of the men had first intercourse with their "steady"; 24 percent of the women and 4 percent of the men with their "fiancé(e)." With respect to less committed relationships, 42 percent of the boys' first partner was a "pickup," 38 percent an "acquaintance" and 26 percent a "short affair." For girls, the corresponding proportions were 7 percent, 21 percent and 14 percent. (Schofield, 1965, p. 89). In other words, the men did not have to define themselves as being in love, nor define the relationship as something special, in order to have intercourse, while the women did.

Another feature of a protomonogamous orientation toward sexual behavior is sexual exclusivity or "faithfulness." If we look at the number of partners with whom college women and men report having had intercourse, we will see once again that the protomonogamous pattern shows up more distinctly in women than in men. In the Simon et al., study, 24 percent of the college senior women have had only one sexual partner,[12] as compared with 15 percent of the senior men. Ten percent of the senior men, and only 1 percent of the senior women, have had ten or more partners.

The third element is persistence: the extent to which lovers sustain an exclusive sexual relationship. Data on how many times respondents subsequently had intercourse with the first partner shows sex difference as well. Among the men, 33 percent never again had intercourse with their first partner, 36 percent one to five times, 23 percent six to twenty times, and only 8 percent were still having intercourse with the first partner at the time of the study. The pattern for women shows almost a reversal: only 13 percent never again had intercourse with their first partner;

---

[12]These percentages are based on the total sample, not just the coitally experienced. Thus the 24 percent of women having only one partner is a very high proportion of the 29 percent who are still with the first partner.

22 percent one to five times; 34 percent six to twenty times; and 29 percent were still having intercourse with the first partner. The percentages for the intermediate two categories are comparable for the two sexes, but the patterns are reversed at the extremes. Almost four times as many women show the pattern of protomonogamous commitment.[13]

SEXUAL INITIATION

In the foregoing discussion, we have seen that most college youth espouse a sexual standard of permissiveness-with-affection, with men interpreting "affection" far less restrictively than women. Coitus still defines a woman's sexual status. Sexual initiation, therefore, remains a decision for women. They anticipate some support from peers but the most powerful source of both instigation and support for intercourse is a male partner. Research indicates that the woman will, in most cases, have a considerable sexual history in common with her partner in first coitus. She has shared with him a sexual intimacy that has increased in degree and exclusivity.

Often, the shared sexual history has been initiated by the male partner. Before this stage of heterosexual involvement, the female child's sexual history has differed markedly from that of her boy peer. The training in passivity and modesty that is part of the socialization of female children seems to have a dampening effect on self-manipulation of little girls, as compared with little boys.[14] Few girls enter the dating–courtship phase with a history of arousing and satisfying themselves sexually, without the instigation, presence or permission of any other person.[15] Their genital

---

[13]A comparable analysis of Schofield's data shows that while the percentages of women and men repeating coitus with their first partner were nearly the same (32 percent and 34 percent respectively), differences emerge with longer duration. More than twice as many women (44 percent) as men (20 percent) had intercourse with their first partner more than five times (Schofield, 1965, p. 68).

[14]Kinsey (1948; 1953) reports that 88 percent on males report masturbating at their mid-teens, as compared with under 20 percent of females.

[15]Gagnon, Simon and Berger (1970) report on rates of masturbation during high school by girls and boys. Many women (60 percent, as compared with 11 percent of men) report

area has been tabooed and they wait like Sleeping Beauty for Prince Charming to awaken them. Beauvoir (1953) discusses the primacy given (for the first time, in many individuals) to genital sensations, and their associated meanings, in sexual initiation: "The organ in which the metamorphosis is to occur is sealed. The young girl needs a man to reveal her own body to her" (1953, pp. 356–364). These quotations convey the image of the woman as waiting and receptive, while agency and activity are attributed to the man. Sexual desire and sexual arousal may lack genital focus for the virgin female. The sensations accompanying penetration, stimulation of the cervix and uterine contractions may be unknown to her. Generally speaking, there is little evidence that vaginal sensation is precisely recognized, localized and/or labeled in females *except* as a consequence of coital experience.[16] Beauvoir says, "Virginal desire is not expressed as a precise need; the virgin does not know exactly what she wants" (1953, p. 352).

Because of the prior taboo on genitality and consequent am-

---

they never masturbated, while at the other end of the distribution 28 percent of the men reported masturbating twice a week or more often (as compared with only 3 percent of the women). In accounting for this difference, Gagnon et al.'s analysis is much like my own. They note, "Males learn to pleasure themselves *autonomously* with nearly total *genital focus* on the physical level" (1970, p. 278; italics mine). They reflect, "The females, in contrast, are clearly less frequently in a situation in which they can privately and self-consciously develop *a commitment to giving themselves sexual pleasure*. Girls enter adolescence with a self-definition that is more passive and reactive . . . there is far less focus on the genitals as pleasure-giving, and a girl's most frequent contact with her own genitals is connected with menstruation" (1970, p. 279, italics mine).

[16] Kinsey notes that the routes by which females and males find their way to masturbation are quite different. Males learn about it from watching others (40 percent), talking about it (75 percent) or being masturbated by other males (9 percent). It seems there is a culture, among males, which provides them with a vocabulary, information, models and an audience for sexual experience. These seem to be lacking for females. The great majority of women (about 70 percent) discover masturbation via self-exploration. This is true not only at young ages but in women in their thirties. Many women, according to Kinsey, know about masturbation among men before they find out about masturbation among women. Some women practice masturbation for years before they ever learn it has a name and a definition. (Kinsey, 1953, 137ff).

These findings of Kinsey's are evidence for a pluralistic ignorance among women, concerning not only their personal sexuality but that of other women. It seems likely that this conspiracy of silence applies to other topics, and not just masturbation. In my own research in progress, college women report they knew about orgasm and homosexuality in men before they learned it occurs in women too. Kinsey opines that women do not discuss their sexual experiences in the open way that men do. Part of this may be attributed to ignorance, and part to the operation of a taboo on female sexuality.

biguity about this aspect of her sexuality, and because of the disapprobation she can avoid only if her sexual involvement is "justified" by the intention to marry, the young woman is extraordinarily dependent on the response of her partner. He has a major role in defining her emergent sexuality. In this situation, the lover is the logical source of such definitions; often he is the only one who knows about the event,[17] and the only one who shares its meanings. The young woman is dependent on her first lover in at least two ways that are important for the development of her sexual identity. First, he provides definitions of his own sensations and hers, where these have not been previously labeled in her experience. Second, he provides validation of her definition of the situation and of herself. This support is particularly important in view of the fact that she (but usually not he) is violating the sexual standard in having intercourse. Consequently she needs to be reassured that "this is love" (hence, that the transitional double standard, or the permissiveness-with-affection standard, applies to her in this situation). The possibilities for mystification and for blackmail are obvious.

Existing research indicates that it is *after* coital experience that women report experiencing sexual desire (Davis, 1970, p. 3), and *after* coital experience that rates of masturbation increase markedly in women (Simon et al., 1970; Kinsey, 1953). Awareness of desire for genital satisfaction and of the means to achieve it might be the starting point for sexual agency or subjectivity in women. If, as is traditionally thought, truly adult sexuality is focused in the genitalia, then sexual initiation might inaugurate an autonomous sexual history for the woman.

It is in this sense that sexual initiation is a significant social transition, even more than a biological event. This event, in a sense, lifts the taboo on genitality, exposing the woman to genital sensations that are new and placing her in a new sexual status.

---

[17] In the Simon et al. (1968) study, 27 percent of the women had never told anyone about sexual initiation as much as six months after the event. By way of contrast, 25 percent of the men had told someone within two weeks. Of the women, only 16 percent had told anyone during this period.

She then has the task of integrating and interpreting a new experience.

However, to equate genitality with sexual agency in women is to disregard the sexual scripts for intercourse and the social context of female sexual activity. The woman's training as an object leads her to experience sexual initiation as controlled by the other person. His definitions of the situation and of the experience dominate. The whole history which has led up to sexual initiation militates against the woman's direct apprehension of her own body, sensations and self.

Conversely, the sexual scripting of intercourse reflects the definition of the male as Subject. Not only initiation of sexual contact, but also positioning of bodies, timing of activities, labeling and defining the experience and, indeed, the whole scenario of sexual encounter tends to be directed by the male. The scripting extends to other areas of sexual interaction as well. The male is in charge not only by virtue of his right to initiate, but also because of the greater experience and expertise that he is assumed to have in our culture. Attitudes toward the desirability of virgin brides versus virgin grooms illustrate this expectation. In Rainwater's classic study, many working-class wives were proud to claim their husbands taught them everything they knew about sex (1960, pp. 104ff.).

The definition of the situation with the male as Subject and the Woman as Object is consistent with past socialization and with sexual standards. There is, in addition, a nice fit between these attitudes and the roles provided in the traditional monogamous marriage. The weight of this combined fit argues that women will learn from their initial coital experience a sexual identity that is consistent with Objectivity, not Subjectivity.

In marriage, as in courtship, the theme of woman as Object is perpetuated. In particular, we see the idea of woman as the man's sexual property: she "belongs to" him, and indeed this is her goal. Making the transition from covert coital activity to marriage "makes it safe to be close." Similarly, accommodating to another's sexual direction is easier than a long process of negotiation about unfamiliar sensations and desires, with an unfamiliar and probably inadequate vocabulary.

Marriage remains the institutional context within which an adult woman's sexual activity must be legitimated. In dating, the pattern of going steady mimics the monogamous orientation of marriage. It is only within this sanctioned relationship that a woman may be both sexual and respectable. Control over access to the legitimate status of married lady is another element that adds to the power of the sexual partner. He retains the initiative, ordinarily, in proposing marriage.

The pervasiveness of this external control over women's sexuality can be seen not only in the power of a lover (prototypically, a husband) over his partner, but in the transactions of obstetricians and gynecologists with their patients, and the deliberations of legislators and judges concerning female citizens. Both the macroevents of women's sexual life (e.g., the menarche, sexual initiation, pregnancy, childbirth, menopause) and the microevents (e.g., the monthly hormonal cycle, menstruation) can be seen in terms of Objectivity and Subjectivity. So, too, with other topics that focus upon women's sexuality: rape, prostitution, lesbianism.

The remainder of this chapter is concerned with women and their bodies and with the political struggle over control of women's bodies. Just as courtship scripts define woman as Object, so do expectations that chart the expected or "proper" behavior in situations where her fertility or sexual object choice are the focus. The woman is viewed as an Object insofar as things may be done to her without her consent or barring her active participation. She is viewed as an Object insofar as someone else's will or self-interest is given priority over hers—whether that someone is a concrete individual, like a baby or a husband, or an abstract collectivity, like society.

The literature on courtship and sexual relations illustrates the constraints that social scripting imposes on behavior that is subjectively experienced as private and personal. The topics reviewed under the rubric of women and their bodies illustrate the larger struggle of control over women.

Women and Their Bodies

Simone de Beauvoir (1952) describes the body as an objective or external manifestation of the self. Clearly, the way the body is treated by others can foster Objectivity or Subjectivity. de Beauvoir contrasts practices of cultivation and activity of the male body with the muffled and mystified female flesh. de Beauvoir perceptively describes the effects on behavior if the body is perceived as weak, inadequate or embarassing. Conversely, being assured of the mastery and integrity of one's body has the opposite effect: "Not to have confidence in one's body is to lose confidence in oneself. One needs only to see the importance young men place in their muscles to understand that every Subject regards his body as his objective expression" (1952, p. 310).

CONTRACEPTION

The projected incidence of premarital coital activity implies a large market for contraceptive services. While information about contraception (and even contraceptive services themselves) is now widely available, it is not always utilized. Obstacles to effective contraception can be both informational and motivational.[18] Both information and motivation are affected by factors such as we have discussed above: the contradictions among sexual standards and the strictures of the female sex role script. These influences are not limited to single women, as the data on abortion clients cited later in this chapter make clear.

Contraception poses a particular kind of motivational conflict for the single woman. On the one hand, becoming sexually active

---

[18]Even among contemporary college populations there is inadequate information about contraception (and related topics), and a desire for more. (Grinder and Schmitt, 1966; Angrist, 1966.) Another issue is the quality of contraceptive information. In most studies of sex information, young adults rely heavily on their peers. The accuracy of the information obtained from peers has rarely been assessed.

violates the more traditional sexual standards. An unwed pregnancy further flouts convention. However, taking active steps to obtain and use contraception violates the female role of Object.[19] Further, obtaining contraceptives ordinarily requires that the woman take on the identity of a sexually active single women in at least the quasi-public setting of a doctor's office or clinic.

This conflict about sexual status seems to immobilize some women, resulting in a delay between the behavior requiring contraceptive action (what the population demographers primly refer to as "exposure to pregnancy") and the contraceptive decision. Not surprisingly, this pattern exposes the woman to a large risk of pregnancy. Pohlman (1969) has observed that those who need contraception most are those who are least likely to use it: persons in relationships that are not committed and not stable. In stable and committed relationships, partners are much more likely to engage in serious discussion and joint decision-making with regard to contraception.

This ambivalence about contraception arises because of the connection, for women, between love, sex and marriage. Oftentimes at the outset of a relationship, a woman is uncertain as to the "intentions" of her partner and the future of the relationship. If she has the assurance that it is heading toward marriage, I suspect, she feels much more at ease in rationally planning for nonfertility. Indeed, this, she knows, is what married couples do. Contraceptive use, for many, may be part of a protomonogamous orientation toward sexual activity.

In a sense, unilateral contraceptive behavior may require (or may signal) a woman's recognition that active sexuality (and the related danger of pregnancy) is part of *herself* rather than part of a sanctioned relationship. For as long as most contraceptive methods are still "female methods" and these are not routinely made available to women at puberty, protection against unwanted pregnancy still requires an active effort on the woman's part.

---

[19]Angrist's study affords evidence that such information is considered *inappropriate* for unmarried college women. Thus her respondents (college freshmen) did not perceive contraception as relevant to their central concerns, which were boys, sex and dating.

Not only the decision to employ contraception but the choice among methods may reflect these same conflicts and quandaries. The uncongeniality of actively taking charge of contraception (or conversely, the desire to do so) may be a factor in user preferences for contraceptive methods. In research recently reported in *Ms.*, House (1973) gives a psychological profile of the users of different common contraceptive methods. Coitus-independent methods (like the pill) are attractive to some women precisely because they contain no reminder of being sexually active. The pill can without effort be incorporated into a daily health regimen and, like a vitamin pill, can be thought of as preventive medicine. The wholesome association is then with health rather than with sex. Similarly, the preference for male- or female-controlled contraceptive methods may reflect passive and active, or Object/Subject orientations toward one's own sexuality.

Attitudes toward contraception seem inextricably intertwined with attitudes of sexual morality and sexual stigma. Attitudes toward unlicensed sexual activity reveal a deep ambivalence. Along with the fear that someone is getting away with something goes the desire to see the norm violator punished or "get caught." Such thinking seems to underlie attitudes toward pregnancy outside of marriage, and the options presented to the single and pregnant woman. Thus Pohlman (1969), in a study of Catholic college women, found that they considered practicing contraception was "more immoral" than conceiving and bearing a child out of wedlock.

"ILLEGITIMACY"

The "unwed mother" has a distinctive and deviant sexual status in our society.[20] Traditional sociological approaches to the phenomenon of "illegitimacy" (e.g., Goode, 1960; Winch, 1970; Cole-

---

[20]The use of the term "unwed mother" is highly value-laden and conveys quite directly the social expectations that impinge on the unmarried woman who is pregnant. A more straightforward and descriptive term, "single and pregnant," has been adopted by Wachtel (1972). This designation is free of the connotation that a pregnant woman must become

man, 1966) tend to see the occurrence of births that cannot be unambiguously placed in the social structure as a problem. This, then, accounts for practices society invents to control or regularize problem births. However, this argument does not adequately account for punitive actions directed toward *unwanted* pregnancies. Nor does it account for the asymmetry of blame attached to the partners in such pregnancies (Vincent, 1961). As far as the social problem goes, males are as responsible for producing unassignable young as are females.

However, it appears that there are other problems presented by out-of-wedlock pregnancies. One is the existence of sexual activity in women; another is self-directedness or agency of women with regard to their own sexuality. These are exacerbated when the woman is single—that is, not under the legal or moral control of a man. The treatment to which the single and pregnant woman has traditionally been subjected—now moderated in many jurisdictions—reflects moral, not social-utilitarian, reactions to unlicensed fertility. The "unwed mother" is the traditional scapegoat for all of those who violate sexual standards, not only for those who "get caught."

The stereotype of the "unwed mother" purveys an image of a female who is the polar opposite of the "good woman" (or "nice girl"). She is "promiscuous," slatternly, insatiable and/or ungovernable—unable to act in her own best interests.[21] "Illicit" pregnancies do not, however, result from a situation of unshackled female sexuality; quite the contrary. The majority of illicit births documented in the research literature germinate in ordinary dating and courting relationships like those described at the beginning of this chapter.

---

a mother and the implicit corollary that the child's interests take precedence over the mother's (see Chapter 2).

[21] Many authors (Bettelheim, 1955; Hays, 1964; Horney, 1967) have written about a dread of women in men and analyzed much of social structure as attempts by men to control or neutralize the attributes of women that are most different and most uncanny—e.g., the capacity to bear children (Bettelheim, 1955) or the possibly limitless orgasmic potency of woman (Sherfey, 1966). Consequently, the images of women who flout such control have a monstrous or witchlike quality.

Pope (1967) cautions against falling into the tautology of thinking that relationships that produce an extramarital pregnancy are abnormal or deviant precisely because they produce such a pregnancy. His research shows that most of these relationships differ in no way from those of "good" women and men. In a study of North Carolina single mothers, Pope found only slight age and educational differences between the partners in premarital pregnancy. His data, in addition, provide more detail about the nature of the relationship of the unwed parents. In this study, the unwed fathers were from the same locality as their partners, were members of the same group of friends, and were known to their partners' families. In other words, these pairs emerged from the normal dating context. The characteristics of these pairings resembled the normal dating pattern in yet another way: the relationships tended to be protomonogamous. Sixty percent of the white single mothers had been dating their partner exclusively for anywhere from six months to over two years, as had 78 percent of the black single mothers. Most of the women said they planned to marry their partners, and between 75 percent and 80 percent of them reported they loved their partners. Moreover, these women were far from promiscuous; like the women in the studies of premarital sexual behavior in college students, most of them (between 40 percent and 70 percent) had been intimate only with the father of the child. These, too, were protomonogamous relationships.

Vincent (1961) challenged the conventional wisdom that asserts that only women who are ignorant, poor and/or retarded get pregnant out of wedlock. He chose to study a population that is less socially visible than the stereotyped "unwed mother." Vincent studied more than a thousand single women giving birth in California, a state that does not record illegitimacy status on the birth certificate. Through the cooperation of physicians in Alameda County, Vincent had access to data for women who were seen in private practice, in county hospitals and maternity homes. He shows quite clearly that past stereotypes concerning the "unwed mother" were based upon the captive populations in county hospitals and maternity homes. When the research includes the relatively privileged women who could afford the temporary migration to California and private care, the apparent homogeneity of the category of single and pregnant women disappears.

Vincent discovered that the unmarried pairs involved in the pregnancies he studied were quite similar to the pairs involved in first marriages in the United States at large. The education of the single and pregnant women in his study was almost identical to that of women entering first marriage in the years 1947–1954, and the education of the alleged partners of the single and pregnant women matched that of the husbands. Moreover, the discrepancy between the males' and females' educational attainment was the same for both groups (Vincent, 1961, p. 75). Ages of partners and their age discrepancies followed the same pattern. Vincent makes the point that couples whose premarital sexual involvement produces an "illegitimate" pregnancy are merely a subset of the larger population of dating couples and in no sense appear to be a qualitatively different group.

Studies of premarital pregnancy demonstrate the connection between inadequate information about contraception and the occurrence of an unplanned pregnancy. Wachtel (1972), Vincent (1961) and Pilpel and Wechsler (1971) all draw attention to the high incidence of premarital pregnancy in the very young age ranges. Pilpel and Wechsler attribute this to the denial of contraceptives and contraceptive information to sexually active minors. They point out that this practice reliably produces extramarital births; in the 1965–1968 period, such births increased 25 percent in the 15 to 19 age range. Having an illegitimate child is the hard way to gain access to birth control. The point that Pilpel and Wechsler are making accords with the attitudinal data we have on college women's information level with regard to contraception and also with reports of the respondents studied by Vincent. Many of the latter expressed astonishment at how easy it was to get pregnant (1961, pp. 38ff.).

Vincent and Pope both note that premarital sexual activity is not subject to nearly the same negative sanction that premarital pregnancy is. Indeed, as I suggested at the beginning of this chapter, sex is the major instigation to marriage in our culture. The permissive standards that predominate among young adults lend further weight to the argument that the sexual activity which permits conception to occur is not likely to decline. As Ann Landers repeatedly observes, young people who have begun a sexual relationship are not going to stop, no matter what a parent says. She advocates contraception as a practical response.

A number of social forces seem to militate against a rational policy of prevention of premarital pregnancy, both at the societal level and at the individual level. This reliably produces a social problem, as we have seen. There are a variety of resolutions to "problem pregnancies," of course. One of these is to give birth and then release the infant for adoption. Attitudes seem to favor having the baby and giving it up for adoption over abortion—in spite of the relatively higher costs for the mother in so doing. Vincent suggests an explanation for this, in terms of sex-role expectations. In his expression, the unwed mother "passes the femininity test" when she accepts motherhood and completes her pregnancy, heroically alone and condemned (1961, p. 81). In this way she perhaps "pays for" her mistake (cf. Pohlman 1969). This solution seems to support the primacy of marriage as a social institution and as a career for women. Rather than making a life for herself and child, the unwed mother is encouraged to repudiate the baby. If she "straightens out," perhaps later there will be another chance for her—i.e., marriage and *legitimate* pregnancy.

This pattern of releasing "illegitimate" babies for adoption supports marriage and the family in another way as well. There is a "market" for (some) babies, composed of persons who wish to be a family but are infertile. The demand for appropriately eligible (i.e., white) babies has for some time exceeded the supply (Vincent, 1961; Wachtel, 1972). At the same time, the supply of black babies has exceeded the demand; upwards of 90 percent of agency adoptions in 1964–1969 were of white babies, as compared with less than 5 percent black, and less than 5 percent of other races. Moreover, only 25 percent of black women interested in having their babies adopted were accepted for even a first interview by an agency (as compared with 50 percent of the white women).

Here is an irony. Although social pressures suggest that it is more respectable for a single pregnant women to carry the child to term, give birth and release it for adoption, it seems that the option of doing so is not equally available to all women.

ABORTION

There is still another option for the unwilling pregnant woman: abortion. Abortion has been the most disapproved of the options of the unwilling pregnant woman and is a subject of continuing controversy.

Although many people are unaware of the history of abortion, it became a crime only in the last century. Statutes defining abortion as a crime were passed, in various jurisdictions, only during the Civil War era (Ladner, 1973, p. 21). Before that time it was not illegal. The new legislation was passed ostensibly to protect women against the dangers to life and health that surgical procedures of that era entailed. Concern for the wellbeing of the mother has been a theme throughout the history of abortion legislation and of demands for repeal or reform. A parallel concern for the wellbeing of children, both born and unborn, has been articulated on both sides of the controversy. At present, the right to abortion affirmed by the Supreme Court in 1973 is under continual challenge. Although the practice of abortion is legal, the rights of practitioners and clients are threatened by disruptive intrusions into clinics by those who oppose women's right to abortion. Continuing legislative pressure and public debate punctuate the controversy. The only single-issue presidential candidate in recent years ran on an antiabortion plank—in 1976. The abortion reform movement is neither new or superfluous in 1979.

Moral disapproval of abortion has often masqueraded as predictions of dire outcomes, especially for the mother. Some of these dire prophecies have a slightly wishful tinge, reminiscent of the doctrine of "maternal deprivation" discussed in Chapter 2. Abortion was assumed to constitute both a physical and a psychological trauma. Hence research focused on the incidence of negative sequelae to abortion, whether these were psychological or physical. When abortion was still illegal, the necessity of secrecy and the potential liability for criminal prosecution added to the psychological stress of undergoing an abortion. Certainly it made research on abortion difficult. An early study by Lee (1969) illustrates both of these difficulties. Lee found that women seeking illegal abortions had to pursue a chain of referrals under conditions of risk and uncertainty.

Research indicates that the psychological horrors of abortion have been exaggerated. In a very extensive review of the literature, Osofsky and Osofsky (1971) found that negative psychological sequelae to abortion were the exception rather than the rule. The American studies, for the most part, reported either on illegal abortions (Gebhard et al., 1958) or on therapeutic abortions. (Niswander and Patterson, 1967; Peck and Marcus, 1966; Kretzschmar and Norris, 1967). Not only were bad psychological aftereffects rare, but any regret was also rare. Niswander and Patterson found that the few regrets expressed by postabortion patients had disappeared at the eight-month follow-up. In Peck and Marcus's study, 98 percent of the patients said they would opt for abortion over pregnancy. Some patients reported that abortion brought about an improvement in their psychological state (Whitington, 1970). In the Osofsky and Osofsky study, 64.6 percent were happy with their abortion decision, and 76.2 percent reported no guilt at all. Overall, 78.7 percent were glad they had decided to have an abortion.

Some studies conducted in other countries afforded longer follow-up periods. These findings tend to show a similar pattern. Where a desired abortion is granted, regret is slight and not lasting. Where abortion is denied, however, the picture is different. Höök (1963) studied 294 women who had been denied abortions in Sweden. He found that 23 percent of them accepted the pregnancy and made a satisfactory adjustment; 53 percent showed symptoms of distress for 18 months, and subsequently adjusted; and 24 percent still showed symptoms of distress at the follow-up, seven to 11 years later. Höok reports no data on the effect of the mother's distress on the children. Another study, however, looks at outcomes for young people born from pregnancies that the mother had wanted to abort (Forssman and Thuwe, 1966). They found higher incidence of delinquency, psychiatric symptoms and consumption of social services among these young people than in a control group of adolescents.

Physical consequences of abortion appear to be trivial. The actual risk involved in abortion is a function of the physical condition of the mother, the stage of the pregnancy and the technique employed, and the quality of the medical care involved.[22] Such a risk should be very slight under conditions of routine antisepsis, medical competence and patient care—in short, where abortion is handled in a sane manner, rather than as an immoral transaction that puts both the patient and the practitioner outside the law.

Nevertheless, guilt and regret over abortion is part of the folklore. These themes are still to be found in the true confessions magazines. Within the last year, a number of the women's magazines have carried first-person accounts of a woman's second thoughts about the readily-obtained abortion. This kind of cautionary literature sounds a note of alarm at women's departure from approved morality.

Although research tends to disarm the prediction that undergoing abortion has bad consequences for women, less attention has been paid to the question of negative consequences of being denied abortion. The research of Höok and of Forssman and Thuwe, cited above, shows some of the consequences of women's being forced to bear unwanted babies. Although parallel research has not been carried out in the United States—perhaps because of pronatalist factors discussed in Chapter 2—existing research does show a substantial proportion of births

---

[22]Tietze and Lewit (1971) found a higher incidence of medical complications following abortion among nonprivate patients, regardless of the stage of their pregnancy. This suggests, once again, that poor women are treated differently from those who can afford their own physician.

resulting from unwanted pregnancies. From the evidence on births, it appears that many resulted from unwanted pregnancies (Bumpass and Westoff, 1970). Some of these women accepted the pregnancy and apparently, by the time of the birth, desired the child. Others would have preferred to terminate the pregnancy. In Cobliner's (1965) study, nearly 50 percent of newly delivered mothers reported that the pregnancy was unwanted at the time of conception. The connection between this factor and the "maternal rejection" with which Cobliner was concerned was not explored. In this study, as in much of the literature reviewed in Chapter 2, the wellbeing of the child is the focus, to the exclusion of concern for the mother's. The focus on the "rights of the fetus" found in much current antiabortion material comes perilously close to denying the rights of the pregnant woman and, in effect, advocates forcing women to bear children against their will.[23]

THE DEMAND FOR ABORTION

Research on abortion in the period just following legalization indicated an enormous demand, previously unsatisfied. Tietze and Lewit (1971) found that the demand did not level off after the initial high incidence; rather, there is a continuing demand for abortion.

The psychology of someone's-getting-away-with-something is evident in fears and arguments attending the legalization of abortion. Fears that "abortion mills" would attract riffraff have proven unfounded. Tietze and Lewit (1971), in a study of 42,598 cases from 12 states plus the District of Columbia, found that 60 percent of the patients were local residents. Another concern that is sometimes expressed is that if abortion is made "too" easy, women too lazy to practice contraception will have recourse to abortion rou-

---

[23]The ethical and legal issues involved in forcing women to bear children, and in the hypothesized "rights"of the unborn have been thoroughly analyzed by Sandra Tangri (1976).

tinely. Although the question has not been thoroughly researched, there seems little reason for women to prefer abortion to contraception, where the latter is available, effective and/or safe. In the Tietze and Lewit study, 47.9 percent of patients were pregnant for the first time; only 3.6 percent had had prior abortions and no prior deliveries (Tietze and Lewit, 1971, table 1, p. 6). Many of those with prior pregnancies were, of course, married women.

Osofsky and Osofsky studied 380 abortion patients seen in a New York State Family Life Program initiated after the 1970 liberalization of the state abortion law. Like the population in Tietze and Lewit (1971), about half of these were single women and half married. Like the population of Lee's study, most (71.8 percent) conceived within a stable and serious relationship.

Data on abortion clients point up once again the inadequacy of contraceptive information and use among sexually active women of many backgrounds. In Osofsky and Osofsky's study, as in Howell's, a large number of the unwanted pregnancies resulted from reported contraceptive failure (24.7 percent in Osofsky and Osofsky; 25 percent in Lee) or inadequate contraception. In the Osofsky and Osofsky study, 59.8 percent of the women knew something about contraception but weren't using it; 15.5 percent had little or no knowledge about contraception. Here again we see the effect of lack of agency with respect to one's own sexuality. As in Vincent's study (1961), women who are doubtful, passive or ignorant about contraception are nonetheless involved in sexual relations and exposed to pregnancy. Without the active intervention of effective contraception, one can, with no exercise of volition, become pregnant. Seeking an abortion represents an assertion of control (or Subjectivity) but, under present circumstances, at great cost, as we have seen. Failing a decision about abortion, the infant is born and a new set of decisions presents itself.

It seems likely that, although the abortion option is the most socially disapproved resolution to an unmarried woman's pregnancy, it is the one most preferred by women. Wachtel (1972) affords some evidence for this conclusion. She shows that in localities where abortion is more readily available, the number of infants available for adoption declines. Examining changes from 1960 to 1970 in number of children accepted for adoption, Wachtel finds 75 percent of areas showing an increase had restrictive abortion laws. Of those areas showing a substantial decrease, 80 percent had liberal abortion laws. If anything, it would seem that these data underestimate the extent to which women take advantage of the abortion option, where it is readily available. These statistics relate to a period before the full effects of the liberalization of abortion laws could be observed.

The demand for adoptable (white) babies is another force in the antiabortion impetus. The existence of a black market in white infants has been asserted in the media. Feminist commentators have pointed out that white women, in particular, may be forced to bear their babies while the poorer black women, equally against their will, may be sterilized. These tendencies betray a conception of women as objects, entities which may be used to fulfil others' varying priorities. Women's right of self-determination in sexuality and fertility is not yet acknowledged by many of the powers in society.

The image of woman as Object is so ingrained in culture that this image can be seen even in the arguments for the right to abortion. Abortion has been urged on behalf of maternal and child health—in the context of marital fertility, rather than of sexual self-determination. Women in need of abortion have been portrayed as victims—pregnant women who have contracted rubella, rape victims or mentally incompetent women (Cisler, 1970, p. 275). Women are not portrayed as sexual Subject—as persons who have the right and responsibility to direct their own lives. At present, the legal right to seek abortion must still be mediated by a figure of authority—now a physician, rather than a policeman. The function of physicians in policing abortions is, however, illustrated in a study by Stewart, reported below.

Although abortion is at present legal, the current situation is far from "abortion on demand." The 1973 Supreme Court decision does not concede the right of women to control their own bodies.

Some of the restrictions on women's "right" to abortion that are still in force include the following: in some states a minor must have written consent of her parents to get an abortion (but not to get pregnant, give birth and release the baby for adoption); a wife must have her husband's written consent; a woman must satisfy a residency requirement. In addition, of course, she must have time and money to travel to a state where she can get an abortion; if the facilities are inadequate she may be placed on a waiting list. Restrictions still apply on how late a pregnancy may be aborted. Currently, public funds may not be used to pay for abortions; hence only women who can command private means are in practice allowed this option. Finally, of course, the woman must have the approval of a physician (or a group of physicians).

All of these restrictions are society's way of denying subjectivity to the woman, with respect to her own sexuality. They are contradictions of women's claim that they have the right to control their own bodies. It is in recognition of this fact that people in the Women's Movement have demanded repeal, and not reform, of abortion laws (Cisler, 1970).

Removal of the legal obstacles does not remove the moral objections of many people to abortion or their desire to prevent others from exercising this choice. Many restraints have been internalized by women, and the force of social taboo continues to operate. The findings of Osofsky and Osofsky (1971) reveal how sensitive women are to the negative sanctions attaching to abortion. Fifty-eight percent of the patients reported that if abortion were still illegal, they would have had the child. This is a fair estimate of the effect of social stigma in preventing women from seeking illegal abortion. We can perhaps use it as an estimate, as well, of the number of unwanted babies who may be in trouble.

Stewart's study (1971) illustrates some of the more subtle ways that women may be punished for seeking abortions, even though these are now legal and they are free from *legal* sanctions. Stewart interviewed 30 obstetricians practicing in an urban setting concerning their attitudes and practice with respect to unwanted pregnancies and requests for abortion. She detected a certain amount of resistance to the "avalanche of females" requesting abortion and found that the physicians' professional decisions in these cases were influenced by their personal values. Stewart, therefore, focused on physicians who rejected abortion on personal grounds but did perform abortions as part of their professional practice. As a way of coping with the conflict they made distinctions among the women applying to them for legal abortions.

In deliberating whether to perform the requested abortion, the physicians used four categories to distinguish among the women:

1. Stupid: women who appeared to have little contraceptive information and/or inadequate sex education. These tended to be rather young patients. They were granted abortions but because of their age were subsequently not provided with contraceptive devices and information.
2. Careless: women who, in the context of a protomonogamous relationship where contraception was accepted and used, had "forgotten" once or twice. They were granted the abortion and counseled to be more careful in the future.
3. Made a mistake: women who conceived in an "unsuitable" relationship (e.g., an interracial couple), judged by the physician to be a passing fad. Where the woman confessed that the relationship was a mistake and the pregnancy was the only link to the unsuitable partner, she was granted the abortion, and she, too, was assumed to have learned her lesson.
4. Promiscuous: women who engaged in sex for fun, rather than as an expression of marriage-type love; who rejected marriage as a goal; who had more than one partner; who were critical or rejecting of the contraceptive ethic and/or of medical competence. These were regarded as "undesirable" patients and were refused abortions. Instead, they were referred to other practitioners who made a specialty of abortion, and whom these physicians regarded as marginal and/or incompetent practitioners.

Stewart's study shows the persistence of a tendency to type women as either good or bad and to disregard their self-definition in doing so. The physicians' acceptance of a permissive (proto-monogamous) standard indicates that the basis for making value-judgments may change over time, but *this in itself does not increase the freedom of women*. Indeed, the study illustrates clearly the enormous power the physicians had over women's lives, based on their personal moral judgments. The decisions of this group of physicians regarding the "promiscuous" women would seem to be in violation of their Hippocratic oath, for they knowingly consigned these women to medical care that they did not believe to be competent.

These physicians accepted the responsibility of "playing God," of judging and punishing "sinners." Their patients' sins consisted of the following: (1) They departed from the conventional strictures on female sexuality. These patients did not structure their sexual expression monogamously, and they did not regard sex as sacred. (2) They had subversive ideas about marriage; unlike the "careless" women, they did not express the intention or the hope of marrying their partners, nor did they engage in sex merely as an expression of their commitments to them; rather, they seemed to seek sexual gratification for its own sake. (3) They were uppity, questioning, or even rejecting the authority and expertise of the physician, especially when it involved their own bodies. They wanted to make their own decisions about their fertility and their health.

We have seen that not all single pregnant women were defined as immoral by the physicians studied. Under some circumstances they were viewed as persons "in trouble" and the physician decided to help them. What, then, are the conditions under which the physician decides whether a woman "in trouble" is salvageable or lost? Acceptance of contraception was one precondition for receiving an abortion. Another group of physicians, who did not object to abortion on either personal or professional grounds, echoed this ethos and added two other considerations. First, they disapproved of recidivism in premarital pregnancy: they would be much less willing to perform repeated abortions on the same patient. Second, they expressed some concern for the women, contending that carrying a pregnancy to term and releasing the baby for adoption would be psychologically harmful to the woman. Another group, those who disapproved of abortion both personally and professionally, did, however, perform abortions for the daughters of their regular patients, albeit unwillingly. They were conflicted about doing so, and would have preferred that the women "live up to their responsibility and *be required* to carry the pregnancy to term" (Stewart, 1971, p. 9, italics mine). They did not express concern for the mother's wellbeing.

The attitudes expressed by these various groups of physicians revealed a range in terms of the degree of Objectivity they enforced or of Subjectivity they tolerated in the women patients. The physicians in the first group insisted on some confession of wrong— ignorance, carelessness, mistakenness—before they would grant an abortion; and they denied it to those who refused to submit. Those whose resistance to abortions was even stronger showed two somewhat contradictory images of woman as Object: on the one hand, they were viewed as innocent victims of "con men," rather than as persons who had knowingly and deliberately engaged in sexual activity. By rights, it seems, these daughters of respected families were still virgins; they had been *done to* but weren't responsible for *doing*. On the other hand, these same physicians showed a need to punish the patients and hold them responsible for their lapse.

It might be argued that the punitive responses to abortion clients, unwed mothers and sexually active single women are due to violation of the female sexual script. Only deviants, it can be argued, are treated as Objects; "normal" women following socially approved scripts are allowed a greater degree of Subjectivity, or self-determination. On the contrary: the now classic critique of standard American obstetrical practice is a reaction against the objectification of women in the birth process. The demand for subjectivity in health and bodily experience has been carried forward by the Women's Health Movement.

One of the earliest critics of standard obstetrical procedures was Niles Newton (1955), who criticized the use of straps and anesthesia as routine measures (often against the express wish of the mother). She noted the mutilating effect of shaving the pubic hair and its dubious contribution to antisepsis (1970).

Newton advocated the procedures and philosophy of Grantly-Read's "cooperative" childbirth. Although these have become better known as "natural" childbirth in the United States since the early writings, such innovations as childbirth preparation and rooming-in are by no means standard procedure. Other innovations, such as the birth chair, are unavailable to most mothers. Any options desired by the mother must still be approved by the attending physician and can be overruled by hospital policy. Perhaps for these reasons, home deliveries attended by midwives have become more popular. Not only does this procedure circumvent many features of hospital births most disliked by patients—high fees, nonindividualized treatment, authoritarian medical hierarchy—but often an entirely different ideology accompanies the different practice. Just as the Lamaze method refers to labor as work rather than as pain, so do many of the female-oriented birth practices emphasize positive aspects of birth, and its relationship to human processes of love, sex and caring that have preceded it.[24] Newton (1955, p. 37) observed that mothers report joy and pride when their control and participation in the work of birth is not abridged. Negative attitudes toward, and memories of, childbirth may be related to insensitive use of anes-

---

[24]Such a positive approach is exemplified in the "amazing birth tales," which introduce *Spiritual Midwifery* (Summertown, Tenn.: The Book Pub. Co., 1978). This book is, in part, a midwife's handbook and, in part, the account of a collective of midwives who operate within a large contemporary intentional community in Tennessee.

thesia and analgesia, which dim the mother's experience of subjectivity in giving birth.[25]

Although more humane and participative methods are known and available in obstetrics, the practices of a particular physician may have been shaped more definitively by his training than by the contemporary spectrum. Both knowledge and attitudes are acquired during professional socialization, and textbooks function as a repository for both. Scully and Bart (1973) content-analyzed 27 gynecology textbooks used in American medical schools over the past 30 years.[26] In examining the information on female sexuality contained in these texts, Scully and Bart grouped them into three "generations," according to major gains in knowledge. Scully and Bart found that the textbooks did not reflect the gains in knowledge, when pre-Kinsey texts (1943–1952) were compared with post-Kinsey, pre-Masters and Johnson (1953–1962) and post-Masters and Johnson (1963–1972). Rather, the texts perpetuated an essentially Freudian view of female personality, along with advice based upon archaic and unsubstantiated sex role scripts. The "factual" statements that provide the context for this sort of advice included (1) the male sex drive is stronger; (2) women are "almost universally generally frigid" (Cooke, 1943, p. 60); (3) women are interested in procreation anyway, not sex; (4) vaginal orgasm is mature; (5) those who "cannot" attain vaginal orgasm are frigid; and (6) clitoral stimulation is immature, inferior and/or autistic. On the basis of such dubious data, many of the texts contained prescriptions for how women should conduct their sexual lives. Presumably the gynecologist was to instruct his female patient; for example: "The bride should be advised to allow her husband's sex drive to set their pace and she should attempt to gear hers satisfactorily to his (Novak, 1970, pp. 662–63)." Many

---

[25] In the studies reported by Newton from 48 percent to 95 percent of mothers delivering under "cooperative" methods needed no analgesia or anesthesia at all (1955, p. 33).

[26] This is one of a number of current studies where feminist scholars have examined teaching materials, TV commercials and the like, in order to categorize and count prevalent images of women. An introduction to the fundamentals of content analysis can be found in Berelson (1952).

of the texts advocate that women should fake orgasm—and one can infer that the wise woman will not only please her husband by this "innocent simulation," but will also learn to kid her gynecologist, too, since vaginal orgasm seems to be so important to him.

Rather than treating pregnancy as a contingent consequence of woman's reproductive capability that provides a living for the obstetrician, the authors of these texts elevate the accident of conception to the central force in feminine personality. Willson et al. (1964, p. 49) state, "One of the central impulses in a woman's life is her desire to reproduce." The authors continue, pointing out that pregnancy is "a milestone on the road to maturity," as well as enhancing the woman's status and demonstrating her goodwill to her husband by making him this "gift." The context of the discussion makes it clear that the authors assume that the pregnant woman is always married, does not work outside the home and has no competing options.

The thinking embodied in the texts studied by Scully and Bart is of more than antiquarian interest. Women are defined in terms of others' objectives: husband's, society's, physician's. Women's self-definitions and feelings do not even enter the discussion. Authority of men over women is assumed. Willson et al. (1964) explicitly define the doctor–patient relationship as like that of parent and child. A slightly more grandiose definition of this relationship is offered by Scott (1968, p. 25), "If like all human beings, he (the gynecologist) is made in the image of the Almighty, and if he is kind, than his kindness and concern for his patient may provide her with a glimpse of God's image."

The gynecology texts illustrate prevalent problems in writing about women, which were analyzed in the introduction and throughout this book. Poorly documented and even counterfactual statements, conservative in content and pejorative in tone, are put forward in authoritative sources. Because of the double standard of scholarship, these tend to escape the challenge and correction they deserve. Such work, when found in textbooks, serves to misinform generations of practitioners, who then preach misinformation to generations of patients, with that divine conviction so faithfully described by Scott (1968).

Paradoxically, it appears that after a decade of "sexual freedom" women are subject to radical restriction, to objectification and to mistaken identity. Clearly, the factors determining the treatment of women are more basic than media events such as the "sexual revolution." The dead hand of history—or pseudohistory—is still writing the sexual scripts, and the combined apparatus of the media, the courts, the clinics and the colleges is still disseminating them. Body politics is still a contested area, as the foregoing reveals. One of the most striking examples of the conflict between patriarchal and feminist orientations toward women is found in the case of vaginal versus clitoral orgasm.

Female Sexuality and Property Rights: Who Owns the Female Orgasm?

The conflict between patriarchal and feminist treatments of female orgasm has both an ideological aspect and a factual aspect, the former often overshadowing the latter.

Although the ideological debate had begun before the publication of Masters' and Johnson's *Human Sexual Response* (1966), their research provided a baseline of factual material of a kind that was previously unavailable. Their definition made it clear that they see orgasm not as a purely physiological phenomenon, but one which is affected by many of the factors discussed in this chapter: "For the human female, orgasm is a psychophysiologic experience occurring within, and made meaningful by, a context of psychosocial influence" (1966, p. 127). Masters and Johnson attempted to deal not only with physiological events but also with psychological and sociological factors in orgasm.[27] The best known

---

[27]A more precise definition is the basis of their objective research measurements: ". . . it is a total-body response with marked variation in reactive intensity and timing sequence" (1966, p. 128). A similar emphasis is found in Clark (1970): ". . . the convulsive, rhythmic

of their findings concern the physiologic events that seem to apply to a wide spectrum of women. Their research revealed four stages in the typical episode of sexual arousal and resolution: the excitement phase, the plateau phase, the orgasmic phase and the resolution phase. Each is described in terms of the bodily changes that characterize it. The question of greatest interest to us here is the border between the plateau phase—when breast, sexual organs and perineum are tumescent, awareness of external stimuli is dimmed, and the body is somewhat tense—and the "explosive," short-term response called orgasm. Subsequently the woman returns to the plateau phase and only gradually does the congestion subside in the resolution phase. Masters and Johnson do not give us a distinct picture of "the" orgasm, except as a region in the graph of physiological arousal.[28]

The subjective reports compiled by Masters and Johnson of the "psychologic" experience of orgasm reveal three stages. In the first stage, women report intense awareness of sensation in the pelvic region, a fleeting sensation of stoppage or suspension and a loss of responsiveness to outside stimuli. The second stage is characterized by a feeling of warmth, which begins in the pelvic area and suffuses the body. The third stage is characterized by a pelvic pulsing or throbbing sensation (which is correlated with Masters and Johnson's measurement of the initial spasm of the orgasmic platform of the vagina). Some women are also aware of rectal-sphincter contraction during this stage.

Rather than being reports on the psychology of orgasm, these are simply self-reports of the physiological events that Masters and Johnson studied in the laboratory. We will have to turn to the reports of other research—and research that is still in the future—to learn about the meanings of orgasm and its context of

---

contractions of the pelvic musculature commonly accompanied by the highest peak of pleasurable feeling as a climax to sexual stimulation."

[28]They concede, "To date, the precise mechanism whereby cortical, hormonal, or any unidentified influence may activate this and other orgasmic reactions has not been determined (*perhaps* by creating a trigger-point level of vasocongestive and myontonic increment) (1966, p. 129, italics mine).

desire and intimacy. One difficulty in conducting such research is that the events of the cycle of sexual arousal do not seem to be sufficiently well known to have acquired social labels and standard social meaning. Nevertheless, there are sensations associated with them—for example, the engorgement of the breasts, labia and clitoris and the distention of the vaginal barrel—of which the individual may be aware. Again, there are bodily changes that may be observable—color changes in the labia and nipples, the so-called orgasmic flush. There are thus (at least) two sets of events occurring in the woman's sexual arousal and release. The partners may attempt to communicate about these—or they may not. With both sets of phenomena there is a difficulty in expressing the experience in words[29] because of the lack of social learning. Consequently, accounts of sexual experiences (orgasm among them) have an idiosyncratic and subjective character. Here once again, the ambiguity of experience leaves open the possibility of the partners' defining the experience for each other. The male, for example, may accept his partner's report that she has had an orgasm.[30]

Research on these phenomena is in its infancy. Data on the psychological events in sex are not, however, inherently less "reliable" than the physical events that Masters and Johnson studied. In fact, my point is precisely that their seemingly stable and "objective" measures do not bear an invariant relationship to the psychological events as these are reported simultaneously by the research subjects. Masters and Johnson acknowledge as much.

---

[29]The sex manuals that are so popular with Americans urge lovers to talk to each other about what they are experiencing (with the emphasis on improving proficiency and efficacy, more than on the sharing of experience). Putting the sexual experience into words is often experienced as an interruption, a trivialization, a rude translation, and many persons resist this demand. de Beauvoir (1952, pp. 371–373) suggests why this might be particularly true of women.

[30]In the light of these considerations, Masters and Johnson's conclusion (1966, p. 134) that the "age-old practice" of faking orgasm is now futile seems premature. I do not believe that we can assume, as they seem to do, that the physiological signs of orgasm are (a) evident to both partners and (b) unambiguously labeled and interpreted. Indeed, a widely-read handbook (Reuben, 1969) is in error on just these points and has presumably taught many readers misinformation on female orgasm.

They stress the necessity of studying the whole person and her total involvement in the phenomenon; however, like many other scientists, they started their research efforts with the easiest phenomenon—that most amenable to measurement. They intend their data to provide a baseline but make no claim to have made a complete study of female orgasm. The study of the psychological events remains to be done.

CLITORAL "VERSUS" VAGINAL ORGASM

Masters and Johnson (1966) systematically studied the conditions of sexual arousal and release in women. They concluded that orgasm is triggered through stimulation of the clitoris. Although this may be brought about by a variety of techniques, one implication is clear: in the absence of adequate stimulation of the clitoris, orgasm will not occur. For many women, vaginal penetration by itself stimulates the clitoris only tangentially or, in many cases, not at all. Current research findings on female sexual functioning thus provide a new context for the ideological conflict between clitoral and vaginal orgasm and decisively challenge the Freudian theory that was dominant for so long.

Freud's developmental theory held that females renounce the "immature" behavior of clitoral stimulation (and orgasms resulting therefrom) in favor of orgasm through vaginal penetration. "True femininity," in Freudian doctrine, required and was evidenced by ability to experience vaginal orgasm and only vaginal orgasm. This ideology was reinforced by social sanctions—delivered, over the generations of Freudian hegemony, by husbands and physicians as well as by psychoanalysts—that both forced women toward "true feminine" vaginal orgasms and away from "immature, masculine" clitoral ones. However, many women must have discovered, as Kinsey did, that clitoral stimulation produces orgasm faster and more reliably than intercourse.[31]

---

[31]Kinsey observed that masturbation can reliably and quickly produce orgasm in women (in less than four minutes, for most). Hence it may be the most effective means to this end (1953, p. 339).

For many of the women who were aware of confusions and contradictions in their sexual experience, therapy was sought as a source of clarification. Freudian therapists resolved the conflicts by discounting the woman's personal experience, reasserting the primacy of vaginal sexuality and instilling a terror of inadequacy if the woman "couldn't" experience vaginal orgasm. Very often a "masculinity complex" was seen as the culprit, and women were warned away from autonomy and achievement and herded back toward their vocation as wives and, especially, mothers. Thus vaginal orgasm represents a classic instance of mystification. Freud's theory of female sexuality was much more a theory of sex roles—or rather, was itself a particular sex role script—than of sexuality. In Freud's writings the two are hopelessly confounded.

The feminist position emphasizing the clitoris as the site of sexual climax is a reaction against the Freudian insistence on the vaginal orgasm. Current evidence on female orgasm makes it apparent why women are less than keen about a doctrine that limits their sexual expression to the vagaries of penetration. Women were being robbed of a basic bodily pleasure, while at the same time being nailed by the pejorative label, "frigid." This is, of course, another instance of blaming the victim.

When reliable, carefully done research does not confirm a theory such as that of the vaginal orgasm, the ideological element in its persistence is made clear. The feminist critique of the idea of the vaginal orgasm focuses on the patriarchal ideology it embodies and the male self-interest it serves. Koedt (n.d.) makes an excellent analysis of the stake men have in perpetuating the dominant ideology of insistence on vaginal orgasm. First, in terms of their sexual satisfaction, the preferred stimulation reliably leading to orgasm is provided by the friction of the vagina. Second, the nonmutuality and inequality of relations between women and men outside the sexual realm is maintained in a situation where men have orgasm and women don't. Third, there is the symbolic investment men have in the penis: it is an appropriate expression of dominance in the sexual situation. There is more than a little phallic narcissism in the male insistence on vaginal orgasm. It insists that women's experience of sexual pleasure mirror the personal and cultural preoccupation of men with the phallus. In addition, there is the power element: the insistence on vaginal orgasm boils down to the demand that women experience (or admit to or fake) orgasm only through the agency of a man. This reinforces the doctrine of women's erotic dependence and heterosexist politics.

Phallic narcissism and male sexual dominance are both threatened by recognizing the clitoris as an analogous organ. The surgical mutilation of women's external genitalia practiced in some societies and the benign neglect practiced in ours would thus have equivalent functions in denying or neutralizing this threat. An interpretation offered for clitoridectomy is to ensure the chastity of women by denying them the inducement to infidelity provided by sexual pleasure. This latter argument is tied into Koedt's fourth point: the fear of the male that he might be sexually expendable. This is the aspect of the feminist celebration of the clitoral orgasm that appears to infuriate the public most. The threat of lesbianism is seen in the same light. This leads to Koedt's final point: the necessity of controlling women's sexuality if the heterosexual institution is to be maintained. Not only lesbianism—the satisfaction of women by each other—but any sexual liberation of women weakens the erotic dependence on man and the willingness to be subsumed by institutions controlled by man. These include, of course, not only marriage and ("legitimate") motherhood, but the economy, the professions and so forth. The fear of widening women's options is always that, given a choice, women will choose something other than the traditional option. This argument is not limited to sexual relations, for Koedt points out that part of the "threat" of lesbianism is the possibility that it involves the nearly irresistible offer of a full egalitarian, human relationship or, in the terms we have been using, the retention of Subjectivity.

The debate over clitoral "versus" vaginal orgasm provides a microcosm of the struggle between women's right to Subjectivity and women's role of Objectivity. The Freudian (and crypto-Freudian) theories of female sexuality contain a theory of feminine personality that denies female Subjectivity in many ways. The counterargument is emphatic, heightened, even hyperbolic. The continuing expansion of factual information about the phenomenon of female orgasm is sometimes overlooked by both camps.[32]

The ideological argument is, however, fundamental. The body constitutes a basic level of experience, a primary image of self and of capability. To permit control of the body, to permit mystification of body parts, functions and experiences is to establish alienation in the very core of identity. Conversely, the body offers a subterranean route to subjectivity for women, even in a society in which most outward forms of power are controlled by men. Consequently the objectification of women's bodies is a pivotal form of social control. Subjectivity can spring from physical strength and skill; hence females, from the earliest years, are not encouraged to acquire athletic skills or to train for occupations involving physical skills. Subjectivity is affirmed in behaviors of assertion, the demonstration of competence, competition. Hence women learn the taboo against competing with men; they learn an exquisitely subtle web of limitations on aspiration and are introduced to the cultural set of consolation prizes. Women can experience initiative, volition and power in sexual experience, hence are forbidden to touch themselves or other women, and are taught by men when and how to have sex, when to conceive, when and how to give birth—in short, when and how to be sexual.[33]

---

[32]Beyond the physiological level, it is likely that there is no such thing as "the" female orgasm. Individuals differ in how they experience orgasm (see Hite, 1974, for first-person descriptions of orgasm), and most individuals can describe differing experiences within their own sexual histories. Many individuals report different sensations corresponding to clitoral stimulation as contrasted with the friction of the penis in the vagina.

Male respondents in a recent study (Pietropinto, 1977) reported that orgasms differ across occasions for them as well. Their reports make it clear that among men, as among women, individuals experience and/or report orgasms in different ways. Vance and Wagner (1976) found that expert judges were unable to discriminate males' and females' written descriptions of their own orgasms, suggesting that at the subjective level the experience is similar.

[33]Through education, experience and introspection, awareness and control can be added

Myopia in the Sex Research Literature

This chapter has emphasized how power relations between the sexes operate to define female sexuality and restrict it. Even the professional research literature incorporates the influence of the power framework by the choice of variables and relationships on which it focuses. Thus for example, the focus upon heterosexual relations and on coitus gives one picture of female sexuality. However, it is by no means a complete one. Rather, it reflects an accommodation to the realities of sexual politics in America. Only sex with men "counts"; any other experience is edited from the sexual history.

The image of the coitally inexperienced woman as a virtual tabula rasa may in part be camouflage. Current research (e.g., Schaefer, 1973) indicates that many women can recall childhood masturbation and other forms of sexual experimentation. However, the politics of heterosexuality are such that this autonomous or preheterosexual history becomes lost or suppressed as the woman takes on the identity of sexual partner—or sexual property. Thus in the most recent research (Hite, 1976; Schaefer, 1973) women express guilt, or a sense of impropriety, in masturbating as adults. The impropriety consists in autonomous self-pleasuring, or the expression of sexual agency. For some women, guilt is moderated if they masturbate with their partner's permission (Hite, 1976, pp. 213–218). As with masturbation, so with homosexual experience: this becomes part of the "lost data" of sexual history. Ordinarily its part in sexual self-definition or sexual identity is minor, since lesbian is not an approved sexual status. The approved sexual status for adult females corresponds to the dom-

---

to the initial bodily experience (e.g., through natural childbirth or alpha-wave conditioning). This can foster competence and heighten enjoyment.

inant sexual script: heterosexual/monogamous/married/permanently.[34]

The vaginal/clitoral conflict illustrates the myopic underestimation of women's sexuality that characterizes not only the popular wisdom but research in human sexuality as well. A "phallocentric" worldview is perhaps responsible for the disproportionate emphasis on coitus in sex research. Coitus remains the focus of research on premarital sexual behavior.

Yet, current research, centered on female sexuality, reveals that women enjoy a polymorphous sexuality that is different from the goal-oriented male focus on intromission and penetration. Although research indicates that detailed sexual codes exist specifying the actors and circumstances appropriate for kissing, necking, light petting and heavy petting, this sequence is overlooked, as though intercourse occurs in a social vacuum. The emphasis on intercourse as the "main event" reveals a perspective that is both traditional and masculine, as I have indicated elsewhere (Laws and Schwartz, 1977, Chapter 4). The monistic emphasis on coitus has, similarly, caused sex researchers to overlook evidence that patterns of sexual behavior in women vary by the type of act. Schofield found that his female respondents, in contrast to the male, reported more experience in noncoital forms of sexual contact and expressed a preference for these. Davis found that some college women applied different sexual standards to petting behavior and to coitus. Petting was limited neither to a single partner (i.e., was not protomonogamous) nor was restricted to relationships with affection. Thus, 28 percent of Davis's female sample had petted with three or more partners, and 55 percent admitted to engaging in heavy petting with one or more partners whom they did not love. One interpretation of this finding is that the realm of the sexual behavior is becoming differentiated for women. Although coitus continues to be perceived as linked to marriage, other forms of sexual experience may come to be more indepen-

---

[34]For an extended discussion of pluralism in sexual scripts and sexual communities, see Laws and Schwartz (1977, Chapter 1).

dent of this framework. In the light of women's preferences for noncoital forms of sexual relating, this may be a significant finding.

Another indication of potential change arises from current contraceptive technology in conjunction with demographic trends. With reliable contraception accessible and prevalent, sexual involvement may have become less consequential for women. As more women have a greater degree of sexual experience for a longer period before marriage, there is the potential for developing a sexual identity that is not overshadowed by a partner or by orientation toward marriage. Sexuality may come to be experienced as an attribute of the personality rather than of a relationship.

There are thus a number of indications—for the most part underestimated in the professional literature—that women's sexuality and women's experience of their sexuality are at variance with the prevalent scripts. At present, however, there is no sexual script in which a woman's status or sexual value is enhanced by her experience. Women's sexual potency is represented only in terms of attracting men or of licensed fertility. What this means is that it is difficult for a woman to develop a sexual identity that encompasses sexual agency, sexual passion and a positive experience of bodily and cultural femaleness. The elements of such an identity can be formed in the individual's sexual history but she must own it rather than being owned. The learning that takes place during a sequence of intimate relationships is in large part learning about the self. To utilize the learning, reflection is required. A necessary component of the development of sexual identity is the recognition that the center and the continuity in experience is the self, rather than a relationship or another person. As new aspects of the sexual self are discovered and defined, they are added to the accumulated self-image as a sexual person (or sexual identity). The sexual self can more easily come into focus in the context of the recognition of the woman as subject in her own life history, sexual and other. In this context, the option of celibacy takes on a dual meaning. On the one hand, it signals a woman's refusal to allow herself to be used as an object by another.

In parallel fashion, it often has the purpose of permitting the individual to reclaim her personal space, time and energy. Thus it is an occasion for "centering," for getting grounded, which may be of increasing significance in the context of women's longer and more varied sexual histories.

Nevertheless, sexual scripts now in force assign the role of Object to women and Subject to men; thus it is unfeminine to exhibit Subjectivity. Yet neither the dichotomy between Subject and Object nor the association of females with Objectivity originates with courtship and the beginning of the sexual career. Processes of sex-typing begin much earlier. However, they are not innate. As we have seen, we are schooled even in sex and even the most personal is politicized. As we have seen, enacting the Object role is not "doing what comes naturally." It takes effort and shrewdness. But self-presentation and self-enhancement as an Object are not all that is involved.

An essential element in Objectivity is what de Beauvoir calls "alterity," or Otherness. The essence of this idea is that the Subject invests the Other with qualities that he does not attribute to himself. These may be valued (as in the literature de Beauvoir cites, where different versions of the Love Object, or "ideal woman" are developed) or disvalued (as in certain psychological monster theories). Both aspects appear in female figures depicted in myths. The fact of the male's controlling the definition and the female's acceptance of it seem to be at the core of de Beauvoir's idea of "the inessential."

Because de Beauvoir is focusing on images of the ideal woman, we do not see in her discussion instances of the Other depicted as alien and threatening. Rather, she offers examples of the "Privileged Other, through whom the subject fulfills himself: one of the measures of man, *his* counterbalance, *his* salvation, *his* adventure, *his* happiness" (1953, p. 233, italics mine).[35] The fun-

---

[35]Simone de Beauvoir notes, however, that if a woman declines the niche of Privileged Other, the alien images are invoked: she becomes a praying mantis, an ogress (1953, p. 233)—or a dyke.

damentally narcissistic nature of this projection is noted by de Beauvoir, in observing that the context of the ideal depends on what a particular writer needs to project. What the diverse formulations of the ideal have in common is that they are *defined by* the (male) Subject: "For each of them the ideal woman will be she who incarnates most exactly the other capable of revealing him to himself" (p. 236, italics mine).

It should be noted that such formulations are not merely the harmless fantasies of artists and dreamers; de Beauvoir asserts emphatically that any woman must accept the role of Other if she is to be considered a "true woman." Moreover, de Beauvoir holds that every girl-child has experienced Subjectivity, so that embracing Objectivity involves a conflict and a process of struggle. It is in this sense that de Beauvoir observes, "One is not born, but rather becomes a woman." (1953, p. 249). In this context de Beauvoir talks about one's "vocation as a female." The choice of words conveys an adventitious rather than an essential attribute— a choice rather than predestination. What de Beauvoir refers to as the "true woman" is an artificial creation, purposely created— as eunuchs were, at one time in history. Her choice of analogy conveys the pain, mutilation and alienation that cutting the female person off from her Subjectivity entails.[36] For de Beauvoir, capitulation to Objectivity is inevitable. The crisis comes with sexual initiation, when the young woman renounces Subjectivity and takes up the yoke of sexual bondage. de Beauvoir is not critical of the concept of woman's erotic dependence on man; hence, for her, to be sexual at all is to be implicated in the politics of heterosexuality. de Beauvoir's formulation does not encompass the concept of sexual agency.

Simone de Beauvoir's insight concerning the Subjectivity in the child's life history is borne out in the research on child development. Processes by which the androgynous child is transformed into the feminine woman are the focus of the next chapter.

---

[36]Reading the literature on female socialization reminds one of the familiar image of Cinderella's stepsisters industriously lopping off their toes and heels so as to fit into the

REFERENCES

Angrist, Shirley. 1966. Communication about birth control: an exploratory study of freshman girls' information and attitudes. *Journal of Marriage and the Family*, pp. 284–286.

———. 1969. The study of sex roles. *Journal of Social Issues*, 25: 215–232.

Bach, George R., and Deutsch, Ronald M. 1970. *Pairing*. New York: Avon Books.

Bart, Pauline. 1967. Depression in middle aged women: some sociocultural factors. Ph.D. Dissertation. UCLA.

———. 1970. Mother Portnoy's complaints. *Trans-Action*, pp. 69–74.

———. 1971. The myth of a value-free psychotherapy. In *The Study of the Future: Explorations in the Sociology of Knowledge*, ed. Wendell Bell and James Mau. New York: Russell Sage Foundation.

Berelson, Bernard. 1952. *Content Analysis in Communication Research*. New York: American Book-Stratford Press.

Berry, Mary. 1978. Constitutional aspects of the right to limit childbearing. Washington, DC: U.S. Commission on Civil Rights.

Bettelheim, Bruno. 1955. *Symbolic Wounds*. London: Thames and Hudson.

Blau, Peter. 1964. *Exchange and Power in Social Life*. New York: Wiley.

Bumpass, L., and Westoff, C. F. 1970. The 'perfect contraceptive' population. *Science* 169: 1177–1182.

Chesler, Phyllis. 1970. Psychotherapy and women. Paper presented at American Psychological Association.

———. 1972. *Woman and Madness*. Garden City: Doubleday.

Christensen, H. T., and Carpenter, G. R. 1962. Value-behavior discrepancies regarding premarital coitus. *American Sociological Review* 27: 66–74.

Cisler, Lucinda. 1970. Unfinished business: birth control and women's liberation. In *Sisterhood Is Powerful*, ed. R. Morgan, pp. 245–289. New York: Vintage Books.

Clark, LeMon. 1970. Is there a difference between a clitoral and a vaginal orgasm? *Journal of Sex Research* 6(1): 25–28.

Cobliner, W. 1965. Some maternal attitudes toward conception. *Mental Hygiene* 49: 550–557.

Cooke, Willard R. 1943. *Essentials of Gynecology*. Philadelphia: Lippencott.

Davis, Keith. 1971. Sex on the campus: Is there a revolution? *Medical Aspects of Human Sexuality* 5, 1:128–142.

---

glass slipper (key to the somewhat enigmatic heart of the Prince)—when of course it was never intended for them anyway. As Cinderella and the Prince fade into the Happily Ever After, our attention is diverted from the leftover and mangled stepsisters. However, I think of them a lot.

de Beauvoir, Simone. 1953. *The Second Sex*. New York: Alfred A. Knopf.

Ehrmann, Winston. 1957. Some knowns and unknowns in research into sexual behavior. *Marriage and Family Living* 19: 16–24.

———. 1959. *Premarital Dating Behavior*. New York: Holt.

———. 1971. Premarital sexual behavior and sex codes of conduct with acquaintances, friends and lovers. In *Human Sexual Behavior*, ed. Bernhardt Lieberman, pp. 191–199. New York: Wiley.

Ellis, Albert. 1949. A study of human love relationships. *Journal of Genetic Psychology* 75: 61–71.

Festinger, Leon. 1954. A theory of social comparison processes. *Human Relations* 7: 117–139.

Forssman, H., and Thuwe, I. 1966. One hundred and twenty children born after application for therapeutic abortion refused. *Acta Psychiatrica Scandanavia* 42: 71–88.

Freedman, M. B. 1965. The sexual behavior of American college women. *Merrill Palmer Quarterly* 11: 33–48.

Freud, Sigmund. 1914. On narcissism: An introduction. In Philip Reiff, ed. *Collected Papers of Sigmund Freud*. Vol. IV, pp. 56–83. New York: Collier Books, 1963.

———. 1918. The taboo of virginity. *Sexuality and the Psychology of Love*, ed. P. Reiff. *The Collected Papers of Sigmund Freud*. pp. 70–86. New York: Collier Books, 1963.

———. 1931. Female Sexuality. In Philip Reiff, ed. *Collected Papers of Sigmund Freud*. pp. 194–211. New York: Collier Books, 1963.

———. 1925. Some psychical consequences of the anatomical distinction between the sexes. *Int. J. Psa.* 8: 133–142.

Fromm, E. 1956. *The Art of Loving*. New York: Harper.

Gagnon, John H., Simon, William, and Berger, Alan J. 1970. Some aspects of sexual adjustment in early and later adolescence. *The Psychopathology of Adolescence*. New York: Grune and Stratton.

Gaskin, Ina May. 1978. *Spiritual Midwifery*. Summertown, TN: The Book Publishing Co.

Gebhard, P. H., Pomeroy, W. B., Martin, C. E. et al. 1958. *Pregnancy, Birth and Abortion*. New York: Harper and Row.

Gilmartin, Brian G. 1964. Relationship of traits measured by the California personality inventory to premarital sexual standards and behaviors. Masters thesis. University of Utah.

Goode, W. J. 1959. The theoretical importance of love. *American Sociological Review* 24(1): 38–47.

Goode, William J. 1960. Illegitimacy in the Caribbean social structure. *American Sociology Review* 25: 21–30.

Gornick, Vivian, and Moran, Barbara K. (eds.). 1971. *Woman in Sexist Society*. New York: Basic Books.

Gough, H. G. 1957. *The Psychological Inventory Manual*. Palo Alto: Consulting Psychologists Press.

Grinder, R. and Schmitt, S. 1966. Coeds and contraceptive information. *Journal of Marriage and the Family* 28: 471–479.

Hacker, Helen. 1951. Women as a minority group. *Social Forces* 30: 60–69.

Halleck, Seymour. 1973. Sex and mental health on the campus. In *Sexual Development and Behavior*, ed. A. M. Juhasz, pp. 250–264. Homewood, IL: The Dorsey Press.

Hays, H. R. 1964. *The Dangerous Sex: The Myth of Feminine Evil*. New York: Putnam.

Hite, Shere. 1974. *Sexual Honesty by Women for Women*. New York: Warner Paperback Library.

———. 1976. *The Hite Report*. New York: MacMillan.

Holter, Harriet. 1970. *Sex Roles and Social Structure*. Oslo: Universitetstorlaget.

Höok, K. 1963. Refused abortion. *Acta Psychiatrica Scandanavia* (Suppl. 168) 39: 1–152.

Horney, Karen. 1950. *Neurosis and Human Growth*. New York: W. W. Norton and Company.

———. 1967. *Feminine Psychology*. New York: W. W. Norton and Company.

House, Aline. 1973. What contraceptive type are you? *Ms.* 2, 1: 7–14.

Insko, C., Blake, R., Cialdini, R., and Mulaik, S. 1970. Attitude toward birth control and cognitive consistency: theoretical and practical implications of survey data. *J.P.S.P* 16(2): 228–237.

Kaats, Gilbert, and Davis, Keith. 1970. The dynamics of sexual behavior of college students. *Journal of Marriage and the Family* 32(3): 390–399.

Kanin, Eugene, Davidson, Karen, and Scheck, Sonia. 1970. A research note on male–female differentials in the experience of heterosexual love. *Journal of Sex Research* 6(1): 64–72.

Kelman, H. C. 1961. Processes of opinion change. *Public Opinion Quarterly* 25: 57–78.

Kephart, W. 1967. Some correlates of romantic love. *Journal of Marriage and the Family* 29: 470–474.

Kinsey, Alfred, C., Pomeroy, W. B., and Martin, C.E. 1948. *Sexual Behavior in the Human Male*. Philadelphia: Saunders.

Kinsey, Alfred C., Pomeroy, W. B., Martin, C. E., and Gebhard, P. H. 1953. *Sexual Behavior in the Human Female*. Philadelphia: Saunders.

Kirkendall, Lester, A. 1961. *Premarital Intercourse and Interpersonal Relationships*. New York: Gramercy Publishing Company.

Komarovsky, Mirra. 1946. Cultural contradictions and sex roles. *American Journal of Sociology* 52: 184–189.

Koedt, Anne. n.d. The myth of the vaginal orgasm. New England Free Press, 191 Tremont Street, Boston, MA 02118.

Kretzschmar, R.M., and Norris, A.S.1967. Psychiatric implications of therapeutic abortion. *American Journal of Obstetrics and Gynecology* 198: 368–373.

Lader, Lawrence. 1973. *Abortion II*. Boston: Beacon Press.

Laing, R. D., and Esterson, A. 1964. *Sanity, Madness and the Family*. New York: Basic Books.

Lamaze, Fernand. 1970. *Painless Childbirth*. Chicago: Henry Regnery Co.

Laws, Judith Long. 1970. Toward a model of female sexual identity. *Midway* 11, 1: 39–75.

———. 1971. Social pressures and self-identity as determinants of female fertility behavior. Paper presented at American Psychological Association.

—— and Schwartz, Pepper. 1977. *Sexual Scripts: The Social Construction of Female Sexuality*. Hinsdale, IL: Dryden Press.

Lee, Nancy Howells. 1969. *In Search of an Abortionist*. Chicago: University of Chicago Press.

Maslow, Abraham. 1942. Self-esteem (dominance-feeling) and sexuality in women. *Journal of Social Psychology* 16: 259–294.

Masters, R., and Johnson, V. 1966. *Human Sexual Response*. Boston: Little, Brown and Company.

Morgan, Robin (ed.). 1970. *Sisterhood Is Powerful*. New York: Vintage Books.

Moss, Zoe. 1970. It hurts to be alive and obsolete. In *Sisterhood Is Powerful*, ed. R. Morgan, pp. 170–175. New York: Vintage Books.

Neal, A. G., and Groat, H. T. 1970. Alienation correlates of Catholic fertility. *American Journal of Sociology* 76(3): 460–473.

Newton, Niles. 1955. *Maternal Emotions: A Study of Women's Feelings Toward Menstruation, Pregnancy, Childbirth, Breast Feeding, Infant Care, and Other Aspects of Their Femininity*. New York: Paul B. Hoche.

Niswander, K. R., and Patterson, R. J. 1967. Psychologic reaction to therapeutic abortion. *American Journal of Obstetrics and Gynecology*. 29: 702–706.

Novak, E. R., Jones, G. S., and Jones, H. 1970. *Novak's Textbook of Gynecology*. Baltimore: Williams and Wilkens.

O'Hare, H. 1951. Vaginal versus clitoral orgasm. *International Journal of Sexology* 4: 243–244.

Osofsky, J. D., and Osofsky, H. J. 1971. The psychological reactions of patients to legalized abortion. Paper presented at the meetings of the American Orthopsychiatry Association, 1971.

Peck, A., and Marcus, H. 1966. Psychiatric sequelae of therapeutic interruption of pregnancy. *Journal of Nervous and Mental Disorders* 143: 417–425.

Peretti, Peter. 1969. Premarital sexual behavior between females and males of two middle-sized mid-western cities. *Journal of Sex Research* 5(3): 218–225.

Pietropinto, Anthony, and Simenauer, Jacqueline. 1977. *Beyond the Male Myth*. New York: Times Books.

Pilpel, Harriet F., and Wechsler, Nancy F. 1971. Birth control, teenagers and the law: A new look, 1971. *Family Planning Perspectives* 3(3): 37–45.

Pohlman, E. 1967. A psychologist's introduction to the birth planning literature. *Journal of Social Issues*, 13(4): 13–28.

——. 1968. Changes from rejection to acceptance of pregnancy. *Social Science and Medicine* 2: 337–340.

——. 1969. Premarital contraception: research reports and problems. *Journal of Sex Research* 5(3): 187–194.

Pope, Hallowell. 1967. Unwed mothers and their sex partners. *Journal of Marriage and the Family* 29: 555–567.

Rado, S. 1933. Fear of castration in women. *Psychoanalytic Quarterly*, III–IV.

Rainwater, Lee, Coleman, R. P., and Handel, G. 1959. *Workingman's Wife*. New York: Macfadden.

Reage, Pauline. 1965. *The story of O*. New York: Grove Press.

237

Reiss, Ira. 1960. *Premarital Sexual Standards in America*. Glencoe, IL: Free Press.

———. 1967. *The Social Context of Premarital Sexual Permissiveness*. New York: Holt, Rinehart and Winston.

Rheingold, Joseph. 1964. *The Fear of Being a Woman: A Theory of Maternal Destructiveness*. New York: Grune and Stratton.

Reuben, David. 1969. *Everything You Always Wanted to Know About Sex*. New York: David McKay Co.

Rubin, Lillian. 1976. *Worlds of Pain*. New York: Basic Books.

Rubin, Zick. 1970. Measurement of romantic love. *J.P.S.P.* 16: 265–273.

———. 1973. *Liking and Loving*. New York: Holt, Rinehart and Winston.

Sartre, Jean Paul. 1966. *Being and Nothingness*. New York: Washington Square Press.

Schaefer, Leah. 1973. *Women and Sex*. New York: Pantheon.

Schank, R. L. A. 1932. A study of a community and its groups and institutions conceived as the behavior of individuals. *Psychology Monographs* 43(2) (whole #195).

Schofield, Michael. 1965. *The Sexual Behavior of Young People*. London: Longman, Green and Company.

Schwartz, Pepper. 1973. Female sexuality and monogamy. In *Renovating Marriage: Toward New Sexual Life Styles*, ed. R. W. Libby and R. Whitehurst. San Ramon, California: Consensus Publishers.

Scott, C. Russell. 1968. *The World of a Gynecologist*. London: Oliver and Boyd.

Scully, Diana, and Bart, Pauline. 1973. "A funny thing happened on the way to the orifice: Women in gynecology textbooks. *American Journal of Sociology*, 78(4): 1045–1050.

Seaman, Barbara. 1972. *Free and Female: The Sex Life of the Contemporary Woman*. New York: Coward, McCann and Goeghegan.

Secord, Paul, and Jourard, Sidney. The appraisal of body cathexis: Body cathexis and the self. *J. Consulting Psychology* 17: 343–347.

Sherfey, Mary Jane. 1972. *The Nature and Evolution of Female Sexuality*. New York: Vintage Books.

Simon, William, Berger, Alan, and Gagnon, John. 1972. Beyond anxiety and fantasy: The coital experiences of college youth. *Journal of Youth and Adolescence* 1, 3: 203–223.

Simon, W., and Gagnon, J. 1968. Youth cultures and aspects of the socialization process. Unpublished.

Singer, Jerome. 1966. Social comparison: progress and issues. *J.E.S.P* (Supplement 1), pp. 103–110.

Slater, P. E. 1963. On social regression. American Sociological Review. 28(3): 339–364.

Smith, J. R., and Smith, L. G. 1970. Co-marital sex and the sexual freedom movement. *Journal of Sex Research* 6(2): 131–142.

———. 1971. Co-marital sex: the incorporation of extramarital sex into the marriage relationship. Paper presented at annual meeting, American Psychological Association, New York.

238

Stewart, Phyllis. 1971. Female promiscuity: A factor in providing abortion service. Paper presented at American Sociological Association.

Stratton, John R., and Spitzer, Stephan P. 1967. Sexual permissiveness and self-evaluation: A question of substance and a question of method. *Journal of Marriage and the Family* 129: 434–441.

Tangri, Sandra. 1976. A Feminist Perspective on Some Ethical Issues in Population Programs. *Signs: Journal of Women in Culture and Society* I(4): 895–904.

Tietze, C., and Lewit, S. "Legal abortions: early medical complications." *Family Planning Perspective* 3(4): 6–15.

Udry, J. R., and Morris, H. M. 1968. Distribution of coitus in the menstrual cycle. *Nature* 220: 593–596.

Vance, Ellen Belle, and Wagner, Nathaniel N. 1976. Written descriptions of orgasm: A study of sex differences. *Archives of Sexual Behavior* 5(1): 87–99.

Vincent, Clark E. 1961. *Unmarried Mothers*. New York: The Free Press.

Wachtel, Dawn Day. 1972. Options of the single pregnant woman. Paper presented at the meetings of the Southern Sociological Association.

Waller, Willard. 1937. The rating and dating complex. *American Sociological Review* 2(5): 727–734.

Whitington, H. G. 1970. Evaluation of therapeutic abortion as an element of preventive psychiatry. *American Journal of Psychiatry*, 126(9): 1224–1229.

Willson, James R. 1971. *Obstetrics and Gynecology*. Second Edition. St. Louis: C. V. Mosby.

Willson, J. R., Beecham, C. T., and Carrington, E. R. 1963. *Obstetrics and Gynecology*, St. Louis: C. V. Mosby Company.

Winch, Robert F. 1970. Performance and change in the history of the American family and some speculations as to its future. *Journal of Marriage and the Family* 32(1): 6–16.

WOMAN

as

Girl-Child

Socialization

In the first two chapters of this book we examined the roles defined for women in two major institutional contexts of our society: employment and the family. We found that courtship, too, is institutionalized, with a defined role for women. In analyzing these roles, we could identify the functions assigned to women and some mechanisms for rewarding conformity and punishing deviance. Yet there is more to it than that. No individual enters into these institutional contexts totally unprepared for her role. Even if she has never enacted the role herself, it is not new for her. She is not like the proverbial person from Mars, for the situation she confronts is intelligible to her. It is governed by many of the cultural assumptions and practices with which she is familiar; she knows the signposts, even if she does not know the terrain. Sex role scripts are, as we have noted, age-graded. Transitions from one stage or status to the next are themselves scripted. The content of these scripts is learned very early in life, as we shall see.

Socialization is a process involving interaction between "old hands" and new recruits. The old hands are representatives of society (or subgroupings within a society), whether they are officially so designated or not.

Socialization is the process by which human beings are shaped for participation in human society. This involves both a cognitive process of learning and a motivational process of adopting values. The individual acquires a repertoire of skills, knowledge and meanings that are held in common with other members of the culture (or subculture). She also learns to value some things and to hate others; to approach or seek certain states and avoid others. She learns to think of herself in certain ways and to be responsive to the approval and disapproval of others. She learns to value fitting in, knowing how to behave and being accepted.

This conditioning of the individual's motivation (sometimes called internalization) is responsible for the collusion between the socialized person and those whose role expectations she meets. For socialization is not, as some writers have suggested, a one-way process of influence and coercion.

The conformity to role expectations that we observe is not attributable solely to sanctions and surveillance practiced by others. Rather, the individual is motivated to take direction from others and to fit into existing structures. This role readiness is the result of socialization, which begins in infancy but continues throughout the lifecycle. Each new demand in socialization builds upon the previously created motivation to think well of oneself, to be accepted, and to be self-consistent.

Though the individual is engaged in a process of learning about the environment from birth, not all learning qualifies as socialization. The kind of learning we call socialization is directed at preparing the individual to fit into society that is already structured and to function effectively in a designated context. *Socialization thus has direction, has a destination.* It is not random learning, and not all learning is rewarded by the agents of socialization. Rather, behavior is shaped toward already established patterns.

A representative definition is the following: socialization may be said to include "those kinds of social learning that lead the individual to acquire the personal and group loyalties, the knowledge, skills, feelings and desires that are regarded as appropriate to a person of his age, sex and particular social status, especially as these have relevance for adult role performance" (Clausen, 1968, p. 7). Brief as it is, this definition draws attention to several aspects of socialization that are distinct and important. It emphasizes the destination, in this case adequate enactment of the appropriate sex role. The individual is pushed or pulled along the path by agents of socialization. Studying sex role socialization requires us to focus attention on the content of the sex role, the agents of socialization and the means by which behavior is shaped toward the intended outcome. In looking at the social terrain of the girl-child in this chapter, we will be able to identify the specific agents of socialization who contribute role pressures, role expectations and sanctions in the development of ideas about the female sex role.

The manipulation of rewards and punishments and of alternatives provided are the means by which primary socialization of infants and very young children is accomplished. The major sanctions manipulated in socialization are those involved in any attempt to persuade or control: social approval or disapproval, and control over outcomes affecting the person to be socialized. By these means children learn to use toilets, table silver and other amenities of culture. They also learn games and manners; they learn to read, to keep secrets and to dress themselves. They learn language and a number of other symbol systems. The assumption is usually made that this learning, which takes place initially in a context of imitation, direct tuition and monitoring of performance and reward, becomes autonomous in time. All subsequent socialization is assumed to build upon primary socialization.

Another aspect of socialization focuses upon the new recruit, and the changes produced by socialization. Products of socialization included learned motives (like the achievement motive), learned cognitions and the larger psychological structure within which these are embedded, which is called personal identity or self-identity. Initially, the sense of self emerges as the individual learns social labels or categories and applies them to the self. One of the earliest and most potent categories is that of gender. Gender identity, or the fundamental sense of oneself as female or male, appears to crystallize at about the age of two and a half, and is considered to be irreversible (Stoller, 1968). Sex role socialization builds upon this basis in personal identity.

The culture provides the individual with ways of making sense of her experience; it furnishes a net which she casts over experience (Hochschild, 1975), and which filters that experience. However, culture does not entirely define or determine the emerging personality. Rather, there is a dialectical relationship between personal reality and social scripts.[1] Identity develops as the individual enacts differing roles across occasions and situations, yet recognizes the continuity of herself. Self-consistency becomes a value, for the self is valued. Thus the individual's identity becomes a standard against which she evaluates options. The self takes an active part in experience and is at least potentially a counterforce to social pressures continuing throughout the lifecycle. The potential active self is of great importance for sex role transcendance. Self expectations and self approval may accord with sex role scripts or may diverge.

Socialization continues over the lifecycle. While primary socialization fits the child to live in human society, later socialization fits the individual for specific roles. The means employed in adult socialization are by and large the same: direct tuition, modeling, the presentation and restriction of information, rewards and sanctions. Some amount of unlearning and relearning is part of normal movement through the lifecycle, as the individual moves from one age-graded status to another. Normally, different role partners and publics become important at different stages: when the young child leaves the nuclear family and moves into the peer culture of school or preschool, she encounters both nonrelative children and nonrelative adults. Marriage, similarly, makes other individuals important: in-laws, providers of various services and

---

[1]For a detailed discussion of this relationship, see Laws and Schwartz (1977, Chapter 1).

the partners of one's associates. Many of these transitions are scripted, and the new socialization is continuous with what has preceded. Other sorts of resocialization are discontinuous, as when the upwardly mobile young person enters graduate school. She is departing from the usual pathway for those who have been her family and friends; yet there are designated agents of socialization in this new milieu who will teach her the role. Discontinuous resocialization can also be initiated by the individual. Women's consciousness raising and psychotherapy are two examples of volitional self-change. In both instances new concepts and new experiences are made available to the individual, and specific others support the change, but the initiative and the control remain with the individual. Sex role liberation is a radical form of self-initiated resocialization. One of the puzzles of this chapter, given the power and diffuseness of traditional sex role expectations and sanctions, is how this occurs. Transformations in identity are examined in greater detail in Chapter 5.

SOCIALIZATION FOR WHAT?

Our definition of socialization points to adult role performance as the end toward which socialization efforts are directed. One of the chief destinations for the young in our society is the attainment of appropriate womanhood and manhood, or femininity/masculinity. Femininity and masculinity are not simple emergents; they do not develop naturally from gender. Being born female does not guarantee the desired outcome; a girl-child must be brought up to be feminine. The same holds for boys; manhood must be achieved, and the achievement judged by others.

Simone de Beauvoir has remarked that the "real woman" is created, for society's purposes, much as eunuchs used to be. She is an unnatural animal, different from plain old regular women. Sex role socialization is the instrumentality invented for the specific purpose of creating femininity and masculinity. In this chapter we will look at the means used to create femininity and masculinity, and the products so created.

AGENTS OF SOCIALIZATION

Formal agents of socialization are designated to bring about a specific contribution to training. Very often these employ techniques of direct and explicit tuition, as for example in formal education. Teachers are formal agents of socialization, but so are parents. Teachers employ lesson plans, curricula, lectures, quizzes, class hours, study halls, homework, report cards. There are explicit routines of defining the content to be learned, the means to be employed in teaching, and the effectiveness or success of the learning. Parents often employ more diffuse and variable methods; their curriculum is the lesson of their own lives and those of previous generations. Much of the content of sex roles is not "taught" at all. Yet few would deny that parents consciously direct and shape their children's behavior toward desired ends, whether these are long-term or short-term goals. Few would deny that parents utilize example, exhortation, approval, material rewards and punishments to induce the child to emit the desired behavior, and parents then sanction it.

Other adults, by virtue of their authority as adults, can take a hand in socializing the young. Peers, too, shape children's behavior along sex role lines by indicating the desired direction and sanctioning behavior. Thus peers, more than adults, may sanction a boy for "sissy" or feminine activities.

Agents of socialization vary in the extent to which they are conscious of enacting this role. In addition, they may be more or less aware of the content to which they are socializing the young. In the case of sex role socialization, people may be unaware of the script and yet forcefully insist on "appropriate" behavior in girl and boy children. They themselves are unconscious of following sex role scripts. Indeed, their own socialization probably did not include any introduction to the what and why of sex roles, only the how. Socialization generally prepares people to fit into the functioning whole somewhere. Most socialized persons can teach someone else what they know, and no more. Much of sex role socialization is just this sort of thing: others are teaching the young to follow the script, without being able to label or analyze the script.

As long as social researchers can define a sex role script, and identify the persons and events that shape young people into comformity with it, we are analyzing sex role socialization.

Looking at the commonplaces of young children's lives, we can identify social pressures that shape them in the direction of established sex roles.

Sex-Typing: Toy Preferences and Beyond

Someone has said that play is children's "work." It is their central occupation in the preschool years. Through play they learn to manipulate objects and solve puzzles. They learn about games and rules. And they engage in much imaginative play: dress-up, adventures and role taking.

Both researchers and parents have become interested in the materials and toys children use in play. Parents have tended to provide children with "sex-appropriate" toys, and researchers have documented that most children know which toys they are "sposed to" play with and prefer even in the preschool years.

Rosenberg and Sutton-Smith (1968) elicited likes and dislikes about play activities from girls and boys in third through sixth grades. The authors started with a set of 180 games, pastimes and activities. Of these, they found 25 items that differentiated boys at a high level of statistical significance and the same number for girls. The remaining items did not show this pattern of exclusive preference but might be chosen by a child of either sex.

Toys, games and activities preferred by girls included dressing up, dolls, playing school, jacks, hopscotch, sewing, cartwheels and so forth. Activities preferred by boys included playing soldiers, bandits, cops and robbers, spacemen, playing with bows and arrows, toy trains, model airplanes, building forts, playing marbles and so forth.

Testing the selected scales in other samples of school children, the authors looked at the degree of overlap in children's preferences. Lack of overlap was a sign of highly developed sex-typing, for it meant that children's preferences did not include activities typical of the "opposite" sex. Rosenberg and Sutton-Smith found more overlap among the girls than the boys: the percentage of girls scoring higher than the mean for boys on the boy-game scale ranged between six percent and 15 percent. The percentage of boys scoring above the female mean on girl-games ranged between four percent and nine percent. In other words, boys showed more sex-typed behavior at this age than did girls. In terms of activity preference, girls were more androgynous than boys.

Hartley and Hardesty (1964) asked girls and boys five, eight, and 11 years old to identify whether mostly boys, mostly girls, or both engaged in a number of activities pictured. They were interested not only in the formation of sex-typed preferences but in the development of consensus about which activities were for girls and which for boys. Of their 56 items, 40 were consensually attributed to one sex or the other, and six consensually assigned to both.[2]

The degree of consensuality was higher for male sex-typed activities than for female. Activities that both girls and boys agreed were implemented mostly by girls included playing with doll carriage, dishes, sewing machine, carpet sweeper and pocketbook, jumping rope, playing jacks, taking dancing lessons and so forth. Activities consensually attributed to boys included playing with toy rifle, truck, soldiers, tool bench, jackknife and erector set, carrying wood into house, climbing trees, shoveling snow off walk, going with man to ball game and so forth. Items consensually assigned to both sexes referred mostly to play locales rather than

---

[2]This number probably underestimates the overlap, since activities on which there was lower agreement (or more spread in the respondents' experience) were dropped out of the analysis. These including playing on the sidewalk, being sent to get groceries, playing in a basement.

play activities: playing at beach, in park, in country fields, on playground, owning and taking care of a puppy.

Data from toy-preference studies reflect the operation of a cultural process that leads and limits persons in our society to different destinations, depending on their gender. They illustrate one of the major functions of sex role socialization, which is to *create* sex differences—especially differences of taste and temperament, of ambition and outlook. The early toy preferences, once established, prepare the way for a series of differences in where and how children play and what demeanors are permitted each gender. For the most part, girl-children are exposed to more physical restrictions than boys: they are expected to stay clean, not to fight, not to play in dangerous places or ways. They are not expected to develop substantial athletic or physical competence, particularly in competitive sports.

The toy-preference studies show us that there is some cultural programming of the materials children use in play and that by the time children reach mid-childhood they have mastered the script.[3] Both girls and boys can report with a high degree of consensus which toys and activities constitute their territory and which that of the other sex. As we have seen, their preferences accord with these boundaries. Moreover, breaching the boundaries is punished, and even very young children are reluctant to engage in contrasex activities. In other words, the learning of sex-typing is not merely cognitive, but has behavioral consequences. Hartup and Moore (1963) found that boys avoided an attractive but "sex-inappropriate" toy to a greater degree than girls did, especially when the experimenter was present. These children ranged from three to eight years old. DeLucia (1963) found that an experimenter of the "opposite" sex obtained toy preferences that were in closer agreement from one session to another with children ranging from kindergarten through fourth grade. Both of these

---

[3]Rabban (1950) has shown that children have mastered these distinctions by the age of five. Kohlberg and Zigler (1961) find that the child of higher intelligence "learns the game" ahead of children with lesser intelligence.

studies suggest a social sensitivity in children with respect to appropriate sex-typing and a behavioral tendency to conform to this social norm when under observation by adults. The sex difference is consistent here. In another study, boys showed more concern about hypothetical others choosing a sex-appropriate item (Ross 1971) at age three to five. Boys also showed more reluctance to play the role of a girl in a "pretend" phone conversation (Sears et al., 1965).

CONDITIONS ELICITING SEX-TYPING IN CHILDREN

In all of these studies, the presence of an adult served as a stimulus eliciting children's previously learned sex-typed behavior. This suggests not only that children perceive adults as rewarding sex-typing, but that adults are models for this behavior. The latter possibility receives support from the finding of Sears et al. in the study cited above, that observing a model of their own gender playing with a "sex-inappropriate" toy helped the children overcome their avoidance. In other words, they were able to follow a model for androgynous or non-sex-typed behavior, just as they had presumably followed a model for sex-typing.

The power of adults to elicit sex-typed behavior reflects variation by social class. Rabban (1950) found that working-class children's toy choices were more sex-typed than were middle-class children's. Girls' toy choices were less sex-typed than boys', with middle-class girls being less restricted than working-class girls. Kohn (1959) had found that working-class mothers encouraged sex-typing in their children more than did middle-class mothers. In another realm, Hartley (1964) too had found social-class differences: more middle-class girls rejected the domestic choices associated with "the" feminine role than did working-class girls.

Pope (1953) investigated some social-class-specific content dimensions of "femininity" and "masculinity." He found that teenagers, in responding to a descriptive paragraph about someone of their own gender, found the hypothetical person acceptable or unacceptable depending on their own social class. The boy with nonmasculine interests is rejected by both middle-class and working-class boys, but middle-class boys accept a studious boy, while working-class boys reject him. Among girls, the middle-class girls rejected a sexy or boy-crazy girl, while the working-class girls accepted her, and middle-class girls found a studious girl acceptable, while the working-class girls rejected her. This study suggests the importance of peers as agents of socialization. They not only communicate content and direction of desired behavior but reinforce it with acceptance or rejection. Responses in Pope's study perhaps mirror the slightly different destinations of working-class and middle-class youth. Socialization does serve the purpose of directing individuals toward their appointed destinations, and it is certainly true that higher education is part of the life plan for more middle-class young people than working-class ones.

Similarly, working-class women marry younger than middle-class women. Being boy-crazy and too effective at attracting boys would be more of a detriment to the middle-class girl, possibly distracting her attention from the appropriately eligible young men she will meet in college.

This is not to say that respondents in Pope's study are aware of the destinations of the individuals they saw described. However, the study does illustrate how socialization forces that are consistent with the overall script are perpetuated by varying agents of socialization throughout the lifecycle. The data on social class effects add further detail to our understanding of the expectations that young women and men must meet in order to qualify as acceptably feminine or masculine.

Outcomes of Early Sex Role Socialization

The principle of sex differentiation that is apparent in toy and activity preferences of young children is not confined to play. Rather, it constitutes a script for adult role behavior as anticipated by the children. At this early age, children are learning a map of the social world in which each will move. They are learning roles, not only their own but the reciprocal ones. Thus the children in Hartley's (1964) study showed evidence of learning reciprocal role expectations: boys had learned that they had dominance over their future wives, and girls had learned that they would have to take those preferences into account.

Iglitizin (1972) queried fifth graders concerning what tasks in the domestic division of labor were appropriate for wives and for husbands. Their perceptions coincided quite closely with the classic study of actual domestic division of labor by Blood and Wolfe: men were to pay bills, go out to work and weed the garden. Women were to wash, cook, scrub, dust and tend a sick child.

Interestingly, when asked to describe a future day in their adult lives, more than 83 percent of boys made no mention of home or family, while better than 25 percent of girls made this sphere their major focus.

Iglitizin found high agreement not only on sex-typing in family roles but in occupational roles as well. The fifth graders judged certain jobs—boss, mayor, taxi driver, factory worker, lawyer—as appropriate for men, and others—nurse, house cleaner—as appropriate for women. As with some studies of toy choices, girls in Iglitizin's study showed less sex-role stereotyping (that is, were less restrictive in assigning jobs by sex) than boys.

The research shows a clear tendency toward sex-typing in both girls and boys. This tendency extends beyond the child's immediate world to structure the perception of adult life. It foreshadows the sex segregation that, as we have already seen, is so large a part of the adult world. Both girls and boys acquire the knowledge of sex-typing and are motivated to choose the "sex-appropriate" materials, much as they will later choose sex-appropriate school subjects and occupations. However, a substantial pattern of difference can also be noted. Though both girls and boys learn the preferences appropriate for their gender, many studies show girls to be less conforming than boys. Their choices cover both female and male domains, while boys hold consistently to a restrictive line (Ward, 1968; Pulaski, 1970). Thus, for example, Ferguson and Maccoby (1966) found that ten-year-old boys showed a more pronounced preference for a variety of activities associated with their sex role than did girls. Girls are less rigid in their sex-typing than boys at early ages. This observation may be at the root of the proposition that girls have "more latitude" in the formation of the social and sexual self, while boys are "socialized more severely." This implies—probably misleadingly—that agents of socialization are more tolerant with girls and more restrictive and/ or more punitive with boys. However, most studies reviewed by Maccoby and Jacklin show no sex differences in parents' behavior with respect to restrictions or punishments (1974, Chapter 9, pp. 330–335).

Tyler (1964), in a study of the development of occupational preferences from kindergarten to high school, concludes that the process of "choice" involves *excluding* categories of options, until alternatives are progressively narrowed down (1964, p. 188). The differences observed in the sex-typing of girls and boys may be attributable to a similar process of exclusion, which is brought to bear on boys earlier than on girls. The research shows that not only are boys more conforming to the masculine sex-type but they vigorously repudiate things feminine. Hartley has found that little boys express misogynistic attitudes, presumably in order to be orthodoxly masculine. The girl's script does not appear to contain a parallel requirement of female chauvinism, nor is there evidence that adult women teach or provide models to young girls for misandry.

Maccoby and Jacklin (1974) speculate that boys are somehow "more interesting" than little girls, hence "attract" more attention and incidentally socialization, which then directs them to a narrower path than girls tread at this early (pre- or elementary-school) age. Feminists have advanced a different interpretation: since men control more resources than women and occupy positions of privilege, they have more at stake in training their successors *and* keeping strong the divisions between the females and males of the coming generation. Many of these divisions are social and psychological (although, as we have seen, many are structural); hence socialization processes that create psychological habits of contempt for women and social habits of exclusively male solidarity are functional.

Men formed by such socialization practices are painfully limited (if privileged), as a number of writers have pointed out (Pleck, 1975; Farrell, 1974). The other side of the coin is that at this stage, girls have an advantage. Although they are by no means free of sex-typing, their repertoires are broader than those permitted to boys. This early experience builds an androgynous core identity that, although it is subject to severe socialization pressures later on, remains a resource for a more complete life. The idea of androgyny—by which I mean identity in which "feminine" and "masculine" attributes are present, accepted, and celebrated —is central to Chapter 5, so we will defer the discussion to that time. The evidence on early socialization shows us, I believe, the foundations of psychological androgyny.

THE SELF AND SEXUAL IDENTITY

It seems unlikely that children acquire their sex-typed repertoire through imitation of adults. Instead it appears that sex-typing relies upon achieving sex categorization, and this starts with the self. Gesell (1940) has found that 66 to 75 percent of children can correctly and stably identify their own gender at age three, but only half can do so at two and a half.

Kohlberg (1966) has argued that one of the earliest organizing schemata in a child's cognitive development is the self, which the child values so enthusiastically that anything associated with it or perceived as similar is likewise valued. At very nearly the same point in development, the child begins to identify herself by gender. This means that gender identity is a central part of the self, and also that it has the emotional investment associated with the self. Sexual identity is, then, a very central category throughout life. However, the personal meaning of gender need not be linked to the cultural sex-typing so pervasive in our own society. Sex-typing appears to be a cultural capability with a developmental threshold. A culture *needn't* teach its young to sort things by gender categories, but ours does, usually between the ages of four and six. Feminine and masculine become powerful concepts, and these are associated with gender. Sexual identity involves not only cognitive elements (the knowledge that this item is "feminine" and that item is "masculine") but also motivational elements (I should or want to do that which is feminine, since I am a girl). As we have seen, individual gender identity becomes a hook on which various kinds of learning are hung or, in more formal terms, an organizing principle, a cognitive category.

Gesell (1940) has pinpointed the timing of the achievement of gender categorization. Stabilizing and correctly generalizing gender categories proceed from this point. Slaby (1973) found that children three to five years old who had attained gender constancy watched same-sex models more than other-sex models when both were performing the same actions on a split screen. This suggests that after the attainment of gender constancy, sex of model affects the probability of imitation, even of cross-sex behavior (Wolf, 1973). Before the gender category becomes part of the child's cognitive equipment, selective imitation of this sort is not observed.

Evidence that the gender category starts with the self and generalizes outward, rather than being introjected and then applied to the self, is found in Thompson and Bentler's (1973) finding that a group of children four to six were sure they'd grow up to be daddies or mommies (as appropriate) but less sure that hypothetical strangers in pictures couldn't reverse their gender.

The gender category is subject to constant increment and elaboration as the individual passes through age-specific and social-class-specific social settings. The sex-typed repertoire we have examined is part of this category. So is the associated motivation.

The significance of this fact is that the individual very early learns to evaluate herself in terms of conformity with a socially valued set of behaviors, knowledge, skills, demeanors and preferences that we call the female sex role. Because femaleness (and, scarcely distinct at this early age, femininity) is accepted as part of the self, it is extremely difficult for the individual to reject sex role expectations. For most people, these are not "external" and imposed by others but are part of the self. Rejecting sex roles means devaluing part of the self. The socialization of most persons in our culture establishes a connection between "femininity" and "masculinity" and being okay. Once this connection exists, it must be broken before sex role liberation can occur.

Sex role polarization is one of the consequences of sex role socialization in our society. Indeed such polarization is one of the goals of sex role socialization. For *socialization commonly involves two complementary processes: shaping the individual toward one set of behaviors or beliefs while simultaneously shaping her away from others*. This is nowhere more true than in the case of sex role socialization, whose goals include polarization of the sexes. In preparing individuals for careers as women or men, sex role socialization must fit them for a world which is substantially segregated by gender.

Thus the socialization of girl-children must uniquely fit them for some options and unfit them for others. This process, already underway in the preschool years, is carried forward during the long period in which young people attend educational institutions.

Sex Role Socialization Within the School

It is possible to identify, within the schools, agents who direct the young toward future role performance, the mechanisms by which behavior is shaped or controlled, and the age-specific elements of sex role that are enforced or reinforced. Agents of socialization within the school setting include teachers, same-sex peers and other-sex peers, the self and the materials of instruction.

The latter is probably most often overlooked, for, like desks and chalk, it seems to be part of an inert environment, not exercising any effect on its own.

Yet research has wondered what picture of the world school children might derive from the materials provided for their instruction. Saario et al. (1972) conducted a comprehensive review of three elements of schooling that might have differential effects and outcomes for girls and boys: readers used in elementary schools, educational achievement tests and sex-differentiated curricula. One of the first things they found was a great disproportion in the use of female and male nouns and pronouns in standard achievement test batteries used in schools. Content of stories was coded in terms of locale where characters appeared (e.g., indoors/outdoors), actions they took, actions that were done to them and consequences they sustained. The content analysis showed significant sex role stereotyping as well. Interestingly enough, Child et al. had undertaken a similar study in 1946, analyzing textbooks published since 1930. Their findings were similar to those of Saario et al., who found that 73 percent of central characters were male and 27 percent female. Child et al. found, too, that female characters were portrayed as timid, affiliative and nurturant, and males as active, achieving, constructive and aggressive. Subsequent studies (Frasher and Walker, 1972; Graebner, 1972) found virtually identical results, with the additional warning that the newer editions within their sample are even more biased than the older ones.

If elementary-school children are learning their lessons then the information they acquire is of two sorts. First, they learn caricatures of the two sexes. Some stories show negative consequences to those who depart from the stereotypes (particularly girls) and positive consequences for those who conform. The second lesson is that of the shrinking or "invisible" female. School books show sex ratios grossly out of proportion with reality and in a direction opposite to reality. This ought to seem peculiar to children (and certainly to teachers) who see classes with roughly equal sex ratios. It "makes no sense"—except in the context of socialization for adult roles. The textbook pictures prepare school children for a *future* world of sex segregation, in which women are not seen in many domains. As children progress through school they will use textbooks that tell them about *no* female political leaders, composers, writers, engineers, admirals, professors, scientists or religious leaders. Later, perhaps, the daily newspapers will regale them with accounts of how men, singly and in groups, work arduously at controlling commodities, legislation, solid wastes and the exchange of inanities between political personages. One might consider it overkill to structure elementary-school readers along these lines but, as we shall see, "realism" is frequently used as a rationlization for educational practices peculiar to women. Perhaps elementary reading texts are a first lesson in "realism."

The question of sex-differentiated curricula has been the subject of much community action and is prohibited by Title IX of The Educational Amendments Act passed in 1972. While the dockets are still full of cases protesting the unequal allocation of educational resources to girls and boys, some changes can be observed. Prior to successful litigation, the kinds of findings Saario et al. reported for the New York City schools in 1970 were (are) quite typical: Seventy-seven courses were designated for males only and thirty-six for females only. Both the sex segregation and the selection of courses offered are of extreme concern in vocational education. For students who are not college-bound, these high-school courses are intended to fit them for economic self-sufficiency and a work career.

Before the passage of Title IX, it was not uncommon for programs like the JOBS program to overlook women completely. In a recent review of vocational education programs (Roby, 1975), the picture is little different. No effort has been made to ascertain where labor needs and opportunities exist, and to orient training toward these ends—at least not for girls. As of 1972, more than 75 percent of women and girls enrolled in such programs were receiving training in home economics or office skills; almost none in the better-paying skilled trades or technical jobs. In fiscal 1974, a total of 94 projects were funded under Section 131(a), Part C of the Education Amendments of 1968; only one of these was provided for women. Roby's report documents many specific forms of "tracking" of women in vocational education, all of which disadvantage them in terms of future earning power and career advancement. Some schools are "for boys only"; programs for boys have a higher faculty–student ratio than programs for girls; per-student expenditures are higher for programs with a high or exclusive concentration of boys rather than girls.

Many parents—and the bulk of researchers—tend to overlook problems in the realm of vocational education. Research on occupations tends to presuppose college training and jobs that lie at the professional end of the spectrum. Yet when we examine occupational "aspirations" of youth, we discover that the forgotten girls in vocational tracks faithfully reflect the dismal future that awaits them.

The emphasis on achievement in American schools focuses implicitly, if not explicitly, in college preparatory tracks. Consequently, achievement tests are accorded much importance, and in the last decade questions have been raised about their "culture fairness"—whether they in fact discriminate against those whose backgrounds do not familiarize them with materials of which the test is composed. This concern has been raised with respect to gender as well as race.

SEX-TYPING IN CURRICULA AND TESTS

In this third area of inquiry, the tests used to assess achievement in school, we find two kinds of biases. First is the ratio of female to male pronouns, and second is sex role stereotyping in the items that make up the tests. Saario et al. found that male pronouns predominated in achievement tests, even when "generic" pronouns were tabulated separately. Many persons argue that the predominant use of "he" shows no bias, precisely because we use this pronoun generically in English. Yet Schneider and Hacker (1972) found that college students selecting pictures to illustrate sociological topics filtered out females when the topic was "Political Man" but not when it was "Political Behavior."

Item content in achievement tests depicted stereotypic situations much like those found in the elementary readers. Girls were shown in domestic roles in indoor contexts, and involved with "trivial" concerns. Saario et al. (1972) found that the degree of sex role stereotyping increased with grade level. While little direct evidence exists in linking the degree of sex stereotyping in materials to students' performance in schools, there is some basis for putting together a plausible argument for there being effects.

Chiu (1973) studied fourth graders' ranked preferences for subject matter of books. A study by Bernstein (1955) suggests that the excitement value of the passages used to test reading competence enhances the scores of both boys and girls. Griffeath (1973) observes that in the most widely used achievement batteries, test items cover content that is much higher up in boys' preference than in girls. In other words, boys are being tested with materials that are more interesting and exciting to them than are girls, a factor that should enhance both attention and motivation to perform well.

All of the above research indicates quite clearly the existence of sex stereotyping in adults who write books, organize curricula and construct tests.

Our review of the characteristics of teaching materials in the schools might lead us to expect that these would have a negative effect on girls' school performance. Perhaps as a result of these factors, in terms of *absolute* levels of performance, girls may not do as well as they could. Pragmatically speaking, however, performance is usually assessed relatively rather than absolutely: by means of comparisons with other groups, with one's own performance under other conditions, etc. The comparison which has attracted the most attention is that between girls and boys. Moreover, as we have seen, sex role scripts prescribe that females not outperform males.

A substantial volume of research has demonstrated that girls outperform boys in school achievement during the elementary-school years (Maccoby, 1966). This finding has occasioned a public controversy, with much talk about the "feminizing" influence of the schools. In other words, violation of sex role prescriptions has been defined as a social problem. The "problem" of the "feminized school" has inspired some of the most bizarre and sexist solutions in the history of American public education (cf. Sexton, 1969).

The "Feminized School" Canard

Much of the controversy has been inspired by the finding that girls' reading achievement outstrips that of boys. The *educational* issue here is whether boys can perform at an adequate (absolute) level in order to cope with the requirements of a complex society, which assumes literacy as a basic skill. The *social* problem is how to counteract the relative superiority of girls and reestablish male superiority. The controversy and concern have centered on the second of these issues rather than the first.

Tregaskes (1972) tested the effects of a program designed to "masculinize" the perception of reading as an activity, with the goal of improving boys' reading performance. The reasoning behind this seems sound, in the light of the facilitating effect of sex role congruence on attention (Bernstein, 1955). But Tregaskes goes further: he assumes that the perception of an activity as feminine will engender hostility in the male child. Tregaskes is not concerned with the misogyny implicit in this kind of thinking, but only with the possible negative instrumentality of poor reading for male goals. In other areas, misogyny may be seen as facilitative of male achievement and does not occasion this kind of concern. In this study the author illustrates a sexist bias that is unconscious and unexamined. While a feminist viewpoint would hold that desirable attributes of each sex are desirable for all persons, the sexist approach attempts to *redefine as* masculine the valued feminine attribute in this case, reading skill.[4]

The expectation of male superiority is so ingrained that its

---

[4]This way of viewing the "problem" is in direct contrast to the feminist approach to sex differences. Since the social origins of most sex differences in personality and ability can be demonstrated, a degree of flexibility is possible. It is no longer tenable to assume "innateness" or fixity in most sex differences which have been studied to date. Hence it is possible to ask which attributes are most socially desirable or which contribute to individual wellbeing, and how they might be made more prevalent through aware socialization practices. Valuable attributes such as nurturance and assertion might be developed equally in women and men.

nonoccurrence requires an extraordinary explanation. The explanation that has gained currency is that the school is a "feminine" environment, presumably because of the high concentration of women in the teaching profession. An additional assumption is that female teachers and/or "feminine" schools act on boy students in such a way as to "feminize" them. This presumably accounts for boys' failure to outperform girls—and calls for strong medicine to counteract the insidious effects of "feminization."

It is hard to tell which is shakier, the logic of this argument or its factual basis. If a preponderance of female personnel makes an organization "feminine," we must then wonder about hospitals and universities as well as public schools. We may have to reconsider history: were the antebellum plantations African in culture, since blacks predominated? But in these instances, as in the public schools, the bosses are from a group that is in the minority but is dominant. The student, like the hospital patient, is under the direct care of a woman, but she is under the direction of a man.

Demonstrating empirically that one institution is "feminine" and another "masculine" would be difficult to do. Certainly it has not been established in the case of the "feminized school." One might argue that the child, who is comparatively powerless in relation to the teacher, may be "feminized" through some process of identification. However, demonstrating that identification has occurred is probably as empirically difficult as establishing the "femininity" of a school. Existing psychological research on the process of identification provides little basis for optimism on this point. Even if we knew more about identification, demonstrating that it had occurred would require before-and-after comparisons, comparisons between girls and boys, and a correlation between self-reports of the identifiers and objective assessment of similarities between identifier and model. Discussions of the "feminized school" do not seriously consider these issues. Of course, the child could be "feminized" by coercion, but this too would require evidence. One could always presume that imitation is a factor, without assuming either identification or coercion, but this should be demonstrable by means of an increasing similarity between students' and teachers' attributes or behaviors. To the extent that sex role similarity facilitates imitation, girls should be more "feminized" by exposure to a female teacher than boys are. What happens to girls remains a question no matter which explanation one favors.

The idea of "feminization" in the classroom would gain some measure of plausibility if the mechanism by which it is presumed to occur were spelled out. Failing that, we fall back on a vague contamination theory, which justifies menstrual taboos and witch burning, as well as compensatory hiring of men in public schools. The contamination theory has the advantage of accounting for the lack of "feminization" of girls: they are already inoculated against femininity.

Of course, logical flaws remain. If schools "feminize" boys (and only boys), this should boost their school achievement. In this case, why is it necessary to increase the proportion of male teachers in order to counteract this effect? The suggestion seems self-serving, especially when coupled with the recommendation that men be offered inflated salaries in order to recruit them (Peltier, 1968). Often this inflated salary scale is justified by analogy with combat pay, or hazardous duty pay—a jovial reminder that associating with women and children is not something a man would choose to do in the absence of some compelling extrinsic incentive.

It is possible that the whole "feminized school" bubble is based on Kagan's finding that second and third graders rated a number of school-related objects (blackboard, desk) as feminine more often than masculine, without taking into account Kellogg's finding that some items are perceived more often as feminine and others more often as masculine. Perhaps more to the point, while boys did perceive school as feminine, girls perceived it as masculine (Kellogg, 1969). What are we to do about this? Shall we bring in more women, to counteract the masculine image of school? Or more men, to counteract its feminine image?

Actually, there is no evidence that either is a solution. In neither Kagan's nor Kellogg's study is there evidence of any behavioral consequence of the children's perception. Yet the feminized school canard supposes that school achievement is affected negatively–in boys—by the perception of the learning environment as "feminine."

Achievement and Sex-Typing in the Schools

Analysis of the material factors operating in the public schools establishes incontrovertibly that school is not the same environment for girls and boys. The school as an institution is one in which sex-typing prevails; that is, the consequences of a given behavior or attribute are different when the individual is a girl or a boy.[5] Some of the most potent of these consequences are the responses of teachers and peers to students' school achievements. Anastasiouw (1965) has shown that teachers rate as more competent boys they consider more"masculine." Sears (1963) found that female teachers rated achieving girls lower than other girls, increasingly so as the year went on. From Sears' study it appears that girls are being punished for achieving; an association is being formed between achievement and bad consequences—for a girl. The other study shows a connection between the "good" attributes of being male and being competent, but goes one step further. The teachers appear to confuse the two approved attributes, for they distorted their evaluations of the "masculine" boys in an upward direction. It appears that if a boy is "masculine," at least some raters will take it for granted that he is competent. The effect illustrated by these two studies has been repeatedly documented in research where older persons were evaluated: college students (Deaux and Emswiller, 1974), artists (Pheterson et al., 1971), professionals (Goldberg et al., 1968) and professors (Simpson, 1970; Fidell, 1970). Work attributed to a male is judged

---

[5]This definition is offered by Mischel (1970) in a fine review of the research literature of sex-typing and socialization.

better by most people, without independent evidence that this is so; and work attributed to a female is downgraded.

Sex-typing and sex prejudice certainly have their effect on the achievement of girl-children in school. Other significant features of the learning situation include conditions of instruction (social versus nonsocial), sex of instructor, sex composition of the class and sex-typing of the subject matter.

A number of studies have found that students do better in an auto-instructional mode than in classroom learning. These studies include black students (Suppes, 1968), girls (Brinkman, 1966), and boys (McNeil, 1964).

McNeil compared his boy students who studied reading in the auto-instructional mode in kindergarten with their own performance in a female-taught first grade classroom, but failed to control on another variable, the sex composition of the class. In order to assert positively that sex differences on this variable exist, one would have to control the other three variables: subject matter, sex of teacher, sex of peers (and perhaps age). Research that adequately controls for the complex interactions among these variables remains to be done. Some studies find no difference in student performance when sex of teacher is varied (Good et al., 1973; Asher and Gottman, 1973; Peterson, 1972), but some have found differences in performance attributable to sex of the peer group. Walter (1972) found that reading performance of first grade girls was best when they learned in an all-girl group (although girls were superior overall to boys). Sex composition did not affect performance of boys at this age, although some studies have found superior performance in same-sex groups among older boys.

A general finding for girls, consistent over a wide age range, is that girls perform better on tasks they perceive as feminine (Milton, 1958). Moreover, girls set higher levels of aspiration and higher standards for performance on tasks they perceive as feminine (Milton, 1958; Battle, 1965, 1966; Stein, 1971). It seems girls permit themselves higher achievement in areas that do not threaten their femininity or their relations with males.

Stein et al. (1971) examined the hypothesis that children's performance is affected by the sex-typing of the task. They found that among sixth graders boys did best on skills labeled as masculine, next on neutral skills, and least well on "feminine" skills. Girls showed a different pattern: performance and aspiration were substantially the same on feminine and neutral skills, but a noticeable pattern of avoidance of masculine-labeled tests was observed. This reaction is consistent with the centrality of sexual identity to personal identity, as that idea was developed earlier in this chapter. From it we can predict that as sex role becomes more salient at puberty, this avoidance tendency will be intensified.

What appears to be happening in elementary school is that achievement itself is becoming sex-typed. Achievement is expected of males and is positively evaluated in males. Achievement is not expected in girls and may be negatively sanctioned in girls. Indeed, nonachievement may be expected of girls. Further research is needed to specify whether school achievement as a whole becomes perceived as masculine, or whether this effect is limited to certain subjects (e.g., mathematics). Certainly by the time students reach college, the teaching profession becomes dominated by males, who provide the models for their disciplines.

By the end of high school, males' achievement has caught up with that of females, and males frequently dominate the top honors in high school. Nevertheless, young women's achievement remains high enough to justify high aspirations. Yet at this point a "confidence gap" is apparent. When we look at the aspirations of high-school graduates we find that females are overrepresented among those who do not go any further. Of the 50 percent of high-school graduates who do not go on to college, 75 percent are women (Sutherland, 1961). This "confidence gap" is found in the graduate school plans of college seniors as well (Baird, 1973). Only the "A" students among women plan to go on to graduate or professional schools, while among men, students with "B" and even "C" averages intend to attend graduate school and pursue careers in the professions.

Current research provides possible explanations of this phenomenon. Studies on the attribution of causality in success and failure reveal sex differences of a particularly interesting sort. Deaux and Emswiller (1974) found that success achieved by men was attributed to skill, while success achieved by women was attributed to luck, when the task was one that was sex-typed masculine. However, men's success was evaluated more highly by both female and male than was women's success, regardless of the task. These results suggest that competence is sex-typed masculine, in such a way that only men may claim it. Furthermore, success in a male is more highly rewarded than success in a female.

Another perspective on the confidence gap comes from recent developments in achievement motivation theory. Raynor (1974) has demonstrated the importance of perceived instrumentality of school grades for future goals. Even where achievement motivation is high, it is not mobilized for tasks that bear no connection to future goals. The instrumentality of school achievement for men's occupational goals is stressed to a greater degree than for those of women. Indeed, the occupations toward which women are directed do not require or reward differential school achievement. In the primary grades, school is sometimes represented as the child's "job." Good grades represent a "job" well done. Increasingly, however, school achievement comes to represent not an end in itself but an instrumentality to future goals of occupational attainment. As students approach the end of their public schooling, the different instrumentality of good grades for females and males becomes increasingly apparent. In addition, the research on the Motive to Avoid Success has demonstrated that for women, success can have the meaning of threat or failure, mobilizing the conflict between competence and femininity.

The evidence suggests that during schooling there develops a sex difference in expectancy. The expectation of reward consequence upon school achievement differs for females and males. In addition, the instrumentality of school achievement for the attainment of future goals differs by sex. And finally, the valence of some outcomes may be purely positive for males, and mixed or negative for females.

Sex role socialization in the schools directs girl children away from achievement as a goal, the more so as achievement comes to be perceived as masculine. At the same time, the expectation that females will make marriage their primary commitment is present from the earliest years.

At puberty, however, a noticeable discontinuity occurs. During adolescence, when dating commences and mate selection looms in the near future, the disjuncture between achievement and femininity is emphasized. As Komarovsky (1946) noted, this discontinuity may be rather sudden, with a swift change in the reward structure. If a woman has been supported and praised by her parents for doing well in college, and they suddenly lose interest in her achievements, inquiring only about her social life, the previous behavior loses social support. The research by Tangri and by Angrist and Almquist cited in Chapter 1 demonstrates the importance of support for career-connected striving. Many college women do not find such support from their female and male peers, much less their professors, and sometimes not from their parents.

The focus now shifts to the female in relation to a potential partner. In Chapter 3 we examined scripting for courtship, which provides strategies and attributes appropriate for a woman who is trying to catch a man. The role expectations for the nubile female resemble those of Objectivity more than Subjectivity at this point. Discontinuity is thus introduced between the androgyny and autonomy of the child and the more restricted life of the adult woman. Another discontinuity occurs as young females become more distant from and different from their male peers.

In adolescence, then, *sex segregation between females and males begins to be enforced.* Young women are expected to retreat from the occupational realms that men have staked out for themselves and involve themselves increasingly in the domestic world reserved for women. As their concern with mating and courtship increases, male peers become judges. To the extent that they, collectively or individually, control a woman's "success" (i.e., achieving marriage) they have a degree of power. When, in a coeducational school setting, they can monitor a young woman's performance, they can readily mobilize the conflict between competence and femininity. The research on the Motive to Avoid Success documents not only women's vulnerability to this conflict but also the frequency with which men use it against women (see Chapter 1).

Given both the strength of motivation for competence and the importance of social acceptance, the potential for role conflict for women is nearly ubiquitous. Perhaps for this reason, it is all too common to find women's adaptation to the forces mobilized by these pressures analyzed in terms of "personality" or motivation. Nevertheless, a careful analysis of situational forces should make it clear when the field of forces in which the individual finds herself, rather than internal states or stable attributes, accounts for observed behavior.

It is unlikely that the characterization of an enormous population of individuals in terms of "a" feminine personality is due entirely to habits of intellectual laziness. Rather, this practice can be seen as a parallel to the kind of work which characterized the study of black people during the early 1960s. It became apparent that the explanation of group differences in terms of psychology has the function of directing attention away from structural conditions that differentiate the groups and restrict opportunities for one group. The traditional psychology of women exhibits the characteristics of a classic example of "blaming the victim" (Ryan, 1971).

Traditional Theories of Feminine Personality

The dominant influence in traditional theories about feminine psychology is Freud. Freud saw the essence of feminine character as comprising passivity, narcissism and masochism. Freud constructed his psychology of women upon the presumed passivity of the female in intercourse. A psychology of receptivity and appreciation was thought to reflect the reactive sexuality of the woman, in contrast with activity and initiation, which characterized the man. Freud saw assertion and ambition in women as inappropriately phallic: they were "masculine strivings" reflecting "penis envy." As we saw in Chapter 3, sexual expression which does not reflect submission to a man (i.e., clitoral sexuality) is similarly unfeminine. Thus in the Freudian psychology of women, anatomy is destiny: psychology recapitulates genital morphology.

In another element of Freudian theory, too, anatomy is destiny. Freud's notion of feminine masochism reflects his perception of menstruation, defloration and childbirth as gory and horrific events. To Freud, for the woman to accept her genitals was to embrace this horror. Hence female sexuality involves pain; and since Freud's theory of feminine personality relies so heavily on this view of female sexuality (Freud, 1925, 1931, 1933), Freud cannot but see the feminine personality as masochistic. In this context he means that the female not only accepts but perhaps seeks pain.

Freud's analysis of feminine masochism lacks any comparative framework. He assumed that all persons experience horror at normal female biological functions, overlooking the possibility that under other cultural conditions these functions occasion either no comment or pride, and the possibility that the reaction he assumed universal was no more than a male projection. Further implications of Freud's theory of feminine masochism have not been explored. For example, are postmenopausal women, since they no longer bleed, less masochistic than they were at an earlier age? Are virgins less masochistic than coitally experienced women? Are child-free women less masochistic than mothers?

Freud's writings on masochism actually deal with three quite distinct types. His discussion of the "feminine type" is circular: to be female is to bleed, hence to be masochistic. The primary or "erotogenic" type of masochism described by Freud is based on his theory of the duality of instincts. The death impulse (Thanatos) becomes split, according to Freud, and some part of it is directed against the self. The self then becomes the object of the destructive impulse, and a number of psychological and behavioral expressions of this event are hypothesized by Freud.

One consequence is the "moral" type of masochism, which Freud says is powered by guilt or the unconscious desire for punishment. This need causes the individual to seek punishment (or, as Horney develops the idea, humiliation, disappointment, heartbreak) and is satisfied by these events.

The "moral" type of masochism appears to be quite different from the "feminine" type in its origins and in the behavior that might be predicted from it. Yet both types are attributed to women. Indeed, it is ironic that although this discussion (Freud, 1924) is based on Freud's observations regarding *male* patients, the idea of masochism is almost exclusively applied to women. It is hard to evade the suspicion that Freud's hypothesis—it is no more than that—has found popularity as a rationalization for the scapegoating of women. The sex role stereotypes of women as docile, unassertive individuals who shun responsibility, risk and glory appear to have something in common with the idea that women are "by nature" masochistic.

For the third element of the trinity, narcissism, Freud once again had a separate theory for women. As a developmental phenomenon, narcissism emerges as a variant in the normal succession of love objects. While the care-taking person is the prototypical choice in anaclitic love, some individuals take the self as object, in narcissistic love. Freud identifies anaclitic object cathexis as typical of men, and narcissistic object choice as typical of women (1963, pp. 69–70). Maternal love, too, is narcissistic in its dynamics, according to Freud (1963, p. 71).

Freud's psychology of women was thus closely tied to his view of female biology and to a social sphere circumscribed by biology. This limitation can be seen in the developments of Freudian psychology of women by such disciples as Helene Deutsch (1944, 1945) and Erik Erikson (1964).

The congruence between Freudian psychology and traditional female sex role is apparent in the following discussion, quoted from an obstetrics/gynecology textbook (Willson et al., 1964, pp. 47ff). The lack of clear distinctions among narcissism, masochism and passivity is also apparent in this discussion. In feminine narcissism,

The woman receives gratification from the idea of being loved and bases an increased sense of her own value on her image of the person who loves her. She says, "I am valuable, important, etc. *because he loves me*" (1964, p. 47, italics mine)

This theme is developed into marriage and motherhood.

As a wife it (narcissism) allows her to be gratified by the success and achievements of her husband. . . .As she raises the child her feminine narcissism rewards her by the pleasure she feels in the accomplishments of the child (p. 47).

Feminine masochism, in this discussion, consists in accepting the female role.

The authors distinguish this from the "neurotic" masochism that seeks suffering as an end in itself; in "feminine" masochism suffering is only incidental! It is difficult to distinguish masochism conceptually from passivity. The discussion of each is studded with "musts" projected onto the woman: she "*must* submit her own needs to build up the personality and strivings of her husband and family;" she "*must* accept the idea that she is given things by her husband and even by her children, rather than assuming an active and aggressive role in attaining these things for herself;" she "*must* be passive and receptive to the male" sexually. However, passivity can be too much of a good thing: the authors introduce the notion of "feminine maturity" in contradistinction to the "*overly* passive woman who is continually waiting to receive without any willingness to give of herself in a *masochistic* or narcissistic manner" (1964, p. 48, italics mine). No more succinct statement of a sexist psychology could be imagined. Not only are women characterized in terms of disesteemed attributes, but they can be additionally faulted if these "innate" attributes "over which they have no control" prove inconvenient to men.

Freudian theory of feminine personality has been so frequently and so trenchantly critiqued that little remains to be said here. By the standards of present-day psychology, the Freudian theory is unconvincing. Systematic observations on the development of the characteristics attributed to women are lacking. No attempt is made to predict specific behaviors or choices. The implied comparison with men is not carried out; hence the discriminant validity of a differential psychology cannot be demonstrated. Moreover, satisfactory interrater reliability has never been achieved, an important failing in a method which relies on retrospection for data collection. Perhaps most damning, alternative causal explanations for even these dubious data receive no systematic test. This failing is particularly severe with respect to instances where the structure of situational rewards and sanctions predicts to "feminine" behavior, rendering personality variables irrelevant. Freud's psychology of women represents neither a major part of his work nor his best effort. His ideological concerns are explicitly stated in a number of places. Freud rejected the claims of his feminist critics that women were equal to men (Freud, 1925, p. 193). In no sense does Freudian psychology attempt an even-handed development of the dynamics characterizing women, men and individuals in general. Rather, Freud is an early example of the double standard of scholarship, in which women occasion a footnote or two to a grand theory.

The work of Erikson, a neo-Freudian, is taken more seriously by contemporary psychologists. Erikson, too, has been criticized for basing a personality theory on the assumption that anatomy is destiny. He postulates an innate conservatism in females, based on their preoccupation with "inner space" (the reproductive tract), as contrasted with an up-and-out male psychology based on phallic imagery. Erikson (1964) bases his theory on observations of young children (a small and unspecified sample) in a play situation. He has been severely criticized for assuming that sex-typed play activities reflect "innate" dispositions, seeming unaware of the extensive research literature that documents the origin of this behavior in social learning.

Erikson, too, exemplifies a special-interest type of psychology, emphasizing differences between the sexes where similarities should be explored. It can hardly be argued that "inner spaces" are found only in females. In fact, a number of inner spaces are more vital to daily functioning, and more continually in use, than the uterus. With a little more imagination, a neo-Erikson could develop a pulmonary or a peristaltic psychology based on the significance of the lungs or digestive tract. Such an integrated psychology would be more powerful than two sex-specific and fragmentary theories. Moreover, the new theory would have no more difficulty with questions of social significance of the inner spaces and the part that labeling plays in socialization than does Erikson's theory.

Erikson characterizes the identity of the young woman in a way parallel with inner space: in his theory, she reserves space in her lifestyle planning and her personal identity, which will be filled by her future mate. This theory fails to take into account the plentiful empirical literature on young women's planning, reviewed in Chapter 1.

Contemporary Psychology of Women

Not all psychology of women follows the psychoanalytic approach. Within the discipline of psychology, there are two traditions within which one might expect to find research on women. The first of these focuses on distinct attributes or predictors, having evolved from the venerable tradition of individual differences (and its offspring, the study of sex differences) through a stage of trait psychology. Although the idea of psychological "traits" has gone out of fashion, very similar entities called personality dimensions or personality variables abound in the current literature. Their number is limited only by the imagination of psychologists and their ability to develop and validate paper-and-pencil measures of new variables. These are judged against their ability to predict behavior, with no concern for their concordance with self-perception. Many such have been validated against behavior in controlled, contrived situations. These situations are intended to simulate a class of real-life situations to which the personality dimension is relevant. Very few personality dimensions succeed in predicting behavior across the range of real-life situations to which they are theoretically relevant. Most personality research does not even attempt to demonstrate the stability of personality variables over any appreciable amount of time. These limitations inspired the critique of trait psychology and the search for alternative approaches. In principle, the trait approach, failing as it does to provide a description of the whole individual, ought to be immune to sexist bias. In fact, however, the thesis of sex differences underlay this tradition, along with the implicit assumption that *the* human being is male. The difficulties with this tradition have been amply documented by Sherman (1971), Parlee (1975) and Sherif (1977).

The other tradition in psychology comprises a set of personality theories, which tend to be schemata at a high level of generality. Some of these present personality as a dimensionally complex constellation, often with a developmental theme, so that personality is understood as a sort of succession of equilibria. Other theorists opt for dichotomous polarities, which are often (although not always) mapped into a masculine/feminine polarity—for example, agency/communion, instrumental/expressive. This preference for dichotomies remains one of the unplumbed mysteries of personality psychology.

Many unresolved issues separate the two traditions. When the prediction of behavior is the goal of personality research, no overall integration is attempted. When the theorist attempts to formulate an overall constellation, systematic observations are not incorporated. Both traditions tend to remain outside the person and neglect the function of the individual's making sense of her experience.

The psychology of women has often been neglected by both approaches. Each treats the study of women as an addendum or exception, leaving the psychodynamic tradition virtually uncorrected. Another limitation common to all three traditions introduces an additional bias. Most personality researchers do not take into account the cultural context; neither race, class nor sex role.

Yet an examination of empirical research on women will show that the variables studied and the hypotheses put forward have their unacknowledged origins in sex role scripting. Sex role congruent traits and behaviors, and only sex role congruent ones, are studied in both women and men. Nurturance in men is studied only in the context of psychological androgyny, as in Bem's research reviewed in Chapter 5.

In a recent review, Denmark et al. (1973) report finding not a single entry on women's motivation for power in *Psychological Abstracts, Sociological Abstracts* and *Educational Abstracts* for the period 1969–1973. So much for research on unfeminine attributes. Research on items in the sex role script is more plentiful. However, the most recent reviews on the empirical literature reveal that widely cited female suggestibility (Eagly, 1978) and lack of aggression (Frodi and Macaulay, 1977) are no more than sex role stereotypes, accepted without due scientific scepticism by many psychologists.

Feminine Personality as Sex Role Conformity

Another perspective on "feminine personality" is to view it as behavior that satisfies sex role expectations. As we have seen, sex role includes all the systematic consequences of being born female or male. Chapter 1 concentrated on the consequences of being *a female* worker, Chapter 2 on the distinctive constraints that operate upon the *female* spouse and parent, and Chapter 3 on the programming of *female* sexuality and intimate relating. The structural constraints and reinforcement contingencies that women have in common militate toward a particular "personality type," which is adaptive as long as these structural conditions prevail.

The traditional triad of female personality traits—masochism, narcissism and passivity—can be retranslated in the light of the circumstances of women's lives. This is in fact what Horney (1967) did, contemporaneously with Freud. Horney analyzed "female masochism" in the light of cultural constraints on women, in dramatic contrast to Freud's context-free, "universal" characterization of feminine personality. Horney thought that what Freudians call "masochism" is simply adaptive behavior, given the disadvantaged position with which women have to cope. Her analysis focused on conditions that militate toward greater "masochism" in the class of women. Societies that exhibit the following characteristics should produce more "masochistic" women than those that do not have these characteristics (Horney, 1967, p. 230):

1. A belief in the inferiority of females
2. Practices that block the avenues for assertion (e.g., in work; in sexuality)
3. Economic dependence of the woman on the family
4. The restriction of women to spheres based on emotional bonds (e.g., the family, volunteer work)[6]
5. A surplus of nubile females in the population
6. An emphasis on marriage, with "weakness" of women being emphasized as a basis for attracting men.

Similarly, narcissism needs to be viewed in a broader light than Freud's formulation, which emphasized a pathological aspect. Narcissism is a rich concept, and one that has been used in a variety of ways. Narcissism may be defined as experiencing oneself as a pleasing entity. Such self-consciousness requires awareness of the self as an object of cognition, but does not necessarily imply objectification. Social psychologists tend to use the term to refer to a normal, rather than abnormal, range of self-appreciation. Self-acceptance has been shown to be related to acceptance of others, rather than being antithetical to it. In a social psychological framework, moreover, narcissism may refer to any aspect of the self, not solely to the physical self or the body. In this context, nar-

---

[6]See Adams, The Compassion Trap, in Gornick and Moran's *Woman in Sexist Society*, (1971). For a detailed analysis of the programming that channels women into these supportive, caring, and helping roles, see Holter (1970).

cissism is akin to self-esteem. Fromm (1956) argues that one cannot love another unless one loves oneself.

The individual acquires an idea about the self, or self-image, as a normal part of early development. The individual becomes an object of cognition to herself, as she is to others. Moreover, the ways she perceives herself is, at least initially, based on how others perceive her (cf. Cooley's concept, the "looking-glass self"). Normal narcissism includes being able to accept another's appreciation of the self and, by extension, to accept the caresses of another.

In and of itself, narcissism does not imply abdication of selfhood and acceptance of oneself as a thing. However, when body and self become commodities for the enjoyment of another and subject to his approval or disapproval, alienation enters into narcissism. Under these conditions little self-confirmation is associated with narcissism.

When self-esteem is divorced from narcissism, we are properly speaking of masochism rather than narcissism. Simone de Beauvoir follows Sartre (1966) in her definition of masochism. It is not masochistic to attempt to fascinate the other by one's Objectivity; that is part of narcissism as we have defined it here. Masochism is seen, rather, in the alienation of the will (or Subjectivity). When the ego is estranged and dependent on the will of another, we properly speak of masochism.

Masochism is inimical to normal adult female sexuality rather than being inherent in it (de Beauvoir, 1952, p. 376). An adult sexual relationship requires not passivity but the establishment of reciprocity. The lovers enjoy a shared pleasure; the woman experiences the pleasure of her own but acknowledges the particular contribution of her partner. Turning Freud on his head, de Beauvoir contends that it is masochism, rather than assertion, which is an immature perversion in women. It is possible, she concedes that a woman might feel a need to punish herself for abandoning her Subjectivity and resigning herself to Objectivity. Masochism, in the standard usage (i.e., seeking pain) is a misnomer when applied to women. It seems more likely that a splitting of events and experience is achieved via programming for vicariousness. As a consequence, painful or humiliating occurrences are not experienced as they would be by the objective observer who has not been subjected to the programming. The masochistic woman is one who accepts vicariousness.[7]

The idea of woman's essential passivity would be better translated as *Objectivity* as well; that is, the availability for others' purposes. Chapter 3 emphasized the commodification of women in the context of the courtship market. In the psychology of women the same idea is expressed in an abstract vocabulary of individual traits rather than social situations. In reality, however, expectations of women do not leave room for passivity. Even in the role of sex object, the woman must exert effortful striving and work to enhance self-presentation as an Object. Women have almost exclusive responsibility for the home and for the family, and these responsibilities are hardly discharged in a passive manner.

Female "passivity" refers, rather, to the role obligation of being responsive to others' initiatives, of reacting rather than initiating. This pliability or compliance[8] reflects the "alterity" de Beauvoir describes. From the male or Subject point of view, the Object is invested with the qualities he wants her to have. The "feminine personality" described here exhibits this characteristic: it is the perfect complement to the male role of Subjectivity.

We thus conclude that "feminine personality" is shorthand for sex role behaviors and attributes designed to complement the behaviors and attributes prescribed for the male in our culture. The vocabulary of individual traits and enduring personality dis-

---

[7]Whether this acceptance is masochistic or normal depends, of course, on the perspective of the person doing the labeling. This is another instance of the concept of *consciousness*. The false consciousness of the woman who is adjusted to her situation is masochistic, from the point of view of the feminist. On the other hand, to experience oppression, isolation and rage, as feminists commonly do, seems unnecessary and masochistic to the normal woman.

[8]Compliance is governed by the presence of rewards and threats. The behavior is not internalized and can be expected to cease when the reinforcements are withdrawn (Kelman, 1961).

positions is misleading, however, implying as it does stability over situations, fixity and independence of situational inducements. Analysis in terms of roles is more apt. For roles are properly defined in pairs. Any role acquires much of its significance in relation to its complement; indeed, it is usually thought that one cannot *be* a mother without a child, or a wife without a husband. More to the point, role expectations and evaluations of role performance are communicated by the role partner. They are not sociological abstractions, nor do they originate with the role incumbent. What is desirable about psychological femininity is the way it meshes with psychological masculinity.

There is complementarity in female and male sex roles, but not parity. Rather, they correspond to the ideas of Objectivity and Subjectivity, as developed in Chapter 3. We shall return to the ideas of Objectivity and Subjectivity after reviewing current research on feminine personality in the light of the sex role approach.

The sex role script points toward the elements we should expect to find in "the" feminine personality—that is, in a person who will fit the role. The role prescriptions define the woman in relation to others—for example, in terms of family roles. We therefore expect that much research would focus on relatedness, desire for relatedness, skills at relatedness, etc. We find women expected to have greater "social skills" or "social competence" than men; we also read that relatedness is more important to females than to males. A number of psychologists have developed hypotheses relating to the personal greater "need for affiliation" in girls.

A number of basic issues remain in contention regarding the affiliation motive. If social relations are more important to girls than to boys, do girls spend more time in the presence of others than do boys? Does the need for affiliation lead the individual to seek quality or quantity in relationships?

Much of the evidence on the social behavior of girls and boys belies the predictions concerning affiliation. Girls tend to have fewer friends, boys to travel in gangs (Maccoby and Jacklin, 1974). Denmark et al. (1975) find that different studies use different measures of the tendency, and there appear to be age differences as well. There is little basis at present for concluding that differences between the sexes are greater than differences within the sexes.

A related prediction is that females are more dependent than males. Maccoby and Jacklin (1971) have demonstrated that dependency, like other "traits", is not unitary, but rather that different indicators are taken as measures of dependency in a variety of research projects. In studies of young children, Maccoby and Jacklin conclude, there is no evidence of girls' greater dependence.

The idea of social dependence as a feminine personality trait is related to the assumed dependence of women's fortunes on the approval of others. One hypothesis has it that girl children are trained to orient toward parents and later toward male partners, whereas boy children are trained toward increasing independence. Insofar as the female individual derives her sense of self-worth from the approval of others (as contrasted with self-approval), she must remain pliable and adaptable, ready to alter her behavior (or self) in response to rewards and threats. However, the necessity of being accommodating and responsive works against the development of a sense of self that might oppose the demands of others. Any evidence of the development of the self as a source of approval or of alternative directions is punished by the other(s).[9] The "responsiveness" and the sole reliance on social support make the woman extraordinarily vulnerable to rejection (which has the meaning of failure, given the motivational pattern we have described).

Some writers would argue that focusing on the marital partner is simply a narrowing of the habit of other-directedness, which is established very early in girl-children. Walstedt (1977) studied the influence of the father in the development of other-orientation in women. In a sample of adult women (aged 34 to 68),

---

[9]In the schizogenic families studied by Laing (1964) the daughters became "problems" only in adolescence, when they stopped being docile and accessible to their parents. This change was perceived as sudden and unjustified by the parents.

those highest in other-orientation showed a distinctive family history. The father had played a patriarchal role, viewing himself, and being viewed by others, as Subject or focus. He had encouraged the daughter in a traditional feminine role and discouraged atypical behavior when she was a child and an adolescent. In particular, he had discouraged the daughter's achievement and heterosexual interests—two avenues of subjectivity, as we discussed in Chapter 3. Walstedt's study conforms to the model of sex role socialization we have developed in this chapter: the creation of the traditional female personality requires socialization *away from* competence and own achievement, as well as socialization *toward* femininity.

The idea of dependence appears to be related to ideas about affiliation and social sensitivity, which in turn harmonize with the theme of women as "expressive specialists" and men as instrumental specialists. Often the expected sex differences appear in the eye of the beholder but not in the observations of the psychologist. Empathy is usually thought of as sensitivity to others' feelings or desires. Practically speaking, empathy seems to have behavioral implications as well. It implies accommodation to, or anticipation of, others' directions. The empathic person is thought to smooth things over for others, and facilitate their activity, whether this be task performance or emotional expression. The behavioral and psychological aspects are confounded in some research. In research with married couples, for example, it is hypothesized that the intimacy of married life will make partners more attuned to each other than pairs composed of strangers. Empathy is here operationalized as skill in predicting the partner's responses—for example, his/her self-description. Stuckert (1963) found wives more accurate in predicting husbands' response than husbands were in predicting wives'. In addition, wives adapted their behavior to their perception of husbands' expectations. "Empathy," in this study, is a one-way street. Corsini (1956) found a similar relationship not only among married pairs but among randomly constituted pairs (i.e., strangers). This suggests that the behavioral tendency of empathy is part of a widely shared sex role script which any woman can enact under the appropriate circumstances.

Conversely, a different response could be expected under different reinforcement contingencies. For social dependence is a behavioral concept, adaptive—at least in some degree—in the context of the power relations under which many women live. Individuals can be trained toward dependency or toward self-sufficiency.

The training does, however, seem to shape women toward a generalized predisposition that I call *vicariousness*. Vicariousness is an integrative concept that subsumes a number of the behavioral tendencies just discussed and specifies the underlying dynamic. Vicariousness involves the expectation that one's own needs can be satisfied through others, as in the notion of vicarious achievement. Vicariousness emphasizes the satisfactions obtainable through substitute achievement, autonomy and authenticity. However, the substitute nature of the satisfaction is not acknowledged, and the convention of social dependence is useful in concealing this. Because of the way a woman is presumed to be connected organically to her family, their achievements *are* hers, rather than merely seeming to be or being just as satisfying as hers. Another element in the rationalization of vicariousness is the argument that the woman has contributed a great deal to the achievements of her spouse and children, such that they would never have come about without her "participation." Finally, she has (freely) *chosen* to use her talents in this way, rather than in a crudely self-aggrandizing way (i.e., direct and palpable achievement). A good deal of mystification (i.e., the systematic reinterpretation of events, feelings and situations) is apparent in the idea of vicarious achievement.

Vicariousness is also incumbent upon the woman in sex. The heritage of Victorian wifehood is the idea that a wife submits to sex in order to give pleasure to her husband. In liberated 20th-century America, women still submit, in order to give pleasure to their lovers. But as we have seen in Chapter 3, their experiences may well fail to include any learning about their sexual pleasure. When a woman has sexual relations only when and how her partner wants to, she may be slow to learn what the stages of her sexual arousal and fulfillment are. She may not have the opportunity to learn the varieties of her sexual pleasure. Her partner may not be as cooperative in seeking her pleasure as she is his; men are not, after all, trained to be vicarious.

The practice of faking orgasm exemplifies the alienation that is inherent in vicariousness. A woman falsifies her own experience in order to benefit someone else. In sex perhaps even more than in achievement, vicariousness is accompanied by mystification. Authoritative sources tell women that they are normally frigid, hence their sexual satisfaction/nonsatisfaction is a nonissue. On the other hand, these same authorities tell them that male sexuality is a raging tide that cannot be gainsaid. Male sexual satisfaction is essential and consequential; female sexual satisfaction is inessential and inconsequential. Those women who are not scared off by these oracular pronouncements and who find their own experience contradicts them are liable to be labeled as sexual deviants (e.g., "nymphomaniacs").

The elements of accommodation and self-effacement constitute the "positive" side of vicariousness; that is, traits trained *into* the female person. Childhood traits of docility and "niceness" are probably the precursors to womanly traits of empathy and self-effacement. Women are trained to make others comfortable, to smooth things over, to build up the egos of their (male) friends, not to say anything if they cannot say something nice. The habit of admiration and appreciativeness is important preparation for deprecating one's own talents and fostering the achievements of one's family.

Women suffer, however, from being trained away from competence, self-assertion, self-appreciation and striving for excellence.

Vicariousness inescapably contains elements of alienation and destructiveness. The problem of "smother love" discussed in Chapter 2 can be seen as an expression of the intense need for meaningul achievement of one whose avenues for achievement are restricted. Further, an individual whose worth is judged on the basis of others' achievements has a stake in manipulating their behavior in such a way that it reflects well on her. Conceivably she must, for her own survival, limit the options and the development of those with whom she is involved. She needs to have them demonstrate her indispensability. One way of doing this is to foster selective incompetence in spouse and children. Because she is shackled to them as a source of the recognition which is essential to maintain her self-worth, she must create shackles for them as well—in much the same benevolent way that hers were created.

The analysis of vicariousness brings "feminine personality" into focus by allowing us to ask the question, Who benefits? If empathy, concern with others' wellbeing, altruism and other "feminine" traits were stable attributes of the person, they should find expression across a wide variety of situations. In fact, they are put in the service of the woman's immediate family. In our society, the major focus of the vicarious orientation is restricted to husband and children. In our society, a woman does not receive the esteem for ministering to or facilitating another woman, a leper or an inmate that she does for confining her efforts to her own family. This selectivity is more consistent with a sex role prescription than with an enduring attribute of the person. Inevitably, it leads us back to a consideration of the complementary concepts, Objectivity and Subjectivity.

Objectivity and Subjectivity

Simone de Beauvoir, in her analysis of the young girl (1952, book II, pp. 306–378) places the dimensions of masochism, narcissism and passivity in the larger context of the struggle between Objectivity and Subjectivity. de Beauvoir sees the young girl pushed toward acceptance of the adult female role, which—especially in its sexual aspect—is defined as Object. The themes of masochism, narcissism and passivity (by which women are so often characterized) are woven into the socialization process with Objectivity as the outcome.

Simone de Beauvoir thinks that adolescence—the social recognition of puberty and nubility, rather than the biological events themselves—brings about a discontinuity in the girl-child's experience of herself as Subject. The occasion is her confrontation with the adult female sex role and particularly sexual initiation. She struggles against it, but in de Beauvoir's view the reduction to the status of Object is virtually inescapable.

Simone de Beauvoir describes the ambivalence that young women feel toward the bodily changes of puberty. Reactions include alienation and horror (see pp. 287ff), a sense of dislocation occasioned by change itself and the sense of loss control. Another part of this ambivalence is due to the recognition of how one appears *as an object* to others. Beauvoir expresses a sense of loss of Subjectivity and an access of Objectivity, both tied to perceptions of the body:

> The young girl feels that her body is getting away from her, it is no longer the straightforward expression of her individuality; it becomes foreign to her; and at the same time she becomes for others a thing: on the street men follow her with their eyes and comment on her anatomy. She would like to be invisible; it frightens her to become flesh and to show her flesh (1952, p. 288).

The major part of the transition from Subject to Object is accomplished via representations to women about their bodies. In puberty, de Beauvoir says, the "dream of passivity" overtakes the woman. The expressions of her femaleness—e.g., menstruation, vaginal lubrication—are involuntary (or passive). Their association is with shameful excretory functions or culpable lack of control (e.g., bed-wetting) not with agency, purpose, directedness, control.

Beauvoir's discussion of the Objectification of women focuses upon ways women come to think of their bodies and their persons. When a woman is induced to relinquish Subjectivity based on mind or will, she is reduced to her body. And if women's bodies are commodities, women are commodities. Thus we say in Chapter 3 that women's physical selves are carved up and summed up in terms of "measurements" and "assets and liabilities." These in turn are subjected to enhancement procedures and then merchandised. Women's bodies are things, objects, commodities. The interchangeability of objects is implied by the view of *woman as Kleenex*, as a mass-produced commodity designed to serve a specific purpose, low cost and disposable. The seller hopes to develop brand loyalty in the consumer, but the whole culture of the commodity market works against her. The woman is herself induced to strive to enhance her attractiveness—that is, her qualities as an Object. Her job is to make men covet her, strive to possess her—not to act, but to cause others to act.

The enactment of the Object role generates an inherent ambivalence. Feelings of gratification and frustration may be simultaneously experienced. The ambivalence engendered by accepting the Object role is troublesome and recurrent. One possible "escape" from it is to embrace the rewarding aspects of objectivity and deny the contempt that Subject has for Object and that Object must, in some way, echo in her self-image. The "escape" is to assume the role of adorable object, or Privileged Other. Narcissism helps keep this desired balance. The positive side of Objectivity is being sought after and being courted. There is a sense of narcissistic entitlement fostered in young women, the premise of which is that beauty commands.[10]

The ambivalence of Objectivity finds expression in exercising power, either covertly or in fantasy. In fantasy or fiction, a kind of magic can be discerned—magic as Beauvoir defines it: passive force. In a typical *Love Comic* scenario, a young woman goes to extraordinary lengths to position herself to succeed as an Object: to be noticed, asked out, fallen in love with, proposed to, married and consigned to the happily-ever-after.

---

[10]Baumgold's (1971) portrait of the Jewish–American Princess illustrates the kind of socialization forces that produce this mentality and also how the J.A.P. experiences herself and her world.

Another pattern of reaction against ambivalence reveals fairly direct hostility that is expressed in a playful or "cute" way. This includes the whole set of techniques of manipulation and impression management that is called "feminine guile". A subset of these are what *Cosmopolitan* purveys as "teddy bear tricks"; things that a woman can do to throw her suitor off balance and keep him off balance. These play on his insecurities and enhance the woman's bargaining position. They are, of course, ways of playing the game; the game is the same one that Blau analyzes, and the woman's goal is the same. The basic mechanism is to assert "power" by invoking the male's fear of competition. Teddy bear tricks do not challenge the assumption that the woman is Object; they only create the fear that other dogs want this particular bone or that once wooed she will not stay bought.[11]

The negative side of Objectivity is alienation—from the body and its pleasures, from competence and pride in one's abilities, and from others who hold power over us. Women's rage, suppressed and denied as it often is, finds expression in symptom formation, as Chesler (1972) and Bart (1967) have shown. Sexual alienation is common among women living in a culture where rape is part of the script for relations between men and women, and where women, in faking orgasm, deny their own experience. The pretense of incompetence and helplessness can contribute to a failure of confidence and lack of zest. And resentment of economic dependency and thankless domestic labor can poison intimate relationships. Often the negative side of Objectivity comes into awareness only when beauty is modulated by age, when marriage is dissolved or an unprepared woman is forced into the labor market.

---

[11]One teddy bear trick is to have friends send the woman postcards with passionate messages from glamorous places and leave them around when the woman has her beau over. Zelda Sayre used a variant of this, the mistaken letter ploy. While she was pledged to Scott Fitzgerald and was waiting for him to make his name before marrying him, she went out with a number of others. Her letters to Scott stressed the trival and/or platonic nature of these relationships, while the letters to them were somewhat torrid. On at least one occasion, Zelda "accidentally" put the letters in the wrong envelopes and mailed them off (Milford, 1970, p. 52).

The character of this alienation is captured rather well in the research on psychological femininity. Psychological femininity is by no means isomorphic with biological femaleness. As a psychological trait, femininity is prey to artifact and to response bias just as other "traits" are. Femininity is not a unitary trait, nor does it covary with other psychological variables. As a measure of adaptation to the conditions of woman's life as Object, however, psychological femininity has many of the concomitants we might predict. A number of studies have found that high "femininity" on standard measures is associated with high anxiety (Gray, 1957; Webb, 1963), and with anxiety about aggression (Cosentino and Heilbrun, 1964). Though "masculinity" and sex role identification are related to social adjustment (Gray, 1957), popularity (Gray, 1957), and self-esteem for males (Connell and Johnson, 1970), this is not the case for females. Indeed, "femininity" seems to be bad for you, whether you are a girl or a boy. The CPI Femininity scale appears to measure poor self-concept in both sexes (Sears, 1970), and anxiety about aggression is associated with "femininity" in both sexes. An examination of some of the standard measures of femininity (cf. Gough, 1952) gives an indication of why this might be so. Any person who endorsed these items as being characteristic of her/himself might be expected to have self-esteem problems.

MOTHERS, FATHERS AND OTHER ROLE MODELS

Oftentimes psychological "femininity" is related to identification with the mother. More to the point, it is related to the kind of sex role model the mother represents. Daughters show better social adjustment when they identify with "more masculine" mothers. (Heilbrun, 1958). Mother-identified girls were less popular with their peers than father-identified girls (Gray, 1959). Here as in a number of other places, the terms "masculine" and "feminine" are misleading. What we are really talking about is mothers who offer an *enriched-feminine* role for their daughters to model, as contrasted with mothers who offer an *impoverished-feminine* role. The androgynous daughter has had the opportunity to learn more capabilities than the solely "feminine" daughter, and this is reflected in her expanded capabilities. Rand (1968) found that career-oriented young women were both more "masculine" and more "feminine" than their traditionally oriented peers. Heilbrun (1958) found that androgynous girls (whom he mislabeled "masculine") were both expressive and instrumental, while the "feminine" girls were expressive only. Connell and Johnson (1970) found sex role identification unrelated to self-esteem for girls— presumably because the low self-esteem of the "feminine" girls and the high self-esteem of "masculine" girls cancel each other out.

These findings confirm our contention that female personality is moulded to fit female roles. The quintessentially (or exaggeratedly) feminine personality is destined for the impoverished female role. Watley and Kaplan (1971), in their study of college women, found that those who chose the Housewife-only lifestyle had the lowest SAT scores. Birnbaum (1970) compared college honor graduates who were not employed outside the house with a group of married professionals and a group of single professionals. This study gives a more complete picture of the impoverished feminine role. Women in the Housewife-only role perceived employment and wifehood as incompatible, attitudes which they received from their parents. In other ways, too, they recapitulated their parental homes: they had a traditional family division of labor, and not a particularly close relationship with the husband. Their marital happiness was lower than that of the Married Professionals group, and their self-confidence was the lowest of the three groups.

The Married Professionals of Birnbaum's study had different parents and different marriages. They perceived their own parents as having a close relationship, and often had employed mothers. In their own marriages there was acceptance of the wife's career and sharing of domestic responsibilities. They viewed their partners as supermen, and themselves as fortunate women. They had higher self-esteem and reported themselves as more competent than either of the other groups. They saw no conflict between career and family commitments, and reported more pleasures associated with family than did the Housewife-only women.

The Married Professionals received more support for both competence and femininity, from both parents and spouse, than did women in either of the other groups.

The Single professionals came from less advantaged backgrounds than either of the other groups, and reported neither closeness nor support for academic achievement from their parents. Both their individual upward mobility and their marital status contributed to a picture of isolation and lack of substantial social support in their chosen lifestyle. It should be noted that although these women rejected domesticity, they did not reject femininity, and found many outlets for nurturance in their teaching duties.

Even within the straitjacket of contemporary sex role definitions, researchers have discovered that a range of feminine roles exists. A number of studies have sought to explain differences between career-oriented women and traditional women. Given the restricted range, these boil down to differences between women whose lives are defined by the role Housewife-only and those who can be defined as Housewife-plus. Very little attention has been paid to women who are not in marital roles.

Most studies have found that, whatever their occupational commitments, most women report themselves as giving priority to their family responsibilities. This is no surprise, given the early sex role socialization we have reviewed in this chapter. With few exceptions, little girls in our culture are exposed to these socialization pressures. Differences in outcomes are attributable to two factors: (1) variant experiences in early socialization, and (2) continuing socialization experiences.

Within the nuclear family, the girl-child who will have high occupational commitment in adulthood is likely to have encountered an employed mother, a "liberated" father or both. Early studies found that an employed mother predicted to a young girl's high occupational aspiration. Sometimes the mother's values predict to daughter's aspiration, even where she has not been employed. In her longitudinal study of high-school graduates, Mulvey (1963) found some women who characterized themselves as highly career oriented, even though they had not been employed since marriage. Presumably the constraints of the family situation prevent some women from pursuing their career interests. In these cases their message to their daughters may be, "Do as I say, not as I do."

The importance of the father is illustrated by Baruch's (1972) findings. She found that the father's acceptance of a dual-role lifestyle was an important predictor of the daughter's expressed intention to have a career. Conversely, Walstedt (1977) has shown that a father who crushes his daughter's achievement and sexual expression produced a daughter with high "other-orientation"— that is, a "feminine" woman. We have already seen that many fathers encourage feminine behaviors in their daughters and fail to encourage other attributes. Some fathers may discourage extrafamilial commitments in their wives while encouraging daughters' achievement orientation. We do not have data at present to tell us how this affects daughters' ultimate choices or, indeed, relations between mothers and daughters.

Early socialization and lifestyle exemplars appear important in Birnbaum's study. Other studies of women's lifestyle planning reveal substantial influence of events and persons encountered later in life. Angrist and Almquist (1975; Almquist and Angrist, 1970) found that college women who could be designated as Career Salient or Traditional in terms of orientation toward future employment differed in terms of relations with peers and professors. The Traditionals were significantly more likely to be sorority members and to be seriously involved in a romantic relationship. The Career Salients were significantly more likely to have experience with male peers in a professionally as contrasted with socially oriented context. They also perceived that their professors thought highly of their abilities, while the Traditionals thought their professors thought poorly of them. Unfortunately, in this study the Traditionals and Career Salients differed in academic ability/achievement.

In Tangri's (1972) study, all respondents were senior honors students at a large midwestern university. Tangri found that college women choosing role-innovative occupations (i.e., occupations in which 30% or fewer workers were female) had often had productive associations with male teaching fellows. Both studies showed that supportive boyfriends were important in young women's pursuing these high aspirations. Trigg and Perlman (1975) found that career-oriented women students perceived support from boyfriends and parents. Women students who planned no career had parents who did not support any career.

Additional research is needed to identify sources of encouragement for continued professional development beyond college. It can be anticipated that as women move into graduate and professional training, their parents may continue to provide encouragement but cannot really validate their competence. Professors and colleagues may become increasingly important for this kind of feedback and support.

Male peers (particularly future or current partners) exercise substantial influence on women's options. Almquist (1974) found that men are still less favorable to married women's employment than are women (50% as contrasted with 67% of women). Komarovsky (1973), similarly, found that college men supporting a truly egalitarian lifestyle were a small minority: seven percent.

We have little research to date on egalitarian families, particularly where husbands' and wives' careers are given equal importance. One marital lifestyle described by Rapoport and Rapoport (1971) has a husband who is more family-oriented than usual combined with a wife who is more career-oriented than usual. In this type of family the development of the parents is parallel. Although the "two-career" lifestyle described by Rapoport and Rapoport may still be rare, it seems not unlikely that it may provide the pattern of the future, as two-earner families become the dominant family form.

Is Socialization the New Determinism?

Feminists, in battling the doctrine of innate female inferiority, have seized upon the two-edged sword of socialization. Their arguments locate the source of the problem in the social system rather than in the individual. Unfortunately, such analyses can be put to ideological purposes not intended by their authors. As we mentioned earlier in this chapter, research on socialization focuses on early or primary socialization almost to the exclusion of continuing socialization. This focus gets an added boost from developmentalists and from Freud, who often claim that the direction and limits of personality are set during the earliest years. In this tradition, primary socialization is often treated as a one-way influence process of agents of socialization upon objects of socialization, rather than as an interaction in which reciprocal shaping of behavior takes place. Given the picture of sex roles that is drawn, this element too adds to the presumptive rigidity of personality. Finally, of course, the self as an agent of socialization tends to be ignored. What all this adds up to is a picture of women as permanently disabled persons—victims, to be sure, of implacable forces of sex role socialization, but beyond help. It might be argued that to give such creatures opportunities or responsibilities beyond their capacities would be the height of economic irrationality, not to mention inhumanity.

The position taken in this chapter holds that neither personality nor socialization is fixed. If the idea of personality has any utility, it must be as *a set of learned adaptations to the significant environment*. Unless the environment is either fixed or absolutely regular, adaptation must be a continuing process. Further, a great deal of the significant environment, for humans, is social. Much of social life is organized into roles, a succession or multiplicity of roles. The individual is socialized into each new role, and role partners act as both agents of socialization and as monitors of role behavior. If personality is fixed and *if* the inoculation of primary socialization lasts a lifetime, it can only be under extraordinary conditions: where roles are fixed and their social supports unchanging. For most of us this is not the case; and we might expect that women, whose lives change markedly over the lifecycle, might be the least static of all.

We need not go beyond the evidence we have reviewed so far to see that expressions of "personality variables" have always been sensitive to variations in external conditions. From the beginning, research on achievement motivation has shown that the volume of imagery is affected by experimental variation of arousal conditions, sex of experimenter, presence or absence of others, sex of others and characteristics of the stimulus cues. These variations are not due to error, but simply remind us that *personality is adaptive, and behavior is contingent upon external conditions*.

In actuality, sex role socialization is not implanted in personality like an electrode of the brain. It is a social process, taking place within social contexts that vary systematically—e.g., by class and race—and idiosyncratically. We have seen that variations in sex role scripts are reflected in the organization of personality. Moreover, the individual can choose to resist or transcend the effects of early socialization. Even from an early age, the individual exercises considerable selectivity with regard to the significant others who surround her. She constructs her identity, and can construct her significant social environment. The social environment, while it undoubtedly has the potential of reinforcing sex role conformity, can equally well support sex role transcendance.

Beyond Socialization

Birnbaum's research demonstrates that different sex role scripts are encountered in the family, the site of primary socialization. In two of her groups, respondents did not deviate from the scripts to which they were exposed as children. Their personality, as measured by Birnbaum, fits their role destination. Only the Single

Professionals opted for a sex role script that differed in major ways from their earliest models.

The next chapter is devoted to a more detailed consideration of factors in continuing growth, particularly that involved in sex role transcendance. This calls for developing the analysis of role modeling, and exploring sources of social support for unscripted and unconventional options.

In this chapter we have noted that *insofar as self-image and self-esteem are tied to conventional sex role scripts, sex role transcendance or sex role liberation is blocked.* In Chapter 5 we will devote more attention to the role of self in directing choice and behavior, as we explore the idea of female subjectivity.

However, sex role transcendance has implications not only for the individual but for the collectivity. In fact, the "liberated" individual can become a liberated parent, and intervene in the socialization process. Once the individual becomes aware of sex role scripting, the potential for intervention becomes apparent. It is not accidental that persons who become aware of the need for freedom from programmed Objectivity give thoughtful attention to alternative sex role socialization. However, change will require systematic and sustained activity commensurate with the systematic penetration of sex stereotyping in the institutions surveyed in this chapter.

The actualization of women's (and others') potential for Subjectivity will require the same kind of integrated and mutually reinforcing patterns that now produce Objectivity with such reliability. No single project, no matter how apt, can reverse the direction of forces toward Objectivity. Liberated parents are finding, to their dismay, that their children develop—usually by the age of four—robust sexists attitudes, sex-typed toy perferences and "plans" for adult life. Persons who are selective about their children's reading materials cannot control the television programming their children ingest. Egalitarian couples find themselves succumbing to a traditional sexual division of labor when their first child is born. Women who do not choose marriage and/

or motherhood find themselves continually asked to justify their choices. Working wives "compensate" for the power potential of their earnings by espousing a male-dominance ideology. "Sensitive" men have to cope with the chivvying of the John Wayne clones who surround them.

The points requiring change are many—in the overall social structure or in an individual life. In the next chapter we turn to signs of the beginning of change.

R E F E R E N C E S

Adams, Margaret, 1971. The compassion trap, in *Woman in Sexist Society*, ed. Vivian Gornick and Barbara Moran. New York: Basic Books.

Anastasiouw, N.J. 1965. Success in school boys' sex-role patterns. *Child Development* 36: 1053–1066.

Armontrout, J. A., and Burger, G. K. 1972. Children's reports of parental child-rearing behavior at five grade levels. *Developmental Psychology* pp. 44–48.

Asher, S. R., and Gottman, J. M. 1973. Sex of teacher and student reading achievement. *Journal of Educational Psychology* 65: 168–171.

Atkinson, John E. ed. 1958. *Motives in Fantasy, Action and Society*. Princeton, NJ: Van Nostrand.

Baird, L. L. 1973. *The Graduates*. Princeton: Educational Testing Service.

Bart, Pauline B. 1967. Depression in middle-aged women: Some sociocultural factors. Unpublished Ph.D. dissertation, U.C.L.A.

Battle, E. S. 1965. Motivational determinants of academic task persistence. *Journal of Personality and Social Psychology* 2: 209–218.

———. 1966. Motivational determinants of academic competence. *Journal of Personality and Social Psychology* 4: 634–642.

Baumgold, Julie. 1971. The persistence of The Jewish American Princess. *New York* 4: 25–31.

Baumrind, Diana, and Black, Alan. 1967. Socialization practices associated with dimensions of competence in preschool boys and girls. *Child Development* 38: 291–328.

Bem, S. 1974. The measurement of psychological androgyny. *Journal of Consulting and Clinical Psychology* 42: 155–162.

Bernstein, M. R. 1955. Relationship between interest and reading comprehension. *Journal of Educational Research* 69: 283–288.

Birnbaum, J. L. A. 1971. Life patterns, personality style and self-esteem in gifted family oriented and career committed women. Unpublished Ph.D. dissertation, University of Michigan.

Blood, R. O., and Wolfe, D. M. 1960. *Husbands and Wives: The Dynamics of Married Living*. Glencoe, IL: The Free Press.

———. 1966. The division of labor in American families, in *Role Theory*, ed. R. J. Biddle and E. J. Thomas, pp. 265–271. New York: Wiley.

Brinkman, E. H. 1966. Programmed instruction as a technique for improving spatial socialization. *Journal of Applied Psychology* 50: 179–184.

Carey, G. L. 1955. Reduction of sex differences in problem solving by improvement of attitude through group discussion. Unpublished dissertation, Stanford.

Chesler, Phyllis. 1972. *Women and Madness*. Garden City, NY: Doubleday.

Child, I. L., Potter, E. H., and Levine, E. M. 1946. Children's textbooks and personality development: An exploration of the social psychology of education. *Psychology Monographs* 60: 1–54.

Chiu, L. H. 1973. Reading preferences of fourth grade children related to sex and reading ability. *Journal of Educational Research* 66: 369–373.

Clausen, John A. ed. 1968. *Socialization and Society*. Boston: Little Brown and Company.

Connell, D. M., and Johnson, J. E. 1970. Relationship between sex-role identification and self-esteem in early adolescents. *Deviant Psychology* 3: 268.

Cooley, Charles Horton. 1902. *Human Nature and the Social Order*. New York: Scribner.

Corsini, R. J. 1956. Multiple predictors and marital happiness. *Journal of Marriage and Family Living* 18: 240–242.

Cosentino, F., and Helbrun, A. B. 1964. Anxiety correlates of sex-role identity in college students. *Psychology Reports* 4: 729–730.

Crandall, V. J., Katkowsky, W., and Preston, A. 1962. Motivational and ability determinants of young children's intellectual achievement behaviors. *Child Development* 33: 643–661.

Deaux, Kay. 1971. Honking at the intersection: A replication and extension. *Journal of Social Psychology* 84: 159–160.

Deaux, Kay, and Emswiller, T. 1974. Explanations of successful performance on sex-linked tasks: What is skill for the male is luck for the female. *Journal of Personality and Social Psychology* 29: 80–85.

de Beauvoir, Simone. 1953. *The Second Sex*. New York: Knopf.

DeLucia, L. A. 1963. The toy preference test: A measure of sex-role identification. *Child Development* 34: 107–117.

Denmark, Florence, and Sherman, Julia. 1979. *The Psychology of Women: Future Directions in Research*. New York: Psychological Dimensions.

Denmark, F., Tangri, S. S., and McCandless, S. 1979. Affiliation achievement and power: A new look, in *The Psychology of Women: Future Directions in Research*, ed. Florence Denmark and Julia Sherman. New York: Psychological Dimensions.

Deutsch, Helene. 1944. *The Psychology of Women: A Psychoanalytic Interpretation*. New York: Grune and Stratton.

————. 1945. *The Psychology of Women, Vol. II*. New York: Grune and Stratton.

Digman, J. M. 1963. Principal dimensions of child personality as inferred from teacher's judgments. *Child Development* 34: 43–60.

Douglas, J. W. B. 1964. *The Home and the School*. London: MacGibbon, 71–75.

Eagly, Alice H. 1978. Sex differences in influenceability. *Psychology Bulletin* 85(1): 86–116.

Erikson, Erik. 1964. Inner and outer space: Reflections of womanhood, in *The Woman in America*, ed. Robert Lifton. Boston: Beacon Press.

Fagot, B. I., and Patterson, G. R. 1969. An in vivo analysis of reinforcing contingencies of sex role behaviors in the preschool child. *Developmental Psychology* 1: 563–568.

Farrell, Warren, 1974. *The Liberated Man: Beyond Masculinity*. New York: Random House.

Fauls, L. B., and Smith, W. D. 1956. Sex-role learning of five-year-olds. *Journal of Genetic Psychology* 89: 105–117.

Faust, Margaret S. 1960. Developmental maturing as a determinant in prestige of adolescent girls. *Child Development* 31: 173–186.

Ferguson, L. R., and Maccoby, E. E. 1966. Interpersonal correlates of differential abilities. *Child Development* 37: 549–571.

Feshback, N., and Feshback, S. 1969. The relation between empathy and aggression in two age groups. *Developmental Psychology* 1: 102–107.

Fidell, L. S. 1970. Empirical verification of sex discrimination in hiring practices in psychology. *American Psychologist* 25: 1094–1098.

Frasher, R., and Walker, A. 1972. Sex roles in early reading textbooks. *Reading Teacher* 25: 741–749.

Freud, Sigmund. 1914. On narcissism: An introduction, in *The Collected Papers of Sigmund Freud*, ed. Philip Rieff, pp. 56–83. New York: Collier Books, 1963.

————. 1924. The Economic problem in masochism, *The Collected Papers of Sigmund Freud*, ed. Philip Rieff, pp. 190–202. New York: Collier Books, 1963.

————. 1925. Some psychological consequences of the anatomical distinction between the sexes, *The Collected Papers of Sigmund Freud*, ed. Philip Rieff, pp. 183–194. New York: Collier Books, 1963.

————. 1931. Female sexuality, *The Collected Papers of Sigmund Freud*. ed. Philip Rieff, pp. 194–212. New York: Collier Books, 1963.

Frodi, Ann, Macauley, Jacqueline, and Thomas, Pauline. 1977. Are women always less aggressive than men? A review of the experimental literature. *Psychology Bulletin* 84 (4): 634–660.

Fromm, Erich. 1956. *The Art of Loving*. New York: Harper.

Gesell, A. 1941. *The First Five Years of Life*. New York: Harper.

Goldberg, Philip. 1968. Are women prejudiced against women? *Trans-Action* 5: 28–30.

Good, T. L., Sikes, J. N., and Brophy, J. E. 1973. Effects of teacher sex and student sex on classroom interaction. *Journal of Educational Psychology* 65: 74–87.

Goodenough, Evelyn W. 1957. Interest in persons as an aspect of sex differences in the early years. *Genetetic Psychology Monographs* 55: 287–323.

Gough, H. G. 1952. Identifying psychological femininity. *Education and Psychology Measurement* 12: 427–439.

Graebner, D. B. 1972. A decade of sexism in readers. *Reading Teacher* 26: 52–58.

Gray, S. W. 1957. Masculinity–femininity in relation to anxiety and social acceptance. *Child Development* 28: 203–214.

Griffeath, Catherine. 1973. Sex differences in reading. Unpublished ms., Cornell University.

Hartley, Ruth E. 1959. Sex-role pressures and the socialization of the male child. *Psychological Report* 5: 457–568.

———. 1960. Children's concepts of male and female roles. *Merrill-Palmer Quarterly* 6: 84–91.

———. 1964. A developmental view of female sex roles definition and identification. *Merrill-Palmer Quarterly* 10: 3–16.

——— and Hardesty, F. P. 1964. Children's perceptions of sex roles in childhood. *Journal of Genetic Psychology* 105: 43–51.

Hartup, W. W., and Moore, S. G. 1963. Avoidance of inappropriate sex-typing by young children. *Journal of Consulting Psychology* 37: 467–473.

Heilbrun, A. B., 1958. Sex role: Instrumental expressive behavior and psychopathology in females. *Journal of Abnormal and Social Psychology* 73: 131–136.

Hess, R. D., and Torney, Judith V. 1962. Religion, age and sex in children's perceptions of family authority. *Child Development* 33: 781–789.

Hochschild, Arlie R. 1975. Attending to, codifying and managing feelings: Sex differences in love. Paper presented at the annual meetings of the American Sociological Association.

Hoffman, Lois W. 1972. Early childhood experiences and women's achievement motives. *Journal of Social Issues* 28: 129–155.

Horner, Matina. 1972. Toward an understanding of achievement-related conflicts in women. *Journal of Social Issues* 28: 157–175.

Horney, Karen. 1967. *Feminine Psychology*. New York: W. W. Norton.

Iglitzin, L. B. 1972. A child's eye view of sex roles. *Today's Education* 61: 23–26.

Ireson, Carol Jean. 1975. Effects of sex role socialization on the academic achievement, educational expectations, and interpersonal competence of adolescent girls. Unpublished Ph.D. dissertation, Cornell University.

Kagan, J. 1964. Acquisition and significance of sex typing and sex role identity, in *Review of Child Development Research*, Vol. ed. I, M. Hoffman and L. Hoffman, pp. 137–167. New York: Russell Sage.

——— and Lemkin, J. 1960. The child's differential perception of parental attributes. *Journal of Abnormal and Social Psych.* 61: 440–447.

Katz, Irwin, 1969. A critique of personality approaches to Negro performance with research suggestions. *Journal of Social Issues* 25: 13–29.

Katz, P. A. 1973. Stimulus predifferentiation and modification of children's racial attitudes. *Child Development* 44: 232–237.

Kellogg, R. L. 1969. A direct approach to sex-role identification of school-related objects. *Psychological Reports* 24: 839–841.

Kohlberg, L. A. 1966. A cognitive developmental analysis of children's sex-role concepts and attitudes, in *The Development of Sex Differences*, ed. E. E. Maccoby, pp. 82–173. Stanford: Stanford University Press.

————— and Zigler, E. 1967. The impact of cognitive maturity on the development of sex-role attitudes in the years 4 to 8. *Genetic Psychology Monographs* 75: 84–165.

Kohn, Mel. 1969. *Class and Conformity*. Homewood, IL: Dorsey Press.

Komarovsky, Mirra. 1946. Cultural contradictions and sex roles. *American Journal of Sociology* 52: 184–189.

—————. 1973. Cultural contradictions and sex roles: The masculine case. *American Journal of Sociology* 78: 873–884.

Laing, R. D., and Esterson, A. 1964. *Sanity, Madness and The Family*. New York: Basic Books.

Laws, Judith Long 1976. Psychological dimensions of work force participation of women, in *Some New Perspectives of Equal Employment Opportunity: The A. T. & T. Case*, ed. P. A. Wallace. Cambridge MA: MIT Press.

————— and Schwartz, Pepper. 1976. *Sexual Scripts: The Social Construction of Female Sexuality*. Hinsdale, IL: Dryden Press.

Levitin, T., and Chananie, D. 1972. Responses of female primary school teachers to sex-typed behaviors in male and female children. *Child Development* 43: 1309–1316.

Lewis, Michael. 1972. State as infant-environment interaction: An analysis of mother–child interaction as a function of sex. *Merrill-Palmer Quarterly* 18: 95–112.

Maccoby, Eleanor E. 1966. Sex differences in intellectual functioning, in *The Development of Sex Differences*, ed. E. E. Maccoby, pp. 25–55. Stanford, CA: Stanford University Press.

————— and Jacklin, Carol N. 1973. Stress, activity, and proximity seeking: sex differences in the year old child. *Child Development* 44: 34–42.

Matthews, E., and Tiedeman, D. V. 1964. Attitudes toward career and marriage and the development of life style in young women. *Journal of Consulting Psychology* 11: 375–383.

McClelland, David C. 1966. Longitudinal trends in the relation of thought to action. *Journal of Consulting Psychology* 30: 479–483.

————— and Atkinson, J. W., Clark, R. A., and Lowell, E. L. 1953. *The Achievement Motive*. New York: Appleton-Century-Crofts.

McNeil, J. D. 1964. Programmed instruction versus usual classroom procedures in teaching boys to read, *American Education Research Journal* 1: 113–119.

Meyer, W. J., and Thompson, G. G. 1963. Teacher interactions with boys as contrasted with girls, in *Psychological Studies of Human Development*, ed. R. G. Kuhlens and G. G. Thompson. New York: Appleton-Century-Crofts.

Milford, Nancy. 1970. *Zelda, A Biography*. New York: Harper and Row.

Milton, G. A. 1958. Five studies of the relation between sex-role identification and achievement in problem solving. Tech. Report #3. New Haven: Yale University Dept. of Industrial administration and Dept. of Psychology.

———. 1959. Sex differences in problem solving as a function of role appropriateness of the problem content, *Psychology Reports* 5: 705–708.

Mischel, Walter. 1970. In *Carmichael's Manual on Child Development Research*, ed. Paul Mussen. New York: Wiley.

Monahan, L., Kuhn, D., and Shaver, P. 1974. Intrapsychic versus cultural explanations of the fear of success motive, *Journal of Personality and Social Psychology* 29: 61–64.

Mussen, Paul ed. 1970. *Carmichael's Manual of Child Psychology*. New York: Wiley.

Parker, V. J. 1972. Fear of success, sex-role orientation of the task, and competition condition as variables affecting women's performance in achievement oriented situations. Dissertation abstracts.

Parlee, Mary Brown. 1975. Review Essay: Psychology. *Signs: Journal of Women in Culture and Society* 1: 119–139.

Peltier, G. L. 1968. Sex differences in the school: problem and proposed solution. *Phi Delta Kappan* 50: 182–184.

Peterson, J. 1972. Effects of sex of E and sex of S in first and fifth grade children's paired-associate learning. *Journal of Education Research* 66: 81–82.

Pheterson, G., Klesler, S., and Goldberg, P. 1971. Evaluation of the performance of women as a function of their sex, achievement, and personal history. *Journal of Personality and Social Psychology* 19: 114–118.

Pleck, Joe. 1975. Issues for the men's movement. Ann Arbor: Unpublished ms.

——— and Sawyer, Jack. 1974. *Men and Masculinity*. New York: Prentice-Hall.

Pulaski, M. 1970. Play as a function of toy structure and fantasy predisposition. *Child Development* 41: 531–537.

Rabban, M. 1950. Sex-role identification in young children in two diverse social groups. *Genetic Psychology Monograph* 42: 81–158.

Rand, L. 1968. Masculinity or femininity? *Journal of Counseling Psychology* 15 (5): 444–450.

Raynor, Joel O. 1974. Future orientation in the study of achievement motivation, in *Motivation and Achievement*, ed. Atkinson, J. W., and Raynor, J. O. pp. 121–155. Washington, DC: V. H. Winston and Sons.

Roby, Pam. 1975. Vocational education and women. Santa Cruz: Unpublished.

Rosenberg, B. G., and Sutton-Smith, B. 1968. Family interaction effects on masculinity-femininity, *Journal of Personality and Social Psychology* 8: 117–120.

Ross, S. A. 1971. A test of generality of the effects of deviant preschool models, *Developmental Psychology* 4: 262–267.

Ryan, William. 1971. *Blaming the Victim*. New York: Pantheon Books.

Saario, Teresa, Jacklin, C. N., and Tittle, C. K. 1973. Sex role stereotyping in the public schools, *Harvard Educational Review* 43: 386–416.

Sartre, Jean Paul. 1966. *Being and Nothingness*. New York: Washington Square Press.

Schneider, Joseph W., and Hacker, Sally. 1972. Sex role imagery and the use of the generic 'man' in introductory tests: A case in the sociology of sociology. Paper presented at the annual meeting of The American Sociological Association.

Sears, Pauline S. 1963. The effect of classroom conditions on the strength of achievement motive and work output of elementary school children. Final Report, Cooperative Research Project No. 873, Stanford University.

Sears, R. R., Rau, L. and Alpert, R. 1965. *Identification and Child Rearing*. Stanford: Stanford University Press.

Sexton, Patricia Cayo. 1969. *The Feminized Male*. New York: Random House.

Sherif, Carolyn 1977. Bias in psychology. Paper presented for the conference "Toward an equitable pursuit of knowledge." Madison, Wisconsin.

Sherman, Julia. 1971. *On the Psychology of Women: A Survey of Empirical Studies*. Springfield, IL: Charles C. Thomas.

Simpson, Lawrence A. 1970. A myth is better than a miss: Men get the edge in academic employment. *College and University Business*, pp. 72–73.

Slaby, R. G. 1973. Verbal regulation of aggression and altruism in children. Paper presented at the First International Conference on the Determinants and Origins of Aggressive Behavior. Monte Carlo.

Smith, S. 1939. Age and sex differences in children's opinion concerning sex differences. *Journal of Genetic Psychology* 54: 17–25.

Stein, A. H. 1969. The influence of social reinforcement on the achievement behavior of fourth grade boys and girls. *Child Development* 40: 727–736.

———— and Bailey, M. 1973. The socialization of achievement orientation in females. *Psychology Bulletin* 80 (5): 345–66.

———— and Smithels, J. 1969. Age and sex differences in children's sex-role standards about achievement. *Developmental Psychology* 3: 252–259.

———— Pohly, S., Pohly, R., and Mueller, E. 1971. The influence of masculine, feminine, and neutral tasks on children's achievement behavior, expectancies of success, and attainment values. *Child Development* 42: 195–217.

Stoller, Robert, 1968. *Sex and Gender*. New York: Science House.

Stuckert, R. D. 1963. Role perception and marital satisfaction—a configuration approach, *Journal of Marriage and Family Living* 25: 415–419.

Suppes, P. 1968. Computer technology and the future of education. *Phi Delta Kappan* 49, 8: 420–423.

Sutherland, M. B. 1961. Co-education and school attainment. *British Journal of Educational Psychology* 31: 158–169.

Tangri, Sandra Schwartz. 1972. Determinants of occupational role innovation among college women. *Journal of Social Issues* 28 (2): 177–201.

Tasch, Ruth J. 1952. The role of the father in the family *Journal of Experimental Education* 21: 319–361.

Thompson, S. K., and Bentler, P. M., 1971. The priority of cues in sex dis-

302

crimination by children and adults. *Developmental Psychology* 5: 181–185.

———— and Bentler, P. M. 1973. A developmental study of gender constancy and parent preference. *Archives of Sexual Behavior* 65: 211–215.

Torrance, E. 1962. *Guiding Greater Talent*, pp. 111–114. Englewood Cliffs, NJ: Prentice-Hall.

Tregaskes, G. K. 1972. The relationship between sex role standards of reading and reading achievement of first grade boys. Ed.D. dissertation, SUNY Albany.

Trigg, Linda, and Perlman, Daniel. 1975. Social influences on women's pursuit of a nontraditional career. Paper presented at the meeting of the Western Psychological Association.

Tyler, Leona E. 1951. Relationship of interests to abilities and reputation among first grade children. *Educational and Psychological Measurement* 11: 255–265.

————. 1964. The antecedents of two varieties of vocational interests. *Genetic Psychology Monographs* 70: 177–227.

Walter, S. C. 1973. An assessment of the effects of grouping according to sex on the achievement of reading in the first grade. Unpublished Ed.D. dissertation, Ball State University.

Ward, W. D. 1968. Variance of sex-role preference among boys and girls. *Psychology Reports* 23: 467–470.

Watley, D. J., and Kaplan, R. 1971. Career or marriage? Aspirations and achievements of able young women. *Journal of Vocational Behavior* 1: 29–43.

Webb, A. P. 1963. Sex role preferences and adjustment in early adolescents. *Child Development* 34: 609–618.

Willson, J. R., Beecham, C. T., and Carrington, E. R. 1963. *Obstetrics and Gynecology*. St. Louis: C. V. Mosby Company.

Wolf, T. M. 1973. Effects of live modeled sex-inappropriate play behavior in a naturalistic setting. *Developmental Psychology* 9: 120–123.

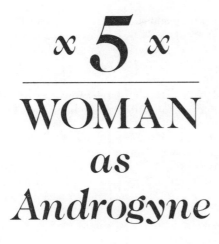

WOMAN
as
Androgyne

The idea of androgyny—a combination or reconciliation of femininity and masculinity—has intrigued thinkers for centuries. In Pythagoras's myth of creation, initially whole entities were split, and through the eons female and male have sought their other half to reunite through mating and recapture wholeness. More recently, creative writers, such as Virginia Woolf, have treated femininity and masculinity as parochial divisions that work against creativity. Quoting Coleridge, Woolf (1957) asserts that the great mind must be androgynous.

The recent resurgence of interest in androgyny was brought about by the publication of Carolyn Heilbrun's book *Toward a Recognition of Androgyny*, in 1973. Heilbrun compiles images and snippets of androgyny through centuries of literature and art, emphasizing the female components of androgyny. Heilbrun's definition of androgyny refers, oddly enough, to a cultural rather than an individual state. Thus, for Heilbrun, androgyny is "a condition under which the characteristics of the sexes, and the human impulses expressed by men and women, are not rigidly assigned" (1973, x). In most usages, androgyny refers to a state of the individual. The uneasy or unspecified combination of feminine and maculine under one skin has been expressed in a number of metaphors, as we shall see. Many of the images employ a metaphor of the body, as in the idea of "psychic hermaphroditism."

The Metaphor of the Body

The freakish image of the psychic hermaphrodite is rooted in the assumed normality of female and male as polarized and real entities. The fixity of female and male bodies and physical function is the original metaphor for femininity and masculinity. One whose body contains elements of both is a hermaphrodite; this is a physical, not a psychic, fact. The unwillingness to accept the physical multiplexity of the hermaphrodite lies behind stigmatizing her or him as a freak. A "psychic hermaphrodite" would be one whose mind contains female and male sex organs—clearly a meaningless notion. Yet transsexualism is commonly confused with hermaphroditism, betraying the confusion between psychic and bodily sexuality. The transsexual is a dramatic phenomenon, for a transsexual is formed by an exceedingly strong *psychic* identification with the "opposite" sex in an individual who is unambiguously male (or female) in physical attributes. With respect to genetic and body structure, the transsexual can be assigned to one or the other gender; there is no ambiguity, no multiplexity at the level of the body. With the transsexual, the body is made to be a metaphor for psychic sexuality, when the transsexual undergoes sex reassignment surgery.

It is the metaphor of the body that misleads us when we read of homoerotic sexual object choice. Because they assume femininity and masculinity to have the stability of the body, researchers and writers search for physical abnormalities that could "explain" an individual's preference for a sexual partner of her own gender. Perhaps within the appearance of normal femaleness or maleness there lurks a biological difference that makes the homosexual "really" discontinuous with heterosexuals. To date, these research efforts have been fruitless. While the metaphor of the body is misleading, its persistence indicates an abiding interest in the fusing of feminine and masculine elements. *It is the combination of feminine and masculine, rather than of female and male, that is our focus in the study of androgyny.* My own definition of *androgyny is a state in which feminine and masculine elements are present, accepted and accessible within the individual.*

The yearning for androgyny finds many expressions. Often it is expressed in dress, as when an individual of one gender adopts the dress common to the other. Dress is ordinarily a means of expression, in which conscious expression of aspects of the self is combined with the anticipation of a designed effect on others. Transvestism builds upon the expressive function of dress, adding on the cross-dresser's image of the desirable Other, which may also correspond to a hidden self. In transvestism there is the fantasy of transformation into another identity. Successful "passing" confirms the achievement of the created identity.

Thus history yields many accounts of cross-dressing as a means of gaining a variety of ends.[1] Deborah Sampson disguised herself as a boy and served valorously in the American Revolution. The theme of the daring girl passing as a soldier is common in literature and opera. In more recent times, accounts of the life of Vita Sackville-West illustrate some of the dilemmas of androgyny and of bisexuality. A member of the intellectual and artistic Bloomsbury community, Sackville-West occasioned a major scandal by fleeing, with her lover, Violet Trefusis, across several continents, pursued by their husbands. This dramatic denouement was part of a history in which Vita attempted a number of means for expressing and unifying her androgyny. At the core of her dilemma

---

[1] Our interest here is thus broader than the traditional treatments of transvestism in the literature of psychopathology. That literature emphasizes the role of cross-dressing for sexual arousal, and thus limits its focus to fetishism. As the discussion shows, cross-dressing can serve many functions, not the least of which is that of ordinary disguise: it allows the individual access to situations and interactions which would not be available to her in her usual dress. The blinders of psychopathology may have caused scholars to overlook the obvious and normal desire to express one's androgyny through dress (see, for example, "My cosmetic confidence," by David Cawley, and "provoking," by Jack Anderson, in *Shocks*, No. 6 (1976).

was what she perceived as a "duality" in her nature. Prophetically, she opines, in the diaries that form the basis of the account, (Nicolson, 1973) that individuals constituted as she was are not so rare as is supposed, and that a future climate of tolerance and candor will permit a more coherent lifestyle for bisexuals. In her own life, she suffered terribly from the constraints and obloquy that surrounded her experiments. The society in which she lived did not permit her to accept and celebrate all aspects of herself, as is reflected in her fictional writings. Vita created a fictional character whose lover says, "'What am I to believe—that she is cursed with a dual nature, the one coarse and unbridled, the other delicate, conventional, practical, montherly, refined?" (1973, p. 143). Her own understanding of her "duality" was that her gentleness and femininity were evoked solely by her husband; in all other contexts her "masculine" personality sought expression. The visible manifestation of this element of herself was a handsome "boy" named Julian, who dressed as often as possible in male clothing. In Vita's account it was her partner Violet who drew the connection for her between the chosen identity and a sexual career with women (1973, p. 104). Vita's solution to the division within her life was to maintain two lives, attempting to keep them separate. Her son reports that at first Vita thought she had discovered a neat division within herself, expressed in two separate lives: she "loved" her husband, Harold, and was "in love with" Violet. She hoped to keep them separate. This proved impossible, and the failure of compartmentalization was agonizing. "When I passed from one to the other, keeping them separate and apart, I could just keep the thing within my control; but when they met, coincided, and were simultaneous, I found them impossible to reconcile" (1973, p. 130).

Vita's compact with her husband required honesty with him. When she extended this honesty to their families, their reactions brought home an alienation and torment that she could evade only in her private intimacies. "I felt so alien from the whole kindly, law-abiding house; I felt like a pariah, and his mother's tolerance only increased my shame. . . . I felt blackened, and I was so unhappy, and felt my alienation from them and my affinity with Violet so keenly that I only wanted to fly where I would not pollute their purity any longer" (1973, 117–118). Vita repeatedly refers to her flights with Violet in terms of liberation, not only from the constraints of the domestic feminine role, but in a deeper sense: the liberation of herself. For both partners, their idyllic, radiant and outlaw life expressed the desire for personal liberty. Both identified the role of women in their society as antithetical to such liberty. The desire for unification of the accepted and outlawed parts of the self was strong. The occasions when they could find expression were like oases in Vita's life.

> . . . we spent five blissful days; I felt like a person translated, or re-born; it was like beginning one's life again in a different capacity (1973, p. 107).

> I never in my life felt so free as when I stepped off the kerb, down Picadilly, alone, and knowing that if I met my own mother face to face she would take no notice of me. I walked along, smoking a cigarette, buying a newspaper off a little boy who called me "sir," and being accosted now and then by women. (The extraordinary thing was, how natural it all was for me.) . . . I personally, had never felt so free in my life. . . . It was all incredible—like a fairy tale (1973, pp. 108–111).

It is clear that in Vita's history transvestism expressed much more than a means to sexual arousal; indeed, this element does not even appear in her account.

The alternation in dress has its own important meaning: that of unification of the self. Virginia Woolf's creation of the figure of Orlando, who alternates gender as she embodies the shifting sensibilities of the centuries, is a means of encompassing in one person the feminine and the masculine. In Greek mythology the character of Tiresias lived for seven years as a woman and seven years as a man. These images express the desire to have the knowledge of female and male under one skin. Sometimes the other is externalized as the "opposite" sex. Sometimes the union is expressed through the metaphor of hermaphroditism, sometimes through transformation of the body from one gender to the other, sometimes through a change of clothes. Change (or seeming change) of the body is used as a metaphor for the transformation of consciousness and the transcendance of sex roles. A range of expressions for these concerns is apparent in current fiction as well. Alan Friedman creates an androgyne who is also a hermaphrodite in his witty book, *Hermaphrodeity*. Marge Piercy offers an androgynous and ambiguous future world within a deceptively realistic account, *Woman on the Edge of Time*. Gore Vidal's broad spoof, *Myra Breckinridge*, contains some of the same elements.

The failure to recognize the body as a metaphor can have disastrous consequences for understanding femininity, masculinity and the relationships between them. As we turn to the research on psychological masculinity/femininity, we will see this error in operation. The metaphor of the body causes psychologists to assume that since female and male are real, femininity and masculinity are equally real, with a common genesis.

Masculinity–Femininity: The Scientific Study of an Artifact

The study of psychological masculinity–femininity (MF) goes back several generations. Among the earliest standard measures of MF is that of Terman and Miles (1936). Contemporaneous with the development of IQ tests, Strong (1936) developed a method for counseling on occupational choice. A MF test was part of this battery. Other standard measures include the Guilford–Zimmerman, the California Personality Inventory/ Gough scale, the MF subscale of the Minnesota Multiphasic Personality Inventory (MMPI). Many other pencil-and-paper measures of MF have been tested over the years. Most take the form of "attitude scales," sometimes with items couched in the third person and sometimes in the first person. An exception is the frequently used Franck Drawing Completion Test, a "projective" measure in which the stimuli are line drawings. Responses to these stimuli are generally taken to indicate "unconscious" masculinity/femininity. Table 5.1 contains sample items from three of the most commonly used MF tests.

In constructing these tests, their authors selected items that discriminated most sharply between females and males, discarding those endorsed by both. In this, of course, they are consistent with the tendency that we have seen in research on children's toy

TABLE 5.1
Selected Items from Standard MF Tests

ITEM	SOURCE	KEY
I am worried about sex matters.	MMPI	T=M, F=F
I like to talk about sex.	MMPI	T=M, F=F
I am very strongly attracted by members of my own sex.	MMPI	T=M, F=F
I think I would like the work of a librarian.	MMPI	F=M, T=F
I think I would like the kind of work a forest ranger does.	MMPI	T=M, F=F
I become quite irritated when I see someone spit on the sidewalk.	Gough Fe	T=F
I want to be an important person in the community.	Gough Fe	F=F
I think I would like the work of a librarian.	Gough Fe	T=F
I like to boast about my achievements every now and then.	Gough Fe	F=F
The thought of being in an automobile accident is very frightening to me.	Gough Fe	T=F
I prefer a shower to a tub bath.	Gough Fe	F=F
Are you afraid of snakes?	Guilford–Zimmerman	No=M
Do you prefer going to a dance rather than a prize fight?	Guilford–Zimmerman	No=M
Would you rather be a florist than a miner?	Guilford–Zimmerman	No=M
Do you feel deeply sorry for a bird with a broken wing?	Guilford–Zimmerman	No=M
Do odors of perspiration disgust you?	Guilford–Zimmerman	No=M

preferences, as well as many other specific areas. This research strategy produces a misleading image of polarization between the sexes. The phenomenon of overlap between the sexes—the psychometric study of androgyny—has come to the forefront of only the most recent research. We will consider this research later.

Standard measures of MF are thus hopelessly entangled in the metaphor of the body. In seeking to "validate" MF against biological femaleness and maleness, their authors sealed themselves off from any meaningful exploration of masculinity and femininity as cultural phenomena. In the MF research, little attempt has been made to map variations in MF onto variations in the biological indicators of maleness and femaleness; the categories of the body are treated as absolutes. Inquiry is thus dead-ended.

A direct consequence of the fallacies inherent in the body metaphor is the conceptualization of femininity and masculinity as completely distinct, much as female and male are distinguished by their sexual organs and their secondary sex characteristics. From there it is but a short step—bolstered by commonsense layman's thinking—to conceive of female and male (and hence feminine and masculine) as "opposites." The operationalization of this conception resulted in the construction of MF scales in which a high F score *meant* low M score, and vice versa. A forced-choice format illustrates most clearly the thinking that was embodied in all these measures: the individual could respond to each item only in a feminine *or* masculine way. The methods of test construction and scoring ruled out the possibility of androgynous response.

Although the body is an inappropriate criterion variable to which to relate psychological MF, its acceptance spared the early researchers the embarrassment of facing the question, "So what?" Subsequent research has revealed many complexities in psychological MF; it is certainly not the brute fact that the fathers of this research tradition imagined. Yet the research spans—clumsily—a real phenomenon; there is some lawful variation, at least in self-report, that is tapped by MF measures. The current critique of sex roles has challenged systems of social privilege built upon presumed sex differences. It is no longer fashionable—or legal—to channel women and men into different occupations or curricula on the basis of traits that are supposed to covary with the body. This sex role critique and the analysis generated by it have increased the impetus to reexamine psychological MF.

The need for reformulating questions about MF has become apparent in the course of research employing the standard measures. The most embarrassing finding in the new research, now amply replicated, is that femininity and masculinity are not polar opposites. Jenkin and Vroegh, in a series of studies (1969, 1971), found that femininity and masculinity are independent dimensions: orthogonally, rather than inversely related. Moreover, they can be measured separately, and both can be meaningfully used to characterize females and males. Jenkin and Vroegh conclude, ". . . males and females unselected as to masculinity and femininity are not adequate criterion groups for an analysis of these constructs." Vroegh found that four dimensions underlay teachers' judgments of preschool girls' and boys' femininity/masculinity. The factors were extroversion/introversion, social adjustment, competence and a fourth factor that the authors did not label. Differences were found among the groups labeled Most Masculine boys (MM), Least Masculine boys (LM), Most Feminine girls (MF) and Least Feminine girls (LF). Compared to LM boys, MM boys were more extroverted, slightly more competent and slightly more socially adjusted. MF girls, compared with LF girls, were more socially adjusted, slightly more competent and slightly more introverted. These findings resemble those of other studies, in that culturally defined masculinity enhances competence, whether in females or males. However, competence and extroversion are part of the male sex-role script and not part of the female.

Jenkin and Vroegh's findings illustrate the complexity of MF and their variable relations with male and female gender. Clearly the components of MF do not hang together in any coherent way. That is, attributes that are culturally considered to be "masculine" are found in "feminine" girls; moreover, "less masculine" boys have more of some masculine attributes than do "more masculine" boys.

Although the metaphor of the body blinded some researchers to the question of variability within gender categories, others working within this tradition were concerned about the lack of correlation among components of femininity and masculinity. Though maleness and femaleness continued to be thought of as unitary phenomena, evidence was accumulating that MF contained a number of distinct elements.

Many researchers have investigated the empirical relationships among the standard measures of MF. Barrows and Zuckerman (1960) note mildly that validity of MF tests must be based on something more than their ability to discriminate the gross gender classes. After all, gender does that. MF must therefore show a systematic and convincing relationship with other variables that are correlated within gender grouping. Moreover, if the MF scales are measuring the same underlying phenomenon, they should be highly intercorrelated. They should demonstrate predictive validity. Not only should MF scores predict outcomes on other measures, but it must be demonstrated that "true" MF, rather than the motive for social approval, experimenter's expectations, social class or other attribute, is the causal factor. That is, they should show discriminant validity: the relationships that are found should be attributable to masculinity/femininity and not to other factors. Other factors can be experimentally manipulated or statistically controlled, but "true" masculinity/femininity should be a fundamental individual attribute, constant across situations. Existing research reveals that MF as presently measured fails to meet the criteria of convergent validity, predictive validity and discriminant validity.

Intercorrelations among the standard measures of MF were not high enough to justify the conclusion that either "femininity" or "masculinity" refers to a unitary phenomenon. Although these personality scales purported to measure the same thing, the data did not bear out this presumption.

Shepler (1951) found the Strong and the MMPI measures of MF correlated $-.499$ for males and $+.551$ for females. The Franck measure was uncorrelated with the Terman–Miles, the Strong and the MMPI in this study. Webster (1956, 1957) found that he had measured three empirically distinct "kinds" of masculinity/femininity. Heston (1948) found that sex-typed interests form one cluster, and personality attributes another. The implications of this are that an individual could have feminine or masculine interests (e.g., music versus hunting) and "feminine" or "masculine" personality (e.g., introspective versus aggressive). Interests and personality could be concordant or discordant; furthermore, each could be concordant or discordant with gender. A female individual can have "feminine" or "masculine" interests, coupled with "feminine" or "masculine" personality, and the same could be true for the male.

An important early study was Nichols' (1962) investigation of MF. Drawing upon a number of the standard measures of MF, Nichols constituted a pool of 350 true–false items referring to many aspects of MF. These responses yielded four scales: an Obvious MF scale, a Subtle MF scale, a Stereotyped MF scale, and a acquiescence response set scale. Fifty-eight items with content referring to true sex differences, on which both females and males agreed, constituted the Obvious scale. Thirty items on which a true sex difference existed, but was not recognized by the students, constituted the Subtle scale. Sixty-one items on which there was consensus about sex difference, but on which there was in fact no sex difference, constituted the Stereotype scale. Thirty-nine items on which there was neither a sex difference nor the perception of a sex difference constituted the final scale. One hundred female and 100 male psychology students endorsed the items for themselves. Another pair of subsamples responded to the items under instructions to answer as a female or as a male.

One way to state the difference among the scales is in terms of a sex-role script. For some attributes, the script specifies that females and males are different, and females in fact characterize themselves differently. For others, the script and self-report are at variance. In the case of Stereotype items, the script is counterfactual: the sex differences are fictional. In the case of the Subtle items, differences are real but are not encoded in the script.

In Nichols's study, the three measures of MF did not show high correlations. The Obvious scale correlates with the Stereotype but not with the Subtle. The Subtle and Stereotype MF were significantly and *negatively* correlated.[2] Most of the standard measures of MF correlated with the Stereotype and not with the Subtle measure, suggesting that the standard scales measure the tendency to perceive nonexistent sex differences, rather than the content of masculinity/femininity. It seems likely that they measure conventionality and the tendency to respond conventionally. Several findings from Nichols' study support this interpretation. Nichols notes that only the MMPI MF scale correlates more highly with the Subtle scale than with the Stereotype. Unlike the others, this MMPI MF scale was developed to discriminate homosexual and heterosexual males, not females and males. Its content may be less heavily contaminated with sex role script than the other scales. In his own sample, Nichols found that females scoring "masculine" on the Subtle scale were the most "feminine" on the stereotype scale. He attributes this lack of congruity to the respondent's defensiveness about sex-atypical interests, which causes her to fake superfemininity on the scale that taps the most exaggerated sex role script.

Nichols notes the tendency for males' responses on MF tests to be more conforming than those of females. This might be interpreted at face value: that is, males are more "masculine" than females are "feminine." It might also be interpreted to mean that the pressures on male to conform to the sex role script are greater than they are for females—or are perceived as greater. This interpretation is consistent with the child development literature and with the theoretical writings on animus and anima, which we will examine later.

---

[2] In a cross-validation sample of 111 males and 102 females the same relationships emerged.

Nichols's findings cause him to be skeptical about the validity of MF measures that have a heavy loading on stereotypical sex role scripting. If there exists such a thing as MF, uncontaminated by motivation to distort self-report in the direction of sex role orthodoxy, the means of measuring it is yet to be discovered. In order to distinguish between these possibilities, we would need a valid and uncontaminated measure of MF to use as a criterion variable.

Research on MF has tended to neglect the question of within-sex variability in whatever it is that these tests measure. An exception is the work that combines a measure of "unconscious" MF with the self-descriptive items typical of other tests. However, the results of a study of Bieliauskas and Miranda raise questions about the validity of any findings based on the Franck test.

Bieliauskas and Miranda (1968) analyzed the aims and validity of measures of MF. According to Bieliauskas and Miranda, MF measures aim to specify aspects of personality in which the sexes tend to differ, and to quantify within-sex differences among individuals Bieliauskas and Miranda focus on the possibly incompatible criteria of face validity and discriminant validity: the content of measures of MF should reflect what we recognize as the properties of females and males (face validity) and should allow us to predict, on the basis of test scores, whether the respondent is female or male (discriminant validity). Because femininity and masculinity are such well-known cultural stereotypes and because sex role conformity is rewarded in our culture, Bieliauskas and Miranda were concerned about the problem of faking on MF tests.

In an experiment that used the Franck test (a nonobvious, "projective" measure) and the Gough (an obvious MF test), Bieliauskas and Miranda sought to discover whether Ss can fake both of these tests when instructed to respond as would a person of the other sex. Their hypothesis was that Ss could fake the Gough but not the Franck. Ss were 90 females and 90 males, college freshmen recruited from single-sex colleges and matched for ability, age and academic achievement. They received instructions

TABLE 5.2

Mean Scores of Female and Male College Students Under Standard- and Opposite-Sex Instructions

	TRUE F	FAKE F	TRUE M	FAKE M
Gough test	34.7	39.2[a]	25.7	22.6[b]
Franck test	18.7	19.2	17.9	18.7

[a] $P > .002$.
[b] $P > .02$.

SOURCE: Bieliauskas and Miranda (1968, Tables 1 and 2, p. 316). Copyright 1968 by the American Psychological Association. Reprinted by permission.

from a tape-recorded male voice. The authors found that under standard instructions both tests discriminated females from males (see Table 5.2). Both sexes were able to fake the Gough. The surprise came on the Franck test: not only were Ss able to fake this "projective" test of "unconscious" MF, but each group, under opposite-sex instructions, produced more sex-stereotypical responses than were produced under standard instructions. In other words, fake females were more "feminine" than true females (even though they were males) and fake males more "masculine" than true males. The authors offer two interpretations of the greater "success" of males in faking the Franck: either males have greater "empathy" than females, or the generally higher scores of males on tests of spatial ability account for their ability to fake femaleness. Of course, any success at faking the Franck casts serious doubt on its validity as a nonobvious measure of "true," much less "unconscious," MF. An equally plausible interpretation of the findings is that males in this sample have greater "unconscious" femininity than females have unconscious masculinity, and that the opposite-sex instructions tapped into this substrate.

The Future of MF and the Study of Psychological Androgyny

The available research indicates that the standard measures of MF tap domains that are dimensionally complex. Femininity and masculinity are not unitary. Furthermore, it is likely that they are made up of different dimensions. When the fathers of MF constructed their tests, they generated items from a number of different areas—occupational, familial, avocational, sexual. The extent to which items cluster and subtests interrelate is properly an empirical question. Continuing to act as though MF were a unitary phenomenon, when the evidence clearly indicates that this is not the case, is a greater error still.

The metaphor of the body seems to lie behind the perpetuation of this error. It is more fruitful to conceptualize MF as the reflection of two sexual scripts—feminine and masculine—which are differentiated according to role spheres—employment, sexuality, family, political participation, interests. This approach allows us to analyze the effect of situational demand upon the specific verbal behaviors which MF tests elicit. The situational aspect of MF has been conspicuously neglected, although the hint is there in Bieliauskas's and Miranda's work, among others. I have suggested in Chapter 1 that married women interviewed *in the home* by *male* researchers are likely to give more "feminine" responses than the same women interviewed in their work places. Future research will have to map the differentiated areas of female and male functioning, with specific attention to social desirability bias in response.

The difficult issues of self-attribution and self-report in MF have seldom been addressed in the existing literature. The approach taken here emphasizes the incentives for traditional responses and suggests that self-report may be systematically biased when elements so value-laden and so central to self-image as sexual identity are being assessed. Disentangling valid self-attribution from verbal conformity calls for a carefully designed series of studies.

In speculating about the direction of future research on psychological differences among women and men, it seems clear that it will be more fruitful to pursue the idea of androgyny than the idea of MF, however defined or redefined. Femininity and masculinity, however defined, take their coloration through social learning, which is tied to the specifics of social experience and social position. Sex-role scripts are age-graded and social-class specific; they are interpreted and reinterpreted in a variety of behavioral contexts in each person's life history. The elements that leave traces in the individual's self-attribution or personality may retain links with gross cultural forms like sex role scripts, but the latter cannot be the effective unit of analysis at the individual level. Sex role scripts are mediated by specific others, in specific interactions with the individual: hence the multiplicity of sex role scripts, reflecting age-graded and social-class-specific individual histories.

The feedback that an individual gets in her history of social interactions has as its referents some items that relate to the female sex-role script and some that relate to the male. Insofar as the self reflects this experience, it too is composed of elements that are related to the cultural conventions of "feminine" and "masculine." Thus the individual is irreducibly androgynous. In each, the selection and combination of attributes can differ.

The form of future research will not emphasize static caricatures of "masculinity" and "femininity" as opposite poles. The appropriate goal for future research is to characterize the individual in terms of a profile of attributes or traits that have demonstrated validity, external as well as internal. Outcome variables in such research might include effectiveness of functioning, feelings of growth, integration, self-esteem—in short, the range of behavioral and self-report measures of interest to psychologists.

Current research that takes androgyny as its focus is a step in this direction. Bem (1974, 1976) in a first attempt to measure psychological androgyny, assessed the discrepancy between measured masculinity and femininity in several samples of college students. The Bem Sex Role Inventory, subsequently used by many researchers, is constructed from admittedly sex-typed self-descriptors ("expressive" items are feminine and "instrumental" items are masculine). In this paper-and-pencil task, Ss indicate how characteristic of them are 20 M, 20 F, and 20 sex-neutral items. Separate scores are constructed for femininity and masculinity. For any individual, the degree of sex role stereotypy is assessed by the t-ratio between his/her F and M scores. The inverse of this discrepancy is used as a measure of androgyny. By her criterion, Bem found that 34 percent of the males in her Stanford undergraduate sample and 27 percent of the females scored androgynous. In her junior college samples, 44 percent of the males and 38 percent of the females scored androgynous.[3]

Bem's research has a good deal to tell us about the restrictiveness of traditional sex roles. Traditionally masculine men and feminine women (those with no significant admixture of contrasex attributes) showed less flexibility in responding to a range of situational demands than did androgynous individuals. Moreover, they showed avoidance of contrasex options and discomfort when they were induced to perform mildly contrasex activities. "Sex-reversed" Ss (those describing themselves in preponderantly contrasex terms) behaved like the androgynous Ss in most experiments.

Bem and associates conducted a series of experiments designed to explore the behavioral consequences of sex-typicality and androgyny in situations designed to tap nurturance and independence. In a standard conformity experiment, Bem found that both masculine and androgynous Ss showed more independence in their judgments than did feminine Ss. Three experiments on nurturance followed. In the first, Bem observed the degree to which Ss involved themselves with a kitten in an experimental room, and found that androgynous women and men and feminine men interacted with the kitten significantly more than either the masculine men or the feminine women, with masculine women falling in between. Feminine women were no more nurturant than other groups in interacting with a baby in another experiment, although their questionnaire responses indicated that they were *attitudinally* more "nurturant." In a third experiment, the feminine women proved to be the best listeners in responding to a same-sex stranger. Bem's experiments suggest a reformulation of the place of nurturance in traditional femininity. In Bem's experi-

---

[3]Though Bem does not offer an interpretation of the differences between institutions in this study, it is tempting to speculate whether the monastic tradition of elite institutions like Stanford is more antithetical to androgyny than that of the community colleges.

ments, feminine women were not more nurturant than other groups in situations where nurturant behavior had to be initiated by the S, but only when it occurred as a response to instigation by another. This finding, together with the results of the conformity experiment, suggests that *responsiveness to others may be the more general feminine role behavior*. The direction or content of the behavior undertaken in response to another's instigation will depend upon the demand of the situation. Nurturance, while it is a socially approved part of the female sex role script, is governed by situational rather than innate factors.

Bem's contribution to the study of androgyny is widely recognized. Nevertheless, the definition of androgyny as the inverse of sex role stereotypy may be faulted as well as defended. By restricting herself to positively valued F and M items only, Bem restricts our knowledge of androgyny and leaves the door open to a response bias in the direction of social desirability. There is no theoretical rationale for supposing that androgynes possess only positive attributes, whether own-sex or contrasex. A more serious problem concerns the fundamental validity of discrepancy measures of self-report variables. Bem reports that her "androgyny" measure is uncorrelated with her measure of social desirability. This is not really reassuring, for it is hard to conceptualize how an individual would be defensive and try to conceal information (e.g., a discrepancy between two scores) that she is not aware of giving. Certainly the Bem measure falls short of operationalizing androgyny as I have defined it. Her measure cannot tell us anything about awareness and acceptance of androgyny. The link to creativity, through accessibility of a wide range of attributes, remains to be explored.

Spence et al. (1975) have taken a different tack in investigating psychological androgyny. In their experiment, college students gave two ratings of 55 bipolar personality attributes: comparing the typical female and male college students and describing the self. The 55 bipolar adjectives were chosen from the Broverman et al. Sex Role Stereotype Questionnaire (1968). The 55 traits were further subdivided into three subscales: male-valued (items on which the ideal rating for persons of both sexes was toward the masculine end of the scale), female-valued (items on which the ideal was toward the feminine end of the scale), and sex-specific (items on which the ideal for females was toward the feminine end plus items on which the ideal for males was toward the masculine end of the scale).

Spence et al. found that ratings of the typical student and self were unrelated. Self-ratings tended to be in a sex-typical direction, but self-ratings and "stereotype" ratings were statistically distinct. Self-ratings were uncorrelated with a measure of sex-role attitudes for the sample as a whole.

Spence et al. found attitudinal differences between androgynous and traditional Ss. Individuals holding traditional attitudes on the Attitudes Toward Women scale (Spence and Helmreich, 1972) were also found to perceive greater differences between the typical female and male college student than those holding more liberal attitudes. Individuals whose self-ratings showed them to be more sex-typical (on both the same-sex valued subscale and the sex-specific subscale) also perceived greater sex differences and were attitudinally conservative.

The Spence et al. findings show substantial evidence of androgyny. The male-valued and female-valued self-descriptors were significantly and positively correlated among both the women and the men. This strongly suggests that both sexes see the ideal or admirable person as androgynous.[4] Both male- and female-valued self-descriptive items were significantly correlated with a measure of social competence/self-esteem. Arguing that possessing male- and female-valued attributes contributes positively to self-esteem, Spence et al. constructed a typology of androgyny reproduced in Table 5.3. Their logic was that the more female- and male-valued traits the individual possesses, the more androgynous she is and

---

[4]Possible contamination by social desirability response bias cannot be definitively ruled out. In two additional samples reported in the same articles, Spence at al. found significant correlations between scores on the Marlowe–Crowne social desirability scale and both the male- and female-valued self subscales. The magnitude of the correlations in no way suggests that the two scales are measuring the same construct.

TABLE 5.3

Distribution of Subjects Classified by Scores Above or Below the Median on Male-Valued and Female-Valued Self Scales

SUBJECTS	CATEGORY 1: LOW MASCULINE— LOW FEMALE	CATEGORY 2: LOW MASCULINE— HIGH FEMALE	CATEGORY 3: HIGH MASCULINE— LOW FEMALE	CATEGORY 4: HIGH MASCULINE— HIGH FEMALE
Males				
N	72	30	64	68
%	30.8	12.8	27.4	29.1
Mean self-esteem[a]	66.82	74.55	87.02	93.73
Females				
N	56	104	30	80
%	20.7	38.5	11.1	29.6
Mean self-esteem[a]	69.66	75.41	92.17	98.73

[a]One-way analysis of variance $p < .001$.
SOURCE: Spence, et al. (1975, Table 4, p. 35). Copyright 1975 by the American Psychological Association. Reprinted by permission.

hence the more enriched. Thus unlike Bem's procedure, which neglects the breadth of personality, Spence et al. consider the High F/High M individual more androgynous than the Low/Low, even though both may be equally "balanced" between F and M. Consistent with their enrichment thesis, they predicted that self-esteem would follow the ordering of the groups as in Table 5.3. In addition to the predicted relationship with self-esteem, Spence et al. found that androgynous Ss reported dating more, earning more honors and awards, and suffering less childhood illness.

From existing research into androgyny, it seems clear that traditional masculinity and femininity are impoverished in ways that complement each other. A good deal of past research has found that the more feminine the woman, the less self-confidence, self-esteem and competence she seems to exhibit (Cosentino and Heilbrun, 1964; Webb, 1963; Connell and Johnson, 1970; Gall, 1969; Gray, 1967; Sears, 1970). The reverse seems to hold true for men. These related findings reflect the realities of a male-dominant society, which is formed to fit men and which rewards masculine traits. The male role has reward value per se; under some circumstances women may be motivated to adopt it, and under some conditions such adoption may be tolerated or even rewarded.

The question of what varieties of androgyny exist is an interesting one. Are androgynes who possess many own-sex and contrasex attributes different from those who, equally balanced, possess fewer? Are there androgynes who would fail to be so classified in Bem's scheme because their attributes were unsextyped? What are the antecedents and consequences of androgyny where feminine attributes are more pronounced, as contrasted with androgyny where masculine attributes predominate? Given a society that rewards masculine attributes and interests, is androgyny more likely to be found among females than among males? This male-oriented type of androgyny was discovered by Stericker and Johnston (1977) in a study of 159 female and 153 male students in an introductory psychology course. Their study included the Rosenkrantz MF scale, measures of achievement motivation and of self-esteem.

They found that self-descriptions of students were gender-appropriate. No overall sex differences in achievement or self-esteem were found. Rather, the degree of femininity/masculinity appeared to affect self-esteem. When achievement motivation and MF were dichotomized, the High F/Low Achievement groups had the lowest self-esteem. The High M/High Achievement group had the highest, but the High F/High Achievement and High M/Low Achievement means clustered very closely with this group. Stericker and Johnson found that achievement motivation and self-esteem were more highly correlated among females than among males. They suggest that achievement compensates for femaleness among this subgroup, while women lacking this avenue to self-esteem show lower self-esteem. The results for males suggest that maleness in itself conduces to high self-esteem, independent of achievement. Masculinity correlates more highly with self-esteem among women than men; the correlation is insignificant among men. Masculinity and achievement correlate independently with self-esteem for men.

Similar results from a study by Ellis and Bentler (1973) reinforce the link between achievement and "masculinity." In a study of 76 female and 76 male college students, Ellis and Bentler compared self-ratings with Ss' ratings of females and males. Ellis and Bentler's study gives an additional sidelight on the restriction of female ambition by sex role orthodoxy. In their study, status seeking among women is related to a large perceived discrepancy between the self and other women. Moreover, status seeking in women was correlated with perceived similarity of self to men. Finally, perceiving women and men as similar predicted negatively to status seeking. This pattern of findings is consistent with my analysis of the psychology of tokenism (Laws, 1975).

Ellis and Bentler found, as did Spence et al., that support of traditional sex role standards is related to perceiving large differences between the sexes, for males. Sex role traditionalism was also related to status seeking in males. Females who espoused traditional sex role beliefs perceived large differences between themselves and the category male, rather than between the categories female and male.

Ellis and Bentler did not find that "sex-reversed" individuals held more liberal sex role attitudes than did traditionally feminine or masculine persons, reinforcing their contention that traditional attitudes are tied to the perception of large sex differences. Liberal sex role attitudes were related to scores on separate measures of liberalism, extralegality and nonreligiosity, for both women and men. Intelligence was an additional predictor of nontraditional attitudes for women but not for men.

In this study, the degree of "femininity" or "masculinity" (as indexed by the discrepancy between self and same-sex others) was unrelated to traditional sex role attitudes. It appears from this finding that the focus of sex role traditionalism lies in the relationship between the self and the "opposite" sex, not in comparisons within sex. In other words, traditional ideas about appropriate roles for women rely upon a contrast effect in which men and women are seen as very different. Ellis and Bentler suggest that masculinity and femininity develop by repudiation of the other category, rather than as a natural outgrowth of maleness and femaleness: "It is suggested that the opposite sex, rather than the same sex, may serve as the primary frame of reference for a person's self concept . . . masculine means 'unlike females'—*not* 'like males,' while feminine means 'unlike males'—*not* 'like females'" (1973, p. 33). Thus, to "qualify" as an adequate female, one must repudiate all things masculine, and the converse is true for males. *Masculinity and femininity are themselves impediments to androgyny.* Ellis and Bentler suggest that the scripts of masculinity and femininity impede individuals' movement in the desired direction of androgyny. Elman et al. (1970) had found that descriptions of ideal females and males were more alike than were typical or stereotypical descriptions—that is, the ideal person is androgynous. Yet "normal" femininity and masculinity require rejection of the androgynous. Ellis and Bentler conclude with this statement of the paradox: "One explanation for the threat that equality seems to pose for some people may lie in the changing 'self–other' discrepancy . . . elimination of traditional, nonfunctional sex determined role standards would result in expansion of the role sphere . . ." (1973, p. 33).

Is Humanistic Psychology the Study of the Androgyne?

Our critique of personality research and its treatment of MF finds the polarity of feminine and masculine a distortion of psychological reality. Alongside this tradition, but emphatically not of it, is the field of humanistic psychology. Its foci have included intrinsic motivation (notably self-actualization) and an emphasis on personal growth. Work on self-transformation and volitional self-change—e.g., "personal growth"—has tended also to come from the humanistic tradition. The focus on self-change has tended to emphasize research and innovation in forms of therapy, however, rather than in social movements like Women's Liberation.

Humanistic psychologists have focused on growth motivation, as distinct from deficiency motivation. They see the creative, exuberant, loving, cooperative individual as normal rather than extraordinary. Maslow's (1955, 1964) work on the self-actualizing individual contends that the normal unfolding of the individual will eventuate in self-actualization. He concedes that experience or the social surroundings can place obstacles in the way of self-actualization but has not dealt with the possibility that the social environment can actively form or elicit self-actualization. According to Maslow, self-actualization is oriented toward a fuller knowledge and acceptance of one's intrinsic nature—the realization of one's potential. Wholeness, liberation and synergy are the hallmarks of that intrinsic nature. Other characteristics include nondefensive coping with everyday life, flexibility, process-orientation and an active and constructive ego. The transcendence of received (social) constraints is part of self-actualization or personal liberation, but these elements have received little attention from humanistic psychologists.

In the humanistic tradition, great emphasis is placed on self-awareness (and its evil twin, repression). Where some aspects of the self are denied or repressed, the individual is divided, and the resources available for functioning are halved. Self-awareness releases energy and multiplies the individual's resources. A long tradition within humanistic psychology has been concerned with the essence of humanness and with the essence of femininity and masculinity. Could this tradition provide the guidelines for the study of androgyny?

The pioneering work of G. C. Jung (1926) discussed femininity and masculinity in terms of archetypes to be found in the psyches of all individuals. Animus (the male principle within the female individual) and anima (the female principle within the male) are concepts that form a link between the individual, in all her particularity, and the collective unconscious. In Jung's system of thought, animus and anima serve the same function as the concept of role does in sociological writing: it is the bridge between individual and culture. It is, in fact, an internalized image of the "opposite" sex role.

Animus and anima are present, in varying degrees, in each

person. Jung sees them as behaving as though they were inner personalities, compensatory to the outer personality. They "find no place in the person's outwardly directed functioning because they disturb his outer adaptation, his established image of himself" (Emma Jung, 1957, p. 1). In other words, conformity to sex role scripts blocks the direct expression—and even awareness—of femininity in men and masculinity in women.

Emma Jung analyzes the functioning and the excesses of anima and animus in two separate papers (1957). The idiosyncratic animus/anima within the individual is formed by (1) the experience she/he has had with representatives of the other sex, (2) the image of the other sex derived from cultural sex stereotypes and (3) the talents and capacities of the individual. The animus/anima is an element of the personality that struggles to come into consciousness; if it is denied, it can declare war on the persona. If the forces of repression are strong, the inner adversary acquires a paradoxical power to distort the personality, interfere with conscious goals or even "take possession" of the individuaal. It is with these excesses or distortions of animus and anima that Jung's analysis is occupied.

Animus in women is identified with logos, a function that includes power, action, language and significance. Emma Jung's analysis focuses on intellective and analytical capacities. The "problem of the animus" is the integration of feminine logos into women's awareness and outward functioning.

The modern form of "problem of the animus" in women is, in Jung's thought, an unavoidable result of the cultural trend toward widening consciousness and decreasing traditionalism in women's lives. Jung contrasts the confrontation with the animus, and the struggle to integrate it, with women's traditional "unconsciousness," or lack of consciousness. She notes that one traditional adaptation is for a woman to mate with an animus figure—a dominant male who embodies the attributes of her personal animus. This is consistent with the idea of vicariousness: the woman "has" a set of virtues, not in her own character but through affiliation with a man who possesses them. However, in so doing she abdicates her own opportunity to develop these attributes. Often she falls into a trap of stereotyped role-playing that diminishes her still further, as Jung shows. Jung observes that the price of this solution to the problem of animus is that a part of the individual is condemned to a shadowy existence (1957, p. 13). The personality is partly robbed of life by the encroachment of the unacknowledged animus (1957, p. 14). Jung observes that women in this kind of relationship generate many psychosomatic symptoms, which complement the perfect contentment they report at the conscious level (1957, p. 9).

When a woman mates with an animus figure, as when a male mates with an anima figure, the relationship is characterized by a compulsive dependence.

> . . . a man to whom the animus image has been transferred is expected to take over all the functions that have remained undeveloped in the woman in question, whether the thinking function, or the power to act, or responsibility toward the outside world. In turn, the woman upon whom a man has projected his anima must feel for him, or make relationships for him, and this symbiotic relationship is, in my opinion, the real cause for the compulsive dependence that exists in these cases (1957, p. 9).

Jung goes on to note that mate selection dictated by the animus/anima is also characterized by a highly unrealistic and unhealthy role playing, in which animus answers anima and the real person is not heard. Jung considers this one of the worst problems complicating relations between women and men (1957, p. 11). Roszak and Roszak capture the flavor of this vicious circle:

> He is playing masculine. She is playing feminine.
> He is playing masculine *because* she is playing feminine. She is playing feminine *because* he is playing masculine.
> He is playing the kind of man that she thinks the kind of woman she is playing ought to admire. She is playing the kind of woman that he thinks the kind of man he is playing ought to desire.
> If he were not playing masculine, he might well be more feminine than she is—except when she is *playing* very feminine. If she were

not playing feminine, she might well be more masculine than he is—except when he is *playing* very masculine.

So he plays harder. And she plays . . . softer.

He wants to make sure that she could never be more masculine than he. She wants to make sure that he could never be more feminine than she. He therefore seeks to destroy the femininity in himself. She therefore seeks to destroy the masculinity in herself.

She is supposed to admire him for the masculinity in him that she fears in herself. He is supposed to desire her for the femininity in her that he despises in himself.

He desires her for her femininity which is *his* femininity, but which he can never lay claim to. She admires him for his masculinity which is *her* masculinity, but which she can never lay claim to. Since he may only love his own femininity in her, he envies her femininity. Since she may only love her own masculinity in him, she envies him his masculinity.

The envy poisons their love.

He, coveting her unattainable femininity, decides to punish her. She, coveting is unattainable masculinity, decides to punish him. He denigrates her femininity—which he is supposed to desire and which he really envies—and becomes more aggressively masculine. She feigns disgust at his masculinity—which she is supposed to admire and which she really envies—and becomes more fastidiously feminine. He is becoming less and less what he wants to be. She is becoming less and less what she wants to be. But now he is more manly than ever, and she is more womanly than ever.

Her femininity, growing more dependently supine, becomes contemptible. His masculinity, growing more oppressively domineering, becomes intolerable. At last she loathes what she has helped his masculinity to become. At last he loathes what he has helped her femininity to become. (*Masculine/Feminine: Readings in Sexual Mythology and the Liberation of Women*, ed. Betty Roszak and Theodore Roszak (New York: Harper & Row, 1969), pp. vii–viii. Copyright © 1969 by Betty Roszak and Theodore Roszak. Reprinted by permission of Harper & Row, Publishers, Inc.)

Jung implies that the traditional solution is no longer a real option for women. With the advance of consciousness, the reduction in fertility and in the arduousness of women's work, women can no longer avoid the pressure to develop intellectually. But even if they do not choose consciousness, it will choose them, and in Jung's words, ". . . if a woman does not meet adequately the demand for consciousness or intellectual activity, the animus becomes autonomous and negative, and works destructively on the individual herself and in her relations to other people" (1957, p. 6). The channeling of women's power of logos solely into family relations may indeed be destructive.

The "problem of the animus" typically takes a different form in current society, where very few women live their lives bounded by the home and their family relations. Most American women have incorporated a variety of competences into their self-images, as into their life histories. The focus of the problem may be the integration of feminine and masculine attributes, rather than the development of animus qualities. Jung notes, "The problem of how to be a woman frequently arises in the midst of the most successful professional activity" (1957, p. 41). She goes on to say, revealingly, "Usually it (the problem) appears in the form of dissatisfactions, as a need of personal, not merely objective values, a need for nature, and femininity in general." In other words, the successful woman is suffering from masculinity poisoning. Jung's prescription for this ailment includes the development of consciousness and a firm feeling of individuality, meaningful work and relationships with other people that establish a bulwark against the inhuman character of the animus (1957, p. 41). Of particular importance is her emphasis on support and solidarity between women: "The relationship of a woman to other women has great meaning in this connection. I have had occasion to observe that as the animus problem became acute, many women began to show an increased interest in other women, the relation to women being felt as an ever-growing need, even a necessity" (1957, p. 41).

The pathway to androgyny, for women, thus requires coming to consciousness and leaving behind a dependent reliance on men. The necessary support for such growth will come from other women, in an unprecedented experience of solidarity. When stereotyped femininity is transcended, a new hunger awakes for a more inclusive and more human femininity and for validation of this androgyny.

Attainment of androgyny, for men, is a different pathway with a different starting point. Jung observes that for the male to embrace his anima is to accept something he has previously thought of as inferior (1957, p. 24). Very little analysis of these obstacles to male liberation is to be found in humanistic psychology. As we have seen in the sex role socialization literature, the repudiation of contrasex attributes, as well as of the "opposite" sex itself, is more virulent among males. The male personality is consequently more impoverished than the female. This has implications for the process of male liberation. Pleck (1975a,b, 1976) has developed an excellent analysis of the difficulties and goals of male liberation. Jung, however, slights the analysis of the obstacles to men's acceptance of the anima. She presents only half of the picture. It is interesting, in this context, that the anima is depicted as infinitely more compelling and alluring than the rather dour animus.

Mythology is rich in anima images and anima stories. The anima figure appears as a nymph, a swan maiden, and an enchanted princess who must be redeemed. The anima figure is often surrounded by an enchantment that cannot be violated. In some anima stories, however, the hero must overcome the enchantment and redeem the maiden, or enter it himself if he is to win his other half permanently. The anima figure is very often invested with esoteric knowledge, usually about nature—sometimes with the gift of prophecy. These attributes dramatize the openness, the mastery of mystery and irrationality that are denied the male persona. The anima mediates the irrational or unconscious for the overly conscious male. Part of the magic of the anima figure is often the power to change her form. As when the contents of the conscious are grasped by rational man, so the anima figure loses this nebulousness and fluidity when confined in a relationship with man.

The hallmark of the anima is the feeling tone that the Other is destined for the hero, that he cannot live without her: she is his other half. The theme of reconciliation or unification of two beings of opposite nature who yet belong together is a central anima theme. Anima adventures have dangers for the hero: sometimes he is won away altogether from the world of men.

The dangers and challenges to the male, and the variations in outcomes, are among the most interesting features of the anima myths. Much work remains to be done, but several themes are apparent. These have implications for men's attempts to incorporate their feminine component and also for their responses to women's liberation. Some of these themes involve representations of other men and the way they relate to the pursuit of the anima.

In the anima story, the hero usually appears alone, without that company of male peers that is so large a part of everday life. Several features of the anima myths recounted by Jung bear upon this significant point. The anima figure sometimes appears in the company of a father figure. Jung interprets this older male as a symbol of the knowledge possessed by the anima. Another possible interpretation is that the presence of the male elder confers legitimacy on the union of the male with his anima: he gives permission. In this connection, it is interesting to examine the theme of patricide in such myths as those of Oedipus and Melusine. Possibly this act frees the male to seek his anima by removing him from the society of men and the solidarity by which they exert social control over him.

Anima stories commonly contain the theme of enchanted forgetfulness. The direction of the action is toward unconsciousness, while in animus stories the direction is toward consciousness. For this reason Jung's discussion of Odin's Thorn of Sleep seems misplaced in the paper on animus. It seems, rather, to belong with Sleeping Beauty's spindle. In both stories sleep is caused via a magic prick. In the story of Sleeping Beauty, the enchanted princess, who is destined to be rescued and possessed by the prince, is thus taken out of circulation for a hundred years. She too is thus removed from the dominion of those who normally control her, and from her normal activities. The magic prick recurs in the story of Cupid and Psyche, where it causes the end of an idyllic though far from egalitarian love affair. There, as Neumann points out (1956), it marks the beginning of feminine consciousness in the sense we have been using.

Other implications concerning male androgyny can be drawn from Jung. In men, the anima is so thoroughly repressed that it must be encountered in indirect ways. The yearning for the anima is expressed often in an ill-defined emotional stirring, a mood of desire for new undertakings, impulses and fantasies (1957, p. 53). Jung's description of this unrest resembles the phenomenon of the "male menopause." The fantasy of entering the unfamiliar and enchanted world of a young girl seems to exemplify the anima feeling. The unknown girl seems to posssess transcendence, universality and exotic knowledge. Her image is in contrast with that of the workaday wife/partner. Perhaps at this stage in life men are even more susceptible to forming a new relationship based upon projection.

For the man, as for the woman, forming a love relationship with an anima figure is a wrong turning on the path to androgyny. It impedes the development of his own awareness, of relatedness, of wisdom. Jung notes, "As long as such a projection exists it is naturally difficult for the man to find a relation to the inner anima, to his own femininity" (1957, p. 82). In this observation Jung seems to foreshadow the large role that gay men have played in the male liberation movement. Gay male activists have rejected the "solution" of projecting their femininity onto an external, female partner. Conversely, among those most opposed to the examination and transcendence of sex roles are married men, particularly those who have or prefer the traditional partnership. Suppression of the anima requires vigorous and continuing effort, which is continually undermined by evidence of emerging animus in women and anima in men.

In Jung's development of the concepts of animus and anima we find a way of thinking about the female and the male androgyne. She provides at least a sketch of the ways in which women and men can begin to know and to integrate the contrasex attributes that are part of them. She acknowledges that this process of growth runs counter to established social roles and will occasion conflict both within the person and between the person and society. She implies that the different histories and positions of women and men in society make it inevitable that their routes to androgyny will be different. Consequently the processes of women's and men's liberation will differ.

The humanistic tradition within psychology would seem a most promising arena for significant progress on these issues. The humanistic emphasis on holism—on integration, on the inclusion of previously disowned parts, on the healing of splits within the personality—has much in common with ideas of androgyny and of sex role liberation. Indeed, the human potential movement, whose major thrust is personal growth in adults, developed from the inheritance of Jung, Rogers, Maslow, Moreno, Reich and others. The promise of Jung has not been fulfilled, however. Theory and practice within the humanistic tradition contain limitations that will continue to block the development of thinking about androgyny and impair individuals' capability of attaining it.

A first impediment is the failure to recognize and accept female animus. Indeed, the word itself has come to mean hostility, and is often taken to mean a threat to men. The threat is twofold: a threat to men's official monopoly on competence and dominance in the world of affairs and the threat of female secession from the roles in which they are useful to men. Because of these connotations, it is preferable to use the term *agency* to refer to the attributes of surgency, competence, decisiveness, self-assertion and self-appreciation that are expected and esteemed in men. The human potential movement has not demonstrated an even-handed commitment to the development of female animus and male anima. The encounter movement, largely developed and led by men, has devoted considerable attention to the enrichment of male capabilities by the addition of traditional female virtues—in short, the search for the anima. Many women participating in groups led by charismatic males have reported the experience of being cast in an anima role, with consequent alienation and a feeling of being cheated. Although "femininity" is celebrated, the appreciation does not include the full range of female humanity. The humanistic view of the feminine includes only positively valued "female" traits. Following Jung, many participants in this movement seek to capture the feminine genius for relatedness. To define women only in such terms, and to reward by approval only the traditional behaviors, is sexist in a quite unoriginal way.

The intellectual, analytical or assertive attributes that women are seeking to develop are not nurtured in such a context.

This curious distortion is projected into treatments of male liberation, in which masculinity is projected to be enriched by nurturance, warmth, sensitivity and the like. The question of the enrichment of femininity receives little attention. Thus issues of women's growth do not receive equal time in groups, tending to be relegated to a therapy context.

The pitfalls of psychotherapy for women have been ably described (e.g., by Tennov, 1975; Bart, 1971; Chesler, 1972), and will not be reviewed here. Equally significant, however, are the implications of relegating women, once again, to a footnote. The integration of animus and anima have meaning only in a context that includes both women and men. Treatments that relegate women to the status of Other retain the distortions in men's images of women and hence impede both the achievement of androgyny in men and change in a society that is inimical to androgyny.

The humanistic emphasis on process and on change should lead to a detailed analysis of the social forces that shape development and impede change. The analysis of contemporaneous forces in the social environment of adults is essential for the understanding of obstacles to androgyny and for the design of interventions that help individuals achieve androgyny. Failure to develop such an analysis is an enduring shortcoming of the humanistic approach. It distorts thinking about male integration by ignoring the system of privilege that must change if men are to change. It distorts thinking about female growth by overlooking the obstacles and the opposition to such growth.

Humanistic psychologists neglect the effects of systematic socialization, not only upon the adult but upon the child. Their view of self-actualization (for example) as intrinsic and immanent leads them to overlook the selective and idiosyncratic acquisition of self-attributes upon which self-actualization builds. Processes of labeling and evaluation are central to the construction of identity. These differ by sex. Sex-typing, or the differential evaluation of attributes when they appear in female or male (Mischel, 1970), is ubiquitous, primary and powerful. In overlooking these processes, humanistic psychologists set up a false polarity of natural versus artificial/cultural, of self-actualization versus socialization, of adult (as spoiled creature) versus child (as noble savage). Certainly there is a germ of truth in this. Sex role socialization does narrow and channel the child's early androgyny, interdicting some of its manifestations. We have come to see how the sexes are polarized and how each becomes a negative ideal for the other. The individual learns to hide his contrasex attributes and to scourge himself in mimicry of social disapproval, when they force themselves into awareness. The conventional outcome of this process is the repression of one's own contrasex attributes and the consequent impoverishment of the individual.

Of the humanists, Neumann (1959) comes closest to taking account of sex role socialization. He maintains that girls and boys originally have a psychic unity that is, however, destroyed by socialization.

The error in this thinking is due to the fallacy of a deterministic view of socialization. Of all psychologists, the humanists, with their emphasis on process and on volitional self-transformation, should be immune to this fallacy. Unfortunately, they seem to take the outcomes of primary socialization as immutable. As a consequence, they overlook the possibilities of primary socialization as a means of nurturing the androgyne.

Another consequence of the neglect of socialization is that humanistic psychology is vague about the contents of personality, including the actual degree of androgyny present in today's women and men. There is a substantial amount of research that demonstrates that the ideal selves of women and men are substantially androgynous. McKee and Sherriffs (1959) found the terms dynamic, independent, courageous and self-confident were part of the description of the ideal woman. Jenkin and Vroegh (1964) found that the traits of the "most feminine" and "most masculine" overlapped, including both agentic and communal traits. Both girls and boys were described as active, dependable, affectionate, intelligent and courteous. The several factors that accounted for the ratings showed differentiated relationships with femininity and masculinity. Items on Vroegh et al.'s Factor IV had expressive/emotional content ("engages in dramatic play," "exuberant, enthusiastic," "flirtatious with opposite sex"). Social Adjustment items (distinguishing good conduct from bad) were much more highly associated with femininity than with masculinity. Competence related about the same for femininity and masculinity, while extroversion was highly related to masculinity and negatively related to femininity. The expressive-emotionality factor had a low negative association with femininity and a moderate positive association with masculinity.

The two constructs, masculinity and femininity, were essentially unrelated in this sample. Morover, the Competence factor in this study was androgynous, being composed of some items that are sex-typed masculine (persistence, confidence) and some that are sex-typed feminine (intelligence, dexterity).

This more detailed picture of the individual is preferable to the global polarities of feminine and masculine. A major obstacle to clear thinking about androgyny is the tendency to confound personality polarities with masculinity and femininity, and these in turn with gender categories; i.e., the metaphor of the body again. Perhaps the prior problem is the tendency to polarize: to construe reality as composed of two and only two elements, and these in some way opposite. Personality theory is full of such polarities: in addition to animus and anima, personalities are sometimes typed as Dionysian or Apollonian. Other examples abound: Gelpi (1975) characterizes female consciousness as dealing in whole rather than parts, in symbolic connections. Male consciousness is characterized in a divergent manner: abstract, analytical, dealing in discriminations. Angyal's (1966) polarities are autonomous/homonomous; Bakan's (1966) are agency/communion. Bakan's ideas of agency and communion can be taken as illustrations of a whole Noah's Ark of personality polarities. Agency includes self-assertion, self-expansion and self-protection; it implies a separate existence, perhaps isolation and alienation. Communion, on the other hand, encompasses the bridging of gaps, being at one with others, participation in larger entities, union. It is perhaps accidental that these poles read like caricatures of the male and female sex roles. By the same coincidence, agency is considered typical of males and communion of females. Bakan diverges from many in being aware of the potential poisoning of the individual by "excessive agency," and the need for communion to make the healthy personality. However, those who employ this polarity still write in terms of importing communion into the agentic (male) personality, rather than asking what impedes us from seeing communion in men and agency in women.

The tendency to polarize may be a flaw of Western thought in general, of the patriarchal mentality, or both. Alan Watts (1963) has analyzed religious mythology of both East and West, examining their central images. In so doing, Watts contrasts the analytical/intellectual mode of knowing with that of image and mysticism. Watts sees myth as expressions that a people take as reflecting the inner reality, not only of the mind but of the cosmos. By means of myth people express things that are difficult to express otherwise (1963, p. 23). The language of description adopted "for convenience" by practitioners of the analytic mode is itself a distortion and ought not, even heuristically, to be thought of as an image of reality. When a language that emphasizes discontinuities and polarizes is accepted as a description of reality, an impoverished reality is also accepted. Jung, more than Watts, deals with the corresponding impoverishment of the individual mind. Both the cultural level of thought—for example, social science knowledge—and the contributions of individual scholars reflect the limitations of such a world view. In the context of Watts's inquiry, Western social science is at the far extreme of impoverishment and is characterized by the excesses of animus described by Jung.

Watts urges the perspective of Eastern traditions, which emphasize a paradoxical but essential unity of what we see as opposites. Both elements are real and essential, and there is no whole without both. The central motif in the myths recounted by

Watts is the transformation of the Many into the One. The polarities are seeming but not real. Their relationship and even combat are dramatized as a prelude to the climactic transformation.

Life and death are examples of polarities that our thought training treats as discrete and which Watts renders as one process—life-and-death. So with the other polarities: good-and-evil, knower-and-known, figure-and-ground, self-and-other, female-and-male. Non-Western traditions retain the fundamental ambivalence that implies reconcilation of seeming opposites that are essential to each other. Conversely, retaining the polarization implies no possible reconciliation or reunification. Our cultural bias is of the Western/polarizing type. In our kind of world, as Watts observes (1963, pp. 15, 29) refusing to accept the polarization is seen as impossible or immoral. It is subversive of the conscious ideals of the social order; it is thus unmentionable or obscene. Such is certainly the fate of androgyny and of the social movements for sex role liberation, which aim to establish the fundamental reality of androgyny. Androgyny belongs to that category of "unthinkable" and "unmentionable" to which Berger and Luckmann have sensitized us.

Humanistic psychology, although it recognizes the existence of anima and animus, is mired in the polarity and provides no real program for the reunification of the individual. In sum, the humanistic vision proves disappointing as a way of understanding androgyny. It fails to keep in focus the multiple processes of recovering androgyny: the relationship between woman and animus, the relationship between man and anima, and the relationship between women and men. I have suggested that a fourth relationship, that between anima and animus, often substitutes for the relationship between women and men. As long as men (including influential humanistic psychologists) persist in dealing with women as anima figures, they impede their own development and that of women.

In the humanistic tradition, the androgynous woman remains a will-o'-the-wisp. The vision is there but is overlaid with distortions and expectations that relate to a partial female person.

Where, then, will we find the female androgyne? One source is the research on creativity, for the creative person emerges as one who has available to her the range of capabilities that society thinks are "owned" by one sex *or* the other.

Androgyny in Creativity

The study of creativity is full of paradox. Not the least of these is the seeming contradiction between the image of creativity as the rare flash of genius and the image of creativity as disciplined inquiry backed up by encyclopedic knowledge. Workers in this field fail to agree even on a definition of creativity. There is agreement on some components of creativity, although different authors form them into different constellations. Current theory recognizes a fourfold nature in the problem of creativity, involving a person, a process, a product and a situation. Situation, in turn, can refer to antecedents of the production of an innovation or to the consequences, as in the adoption of an innovation.

Early research on creativity took science as its paradigm case and overlooked the forest of male institutional settings in trying to examine the tree of scientific productivity. Since the thaw in the Cold War, research in creativity has moved into areas other than competitive science. The possibilities for appreciating the role of androgyny in creativity appear better at present. Some researchers focus on analytical and intellective components of creativity, and others on expressive or "regressive" aspects. To emphasize one to the neglect of the other is to overlook the fundamentally androgynous nature of creativity. Both are aspects of the creative process. What is exceptional about the creative person is the accessibility to her of both the disciplines and the play aspects, both the persistence and the inspiration.

Lowes observes, ". . . the inscrutable energy of genius which we call creative owes its secret virtue at least in part to the enhanced and almost incredible facility with which in the wonder-working depths of the unconscious the fragments which sink incessantly below the surface fuse and assimilate and coalesce"

(1927, pp. 59–60). This comment highlights the importance of accessibility of the associatively rich material that the creative person has stored. Lowes states explicitly that the combination and recombination need not take place at the conscious level or as the result of conscious manipulations.

Eiseley's (1965) comparison of Darwin and Coleridge, who are often treated as exemplars of polar types of creativity, documents the presence of flexible, androgynous processes in the work of each. Coleridge's fantastic works are shown to be built upon the work of others and constructed upon meticulous notes and plans. Irrationalities and discontinuities in Darwin's work reveal the intuition and the "magical" transformations that he explicitly denied. Thus Eiseley's analysis reveals the presence, in both geniuses' work, of methodical note taking, wide reading and inspiration.

CREATIVE PERSON AND CREATIVE PROCESS

Creativity is thought of as stimulus-seeking activity. Current thinking emphasizes that the creative person often constructs a problem or finds a problem that others have not seen. Newell, Shaw and Simon view creativity as problem solving, emphasizing that its product must have both novelty and value in the culture; that creative thinking requires modification or rejection of previously accepted ideas; that the problem requires high motivation and persistence, and that the problem as initially posed lacks definition, so that part of the task is to formulate the problem (1962, pp. 65–66).

Torrance (1965) defines creativity as the process of becoming sensitive to problems, deficiencies, gaps in knowledge, missing elements, disharmonies and so on; identifying the difficulty; searching for solutions, making guesses . . . testing and retesting these, and finally communicating the results (1965, pp. 663–664). Current perspectives emphasize sustained searching, judgment and commitment more than the instantaneous flash of insight.

A major component of creativity is divergent thinking, a kind of intellectual nonconformity that enables the creative individual to break set, to combine elements in original ways, to see unlikely connections. Creative individuals, when compared with others in their own field, tend to show a preference for graphic stimuli that are asymmetrical rather than symmetrical. A parallel dislike for solutions that are too neat may lead the divergent thinker to seek and to work with paradox.

Many students of creativity have noted a playfulness, vividness or impulsiveness that is characteristic of creative process; Barron (1969) has referred to this, in the Freudian parlance, as regression in the service of the ego. That is, within the framework set by training and discipline, the creative person functions in a way that is somehow childlike. This "regressive" functioning remains in the service of the ego—that is, its focus is the problem that the scientist or artist has chosen.

In a recent book, Csikszentmihalyi (1975) has explored autotelic, or intrinsically motivated activities, focusing on play. The subjective experience that is common to the many forms of play he examined may be called "the flow experience," in which action and awareness are merged, ego and environment unified in a way that does away with awareness of an observing self outside the experience.

SITUATIONAL FACTORS IN CREATIVITY

Situational factors are paramount both in the production of innovations and in their subsequent "career."

Andrews, studying creative sociologists, emphasized situational factors that facilitate high productivity: high autonomy and security, a project of limited scope, high motivation and extraproject interests (1975). He notes, however, that lacking these favorable surroundings, the creative person produces less. Studies of the placement of women within a broad range of fields establishes that women are disadvantaged with respect to situational factors.

Like other set-breaking activities, the "flow experience" studied by Csikszentmihalyi is facilitated by situational factors. It is more likely to occur, according to Csikszentmihalyi, when the individual's capacities are well matched with environmental demands, when the focus of environmental demands is limited, and when there is little ambiguity in past reward and future expectations from the environment. Women whose workday and workspace are subject to intrusions and whose success is less than that of comparable males are clearly facing nonoptimal conditions.

The probability of succesful (i.e., accepted) innovation on the part of women is also conditioned by situational factors.

THE CAREER OF INNOVATION

Innovation must be properly publicized and taken up by others in order to have its effect. Networks are essential in helping an innovation have its proper impact. The rose can indeed blush unseen in a desert. In order to have impact, the creative product must be taken up and touted by influentials. Lasswell's (1959) observations on this process do not make for euphoria among creative women. The probability that an influential judge will recognize and foster an innovation is related to the degree to which the judge will be benefited by it and the perceived similarity between the judge and the innovator in values, personality, contacts and the like. To the extent that influentials are males and females are perceived as unlike them, the second condition will not be met. The findings of Caplow and McGee (1961) on the academic profession can probably be generalized to other occupations. They observe that hiring a woman cannot help a department's prestige: women don't count; they are simply not in the game at all (1961, pp. 111). Thus there is no perception of benefit in fostering the career development of women. In a related finding, Rosenberg and Fliegel (1965) found that art dealers and gallery owners refused to exhibit women painters because they thought they would not sell. Of course, painters who cannot get exhibited find it almost impossible to sell their work and gain recognition. Such "failures" can, according to Andrews's finding, depress subsequent productivity. Successful innovation probably

344

requires, in addition to genius, a "resonator" (or Wife of the Genius?), intellectual collaborators and a circle of apostles. The applicability of these requisites to science and to academic scholarship can be readily seen. The data on occupational placement of women doctorate holders are relevant here. Women doctorate holders are disproportionately concentrated in institutions where they have no access to graduate students (apostles), to equipment needed for research or to a laboratory of one's own. Their teaching loads tend to be higher than average, leaving little time for concentration and scholarship. To the extent that their gender-status isolates women academicians from their male peers, they lack the sponsorship and access to networks of opportunities and contacts that facilitate advancement. Feldman (1973) found, in a study of female and male graduate students, that most women were without a sponsor. A woman who had a sponsor, however, perceived herself as more original and dedicated than other women. It seems that acceptance generates a self-fulfilling prophecy, and those with this perception in fact produced more.

SEX AND CREATIVITY

Much of the research on creativity overlooks women, and very little of it attempts to study creative women in depth. Even so, the empirical research on creativity shows the incursions of sex roles on creativity, particularly in females. Helson (1961) found that high-aptitude junior-high-school boys were more likely to be fascinated by mathematics, girls by art. However, she notes that creating works of art may not advance other purposes of girls (occupational ones, for example) to the extent that creating works of science does for boys.

Torrance (1972), in following up a sample of high-school seniors 12 years later, found that high-creative females were more likely to have a career as well as a family than were low-creative females. The number of children was negatively correlated with aspiration and with quantity and quality of creative output in women. Kogan and Pankove (1972) tested creative individuals and followed them up five years later. The ratings achieved by boys were stable but those of girls were not. Both of these findings suggest that researchers should be sensitive to situational factors and life events that impinge on women's creativity.

The confidence gap appears among creative women as it does among the average. Kurtzman (1967) and Werner and Bachtold (1969) found gifted adolescent women to be less dominant and self-assured than their male counterparts. In Helson's research (reported below) male art students were far more likely to name themselves artists than were their female peers.

Other work is more suggestive than conclusive. Creative college women show more regression (as measured by Rorschach) than creative males (Pine and Holt, 1960). Bowers (1971) found hypnotic susceptibility to be related to creativity in women and the reverse in men (1971).

Welch (1975) has developed a conceptual model for the relationships between creativity and masculinity/femininity. Along a dimension of "intellectance" Welch locates a tendency to abstraction, motivation for manipulation and expression of ideas, an interest in comprehension. Associated with the dimension of "origence" (which is uncorrelated with intelligence) are a preference for an unstructured versus structured world, an implicit versus explicit world. Welch tentatively identifies a tendency toward extroversion with origence. In a population of more than one thousand talented adolescents, intellectance was associated with masculinity and origence with femininity—*in both females and males*. Creativity is associated with a blending of femininity and masculinity and of origence and intellectance. Welch proposes a typology composed of high and low ends of both dimensions, with hypotheses about the kind of antecedent family constellation for each of four cells. Feminine behavior and mother identification should characterize persons high in origence and low in intellectance. Masculine behavior and father identification should characterize those who are high in intellectance but low in origence. Persons high in both dimensions should be androgynous, rejecting sex role traditionalism and manifesting behavioral traits associated with both genders. (Identification is with the self rather than with either parent.) Those who are low in both should show conventional sex role behaviors congruent with gender.

Helson goes further, suggesting that the conventional person represses contrasex attributes, while the creative person accepts them. Contrasex attributes thus remain rudimentary or primitive in the conventional person, while they may be developed in the unconventional person and contribute to creativity. This thinking is consistent with Jung's thinking about anima and animus.

STUDIES OF CREATIVE WOMEN

Helson (1975) reports the results of a series of studies of creative adults undertaken by the Institute of Personality Assessment and Research (IPAR). These included matched samples of female and male mathematicians, artists and authors of children's books.

The sample of female mathematicians was drawn from among those earning doctorate degrees in math from elite graduate institutions between 1950 and 1960. Of 44 participants, all were achievers, and 16 were evaluated as highly creative by judges expert in their specialties. A comparison group of male mathematicians was created by augmenting Crutchfield's (n.d.) sample. Helson observes (1975, pp. 18–19) that the female mathematicians combined sensitivity, flexibility and absorption in mathematical research but held peripheral positions in the hierarchy of the professional community. If the criterion for inclusion in the study had not been quality but quantity of work, the women would not have appeared in the study at all. This observation highlights the problem of recognizing female talent in a sexist society. When we assume an open society, we are assuming that equal opportunity allows the talented to rise to the top. However, when we restrict our talent search to top positions, we leave out those whose access to those positions has been barred by custom. The provocative question, "Why are there no female geniuses?", needs to be asked a different way: "How do we overlook female geniuses?"

The female mathematicians' self-descriptions contained many attributes common to achievers, attributes that are "male-valued" in our society. They valued intellectuality and thinking; they prided themselves on being objective and rational, and they valued independence and autonomy. The female mathematicians showed unconventional thought processes, nonconformity and rebelliousness. Unlike male stereotypes (but perhaps like geniuses in all fields), they reported fluctuating moods and were characterized as interesting, arresting people and as self-dramatizing. The IPAR observers described this group as individualistic, courageous, original, complicated, emotional, imaginative, artistic, preoccupied and self-centered. The comparison group of women was characterized by the observers as cheerful, active, appreciative, reliable, sympathetic, organized, realistic, helpful, cooperative, conventional and considerate.

When all groups of writers and mathematicians were compared, both creativity and field of endeavor showed significant effects. Mathematicians as a group were more disciplined, objective and abstract-minded than writers. They scored higher on wellbeing, responsibility, self-control, socialization, tolerance, psychological-mindedness—but lower on femininity. The effects for creativity contradict these findings to some extent. When creative people are compared with their less creative peers, flexibility is found to be positively related to creativity, while wellbeing, self-control, communality and achievement via conformance are negatively related.[5] In addition, the authors found sex differences: males scored higher on self-acceptance and social presence and lower on femininity.

Within the group of women, creativity was related positively and significantly to flexibility, achievement via conformance, communality, dominance, sociability and self-acceptance. Among men, only self-control was significantly (and negatively) related to creativity.

---

[5]The study of male mathematicians was conducted by mail, so no observed ratings were available on them. Both groups completed the California Personality Inventory.

When creative women are compared with less creative women, differences by field of endeavor appear. The creative female mathematicians score more feminine than other female mathematicians, while creative female writers score less feminine than other female writers.

Interaction effects of sex with creativity are more numerous among the mathematicians than among the writers. Creative male and female mathematicians both score high in flexibility, but the women score low on sociability and self-acceptance, and the men score high. Helson relates this difference to the different positions they hold in the profession with respect to prestige and success.

Helson followed up the sex differences in further personality research. Using a specially constructed Q sort methodology, she isolated a distinctive work style that differentiated the creative female mathematicians both from other women and from the creative male mathematicians. This work style employs unconscious as well as conscious processes; the self is totally absorbed in the work and the effort is directed inward. In this mode of functioning, which Helson calls matriarchal after Neumann's usage, the ego is not assertive against the environment. Rather, the individual withdraws from the social environment to complete the creative process.

Helson found this work pattern to be characteristic of the writers more than of the mathematicians, and of the women to a greater extent than of the men. This work style seems well adapted to the artist who must work alone, often without institutional affiliation.

Helson's work maintains an appropriate focus upon the context within which the creative individual works. It is essential, when reading about the personality and vicissitudes of the creative person, to examine how well the data fit the experience of women. The "matriarchal" creative style would seem to be well suited to the woman who must often do her work without benefit of institutional supports—typists, office, someone to buffer interruptions, the deference accorded to office. The mechanism of social withdrawal seems to fit the image of the free-lance artist or writer, and it would be easy to assume that this characterizes the creative person who works at home. Home is, however, the least conducive environment for uninterrupted concentration, as we have seen in Chapter 2. Most women who are at home have household and family responsibilities that constantly infringe on their work.

The interruptions that plague the day of most women find parallels in interrupted careers and interrupted talents. The lack of stability that Kogan and Pankove found in creative girls' creativity contrasts with a stable history for boys. Behind this difference lies the encouragement and staging of achievement in talented boys, which has no parallel in talented girls.

Thus, after reviewing the research on creativity we are brought to the conclusion that ability, or even demonstrated achievement, is not sufficient to guarantee the realization of creative potential. We are brought back to Virginia Woolf's insistence on a room of one's own. That room stands as a proxy for resources sufficient to permit the individual to work on her major projects. The room, and the lock on its door, stand for personal space that one can arrange as best suits the requirements of one's work, for the security of uninterrupted time and unmolested materials.

Androgyny Now

The literature on creativity feeds both optimism and cynicism. Descriptions of the creative process communicate androgynous functioning vividly: the accessibility of a wide range of attributes and modes of thought, the disciplined and knowing use of associations between divergent images and information. On the other hand, it is equally clear that the same obstacles impede women's achievements in this realm as others.

Yet androgyny exists—not only in children but in adults.[6] The links between the two will be considered at this point.

---

[6]Androgyny is to be found in unexpected places. The former heavyweight champion of the world has characterized himself in unmistakably androgynous imagery, by the capacity to "float like a butterfly/sting like a bee." Androgyny has been big business in the profit-making sector for a generation, in the form of "sensitivity training" for managers.

In Chapter 4 we reviewed evidence on toy and play preferences of young children, discovering a large set of activities and toys for which girls' and boys' behaviors and preference overlap. We also discovered the tendencies of others to encourage sex-typed behaviors and tastes and to discourage "sex-inappropriate" ones. The pattern for toy preferences seems to be repeated in many other realms of social life—for example, in the process of occupational "choice." Children seem to learn to *exclude* large categories of occupations from active consideration, with peers, parents and guidance counselors providing the social approval for "sex-appropriate" choices.

The evidence seems clear that preferences in all realms that are sex-typed are shaped by social approval. The evidence is less clear with reference to the effects of negative sanctions. This question is of particular importance for the survival of androgyny, present in children, into adulthood.

If early experience shows a reality of androgynous capabilities for most persons and sex-role socialization consistently favors only a subset of these, what becomes of the rest? If these capabilities are punished, their expression will be inhibited, but they will not necessarily be forgotten. If they simply fail to be rewarded, they may drop out of the individual's repertoire. This leaves the question of whether they can be resurrected again, given a situation of favorable social support or actual reward. The evidence for androgyny in adulthood suggests that there may be some carryover—perhaps only in some persons, or perhaps in all.

The existence of that middle ground of non-sex-typed activities in childhood suggests that most individuals' learning will include experience in this realm as well. One question for future research is the degree to which individuals differ in their exposure to non-sex-typed experiences, and the effects of this comparative freedom from sextyping on androgyny and creativity.

If the overall script of sex role socialization is to limit each gender to nonoverlapping and restricted options, most persons will feel more comfortable within these boundaries. But what is the effect for those whose history contains relatively more non-sex-typed or cross-sex-typed items? Presumably if they do not know that they are "out of step," they will not suffer the social embarrassment and sense of personal inadequacy that haunts the aware misfit. On the other hand, these individuals have access to a broader range of possibilities and may develop a more inclusive range of competences and attributes, than is the case for the "normal" American child. This kind of developmental history may be the ground within which the androgynous person is nurtured— that is, a person who contains, and is comfortable with, attributes that others consider "feminine" and "masculine." Indeed, some studies of achieving women suggest this kind of background as an antecedent condition.

Yet another possibility for the development of androgyny is evidenced by the existence of a sizable proportion of children of both sexes preferring toys or activities that are sex-typed for the opposite sex. When children score above the mean for the *other* sex in their preference for activities sex-typed for that sex, it suggests that they do not habitually limit themselves to the script provided for them.

The issue of labeling interacts with the question of sex-role stereotyping. When a child is exposed to adult models who are androgynous—that is, exhibiting contrasex attributes—is the development of an androgynous identity facilitated or impeded if the adult's attributes are sex-labeled? To the extent that persons of each gender learn to think of the other as a negative identity, interposition of contrasex labels may inhibit imitation or modeling. On the other hand, when the androgynous model is not interdicted by such labeling, modeling may be enhanced. A number of studies indicate that identification is facilitated by nurturance *and* by power in the model. Mussen (1961) found that masculine identification in boys was facilitated by fathers who combined masculinity with feminine warmth. Reports of achieving women show an androgynous father, as well as the more common modeling of multiple roles by the mother. Conscious modeling of androgyny represents a step beyond such a fortuitous combination of "feminine" and "masculine" attributes. Parents can shape their children toward sex role transcendence, just as they have, in the past, shaped them toward traditional sex roles.

Another source of modeling for androgyny is to be found in "opposite" sex siblings. Findings from a study by Rosenberg and Sutton-Smith (1968) suggest that we should look at sex ratios within the family as well as relations between same and contrasex parents with children. When responses of 160 college women were compared with those of their parents and siblings on the Gough Femininity scale, complex interactions emerged. In families with two girls, the scores of mother and daughters are highly intercorrelated but the father is different. In families with a boy and a girl, the scores of father, mother and son intercorrelate, and the girl is an isolate, with high identification with the mother.

Data such as these indicate that the forces for sex role acquisition are more various than is sometimes supposed. Another influence in the development of sex typing versus androgyny is suggested by some of the work in developmental psychology. Kohlberg (1966) has studied children's maturational timetable for recognizing constancies in the world around them. He located gender constancy at about age five (1966, p. 94). At that time the child realizes that gender is invariant: if she is a girl, she can no more turn into a boy at will than a cat can turn into a dog. Kohlberg's work has two implications of paramount interest. First is the emphasis on active mastery of the environment; in the case of sex roles, this means learning the script. Thus the acquisition of sex role stereotyping (and the use of such stereotypes in self-definition) may be part of a developmental process of adapting to and mastering the world. Since, as we have stressed throughout this book, gender is one of the cultural categories most frequently used to structure social life, learning its many meanings is a task the young child must master. Kohlberg observed that brighter children master it at earlier ages—and also abandon it at earlier ages. More differentiated ways of dealing with the world become *more* adaptive, and as the individual masters these, she moves beyond simple stereotyping.

Pleck (1973a) suggests that the development of sexual identity is a process analogous to that of language development. The ripening of a general capacity for language use is essential and forms the foundation for the acquisition of all language. Research demonstrates a developmental threshold for the expansion of this capacity: if an individual has not learned other languages (in addition to her native language) by the age of about fourteen, it becomes virtually impossible for her to do so. Following Pleck's analogy, we fear that people can get fixated at a rudimentary level and fail to develop the much greater capacity for personal growth that is in evidence.

Rebecca and her associates (1976) echo the idea that early sex role learning is lacking in subtlety; its content emphasizes stereotyping and self-definition by reference to opposites (e.g., as Ellis and Bentler observe, I am a boy in part because I am a not-girl). A more evolved level of development moves away from rigid polarities and incorporates more individuality.

Adult life demands more sophisticated coping than does childhood. The discomfort experienced by the more sex role stereotyped subjects in Bem's experiments reflects the difficulties they had with a situation that demanded a broad repertoire and flexible functioning. Mussen's (1961) findings concerning the social adjustment of adolescent and adult males and the low social adjustment and self-esteem of many "feminine" women underscore this point. Mussen found that males who exemplified stereotypical masculinity showed high social adjustment in high school, but much worse adjustment as adults. Similarly, those who succeed in becoming what our society designates as feminine find that they have become ineffective. Sex role socialization works too well, producing a trained incapacity for the demands of adult life.

The effects of sex role socialization in forming self-identity cannot be overlooked. However, it is possible, as I have observed in Chapter 4, to exaggerate primary socialization into a near-total determinism. A perspective that emphasizes social pressures exclusively can overlook the role of personal identity in directing and selecting experience, even from an early age. Personal identity

354

acquires a functional autonomy and is much more than a mirror of social pressures.

Two aspects of personal identity have the potential of working against social pressures. First, the individual values the self and will defend herself against pressures to behave or believe in ways inconsistent with that self. While social approval is a powerful motivator, self-approval may be equally powerful. Normally, the self is positively valued, and the sentiment of self-esteem or self-regard or self-love can be a powerful force that is largely independent of social evaluation or social esteem. Second, the individual has the capacity to reflect on the self, on experience and on the consequences of various options. Though the study of sex roles emphasizes the *social* construction of reality, the self can also be an agent of socialization and resocialization. This potential is seen more clearly in instances of volitional self-change. The most striking example is consciousness raising, which will be discussed later.

Given the above analysis, it can be seen that contrasex attributes may well become part of self-identity and partake of positive self-evaluation, which anchors them and makes them resistant to change. The individual learns to characterize herself in the terms that others use. Further, she is more likely to incorporate items that are remarked upon (perhaps because they are atypical). This prediction is consistent with Jones's (1972) theory of self-identity, and with findings that sex role-atypical behaviors are noted and reported more than sex role-congruent ones by observers rating children. Self-reports of achieving women, as compared with non-achievers, seem to bear this out. Gysbers et al. (1968) and Birnbaum (1971) have found that career-oriented women describe themselves as intellectual and achievement-oriented—both attributes that are considered sex-atypical. Tangri's (1972) role-innovative college women describe themselves as less feminine than do traditionals (though by no means as "masculine"). These findings suggest that traits that are considered remarkable are incorporated and become part of self-report. This may well be the fate of contrasex attributes, with implications for the accessibility of androgynous characteristics in the adult.

Thus in summarizing the evidence for androgyny now, we may say that the androgyny apparent in children is not totally extinguished by sex role socialization. In fact, we have discovered a number of factors that militate toward the entrenchment of androgyny. Additional considerations make it clear that there is much potential for expanding androgyny in both women and men. Before turning to these possibilities, however, it is worthwhile to review what androgyny is and is not. Androgyny is not a chimera, as some contemporary writers believe (Goldenberg, 1976). It is not the exclusive property of women. It is not hermaphroditism or transsexualism. It is not sex role reversal. And it is not a social order; it is not a social structural concept at all, but rather a concept of the individual. Androgyny is, rather, that state of the person in which "feminine" and "masculine" attributes are accepted, valued and available for living.

There remains a contradiction between androgyny as a desirable way of living and the patriarchal society in which we live. Any analysis of the future of androgyny must emphasize the constricting effects of situation and social control, even more than of socialization. The empirical literature makes it clear that both females and males who are creative function in androgynous ways. It is also clear that the social situation supports and reinforces the full utilization of capabilities to a greater extent for males than for females.

The creativity literature tells us what the research on MF and humanistic psychology have already told us: the expression of androgyny is ordinarily blocked in our society. Socialization narrows the androgynous range of children's preferences and attributes, and social control inhibits the actualization of the inner traces of androgyny in adults.

In thinking about how to make the world a "safer" place for androgyny, therefore, we must reexamine the factors that make our own androgyny inaccessible to us. In general, we conclude, social evaluation blocks our access to our contrasex attributes.

First, female traits are devalued in our society, causing both women and men to grasp them with less than enthusiasm. Contrasex attributes, however, are tabooed for both women and men. Consequently the expansion of repertoires by incorporating or acknowledging contrasex attributes is risky. In doing so the individual moves against social support and, in the eyes of many, endangers her primary sexual identity. The woman is doubly vulnerable in this: although her primary identity is a devalued or deviant one, movement away from it exposes her to greater sanctions precisely because of her initially low power position. Women who stand up for themselves and their sisters, or who challenge men's monopoly on power or dominance, are said to "lose their femininity." It is with this kind of threat that the battle of the sexes is waged. Chesler (1972, p. 297) notes that the battle between the sexes goes unnoticed because women take losing for granted, and men take winning for granted. Women are trained to be losers—men to be winners. Although officially they are not antagonists, these traits characterize their interactions. Ophelia is cited as a "good loser"; Medea as a "bad loser" (Chesler, 1972, p. 297). A male feminist may be a traitor to his class, but one does not hear that he "loses his masculinity" by espousing the cause of women's rights.

Paths to Androgyny

It is clear that the liberation of women and men involves different tasks, with different starting points, requiring different changes. A woman who leaves behind the restrictions of femininity does not put on the straitjacket of masculinity. Knowing the family as we do (to borrow from James Baldwin), why would we want to marry into it? The fantasy that the outcome of sex-role liberation will be role reversal ignores both the starting points and the goals of the Women's Movement. The failure to see any alternative to femininity but masculinity is a symptom of the problem of sex roles. Reality is polarized and the polarities become, for many

357

people, reality. The solution of the dilemma created by this means requires seeing through the polarization to an androgynous reality.

One starting point is suggested by Jungian thought. For women, the movement toward androgyny must begin with the excavation and rehabilitation of the animus. Jung suggests that the challenge for women in incorporating their animus is to overcome lack of pride or self-confidence (1957, p. 23). The confidence gap in women appears to support this analysis. Women's competence, often unacknowledged even by themselves, corresponds in part to the idea of animus. The current vogue in assertion training for women is a direct effort at intervening in this pattern and turning it around. Proponents of assertion training make a clear distinction between appropriate self-assertion, which stops short of harming others, and aggression, which is aimed at a target and can have the purpose of causing harm.

However, there are other obstacles to the rehabilitation of the animus. The history of repression, within the individual, and the history of patriarchy, in society, combine in an image of masculinity as deformed and undesirable. The woman reaching for androgyny may, as Jung supposes, be reaching for something she always admired but thought was out of her reach. In our day, however, she must also deal with her alienation from the brutalities and excesses of masculinity as she has encountered it in the "man's world."

The debate about the nature of androgyny—Is it M plus F? Is it neuter?—must be seen in the context of the politics of sex roles. Whether androgyny is seen as the incorporation of feminine qualities into the male, or the stripping away of artificial, culturally male trappings, it represents (always from a male point of view) a reduction in status. However constraining the male role, it encompasses many privileges that are based in part upon keeping women out: the wage inflation of the male labor market, the rights guaranteed under the Fourteenth Amendment, access to many specialized environments, rights of dominance in sex and family, to name a few. It is more apparent in the case of men than of women that moving toward androgyny will mean occupying a different space in the world. The pursuit of the anima has implications for the individual man's power position.

Actualizing androgyny will, for most men, mean moving toward expressivity, nurturance and play—away from control, dominance of others, the exclusive valuation of people in terms of power and money. As Emma Jung observes, the man reaching for androgyny must embrace something he previously thought valueless. From the perspective of the status quo, he has a lot to lose and literally "nothing" to gain.

Pleck (1975a) makes the point that both women and men are mutilated by sex role socialization as it stands in America. In that sense, both are oppressed. Pleck does not say, however, that both are equally oppressed, for the position of women and men in society is very different (1975a, p. 20). In particular, the power position of men affords them greater resources to direct to whatever purpose (including change), making them less vulnerable to those who oppose them. Moreover, the power analysis makes it apparent that men are not likely to initiate major changes in a status quo that benefits them as a group.

Even the more modest goal of personal growth toward androgyny is blocked by the stranglehold of sex roles on our thinking. Because of the way we have been taught to think of ourselves and "the other," both women and men have a stake in a polarized and impoverished view of the sexes. Yet this view has been challenged powerfully and inescapably by the current generation of feminists. Feminists have rejected the images of women purveyed by patriarchy and the right of men to "name" how women are and should be. Many women silently echo these challenges: the shoe no longer fits. Yet the feminist path seems risky (it is) and radical (it is). Is there not some middle way? Aren't there some tolerable, even pleasing, images of women available to all—short of revolution? At present, our image of potential androgyny is blurred by the status quo. We concede that the androgyne is imperfectly rendered in any empirical tradition that has its roots in the-way-things-are. What about the way things were? Or the way things might be? Will we get a clearer image of androgyny if we review the history of matriarchy? What does the Amazon Vision have to tell us? What of feminist/utopian writing of our own time?

The Great Goddess and the Amazon Vision

Women of the current generation show a vivid interest in heroic women, from the labor organizers of the 1930s back to Joan of Arc and even further back, beyond the reaches of written history, to goddesses, priestesses, queens, and Amazons. Elizabeth Gould Davis, in her book, *The First Sex* (1971), draws together a stellar sisterhood of goddesses and queens, whose history she seeks to uncover. She argues, following Bachofen (1967), that mythology recounts real events in the history of the human race, whose record, far predating writing, descends to us through oral history. Davis begins with myths of a female creatrix and assembles the pantheon of female gods and rulers. The Babylonian deity was Tiamat, "Mother of the Gods, Creater of All." The creative principle of earliest Greek mythology was a female intelligence called Metis (later transformed, like so many of the goddesses Davis discusses, into a male figure). Davis also associates Ishtar/Astarte (the Sumerian chief deity) with the figure of Tiamat. Tiamat appeared out of the primeval sea and imparted much wisdom and technology to man. If Tiamat was a historical figure, she may have been queen of the Thracian/Anatolian remnant of the lost civilization who traveled down the Euphrates by boat. Another early avatar was Queen Basilea, who reportedly predated Poseidon as ruler of Atlantis and with whom the cult of the bull is first associated. She was a warrior queen—perhaps the precursor of Celtic rulers like Boadicea. She was said to be the daughter of Gaia, the primeval goddess of Hellenic myth, who created the world from chaos (and was Cronos's mother).

Such heroic figures are far more than imaginative constructions, according to Davis. Before the ancients, antiquarians acknowledge, high civilizations existed whose achievements were unmatched by classic and medieval men. The existence of a common

Indo-European language from which the ancient languages of Latin, Sanskrit and Greek developed suggests a culture highly developed in all ways, which predates written history and so must be divined through other traces. Davis solves the mystery of high civilizations that preceded ancient barbarism by reconstructing the rule of women, or gynocracy whose deity was the Great Goddess.

Davis relies on physical artifacts, imaginative speculation, historical analysis and myth to construct a picture of the possible matriarchal precursors of "our" Western tradition. Davis theorizes that Anatolia was the last outpost of the early matriarchal civilization and the only one whose relics are known to us. Druidism was the religion of this archaic civilization, once common to the regions from the Baltic to Gibralter. Davis links the existence of ancient maps whose accuracy exceeded that of the medieval period in which they were lost to the stories of the "ancient mariners" who circled the globe and initiated similar cultural practices in areas that had no common ties. Davis sees the ancient mariners as a race of women, whose home base was Crete. The prevalent myth of fair-haired strangers of miraculous character suggests to Davis a link between the Druidic Celts and the seafaring mariners. The Celts' ancestors, according to one account, originated on an island located somewhere off the coast of Spain, placing them in the Anatolian/Mediterranean neighborhood. This culture was ruled by a woman, according to Herodotus. The religious and the scientific knowledge of this culture survived in the mountain retreat of Thrace. Thrace was the home of Orpheus and his teacher, Pythagoras, who taught Orpheus the ancient wisdom that had been repudiated by many of Pythagoras's contemporaries. Thrace was cited as the home of witchcraft (woman-wisdom) in ancient times, and the Amazons were reputed to make this region their home. Thrace was also the origin of Druidism, according to Davis. Common to religious observance of these peoples are the symbols of matriarchy, the plow and yoke (invented by the agricultural women) and worked gold. Many Celtic fairies and fairy queens (including Morgan Le Fay of Arthurian legend) are rendered as mermaids and emerge from watery homes to converse with man, as Tiamat was reported to do. The goddess of Thracian (and Druid) worship was Diana, a far more ancient goddess than Apollo's twin who appears in the more familiar Greek mythology. The Eleusinian mysteries were part of her worship, strictly governed by her priestesses. Orpheus, by some accounts at least, was a renegade Druid, and was murdered by the maenads (Diana's priestesses) for revealing the ancient wisdom to those who were not initiates.

From Thrace too, according to Davis, came a generation that founded "prehistoric" towns recently excavated by archeologists, in whose ruins are found many artifacts associated with the cult of the Great Goddess. Davis summarizes the results of the archaeological investigations to support her picture of the gynocratic societies that worshipped the Great Goddess. Mellaart's (1966) reconstruction of Çatal Hüyük portrays a society at peace for a thousand years, where pets were cherished and domesticated animals used for wool and milk but not for meat. The supreme deity was a goddess, and human and animal sacrifice was unknown. Women, as heads of household, were buried with far more reverence than men. The association of the cult of the Great Goddess and the worship of the bull suggests a link to Minoan culture, which Davis had suggested. Some scholars of ancient societies see economy and law as revolving around women; Davis assigns most of the most crucial discoveries of primitive humankind to women. Even the stone megaliths whose construction and origin have mystified the generations are ascribed to what Davis calls the matriarchal period.

The link between prehistory and the Greek historians (or mythologers) is speculative. Davis relies on Hesiod for an accounting of the "ages of man" in Greek history. He bewails the coming of patriarchy and the eclipse of a pacific, productive tradition.

Davis dates the patriarchal challenge at the fall of the city-states of Sumer about 2500 B.C. Some accounts assign this period in time to the Amazons, who are characterized as warlike and who, in many ancient accounts, battled the male invaders to preserve the matriarchal civilization. The new conception of the Amazon arose as the attacks by male nations threatened the matriarchal order. A more militant and androgynous race was needed to counteract the threat of patriarchy. The current revival of the Amazon Vision is, similarly, a reaction against the extremes of patriarchy.

In Amazon societies, the contemporary division among role spheres was unknown: women were warriors *and* mothers. We do not hear much about "role conflict" among Amazons. Within the Amazon nation there were tribal differences. As tradition has it, some tribes crippled male infants and retained them as slaves whose functions were domestic labor, spinning and child care. In others, males were kept in camp, rather like concubines. The Libyan Amazons had universal compulsory military service, with marriage permitted only after this period. Amazons did not nurse: their children were raised on mare's milk and cared for by men.

Amazon societies, thus described, have many similarities with societies modeled upon the image of the Great Goddess. The Amazon is, however, distinct from the old matriarchal religion and the social order it embraced. Diner (1965) identifies Amazons as a daughter clan, incorporating androgynous rather than solely female principles. The mother clan divided out the masculine principles, exiling the young males from the clan. The Amazons incorporated both, thus healing the division. The idea of the Amazon canceled the earlier order. Nevertheless, patriarchy won this battle.

The triumph of a patriarchal order coincided with a transformation of both myth and history. Davis's excavation is crucial to the exposure of the more ancient gynocentric culture, deliberately veiled by chroniclers of the succeeding eras. It is these that are taught as "our" history by the official organs of enculturation—the schools.

The story of Hercules illustrates the patriarchal transformation of Greek mythology. The historical Hercules was a slave of the Lydian queen, Omphale, who, in sport, assigns him the ten labors, (many of which call for him to do what was in their society woman's work). Davis shows, too, that many Old Testament stories are borrowed from the Babylonian and Sumerian epics (appropriately transformed by the patriarchal Semites).

The importance of this magical body of material compiled by Davis lies not in its historicity. Its significance lies in the figures of heroic women that it offers us; in the articulation of the attributes of a gynocentric culture; in restoring continuity through the ages of goddesses, witches and women whose history was eclipsed by patriarchy. If this be myth, it is myth in Watts's sense; the expression of an inner reality that is perhaps at variance with a seeming reality of the outer world.

By their very existence these myths challenge the partriarchal reality. The resurgence of interest in them, and of other woman-lore, is subversive of the social order of male dominance. In ancient times, the survivors of an even more ancient religion were persecuted, as were witches in the Middle Ages and feminists today. Interest in the goddesses and rulers in the matriarchal line is not mere nostalgia nor escapist fantasy. Rather, these images are a source of inspiration and an antidote to the miniaturized images of woman that surround us in our own age. Inspiration serves an essential function as women recognize the necessity for changing the social order and the imperative for taking the change-agent role themselves.

The reconstruction of the Great Goddess is an antidote to the seeming eclipse of matriarchal values in a patriarchal age. Women's history, too, reminds us of lives and contributions whose existence is implicitly or explicitly denied. However, inspiration is nearer than the historic past. In our own time there is Wonder Woman.

The image of Wonder Woman captivated me in the 1940s and, after the parched period of the 1950s, reemerged coincident with the rise of the new feminism. She was beautiful (of course) and had superhuman powers (of course). He preeminence was earned in contests with her peers (as Steinem points out), rather than being artificially conferred by her creator, Marston. Her wonderfulness was achieved, rather than ascribed. On the other hand, it was clearly not of this world, but symbolized Wonder Woman's

tie to another, superior (but no less real) world, Paradise Island—
the home of the Amazons. The images of female community in
Wonder Woman have no parallel in the comic book world. Paradise Island was a model society, with harmony between generations, games of physical skill, art, science and magic being
pursued by serene Amazons. The Amazons are freed from reproduction: Wonder Woman is sculpted by her mother, and then
Aphrodite breathes life into her. Queen Hippolyte governs her
empire and dispatches Amazons to right wrongs in the manmade
world. Her implacable enemy is Mars, who seeks always to steal
her magic girdle through strategems of courtship.

Wonder Woman is the only female member of the Justice
League of America, the externalized collective conscience-and-
trouble-shooter of a wicked world. She acts out the more civilized
matriarchal values of Paradise Island in her adventures in the
world.

Wonder Woman is much less violent than the other superheroes
of comic book life. In her adventures, there is not only less blood-
shed but less hatred. Force is tempered by love and justice.
Wonder Woman often converts her enemies. Wonder Woman's
efforts are aimed at the restoration of peace and just functioning.
When villains get their just desserts, it is often by being caught
up in their own machinations.

Wonder Woman has feminine articulateness, enunciating her
values while engaging in hand-to-hand combat. She is a role model
to women who are ineffectual or fearful.

Her magical accessories have none of James Bond's gadgetry
about them. The transparent airplane is an emblem of her combination of beauty and power. The magic of her golden lasso is
positive, not destructive: it compels the person bound by it to tell
the truth. The Amazon cuffs lend themselves as well to play as
to self-defense; Wonder Woman often makes a game of "bullets
and bracelets."

Wonder Woman is filial—or perhaps sororal. She exceeds male
heroes ("*swifter* than Mercury, *stronger* than Hercules") but not
female ("*as* beautiful as Aphrodite, *as* wise as Athena"). Some

ambiguities remain. In her double life, Wonder Woman/Diana Prince presents two quite different images. Even in the 1940s I was aware of the symbolic meaning of hiding her behind glasses and a dowdy hairdo. When Wonder Woman negates her Amazon excellences to blend in with the male world, she is a wallflower. Her paramour, Steve Trevor, loves her as Wonder Woman, yet cannot win her. And Trevor, though he clearly wants the super-woman, does not come forward with suggestions about how he might modify his role in a permanent partnership. Marston provides no resolution of this dilemma.

As a child, I had the same puzzlement concerning this lack of a happy ending that Steinem confesses. The message is clearer to me now: there is no happily ever after for Wonder Woman in a man's world. That is why she is Wonder Woman and not Cinderella.

The 1960s saw an abortive revival of Wonder Woman, transformed appropriately for that decade. The "new" Wonder Woman sported a Jackie Onassis hairdo, a white jumpsuit and a guru called I Ching. She had mysteriously lost her superhuman powers and, significantly, the memory of her Amazon history and home community. She would occasionally engage in self-defense, without notable competence and often had to be rescued. She rescued few women and inspired none.

This ersatz Wonder Woman would not do. She disappeared, and was replaced by the real and timeless Wonder Woman. The attempted cooptation of the heroine of our time should, however, serve as a reminder of how female heroes are reduced in the patriarchal telling. Chesler's retelling of the Demeter—Persephone myth can also be seen as a cautionary tale. The rape of Persephone disrupts forever the blissful union of Demeter with her daughters, Psyche, Athena, Artemis and Persephone. Once the dominance of men is established, options (even for goddesses) are radically reduced. Psyche, whom Chesler links with Cinderella, takes flight into domesticity and romance. Athena, electing to be twice-born from Zeus' forehead, turns her back upon Demeter and acknowledges only the powerful male parent.

Artemis, the virgin huntress, is transformed by Chesler into the mother of the Amazon tribe. The Mother is turned into the archetype of the wicked stepmother. As the daughters (along with everyone else) turn away from this figure, the division among women is planted. The reunion of Demeter and Persephone is changed into the mother's holding the daughter captive, and the policing of women by women begins. After the rape, nurturance is lavished on husbands and sons, no longer on daughters. Daughters are unmothered, as Rich observes. The scope of Earth Mother virtues is no longer that of a goddess but is restricted to the benefit of a small nuclear family.

Wonder Woman lives. Yet in counterpart to themes of women's strength, intergrity, sense of proportion, solidarity and compassion are the continual pressures of misogyny and male dominance. Women are often disenfranchised and sometimes divided. The forces of oppression seem far stronger.

Yet Mary Daly (1973), writing on women in the Christian tradition, sees misogyny as having positive outcomes for women. Being treated as Other is so alienating, so invalidating for women that it precipitates them into the process that eventuates in liberation. The first step is the hardest: to confront the threat of nonbeing. Daly's position on this is that the "threat" is no threat, contingent on displeasing the dominant group, and avoidable by good behavior: the damage has already been done to women. In patriarchal thought modes, women are nonbeings, and the behaviors informed by this thought invalidate and negate women a thousand times a day. The real terror is not what men will do to us, but the terror of the unknown: if we reject the names men have for us and the images they have created, what will we be? Facing this fear begins what Daly calls the fall through terror to adulthood. The adulthood thus won permits self-affirmation that is totally distinct from the previous negation and that occurs in the company of peers. Adulthood permits a radical vision not accessible to those remaining in the patriarchal tradition. This is a new consciousness that is, in Joan Roberts' phrase, "noncontingent" (1976, Chapter 2). From this point of view, Daly asserts that women's reality is radically discontinuous with patriarchy's images of us. The connection between the two must go. Men can keep their images of women as Other, or they can keep relationships with women, but not both. This is a dilemma for men, rather than for women. Daly, like other feminist scholars, comes to these conclusions from an analysis of the materials of her own field—in this case theology. Daly reviews the products of a patriarchal theology, finding many links with a secular society molded by male dominance.

Daly anatomizes the phallic morality that produces rapism, genocide and war. Her analysis is brillant and well exemplifies the power of naming that feminists have now reclaimed. All three phallic evils have in common the insistence on reducing living persons to the status of Other. Things can be done to Other that would be heinous offenses if done against Us. The cause of creating Others seems to be the old familiar denial and projection of disowned parts of the self. Daly does not, however, take the burden of this problem upon herself: it is a problem that men must solve: they must bear the consequences. When woman as Other ceases to exist (as she has already begun to do), she may have to be reinvented. This is perhaps the context of a quote from Aquinas: "Take away prostitutes from the world and you will fill it with sodomy" (1973, p. 61). Their problem, not ours.

The proper focus of women's work and thought is our being, not Otherness. This being is achieved, not ascribed, and it is in process. Its language is experiential, existential, resembling "feminine" or "matriarchal" forms of thought more than masculine. It is the language of liberation, feminism, humanism. Following this focus, Daly excavates a women's history within Christianity, enumerating the "women-sisters" who traveled with Jesus; the property-owning Beguine communities that were brought under the control of male orders; the doctrine of sophiology; the female prophets in the tradition of the Montanist heresy; and Dame Julian, a 12th-century mystic whose revelation was that God is a mother. In Daly's view, the Ultimate Reality, or God, manifests itself in differing ways down the centuries. In Daly's view, Jesus was not the last Word. Indeed, Daly asserts, the postpatriarchal manifestation is the Women's Movement.

Daly's work exemplifies the new perspectives that are possible when patriarchal lenses are set aside. When women take to themselves the power of naming, new views both of society and of self emerge.

The process of change that Daly describes is identical with the process of consciousness raising, the experience by which persons become feminists.

Consciousness Raising and the CR Group

The "CR group" is the fundamental organizing tool of the Women's Liberation Movement. A small group of women, usually not less than six or more than twelve, meet regularly to share experiences and give support. Only members of the group are present at their meetings, and what is shared is held in strict confidence. Some groups are open to new members at any time, but most crystallize after a few meetings and take in new members only to replace those who are lost. Most groups seem to follow a natural history that takes from six to eighteen months; few groups continue to meet longer than two years.

The sharing of information begins at the level of personal experience and moves to the political—that is, to analysis of the power relationships embedded in everday interactions and of the social structure that forms these.

Consciousness raising has both and individual and a group aspect. The group aspect involves female solidarity (or sisterhood) and commitment to social action, both of which will be dealt with here. The individual experience begins with a sharing of feelings and experiences. Often these are negative feelings about the self, which the safety of the group makes it possible to acknowledge. In a women's group, the woman hears her own experiences told again and again by women who differ from her, often in ways to which she has been taught to feel inferior. If a woman who has straight hair, and/or straight teeth, and/or a ph.D. and/or regular orgasms and/or adoring children feels as angry or depressed, "fails" in just as significant ways, cannot believe in herself, then it becomes apparent that this is no coincidence. To raise consciousness is to bring to awareness the existence of sex role scripts, their effects, the power implications of such scripts, and the fact that they are part of social structure, impacting on individual women because they are women and not because they are individuals.

The process of change begins with a renunciation of myths and mystification, of false consciousness, of the mask of civility. Then the face of oppression is seen and its ubiquity, its brutality, its historicity. Then come terror and pain and rage. But all the while the individual is supported by the strength of sisterhood. Meanwhile she feels, for the first time, the keenness of an unfettered sight and thought. Here enters joy and the feeling of soaring—and finally, back to the world, and a new way of being-in-the-world.

The raising of consciousness means an *irreversible* transformation of consciousness. The power of naming, when used by women, gives us new ways of knowing our own experience. The feminist adage that the personal is political can also be seen as an instance of the power of naming. Women's pain is "merely" personal under patriarchal ontogony, for women are nonbeings. The implication is that women's complaints are unfounded and certainly ill reasoned. On the contrary, feminists name the personal as political. Taking injustices against women seriously requires different actions in the world. Thus the link to social action is an integral part of feminism; it is not something that happens "after" consciousness raising.

Feminism and Social Change

The Women's Movement is not an organization, much to the mystification of reporters and lobbyists. It does not have officers, a charter, a phone number or even a cable address. Women's

Liberation is a social movement. Several good accounts of the rise and development of the current Women's Movement exist (Freeman, 1975; Ware, 1970; Friedan, 1976), making it unnecessary to attempt here what has already been done better. Nor shall I attempt to designate which are "the" issues and priorities of the Movement; that deserves a long, thoughtful book to itself, and many distinguished contributions already exist.

It may be useful, however, to recall that a major contingent of the foremothers of the current Women's Movement consisted of disaffected women from the political left, who found themselves excluded from full participation in "revolutionary" action just as their nonpolitical sisters were from the male establishment of the straight world. Feminists remain skeptical of any "revolutionary" program or society that "hasn't gotten around to" equality for women.

The Women's Movement relates directly to the themes developed throughout this book. The idea of agency or of subjectivity (as contrasted with objectivity) underlies many of the specific goals of the Movement. Agency is the exercise of full options, without asking permission or incurring penalty. Demands for control over our own bodies relate to the concept of agency. Control over reproduction is basic. A review of the Amazon Vision and other feminist utopias underscores the requirement of liberation from unwanted pregnancy and from health dangers associated with pregnancy, contraception and childbirth. In addition to the dangers directly associated with these processes, it is clear that women's reproductive capacities are too often used as an excuse to deny women other options.

Women do not have equal rights under the law of this land. The rationales for keeping women as second-class citizens relate to the expectation of marriage, motherhood and financial dependence. In many financial transactions women are denied the independence that they have earned: many discriminatory practices in mortgages, credit arrangements, social security benefits have been protested, and many remain to be corrected. The power of naming includes the rights to define; whether women or others

371

have the right to define women is contested in a thousand lives every day. The right of women to keep, use, change or invent their own names is currently in litigation.

Change in women's roles means change in every aspect of society. When parenthood is viewed as an option that may be chosen, instead of an inevitability, the ground of discussion shifts. Parenting is a human relationship—not a biological event. If quality of parenting is the issue, then men, as well as women (married, unmarried, heterosexual or homosexual), are eligible for consideration. Yet at present, when lesbian mothers choose to keep their children, they are opposed by the forces of patriarchy.

Equal opportunity and equal rights in employment have been major concerns of feminists. Economic self-sufficiency is essential for autonomy, and although paid employment is not the only means to this end, it is the one that is the most respected. The importance of an esteem income is often overlooked when women's work is discussed. Housewifery is not only unpaid, it is unrecognized. The Wages for Housework movement asserts the value of domestic labor, by translating it into cash terms. This means, of course, translating it into male terms. Women's work has always been claimed to have other "value." Feminists claim it can have money value, too.

It is interesting that public opinion supports one issue that has been of paramount importance to feminists—that of equal pay for equal work. Yet the issue of who controls women's bodies, women's fertility and their children is hotly contested. Women's power subverts male dominance wherever it appears, and the power of women over children and reproduction is particularly impressive. The potential of women's sexual freedom is even more explosive, especially when sexuality can be divorced from fertility and from the obligation to satisfy men's demands. Sexual pleasure is so powerful an experience of subjectivity that to bring it under women's control is revolutionary.

Feminism and Personal Change

To say that feminists have raised these issues is not to say that we have prevailed. And to say that efforts are directed toward social change "out there" is not to say change need not occur "in here." Indeed, changing women's minds and changing men's minds are intimately related; some of the obstacles are the same. Sex role scripts define women as being certain ways; individuals' expectations communicate the same definitions. Sex role scripts are more than role prescriptions that go with particular positions; these are the way men define women (all women) to be; women must complement the way men define themselves. "Feminine personality" as we have discussed it here is the result. The crux of the feminine personality tailored to patriarchy is Objectivity.

Objectivity includes the obligations to be vicarious, masochistic, narcissistic, dependent, competitive with women and the obligations *not* to be initiating, independent, challenging, appetitive, agentic or competitive with men. One function of vicariousness is, of course, to neutralize Subjectivity (or to render it "unnecessary"). Empathy is a one-sided virtue that does not imply a process of give and take, of mutual accommodation. It is adaptive in a society where (only) women are expected to accommodate.

Liberation from sex roles means the refusal to be what men require and refusal to complement their own role definitions. Liberating women requires both changing this personality and changing the expectations of others.

The process of change poses an enormous challenge, and several possible starting points are apparent. Nevertheless, feminists have taken the responsibility to begin the process by changing ourselves. Hence we start with consciousness raising, rather than with fund raising. The terrors of change are not to be underestimated. Nevertheless, no feminist asks another woman to do what she has not done herself.

373

The feminist challenge to the existing system of sex roles has become so powerful and so prevalent that many individuals are threatened by it in a fundamental way. If they concede that femininity has been demolished, they find themselves at the edge of an abyss. The appropriate response is terror. It is literally unimaginable, unthinkable that personal integrity as a female can survive the feminist holocaust—as long as sex roles are seen as real, basic, and irreducible features of humans. This brings us to a paradox: the transcendence of sex roles requires the prior awareness of a feminist perspective. Without the naming, analysis and critique of sex roles, androgyny does not become apparent as a solution to the constriction and impoverishment of the person. Hence consciousness raising is an essential first step. Although media exposure and the appearance of feminist literature make the analysis of sex roles accessible to everyone, the individual who strives to come to consciousness "on her own" does without the support of the group, which is exceptionally difficult.

It might be argued that following the sex role script is the safer and more comfortable course for most women. Over the long run, however, it is an unstable solution. The ambivalence endemic to accepting the Object role (which I discussed in Chapter 3) recurs and grows. Confrontation can be postponed, but not ultimately escaped. The bitterness of a woman who has enjoyed the variation of Privileged Object, only to find it temporary, may be greater than that of a woman who has always felt like an outsider.

Pessimism about the prospects for change, or inordinate fear of moving toward change, may both be symptoms of women who have been inadequately "sistered." Certainly the woman who tries to change without support has long odds against her; and the woman who seeks to change society is extremely vulnerable if she is not supported by her sisters.

Fears, false starts and false consciousness notwithstanding, the direction of change is away from the sex role script and toward a new self. Appropriately enough, one focus of feminist thought is *self*ishness—healthy, appropriate selfishness. This selfishness is a move away from vicariousness and the whole "feminine" personality type based upon it. Within the framework of the feminine sex role, selfishness in a woman is shocking and deplorable. Yet self-love is a prerequisite to loving others. A current bestseller teaches us (but perhaps not including women) how to be our own best friends. A friend is someone you know is on your side. Women need to befriend each other. For many women it is easy to nurture others but difficult to recognize their own need for nurturance. Still harder, for many women, is to give priority to their own needs.

Chesler's prescription is toward inspired *selfishness*: a love of skill, strength and achievement in ourselves; withdrawal of energy and loyalty from interactions and institutions that are not supportive of our best; investment in female survival; reticence toward unnecessary and unproductive compromises. Women must start saving themselves before their daughters, their daughters before their husbands and sons, and all before "saving the world." But selfishness is still a dirty word: if the dominance of a patriarchal value system needed proof, the history of this epithet could provide it. Popenoe (1974) anatomized prejudice toward childless persons in a study in which he asked others (not the childless ones) to explain this anomalous status. The modal "explanation" (31 percent) was "self-centeredness." In a more recent study of awareness of the Women's Movement among Army wives stationed overseas, Dubrofsky (1977) found that negative images of the Movement were associated in these women's minds with the advocacy of "selfishness."

The feminist community is characterized by distinctive values. Foremost among these is affirmation of women. "*Self*ishness" in women is appropriate because women are worthwhile; hence selfpride, self-assertion, self-defense and self-sufficiency are virtues. Within a matriarchal or prefeminist culture these virtues would pass unremarked. But feminism thrives in a patriarchal culture that has left its mark on all of us. Consequently feminists, too, sometimes fall into the trap of mistaken identity—*of responding to women as though patriarchal images were true*. When this happens, feminists can repudiate competence in themselves and their sisters because they associate it with "masculinity." The literature of the Women's Movement contains several moving accounts of women with gifts to share who are rejected by their sisters (dell'Olio, 1970; Joreen, 1976). Often those who have the confidence to challenge the male society are invalidated by their sisters with the label "male-identified." This illustrates an abuse of the power of naming that women are taking back, for feminists can, of course, be hurt much more by women than by men. If these women are lost to the Movement, it is a triumph of false consciousness—in this case meaning that women have chosen to identify with their weakness rather than their strength. Antifemale sentiments include the belief that one cannot be enhanced or protected by the success or power of any other woman (Chesler, 1972, p. 275). In my experience, however, the feminist commitment of the rejected feminists is too strong for such women to abandon the struggle. Only, they resign themselves to working for change without the support of sisterhood, which feminists hold is the birthright of every woman.

The distinctive commitment of feminism is apparent when we look at the ambiguous concept, "the liberated woman." I not infrequently meet women who say, "I don't need Women's Lib. I'm already liberated." By this they mean that they do not suffer from the oppressions that the Women's Movement has brought to public awareness. Sometimes they are individuals of great personal achievement, more often individuals who find themselves in position of personal privilege. They are not feminists if they do not concern themselves with the position of other women—all other women. And they are not feminists if they lack insight into the factors that helped them up and that hold other women down. Possessing more resources than the average woman, they are in a position to help other women; but unless they have a feminist consciousness, they are unlikely to do so.

Female Solidarity and Sisterhood

Female solidarity is one of the best-kept secrets of patriarchy. It is to the advantage of patriarchy to deny that emotional support, understanding of our lives and needs, skills and knowledge, and love can be had from women (and at a better price than from men). Yet we have records of female solidarity that go back at least as far as colonial times. In the diaries and letters of colonial women, Mary Beth Norton (1976) has found evidence of lifelong bonds within the family of women that survived the rigors of frontier life, marriage, bereavement and age. Carroll Smith-Rosenberg's (1975) analysis of relationships among women in the 19th century gives evidence of passionate attachments and a depth of caring that are an emotional oasis in the mundane business of marriage and family life. In our day, meetings and reunions among women that are trivialized in traditional forms of humor (e.g., "hen parties") may have the same quality of heightened vitality and "time out" from a life dominated by oppressive male institutions. Emma Jung observed that female relationships are a life-sustaining necessity, particularly for women immersed in (but excluded from) the male world.

From this perspective, it is not so incongruous to find consciousness raising groups being organized under the auspices of the YWCA, or women's labor unions taking a feminist position on abortion. Women's organizations have traditionally undertaken many projects that benefit the larger community. They may not have come out on "the" woman issue, but they have concerned themselves over the years with women's issues: child care, child welfare, maternal and child health, etc. Awareness of the underground (or in the closet?) women's community makes many traditional female functions worth a second look by feminists. In the last few years, several analyses of women in their role as volunteer have appeared (Mueller, 1975).

Thus relations with women are accessible to us all, even in a "man's world." Moreover, the perspective of sisterhood is causing us to look at traditional women's groups and women's activities with greater appreciation.

Yet if all women are sisters, still not all women are feminists. The specific kind of support that committed feminists give each other has no substitute. The ongoing importance of the women's group has perhaps been underestimated in feminist thinking thus far.

The classic "career" of the emerging feminist does involve participation in consciousness raising, a movement from personal pain and anger to social action, through the crucible of sisterhood. Coming to a state of feminist awareness *is* a change in consciousness, and it is probably irreversible. Through the process of consciousness raising, many things become possible for the individual that did not seem so before. Nevertheless, in a sexist society women continue to need community. While the CR group may be a way-station in the individual's emergence, it should not be left behind too hastily. Support is a necessity of survival. The woman who has committed herself to feminism may feel stronger than ever before, but she is in much greater danger. If she chooses to fight for change in a man's world, she will need a great deal of support. The commitment and support of feminists for one another has a special quality because of the political analysis that underlies it. Feminists, more than other women, recognize that support is essential for survival and for effecting change.

The women's community has another important function. In celebrating and supporting traditionally female characteristics, the women's community not only serves as a buffer against misogyny, but actually counteracts stigma and redefines it into strength. The example of the transformation of "selfish" from epithet to approbation is an example of this power. It is the collective affirmation that makes it so: sisterhood *is* powerful.

The local "women's group" can also be viewed as a powerful force in continuing resocialization. Sex role behavior is subjected to continuing scrutiny and influence—which is as it should be. Making the initial change was a step-by-step procedure achieved with lots of support; maintaining change is the same.

"Inner" and "Outer" Space

Daly (1973) characterizes the achievement of consciousness in terms of stepping through a door that is invisible from the other side. Daly, in fact, characterizes women as occupying a "new space" in new time. The new space is distinctive in that women share it, women form it to fit their own needs, and women define its boundaries. The "women's community" so defined can be a physical space, an enclave within the patriarchal community, or it can be defined in terms of networks of commitment and mutual aid. Daly's new space is a kind of feminist utopia, the destination of the journey to consciousness. However, it is more a kingdom of the spirit than of the social world. Her map is correct and a true guide to a new place. Its logic, however, leads to her prescription that feminists should choose sites on the periphery of patriarchy. Though defensible, this advice is unsatisfying in its implications for social change. Daly tells us how to construct a new space, not how to transform the old. It is possible for feminists to create and maintain by these means a collective space, a small society that meets their needs and embodies their values. Insofar as the goal of feminism is to create a better life for individuals, success is theirs. For that fortunate few, the old space of patriarchy may be essentially irrelevant.

However, that life must eventually be available to everyone or feminism has failed. The women's community is essential for the survival of those who are committed to work for change. How impermeable the boundaries must be, and how permanent residence therein, are points on which feminists differ.

Women who have won their way to consciousness are in a new space and possess the freedom to define themselves and their future way. Yet in addition to a focus on "freedom from" patriarchy and its distortions, we are also in search of "freedom to." Freedom to implies not only the capacity to take action, but also a direction for action. There is wide diversity among feminists on the issue of the extent to which one must be involved with male society in order to pursue the goals for which female solidarity has freed us. Total withdrawal has its appeal. But as Solanas (1971) observes, "dropping out" is no policy for women (though an excellent idea for men): most women were never "in" in the first place. The burden of change still rests with women. Of course it would be easier for men—starting from where they are—to turn society around, than for women. But women are more likely to. This work is not unprecedented, after all. Wonder Woman shines, in part, by contrast to the man's world in which she struggles—against great odds. Her adventures are not set in the Amazon utopia of Paradise Island, where things are as they should be. Her mission—with the support of her mother and sisters—is to the misbegotten.

Beyond Androgyny: The Feminist Future

The process of the individual's recovery of androgyny is distinct from the process of the Women's Movement. The liberation of individual women, through processes of change and expansion such as we have examined in this chapter, is only part of the tide of the Women's Movement. Women's Liberation refers to the liberation of all women, of women as a class, not solely of those who are able or ready to initiate their personal liberation. The program of Women's Liberation is inescapably a program of social change. Androgyny lacks a political program. It may or may not be reactionary, as Secor (1974) and others contend, but as we have seen, most treatments of this concept lack an analysis of the current situation and a plan for social change. This being so, the idea of androgyny could remain an unattainble ideal, a voguish pie-in-the-sky idea. Moreover, even if androgyny in the individual is attainable, it cannot of itself avail anything for social change. Plaskow detects the weakness of the "otherworldly" search for self and meaning: if the search is not oriented toward social life, it leaves political power in the hands of men who will exercise it according to their own world view (1976, p. 337). A stance of political "neutrality" in fact supports the status quo. This is inconsistent with a feminist perspective.

Patriarchal and postpatriarchal consciousness exist simultaneously in our time and in our hemisphere. Attempts to express this simultaneity and discontinuity have relied heavily on spatial metaphors. As we have seen, the ideas of woman-space (and man's world) have a long history. There is a historic imbalance in the allocation of space to women and men. In our cultural mythology, woman's place/space has been reduced to the home. Other spheres of life become male territory, by dominance if not by predominance. Students of body language have observed that men even claim a larger amount of personal space than women do.

When Virginia Woolf referred to a room of one's own, she meant a place to which woman might withdraw to do her own work. The "matriarchal" mode of intellectual creativity described by Neumann, similarly, utilizes withdrawal. The "room of one's own" is thus a closet; a woman's serious, self-directed work is "in the closet." In the closet one is free to divest herself of the garment of femininity and be a whole person. "In the closet" one is free of the presence of others, who by their expectations elicit stereotypical sex role behavior. In our present society, this freedom thrives "in the closet"; in a future world, we will all come out.

Thinkers like Daly argue persuasively for a new space for and by women that has nothing to do with patriarchal territoriality. This new space is not a utopia but a present reality; it is good in itself and is essential for the major goal of female survival. Yet I hold that women should be doing their work in the world, not in the closet. This closet is too damn small. Changing the world "out there," not only "in here," is the task of Women's Liberation.

REFERENCES

Andrews, Frank. 1975. In *Perspectives in Creativity*, ed. I.A. Taylor and J.W. Getzels. Chicago: Aldine.

Angyal, A. 1941. *Foundations for a Science of Personality*. Commonwealth Fund.

Bachofen, J.J. 1967. *Myth, Religion and Mother Right*, tr. Ralph Manheim. Princeton, NJ: Princeton University Press.

Bakan, D. 1966. *The Duality of Human Existence*. Chicago: Rand-McNally.

Barron, Frank. 1969. *Creative Person and Creative Process*. New York: Holt, Rinehart, and Winston.

Barrows, G.A., and Zuckerman, M. 1960. Construct validity of three masculinity–femininity tests. *Journal of Consulting Psychology* 24: 441–445.

Bart, Pauline. 1967. Depression in middle aged women: some sociocultural factors. Ph.D. dissertation, UCLA.

———. 1970. Mother Portnoy's complaint. *Trans-Action*, (November–December) pp. 69–74.

———. 1971. The myth of a value-free psychotherapy, in *The Study of the Future: Explorations in the Sociology of Knowledge*, ed. Wendell Bell and James A. May. New York: Russell Sage.

Bem, Sandra T. n.d. Beyond androgyny: Some presumptuous prescriptions for a liberated sexual identity. Unpublished paper, Stanford University.

———. 1972. Psychology looks at sex roles: where have all the androgynous people gone? Paper presented at the UCLA Symposium on Women, May 1972.

———. 1974. The measurement of psychological androgyny. *Journal of Consulting and Clinical Psychology* 42: 155–162.

———. 1976. Probing the promise of androgyny. In *Beyond Sex-Role Stereotypes: Readings Toward a Psychology of Androgyny*, ed. A.G. Kaplan and J.P. Bean. Boston: Little, Brown.

Bernard, Jessie. 1964. *Academic women*. University Park, PA: The Pennsylvania State University Press.

Bieliauskas, V.J. Miranda, S.B., and Lansky, L. 1968. Obviousness of two masculinity–femininity tests. *Journal of Consulting and Clinical Psychology* 32: 314–318.

Birnbaum, Judith A. 1971. Life patterns, personality style, and self-esteem in gifted family oriented and career committed women. Unpublished Ph.D. dissertation, University of Michigan, Ann Arbor.

Block, Jeanne H. 1973. Conceptions of sex role: some cross-cultural and longitudinal perspectives. *American Psychologist* 28(6): 512–526.

Bowers, K.S. 1971. Sex and susceptibility as moderator variables in the rela-

382

tionship of creativity and hypnotic susceptibility. *Journal of Abnormal Psychology* 78: 93–100.

Caplow, Theodore, and McGee, Reece J. 1961. *The Academic Marketplace*. New York: Science Editions.

Chapman, Jane Roberts, ed. 1976. *Economic Independence for Women*. Beverly Hills: Sage Publications.

Chesler, Phyllis. 1970. Psychotherapy and women. Paper presented at American Psychological Association.

———. 1972a. The Amazon legacy, in *Wonder Woman*. New York: Holt, Rinehart and Winston.

———. 1972b. *Women and madness*. Garden City, NY: Doubleday.

Connell, D.M., and Johnson, J.E. 1970. Relationship between sex-role identification and self-esteem in early adolescents. *Developmental Psychology* 3: 268.

Cosentino, F., and Heilbrun, A.B. 1964. Anxiety correlates of sex-role identity in college students. *Psychology Reports* 14: 729–730.

Csikszentmihalyi, Mihaly. 1975. *Beyond Boredom and Anxiety: The Experience of Play in Work and Games*. San Francisco: Jossey-Bass.

Daly, Mary. 1973. *Beyond God The Father*. Boston: Beacon Press.

Daniels, Arlene Kaplan. Room at the top: Contingencies in the voluntary career. *Social Scientist* 43: 41–56.

Davis, Elizabeth Gould. 1971. *The First Sex*. New York: G.P. Putnam's Sons.

Deckard, Barbara. 1975. *The Women's Movement*. New York: Harper and Row.

dell'Olio, Anselma. 1970. Divisiveness and self-destruction in the Women's Movement. *Chicago Women's Liberation Newsletter*. (August).

Diner, Helen. 1965. *Mothers and Amazons: The First Feminine History of Culture*. New York: The Julian Press.

Dubrofsky, Lynne R., and Batterson, Constance T. 1977. The military wife and feminism. *Signs: Journal of Women in Culture and Society* 2 (3): 675–684.

Eiseley, Loren. 1965. Darwin, Coleridge, and the theory of unconscious creation. *Daedalus* 94 (3): 588–603.

Ellis, L.J., and Bentler, P.M. 1973. Traditional sex-determined role standards and sex stereotypes. *Journal of Personal and Social Psychology* 25(1): 28–34.

Feldman, Saul. 1973. Impediment or stimulant? marital status and graduate education. *American Journal of Sociology* 78(4): 982–995.

Franck, K., and Rosen, E. 1949. A projective test of masculinity–femininity. *Journal of Consulting Psychology* 13: 247–256.

Frazier, James. 1958. *The Golden Bough*. New York: Macmillan.

Freeman, Jo. 1975. *The Politics of Women's Liberation*. New York: David McKay.

Friedan, Betty. 1976. *It Changed My Life: Writings on The Women's Movement*. NewYork: Random House.

Friedman, Alan. 1968. *Hermaphrodeity*. New York: Avon Books.

Gall, M.D. 1969. The relationship between masculinity–femininity and manifest anxiety. *Journal of Clinical Psychology* 25: 294–295.

383

Gelpi, B.C. 1975. *Adrienne Rich's Poetry*. New York: Norton.

Goldenberg, Naomi. 1976. A feminist critique of Jung. *Signs: Journal of Women in Culture and Society* 2(2): 443–450.

Gough, H.G. 1952. Identifying psychological femininity. *Educational and Psychological Measurement* 12: 427–439.

Gray, S.W. 1957. Masculinity–femininity in relation to anxiety and social acceptance. *Child Development* 28: 203–214.

Guilford, J.P., and Guilford, R.B. 1936. Personality factors, S,E,M, and their measurement. *Journal of Psychology* 2: 1956. 109–127.

Guilford, J.P., and Zimmerman, W.S. 1956. Fourteen dimensions of temperament. *Psychology Monographs* 70 No. 417, p. 10.

Gysbers, N. 1973. *Developing Careers in Elementary School*. Columbus, OH: Merrill.

Harris, Daniel A. 1974. Androgyny: The sexist myth in disguise. *Women's Studies* 2: 171–184.

Hartmann, Heidi. 1975. Comment on Marnie W. Mueller's "The economic determinants of volunteer work by women". *Signs: Journal of Women in Culture and Society* 1(3): 773–777.

Heilbrun, Carolyn G. 1973. *Toward a Recognition of Androgyny*. New York: Alfred A. Knopf.

Helson, Ravenna. 1961. Creativity, sex and mathematics. *Proceedings of the Conference on The Creative Person*. Berkeley: I.P.A.R.

———. 1975. Creativity in Women. Paper presented at the conference, New Directions in the Psychology of Women. Madison, WI.

———. and Crutchfield, R.S. 1970. Mathematicians: The creative researcher and the average Ph.D. *Journal of Consulting and Clinical Psychology* 34: 250–257.

Hesiod. n.d. *Works and days*, as quoted in Plato, *Republic*, in *The Works of Plato*, tr. Benjamin Jowett. bk. 5. New York: Tudor.

Heston, J. 1948. A comparison of four masculinity–femininity scales. *Educational and Psychological Measurement* 8: 375–387.

Jenkin, Noel, and Vroegh, Karen. 1969. Contemporary concepts of masculinity and femininity. *Psychological Reports* 25: 679–697.

Jones, E.E. 1972. *Attribution: Perceiving the Causes of Behavior*. Morristown, NJ: General Learning Press.

Joreen. 1976. Trashing: The dark side of sisterhood. *Ms.* 4(10): 49ff.

Jung, C.G. 1926. *Psychological Types*. Chapter 11, New York: Harcourt, Brace.

Jung, Emma. 1957. *Animus and Anima*. Zurich: Spring Publications.

Kogan, N., and Pankove, E. 1972. Creative ability over a five year span. *Child Development* 43: 427–442.

Kohlberg, Lawrence. 1966. A cognitive-developmental analysis of children's sex-role concepts and attitudes, in *The Development of Sex Differences*, ed. E. Maccoby. Stanford: Stanford University Press.

——— and Zigler, E. 1966. The impact of cognitive maturity on the development of sex-role attitudes in the years 4–8. *Genetic Psychology Monographs*.

Kurtzman, K.A. 1967. A study of school attitudes, peer acceptance, and personality of gifted adolescents. *Exceptional Children*. 33: 157–162.

Lasswell, H.D. 1959. The social setting of creativity, *Creativity and Its Cultivation*, ed. H.H. Anderson. New York: Harper.

Laws, J.L. 1975. The psychology of tokenism: An analysis, *Sex Roles* 1(1): 151–174.

Lifton, Robert, ed. 1964. *The Woman in America*. Boston: Beacon Press.

Lowes, J.L. 1927. *The Road to Xanadu*. Boston: Houghton Mifflin.

Lunneborg, P. 1970. Stereotypic aspects in M–F measurement. *Journal of Consulting and Clinical Psychology* 34: 1.

McCarthy, D., Anthony, R.J., and Domino, G. 1970. A comparison of the CPI, Franck, MMPI and WAIS masculinity–femininity indexes. *Journal of Consulting and Clinical Psychology* 35: 414–416.

Maslow, Abraham. 1955. Deficiency motivation and growth motivation. *Nebraska Symposium*, 1–31.

———. 1965. Self-actualizing people: a study of psychological health, in *The Self: Explorations in Personal Growth*, ed. C.E. Moustakas, pp. 160–95. New York: Harper.

Mellaart, James. 1967. *Çatal Hüyük*. New York: McGraw-Hill.

Mischel, Walter. 1970. Sex-typing and socialization in *Carmichael's Manual of Child Psychology*, ed. P.H. Mussen, vol. 2, pp. 3–72. New York: Wiley.

Moreno, Jacob. 1953. *Who Shall Survive?* Sociometry Monograph, No. 29.

Mueller, Marnie W. 1975. Economic determinants of volunteer work by women. *Signs: Journal of Women in Culture and Society* 1(2): 325–339.

Mussen, P.H. 1961. Some antecedents and consequents of masculine sex-typing in adolescent boys. *Psychology Monographs* 75: 506.

Neumann, Erich. 1954. On the moon and matriarchal consciousness. *Spring*, pp. 83–100.

———. 1956. *Amor and Psyche*. Princeton: Princeton Univ. Press.

———. 1959. The psychological stages of feminine development. *Spring*, pp. 63–97.

Newell, A., Shaw, J.G., and Simon, H.A. 1962. The processes of creative thinking. In *Contemporary Approaches to Creative Thinking*, ed. H.E. Gruber, G. Terrell, and M. Wertheimer. New York: Atherton Press.

Nichols, R.C. 1962. Subtle, obvious, and stereotype measures of masculinity–femininity. *Education and Psychological Measurement* 22: 449–461.

Nicolson, Nigel. 1973. *Portrait of a Marriage*. New York: Atheneum.

Norton, Mary Beth. 1976. "My resting reaping times": Sarah Osborn's defence of her "unfeminine" activities, 1767. *Signs: Journal of Women in Culture and Society* 2 (2): 515–529.

Pagels, Elaine H. 1976. What became of God the Mother? Conflicting images of God in early Christianity. *Signs: Journal of Women in Culture and Society* 2(2): 293–304.

Piercy, Marge. 1976. *Woman on the Edge of Time*. New York: Fawcett Crest Books.

Pine, F., and Holt, R.R. 1960. Creativity and primary process: A study of adaptive regression. *Journal of Abnormal and Social Psychology* 61: 370–379.

Plaskow, Judith. 1976. On Carol Christ on Margaret Atwood: Some theological reflections. *Signs: Journal of Women in Culture and Society* 2(2): 331–340.

Pleck, Joseph H., 1973a. New concepts of sex role identity. Paper presented to the Society for the Scientific Study of Sex.

———. 1973b. Social science and sex role change. Cambridge: Unpublished paper.

———. 1975a. Issues for the men's movement: Summer 1975. Unpublished ms.

———. 1975b. Masculinity–femininity: Current and alternate paradigms. *Sex Roles* 1(2): 161–179.

———. 1975c. The psychology of sex roles: Current data and its social implications. Paper prepared for the Aspen Workshop on Women and Men, August 1975.

———. 1976. The male sex role: Definitions, problems, and sources of change. *Journal of Social Issues* 32 (3): 155–164.

Popeoe, Paul. 1974. Motivation of childless marriages, in *Pronatalism: The Myth of Mom and Apple Pie*, ed. Ellen Peck and Judith Sanderowitz, pp. 278–284. New York: Thomas Y. Crowell Co.

Rebecca, Meda, Hefner, Robert, and Oleshansky, Barbara. 1976. A model of sex-role transcendance, in *Beyond Sex-Role Stereotypes: Readings Toward a Psychology of Androgyny*, ed. A.G. Kaplan and J.P. Bean, pp. 89–98. Boston: Little, Brown.

Reich, Wilhelm. 1973. *The Function of The Orgasm: Sex-Economic Problems of Biological Energy*, tr. V.R. Carfango. New York: Farrar, Straus, & Giroux.

Rich, Adrienne. 1976. *Of Woman Born: Motherhood as Experience and Institution*. New York: W.W. Norton.

Roberts, Joan, ed. 1976. *Beyond Intellectual Sexism; A New Woman, A New Reality*. New York: David McKay.

Rogers, Carl. 1954. *Becoming a Person*. Ohio: Oberlin Publishing Co.

Rosenberg, B., and Fliegel, N. 1965. *The Vanguard Artist: Portrait and Self-Portrait*. New York: Quadrangle.

Rosenberg, B.G., and Sutton-Smith, B. 1964. The measurement of masculinity and femininity in children: An extension and revalidation. *Journal of Genetic Psychology* 104: 259–264.

Rosenkrantz, P., Vogel, S., Bee, H., Broverman, I., and Broverman, D.M. 1968. Sex-role stereotypes and self-concepts in college students. *Journal of Consulting and Clinical Psychology* 32: 287–295.

Roszak, Betty, and Roszak, Theodore. 1969. *Masculine/Feminine: Readings in Sexual Mythology and The Liberation of Women*. New York: Harper & Row.

Secor, Cynthia. 1974. Androgyny: An early reappraisal. *Women's Studies* 2: 161–169.

Shepler, B.F. 1951. A comparison of masculinity–femininity measures. *Journal of Counseling Psychology* 15: 484–486.

Sherriffs, A.C., and Jarrett, R.F. 1953. Sex differences in attitudes about sex differences. *Journal of Psychology* 35: 161–168.

Smith-Rosenberg, Carroll. 1975. The female world of love and ritual: Relations between women in nineteenth-century America. *Signs: Journal of Women in Culture and Society* 1(1):1031.

Solanas, Valerie. 1971. *The S.C.U.M. Manifesto*. New York: Olympia Press.

Spence, Janet T., and Helmreich, R. 1972. The attitudes toward women scale: an objective instrument to measure attitudes toward the rights and roles of women in contemporary society. *Journal Supplement Abstract Service Catalogue of Selected Documents in Psychology* 2: 66–67.

Spence, Janet T., Helmreich, R., and Stapp, Joy. 1975. Ratings of self and peers on sex role attributes and their relation to self-esteem and conceptions of masculinity and femininity. *Journal of Personal and Social Psychology* 32(1): 29–39.

Steinem, Gloria. 1972. Introduction. In *Wonder Woman*, New York: Holt, Rinehart and Winston.

Stericker, Anne B., and Johnson, James E. 1977. Sex-role identification and self-esteem in college students: Do men and women differ? *Sex Roles* 3(1): 19–26.

Strong, E.K. 1936. Interests of men and women. *Journal of Social Psychology* 7: 49–67.

Tangri, Sandra S. 1972. Determinants of occupational role innovation among college women. *Journal of Social Issues* 28(2): 177–199.

Taylor, I.A., and Getzels, Jack. 1975. *Perspectives in Creativity*. Chicago: Aldine.

Tennov, Dorothy. 1975. *Psychotherapy: The Hazardous Cure*. New York: Abelavd-Schuman.

Terman, Lewis, and Miles, C.C. 1936. *Sex and Personality*. New York: McGraw-Hill.

Torrance, E. Paul. 1965. Scientific views of creativity and factors affecting its growth. *Daedalus*, 94 (3): 663–682.

———. 1972. Creative young women in today's world. *Exceptional Children* 38: 597–603.

Vidal, Gore. 1974. *Myra Breckenridge*. New York: Bantam Books.

Vroegh, Karen. 1971. Masculinity and femininity in the elementary and junior high school years. *Developmental Psychology* 4:254–261.

Wallstedt, Joyce Jennings. 1977. The altruistic other orientation: An exploration of female powerlessness. *Psychology of Women Quarterly* 2: 162–176.

Ware, Celestine. 1970. *Woman Power: The Movement for Women's Liberation*. New York: Tower Publications.

Watts, Alan W. 1963. *The Two Hands of God: The Myths of Polarity*. New York: Collier Books.

Webb, A.P. 1963. Sex role preferences and adjustment in early adolescents. *Child Development* 34: 609–618.

Webster, H. 1956. Personality development during the college years. *Journal of Social Issues* 12(4): 29–43.

Welch, G.S. 1975. *Creativity and Intelligence: A Personality Approach.* Chapel Hill, NC: Institute for Research in Social Science, University of North Carolina.

Werner, E.E., and Bachtold, L.M. 1969. Personality factors of gifted boys and girls in middle childhood and adolescence. *Psychology in the Schools.* 6: 177–182.

Wonder Woman. 1972. New York: Holt, Rinehart, and Winston.

Woolf, Virginia. 1973. *Orlando: A Biography*, New York: Harcourt, Brace, Jovanovich.

Woolf, Virginia, 1957. *A Room of One's Own*, New York: Harcourt, Brace, and World.

Index

Morse, N. C., 53, 54
Mother(s). *See also* Motherhood
  employment of. *See* Maternal
      employment
  need for power, 143–145
  need for self-actualization,
      145–150
  as victim of "maternal
      depriviation," 124, 143,
      150–151
Mother–child bond, 123
Mother–daughter relationship,
      150–151
Motherhood. *See also* Mother(s)
  confounding of institutional and
      relationship aspects of, 148
  feminine fulfillment through, 122
  as honorific status, 122, 124, 125
  idealized script of, 114
  incentives of, 124
  mandate, 150
  role expectations of, 126
  role requirements of, 143
  toleration for, 142–143
Motivation. *See also* Achievement
      motivation; Work motivation
  definition of, 49
  economic, 21–22
  extrinsic, 52, 54
  intrinsic, 52, 53, 326, 343
  and socialization, 241
Motive to Avoid Success, 10, 60–64,
      266, 268
Mueller, Marnie W., 377
Multiple roles, 5, 87, 137–141,
      152–153. *See also* Dual roles
Mulvey, M. C., 46, 47, 48
Mussen, P. H., 352, 354
Mystification, 176
  of body parts, 228
  definition of, 89, 177–178
  and education, 103
  and marriage relationship, 118
  and vaginal orgasm, 226
  and vicarious achievement, 282,
      283

and wife, role of, 114–115
Myth(s). *See also specific myth*
  of "the" breadwinner, 35
  definition of, 67, 339, 364
  of female mobility, 70
  of heroic male professional, 54
  of land of opportunity, 37
  as projections, 68
  as reasons for discrimination, 69
  as social control mechanisms, 68
  of work motivation, 6

Naming, power of, 4, 7, 11, 359,
      369, 370, 371–372, 376
Narcissism, 268, 270–271, 275,
      276–277, 284, 286
  phallic, 226, 227
Natural childbirth, 219
Needs, paradox of women's
      disappearing, 7, 72–73. *See
      also specific need*
Networks, 379
Neumann, Erich, 333, 337, 381
Never-married women, labor force
      participation of, 20
Newton, Niles, 218, 219
Nichols, R. C., 314, 315
Nicolson, Nigel, 307
Niswander, K. R., 210
Norris, A. S., 210
Norton, Mary Beth, 377
Novak, E. R., 220
Nuclear family, 99, 144
Nurturance, 123, 144, 290, 320–321,
      352
  need for, 375
Nye, Francis Ivan, 131, 132

Oakley, Ann, 105, 109, 110, 111,
      112, 113, 114, 143, 150, 153,
      154, 157, 161, 162
Objectivity, 9, 232, 278, 279,
      284–287, 295, 373, 374. *See
      also* Woman, as object;
      Woman, as sex object
Obstetrics, 218–219, 220–221